PSYCHOLOGY

*****

Essence of the Human Soul

ANTONIO ROSMINI

PSYCHOLOGY

Volume 1

Essence of the Human Soul

Translated by
DENIS CLEARY
and
TERENCE WATSON

ROSMINI HOUSE
DURHAM

Translated from
Psicologia
Critical edition, vol. 9, Stresa, 1989

Typeset by Rosmini House, Durham
Printed by Bell & Bain Limited, Glasgow

ISBN 1 899093 25 7

Note

Square brackets [ ] indicate notes or additions by the translators.

References to this and other works of Rosmini are given by paragraph number unless otherwise stated.

Abbreviations used for Rosmini's quoted works are:

AMS: *Anthropology as an Aid to Moral Science*
CS: *Conscience*
ER: *The Essence of Right,* vol. 1 of *The Philosophy of Right*
NE: *A New Essay concerning the Origin of Ideas*
PE: *Principles of Ethics*

Foreword

This translation of Rosmini's *Psychology* has been carried through
and sustained by the conviction that the work, first published in
Italian in 1846–48 at Novara, has great practical relevance today.
Such a judgement, applied to a book almost unknown in English-
speaking countries, despite the existence of a previous English
version by William Lockhart (London, 1884), needs solid justification. Some explanation must also be given a number of words which
have been difficult to translate from Rosmini's Italian.

A. The relevance of the work is best substantiated by Rosmini's
own *Preface, Introduction* and *Definitions* which indicate immediately, at the very beginning of the book, a treatment of psychology
almost unknown to the general reader in modern days. We are
dealing, he says, with metaphysics, with a philosophical study
devoted to the ultimate reasons for the existence and development
of a reality called 'soul'.

Such an assertion gives rise almost inevitably to sceptical questions about the viability of the project, or even to out-of-hand rejec-
tion of the possibility of any genuine exploration along these lines.
Today, and for some time now, it has been common ground amongst
philosophers and others that soul and spirit can and must be
consigned to the mental scrap-heap. Nevertheless, the classical
problems remain: debate about life after death, about the relationship between soul and body, about the constitution of the human
personality with its innate and acquired duties and rights persists
and will persist as long as human beings exist. Human thought, if it
is thought in any true sense of the word, must consider in depth
whether life on earth is simply progress towards the grave or
preparation for existence in a world beyond.

Rosmini's *Psychology* continues his *A New Essay concerning the
Origin of Ideas*, where he dealt with the problem of knowledge, and

his *Anthropology as an Aid to Moral Science*, in which he considered the elements of human nature insofar as they are intimately connected with moral action; in it Rosmini attempts to consider globally all that can be said philosophically about human nature. This global consideration does not go beyond the limits imposed by human reason in its search for information about itself; it does not deal with life in the hereafter as it is presented by religious revelation. But it does set out the principles whose denial would make nonsense of revelation about a future life. If, in fact, there is no soul, statements about its existence in a world beyond have the same standing as answers to the once fashionable philosophical question: 'Is the present king of France bald?'

This is not the place to attempt a synopsis of Rosmini's study of the soul in its essence, its development and its laws. He himself has more than enough to say about these matters. Moreover, his method, which always offers admirable on-going summaries of what has been said or is yet to be said in various sections of his work, fulfills any need or synthesis. One example amongst many can be found in the following words:

> In the preceding book [1], I indicated consciousness of ourselves as the source from which psychological teachings have to be drawn. At the same time, I established the *principle of psychology*, which lies in the *essence of the soul*. This principle, I said, consists in a *first, immanent and wholly substantial feeling*. The present book [2] and the three following are dedicated to explaining (through meditation on that feeling) and revealing (by careful analysis) the elements, characteristics and attributes of the essence of the soul, and excluding those which have been falsely attached to it. Our teaching, therefore, will be partly negative and partly positive. In other words, I shall say what the soul is not, and what separates it from other substances; and I shall also indicate what it is in itself.
>
> (*Psychology*, vol. 1, *Essence of the Human Soul*, 124)

Emphasis *is* needed, however, on Rosmini's approach to the study of psychology. He places the greatest importance on exhaustive observation of the content of self-perception. This content, observed at length and in surprising detail, becomes the standard according to which reasoning about the existence and nature of the soul may be judged. In other words, Rosmini is not constructing a 'model' which may or may not serve as a kind of paradigm for some hypothetical, incomplete science; he is, according to his own affirmation, indicating reflectively and reflexively the reality to which he and his readers can turn constantly as they analyse what they perceive, and bring together synthetically the results of their analysis. The true excitement of philosophy consists in coming back to the starting point, and seeing it anew. Chesterton's exuberant remark about his own method, and its consistent return from reflective to direct thought, is equally applicable to Rosmini's *Psychology*.

> What could be more glorious than to brace one's self up to discover New South Wales and then realize, with a gush of happy tears, that it was really old South Wales. This at least seems to me the main problem for philosophers, and is in a manner the main problem of this book. How can we contrive to be at once astonished at the world and yet at home in it?
>
> (*Orthodoxy, Introduction in Defence of Everything Else*)

Recognising what we know about the soul through direct perception is not, however, as easy as returning to 'old South Wales'. 'Know yourself', in the sense of 'acknowledge what you already know of yourself', is difficult, and made more difficult by our imagining that we have already recognised ourselves sufficiently, due to our modern inability to concentrate closely on anything, and in particular through our ever-present incapacity to distance ourselves from the overlay of habits and customs which hide the depths within. The successful philosophical psychologist is like an archaeologist engaged in aerial photography: he shows from above what has been trampled underfoot for thousands of years.

Philosophically speaking, the difficulty of sufficiently accurate observation in psychology is overcome by adherence to two simple, yet profound principles enunciated by Rosmini in his *A New Essay concerning the Origin of Ideas* (vol. 2, 26–27).
First:

> When explaining facts about the human spirit, we must not take into account less than is necessary for the explanation. The reason is clear: as long as we take into

account less than is needed, it is impossible to posit a sufficient explanation of the facts...

Second:

> In our explanation of these facts, we must not take into account more than is required. Non-essentials are gratuitous to the explanation and, as entirely gratuitous, can be gratuitously denied.

Rosmini follows these principles throughout his *Psychology*. If this is kept in mind, the reader has a key with which to unlock the many difficult passages presented by the work.

B. Mention must also be made, as we said, about difficulties of vocabulary inherent in the translation of this work. Besides the normal obstacles associated with Rosmini's wordiness and erudition, specific problems of translation have arisen in *Psychology* through his use either of words which he coined in Italian or of words which cannot be put into English without placing great strain on the language. The translators feel that many of these difficulties have been overcome, and present no further problem in English. Five words, however, require special explanation if enigmas and irritation are to be avoided. In Italian, these words are: *ente, organato, intestino, sensilità* and *tocco*.

Ente

The straightforward translation of ente (present participle) is 'being'. Italian, however, like Latin, has another word, essere (infinitive) (Latin: *esse*) which is also translated as 'being' in English. But when both words are expressed as 'being', the subtle, and not so subtle, differences in meaning between *ente* and *essere* are lost in translation, despite their importance in the original text. These differences are often overlooked, of course, even by native Italians, not all of whom are philosophers. On one occasion, Rosmini wrote to his proof reader, rather sharply it must be said:

> Leave *ente* or *essere* as you find them. I did not use them haphazardly.
>
>   (to Fenner, *Epistolario completo*, vol. 5, 749).

The multiple differences in meaning between the two Italian

words cannot be fully explained here. It is sufficient to state that Rosmini's use of *ente* is dealt with under forty-seven separate entries in Bergomaschi's immense *Dizionario antologico del pensiero di Antonio Rosmini* (CD-Rom, Centro Internazionale di Studi Rosminiani, Stresa, 1998). One example, however, will be especially useful.

Niccolò Tommaseo, the great Italian lexicographer, had included an article on *ente* and *essere* in his *Dizionario dei Sinonomi*. Writing to him about this, Rosmini elucidated his own understanding of the words:

> *Ente* [ens] suitably expresses both that which HAS *essere* [being], and *essere* itself or, to use a pleonasm, that which *essere* IS. *Essere*, on the other hand, means simply *essere*, that which is *essere*, the act and nothing more. But everything that HAS *essere* and is not itself *essere* is contingent; while *ESSERE* itself is necessary. In my opinion, therefore, we say more correctly *gli enti* [entia] when we are speaking about contingent *esseri* [beings], and *essere* and *esseri* when speaking about necessary *esseri*.In a word, *essere* is act. In so far as *enti*, contingent things, have act, they participate in *essere*, although they are not themselves *essere*.
>
> (*Epistolario Completo*, vol. 4, 338–339)

In a note to this letter, Rosmini comments on *De Divinis Nominibus*:

> In this book, we read that God is himself *esse* (εἶναι) for those things which are (τοῖς οὖσι). This applies not only to *entia* (τα ὄντα) but also to the *esse* itself of *entia* (τὸ εἶναι τῶν ὄντων).

It is clear from these illustrations that the use of 'being' to indicate both *ente* and *essere* would at best confuse and at worse mislead the reader. We have, therefore, used the word *ens* (plural: *entia*) to translate the Italian *ente*, and reserved 'being' to translate *essere*. A tenuous support for this practice will be found in the *Oxford English Dictionary* under the entry *ens*, although the exact meaning of the word in *Psychology* will have to be taken from its use in context rather than from explanations given in *OED*.

Organato.

There is no support, however, for the use of 'organated' as a translation of the Italian *organato*. *Organato* is not a current word in Italian, nor was it current in Rosmini's day. It was minted by Rosmini to indicate a state of affairs to which, according to him, he was drawing attention for the first time. The best introduction to his use of this word, and the root from which it springs, is found in his *Teosofia*.

> The word 'organism' is sometimes used by me, as it is by other philosophers, to mean in general every discernible multiplicity in an ens which does not detract from the ontological unity of the ens. But the first, proper meaning of the word is that applied to the living, organated body.
> (vol. 6, *Il Reale*, chap. 42, p. 225).

In other words, 'organism', 'organisation', 'organated', and other words etymologically related to them, often have a much wider use for Rosmini than their present-day application, even in Italian. He speaks, for example, of the 'ontological organism of an ens', a phrase intended to designate the 'intrinsic order of the ens' (*ibid*., p. 104). If this is kept in mind, 'organated' in English will help the reader to understand that even in relationship to the living body, Rosmini is not considering simply the bodily organs but the body with its multiplicity insofar as this multiplicity does not detract from its unity.

Intestino

Rosmini uses this word adjectivally in the sense of 'internal' rather than in its modern, substantive meaning of 'intestine'. His obvious preference for *intestino* rather than *interno* when referring to elements related in some way to sensation has been respected by our use of 'intestine' as an adjective, a revival of an archaic usage which we hope will be understood as a suitable solution when seen in context.

Sensilità

This is another word coined by Rosmini and transcribed by us into English to express a notion necessary to Rosmini's philosophy, but scarcely referred to by others. For him, the animal feeling principle, or soul, is undoubtedly unextended. At the same time, what is felt, the term of feeling, is often extended. 'Sensility' describes the relationship between the unextended feeling principle and its extended term.

> The relationship between the feeling principle and extension is not a relationship of size, according to which two extended things are measured with one another. It is a relationship of sensility.
>
> *(Anthropology as an Aid to Moral Science*, 232)

Rosmini acknowledges that he has invented a new word for his purposes.

> I called this relationship between the extended element and the sentient principle a relationship of sensility.
>
> *(Psychology*, vol. 2, 1126)

We have tried to respect his new use of language.

Tocco

Here again Rosmini states clearly that he has 'invented a word' (*Teosofia*, vol. 6, chap. 50, p. 81). In this case, he wished to express the variation arising in sensation (*sensazione*) or feeling (*sentimento*) from the action on the sentient principle of one being (*essere*) rather than another. The distinction in 'touch' or 'feel' between one kind of sensation and another (sight differing from hearing), and between sensations of the same kind (different qualities of sound, for example) is what he has in mind. But by using *tocco* in this sense, Rosmini was adapting an already existing word to his purposes rather than inventing a new one. Our own conclusion is that we can achieve his aim in English by using the word 'feel', which is already employed in a non-philosophical sense to indicate something similar to *tocco*. We speak, for instance, of 'the feel of a painting' when we mean to express its total effect upon us in contradistinction to that experienced when we contemplate other works by the same artist or by different artists. To avoid possible ambiguities, however, we have consistently used 'feel' in inverted commas to translate Rosmini's *tocco*. An example will be helpful:

> Although the 'feel' of a sensation can vary in kind and degree according to the difference in the extended term and in the intestine movements in the term, we can easily see that the 'feel' (a positive quality of sensation) is neither

extension nor movement, but always the varied act of the smple, a sensation may vary in 'feel' but not in extension. Thus while the sensation both of the eye and of the touch can terminate in one and the same extension, the sensations differ greatly and have a very different 'feel'.

(*Psychology*, vol. 2, 1999)

DENIS CLEARY
TERENCE WATSON

Durham,
March, 1999

Contents

Preface to the Metaphysical Works   3

INTRODUCTION
I. Classification of the sciences: complete and incomplete sciences   15
II. Unity of the science dealing with the human being — subsidiary sciences   17
III. Anthropology — Psychology   18
IV. Ideology and psychology — they provide the rudiments of everything that can be known   19
V. Psychology — Cosmology   26
VI. The method to be used in psychological research   28
VII. Christian Wolff's division of psychology into two sciences, one called *empirical,* the other *rational psychology,* is excluded   28
VIII. The *synthesism* inherent to method and distribution in the philosophical sciences   31
IX. The division of psychology   36

DEFINITIONS   39

Part One

Essence of the Human Soul

Book 1
The source and principle of psychology

CHAPTER 1. A concept of soul must be sought free from everything that operations of the mind may have added when composing it   48

CHAPTER 2. *Myself* does not express the pure concept of the soul   49

CHAPTER 3. The pure notion of the soul can only be attained from *myself* by stripping *myself* of all that is foreign to this notion   52

CHAPTER 4. A start to expropriating *myself* of everything not pertaining to the pure notion of soul   52

CHAPTER 5. The human soul is a substantial feeling which expresses itself through the word *myself*   60

CHAPTER 6. Opinions of philosophers
Article 1. Philosophers who did not know where to seek the essence of the soul   61
Article 2. Philosophers who remain unaware of the fundamental feeling   64

CHAPTER 7. Proofs of the fundamental feeling   65

CHAPTER 8. The essence of the soul is in the fundamental feeling in so far as this feeling is substance and subject   69

CHAPTER 9. The principle of psychology   70

CHAPTER 10. How to apply the principle of psychology to deduce the special information that forms the science of the soul   73

Book 2

Some properties of the essence of the soul

[INTRODUCTION]   82

CHAPTER 1. The unity of the soul in each human being   82

CHAPTER 2. The substance of the soul is the sole principle of all operations   83

CHAPTER 3. The spirituality of the soul is proved directly through consciousness   84

CHAPTER 4. The immortality of the soul proved directly from consciousness   85

CHAPTER 5. The identity of the soul in its different modifications

Article 1. The difficulty explained   87
Article 2. A start to solving the problem   89
Article 3. Continuation   90
Article 4. Continuation — The feeling and intelligent subject
remains the same whatever change takes place in the terms of
its actions, or in the actions themselves   94
Article 5. The sentient subject and the intelligent subject in
human beings are one subject, not two   99

CHAPTER 6. The nouns 'substance' and 'subject' applied to
the human soul   101

CHAPTER 7. A question about the invariability of the soul,
and the changes to which it can be subject   103

Article 1. Removal of what is first felt and what is first
understood   103
Article 2. Removal of what is understood   104
Article 3. Removal of what is felt   104
Article 4. Addition or change to what is first felt   105
Article 5. Addition to what is understood   106

CHAPTER 8. The difference between the human soul, pure
intelligences and animal souls   108

CHAPTER 9. Relationship between the substance of the soul
and human nature

Article 1. The soul is the form of the human being   109
Article 2. How that which is first understood is the form of he
intelligent principle   110
Article 3. How that which is *first felt* can and cannot be called
the form of the sentient principle   110
Article 4. The sense in which the body can be called
matter of the soul   115
Article 5. The sense in which the soul is said to be the form of
the body   119

CHAPTER 10. The reality of the soul   121

CHAPTER 11. The finiteness and infinity of the human soul   123

Book 3
The union and mutual influence
of soul and body

[INTRODUCTION]   132

CHAPTER 1. The sensitive soul is united with the body by
means of feeling   133

CHAPTER 2. The union of rational soul with body comes
about by means of an immanent perception of animal
feeling   135
Article 1. Rational activity contains sensitive activity   135
Article 2. Rational activity contains sensitive activity in a way
proper to itself   136
Article 3. It follows that the rational principle is united to the
body through immanent perception of the animal feeling   139
Article 4. Distinction between the individual, fundamental
feeling which constitutes the human being and the primal
perception of the animal feeling where the nexus between
soul and body is located   140

CHAPTER 3. The nature of the first perception by which the
rational principle constantly perceives its own animal-
fundamental feeling and thus unites itself to the body   141

CHAPTER 4. How philosophical meditation, in analysing the
animal feeling perceived by the soul, distinguishes the
subjective body and recognises it as having the same nature
as extrasubjective bodies   142

CHAPTER 5. Concerning Averroes' opinion that the body is
united to the rational soul by means of the intelligible species   144

CHAPTER 6. Descartes' teaching that thinking is essential to
the human being   147

CHAPTER 7. The activity and passivity of the soul relative to
the body to which it is united
Article 1. The relationship between formal and efficient cause   148
Article 2. How the nexus between soul and body by means of
the primal perception explains the activity and passivity of
the rational soul relative to the body it informs   149

Article 3. The activity of the rational soul on the extrasubjective body 153

Article 4. Can the rational soul cause animal movement harmful to the animal? 153

CHAPTER 8. Can the pure intellect act effectively on the body? 154

CHAPTER 9. The efficacy of the acts of the rational principle on the body

Article 1. General extension of this efficacy 156

Article 2. Efficacy of the special acts of the rational principle 156

§1. *How the body is changed by the rational principle through acts of intelligence*

A. Perceptions, and an explanation of their spontaneity 157

B. Imagination 158

C. Memories 160

D. **Rational feelings** 161

§2. *How the body is changed by the rational principle through acts of the will* 165

CHAPTER 10. The conditions necessary for the rational principle if it is to produce the movements it wishes in its own body 167

CHAPTER 11. Propagation of the movement stimulated by the rational principle and beginning in the body; the parts to which it spreads

Article 1. Summary — Voluntary and involuntary nerves and muscles 173

Article 2. Parts of the body where movements stimulated by the rational principle begin 174

Article 3. Continuation — Location of movements stimulated by the rational instinct and by the will — The double nervous system 176

CHAPTER 12. Causes of the errors of the animistic school 181

Article 1. First cause 182

Article 2. Second cause 183

Article 3. Third cause 189

Article 4. Fourth cause 191

CHAPTER 13. The soul's activity on the extrasubjective body 192

Book 4
The simplicity of the human soul and the questions to which it gives rise

[INTRODUCTION]   202

CHAPTER 1. The meaning of simplicity   203

CHAPTER 2. Classification of the proofs of the simplicity of the soul   203

CHAPTER 3. The simplicity of the soul shown from the properties with which the soul is furnished   203

CHAPTER 4. The proofs of the simplicity of the soul from its operations in general   205

CHAPTER 5. Proofs drawn from the passive and active operations of the soul   207

CHAPTER 6. Development of the proof of the simplicity of the soul from the nature of the continuum   208

CHAPTER 7. Development of the proof drawn from the opposition existing between extrasubjective phenomena accompanying sensation, and sensation itself   212

CHAPTER 8. Some proofs, given by the ancients, for the simplicity of the soul coincide with our own   215

CHAPTER 9. How the sensitive soul can multiply but not divide   217

CHAPTER 10. Continuation — Multiplication of polyps   222

CHAPTER 11. Causes of death and of generation   224

CHAPTER 12. Causes of different organisation in animals   226

CHAPTER 13. The law according to which the sentient principle carries out the organising function   228

CHAPTER 14. Spontaneous generation
Article 1. Various opinions about the truth of spontaneous generation   233

Article 2. Does the opinion of spontaneous generation favour the materialists' system? 235

Article 3. Animals considered by antiquity as emerging from apparently brute matter 237

CHAPTER 15. The hypothesis that all particles of matter are animated 238

Article 1. The hypothesis that all particles of matter are animated does not favour materialism 239

Article 2. The hypothesis does not favour pantheism 239

Article 3. Opinions about the animation of the particles of matter

§1. *Indian philosophers* 241

§2. *Greek and Italian philosophers, and those of other nations* 245

§3. *German and English philosophers* 248

Article 4. Does the hypothesis of animation contradict common sense? 252

Article 5. Does the hypothesis of the animation of the elements harmonise with the progress of the natural sciences? 253

Article 6. Apparent life and latent life 253

Article 7. Three forms or levels of sensitive life: life of continuity, of stimulation and of self-renewing stimulation 254

§1. *The first kind of life (non-apparent): a feeling of continuity* 255

§2. *The second kind of (non-apparent) life: a feeling of simple stimulation* 256

§3. *The third kind of (apparent) life: a feeling of perpetual stimulation* 257

Article 8. Different organisation is the cause of the varieties of life 258

Article 9. Sensitive and insensitive parts of the animal 259

Article 10. Important questions still to be solved 260

Article 11. Direct proofs of the life of the first elements; these proofs make the hypothesis practically certain 260

CHAPTER 16. Unlimited space as the term of sensitive souls 262

CHAPTER 17. Individuality

Article 1. The concept and nature of individuality 265

Article 2. Individuality of the human being in so far as it is rooted in intuition 267

Article 3. Individuality in animals 269

Article 4. Human individuality in so far as it is founded in the perception of an individuated animal feeling 271

CHAPTER 18. Living fluids 273

CHAPTER 19. Animal death 285

CHAPTER 20. The source of animal life 289

CHAPTER 21. The simplicity of the human soul relative to the intellective principle 294

CHAPTER 22. The simplicity and oneness of the rational soul 298

CHAPTER 23. The origin of the intellective soul 304

Book 5
Immortality of the human soul
and
death of the human being

[INTRODUCTION] 310

CHAPTER 1. The concept of death, and the concept of annihilation 311

CHAPTER 2. Can sensitive souls cease to exist?
Article 1. Sensitive souls cannot cease to exist through any action on the part of natural forces 311
Article 2. Sensitive souls are not destroyed by the Creator 313
Article 3. Confirmation of the existence of elementary life 313

CHAPTER 3. Origin and confutation of metempsychosis 314

CHAPTER 4. The concept of human death
Article 1. Death in human beings consists in the cessation of the primal perception of the fundamental feeling 316
Article 2. The conditions giving rise to the primal perception and consequently to human life 317

CHAPTER 5. How human nature is constituted 318

CHAPTER 6. The intellective soul never loses its individuality; it is immortal 321

CHAPTER 7. The first thing that human beings understand 322

CHAPTER 8. Why the human soul no longer perceives the body when the organisation is dissolved 325

CHAPTER 9. Why the human soul is joined to only one body, and to this body rather than that 328

CHAPTER 10. Can the intellective principle abandon the body spontaneously in the absence of disorganisation? 328

CHAPTER 11. Why human beings find death repugnant 333

CHAPTER 12. Does the separated soul retain any inclination to unite itself with the body? 334

CHAPTER 13. The preceding teaching about the union of soul and body avoids the opposite errors 341

CHAPTER 14. Further proofs of the immortality of the human soul 350

CHAPTER 15. Conclusion 355

Appendix 358

Index of Biblical References 372

Index of Persons 373

General Index 375

PSYCHOLOGY

Preface
to the Metaphysical Works

(1) It is strange to see the words *Philosophy* and *Metaphysics* still used without a consistent meaning. A short time ago, we even heard some French philosophers maintain that these words could not be defined. If this were so, the words should be banned from human language. But because people do in fact use them, it is certain that they have some value, inconsistent though it is. It will be helpful if we examine the reason for this inconsistency.

(2) *Philosophy* is a word invented by the founder of the Italic school. Cicero describes how Leontius, king of Phliasi, asked Pythagoras to state the art which gave value to his life. The reply was simple: he knew no art; he was a philosopher.[1] From that moment, people who engaged in the investigation of the most important truths were no longer called 'wise' (σοφοί), but 'philosophers' (φιλόσοφοι), that is, lovers and seekers of wisdom.

This remark of Pythagoras was an extremely noble, moral statement whose intimate truth is felt by all. No one, as we know, can call himself wise. The darkness besetting our intellect is profound; our ignorance as mortals is extreme even after a lifetime of meditation. Prolonged efforts and innumerable frustrations, often accompanied by error, bring forth as their fruit only a tiny particle of truth. God alone has the right to be

[1] *Tuscul.*, bk. 5: 3.

called wise; it is a lie and pride to call human beings wise. In uncovering this lie and rebuking this pride, Pythagoras made philosophical humility the solid base for the investigation of what is true. However, the words 'philosophy' and 'philosopher', although providing a better direction for systematic knowledge and its lovers, did not determine the matter of their research. In this respect, the meaning of the words remained vague and uncertain.

(3) Andronicus of Rhodes, who put Aristotle's works in order, placed the books dealing with ens after those on physics. This seems to have been the origin of the word 'metaphysics' (from μετά and φύσις) which means 'after physics'. 'Metaphysics', like 'philosophy', was pressed into use without its indicating any matter for the mind to work on. It did nothing more than show the place assigned to the ontological works in the Aristotelian corpus.

(4) The origin of the two words 'philosophy' and 'metaphysics' illustrates clearly enough that they were not employed in the first place to point to a determined subject of some academic discipline. When used, these scientific words could be freely applied to different branches of systematic knowledge. This accounts for their different meanings.

(5) Today, however, solemn words of this kind, used so frequently, cannot be ignored. At the same time, common sense will not be satisfied if the words circulate freely and lawlessly, like wandering vagabonds whose name and way of life is unknown to their fellows.

(6) It is the duty of philosophers alone to determine their meaning. The words have been put into use not by the masses but by philosophical schools. People will be happy enough to accept the law laid down by philosophers, provided the latter agree amongst themselves about the use of the words.

(7) Considerations of this kind have made me attempt to fix the meaning of the word 'philosophy' by defining it as 'knowledge of the ultimate reasons'.[2] I felt the need to determine the value of this word as soon as I contemplated the UNITY of wisdom, which philosophy studies and loves. It is impossible for the spirit to admire wisdom in its sublime unity unless we

[2] *Sistema filosofico*, 1–9 [Turin, 1844].

(3)–(7)

understand that philosophy, precisely because of its unity, is susceptible of a single definition, without which it could never be written methodically and scientifically.

(8) But the value we give to the word 'metaphysics' must be such that people will not be too unfamiliar with the concepts already attached to it. In other words, we need to adopt some means of reconciling its opposite senses. We must remove its vague, uncertain use and establish a fixed, unchangeable meaning as a point of reference for those who employ it.

(9) Previously, 'metaphysics' was sometimes used synonymously with 'philosophy', sometimes as the equivalent of 'ontology'. Later, 'ideology', when it came into use to indicate teaching about ideas, appeared to have been separated from the body of metaphysics, together with logic which is as it were a corollary and appendix of ideology. As a result, many Scholastic treatises called *Elements of Logic* and *Metaphysics* were placed one in contradistinction to the other. This is my way also. 'Ideology' (to which I reduce 'logic') is the science of ideal being; 'metaphysics', unburdened from the part of knowledge which deals with ideas, is then left to us as an extremely suitable word to indicate that group of sciences which deal philosophically with teaching about real entia. We thus have two groups of clearly distinguished philosophical sciences, one composed of ideological, the other of metaphysical sciences.

(10) This definition has to be considered at greater length.

First, we have to note the difference between metaphysics and physics, both of which deal with real entia.

Physics has no rightful place amongst philosophical sciences. It remains there because of the vague meaning of the word 'philosophy'. But as soon as the meaning of this word has been restricted to 'teaching about the final reasons', both physics and mathematics are excluded from philosophy, together with all the natural sciences, as they are called, which take note of the phenomena and laws of real entia without investigating their final reasons.

Moreover, these sciences do not extend further than real, corporeal entia. Metaphysics on the other hand, as part of philosophy, cannot fulfil its responsibility in seeking the final reasons of real entia unless it considers them in all their universality and in their entire fulfilment. In other words, it must ascend to those supreme principles or first causes which embrace all real *entia*. The reasons for things are not final unless they are totally universal and absolute. The unity of philosophy must be accompanied by UNIVERSALITY, philosophy's other most noble characteristic.[3]

(11) Second, care must be taken to understand that in defining metaphysics as 'philosophical teaching about real, complete *ens*', or 'teaching about the final reasons of real *ens*', we do not intend to indicate reality alone as the object of metaphysics. In fact, reality alone, cut off from the idea, is the object neither of science nor of cognition, as we showed elsewhere.[4] It is not yet *ens*, but on the way to being *ens* (μὴ ὄν). It has no reason for itself in itself. The reason for things is always an idea[5] so that real things become the object of knowledge only when they are apprehended or considered in relationship to the idea, through the idea and in the idea. Naked reality is perceived only by feeling; it cannot be perceived by intelligence and is not, therefore, *per se* an object of knowledge.[6]

[3] Cf. the preface to the first and second volumes of the *Opuscoli filosofici*, Milan, 1827–1828, and to *A New Essay concerning the Origin of Ideas*, Durham.

[4] *NE*, vol. 2, 410; *Sistema filosofico*, 1–8.

[5] *Principles of Ethics*, fn. 2, and *Storia comparativa e critica dei sistemi intorno al principio della morale*.

[6] Hence, contingent realities, which do not have the *idea* in their nature, are not *per se* knowable as God is, in whom there is contemporaneously real and ideal being.
Note that it is easy to err by believing that certain sciences which deal with individual things, such as astronomy which concerns the sun, moon and other stars, consider purely real, subsistent being. To realise that the theory of these stars does not stop at their subsistence, it is sufficient to consider that even if the Almighty were to annihilate all the stars in heaven, the theory would be no less true. If the Almighty were to annihilate sun and moon, and create another sun and moon equal to those annihilated, astronomy would suffer no change whatsoever; it would be true applied to the newly created stars as it was of the preceding stars from the observation of which human beings had drawn astronomy. And this despite the fact that their reality was no longer the same as before. Here we have a clear proof that material individuality, which serves us as a means and an *occasion* of attaining knowledge of such sciences, is not their *object*. Indeed, it is only an example, on the basis of which the mind considers theory, which is valid for all similar cases. We have already considered more at length how the understanding always

(12) The definitions I have established for philosophy and metaphysics could appear to some people as contradictions. They may object: 'If philosophy is knowledge of the ultimate reasons, and reasons are always ideal beings, how can it be said that one part of philosophy, that is, metaphysics, embraces real things?' I reply: 'Metaphysics does not in any way embrace real things (which are the term of feeling), but philosophical teaching about real things (cf. (9), (11)).'

(13) Philosophy is knowledge of the final reasons and precisely under this aspect has to deal with what is real. It is necessary to speak about real things in the teaching concerned with final reasons.

First, because *reason* has meaning relative to that of which we seek the reason. Here, we are seeking the reason for real things which of themselves do not constitute the proper object of philosophy but only its occasion and condition. Philosophy deals with real things because it deals with their possibility and their sufficient final reasons.

Second, because the first reason demands a real being co-essential to it, as we have seen.[7] It cannot be fully known, therefore, without the teaching about that first reality which constitutes it not as reason, but as complete, absolute ens which contains the reason of all things in its depths. Philosophy must deal with this absolute, subsistent reality as its first proper object, as the completion of this object.

(14) Having said this, we can examine critically the three principal definitions of philosophy given so far.

Some authors are incapable of moving away from what is real. Materialists are necessarily bound to this kind of philosophy. For them, only negative philosophy is possible, or rather the destruction of philosophy. Hobbes' definition of philosophy is an example of this. He makes philosophy consist in the knowledge of effects and of phenomena by means of causes and generation, and in the knowledge of causes and generation by means of effects and phenomena. But if the discussion starts from phenomena and effects alone, rather

terminates its act in ideas, even when it considers what is real (*Teodicea*, 617–641, and elsewhere).

[7] *NE*, vol. 3, 1456–1460.

than from the ideal object, only proximate causes, or rather the *laws* according to which feelable things may change, can be known. This definition destroys philosophy. All that remains is physics and the natural sciences which usurp the title 'philosophy'.

(15) The second mistaken definition is given by subjectivists who reduce every ideal object simply to a modification of the human spirit. For them, philosophy is 'the science of human thought', as Galluppi says.[8] But human thought is only the instrument used by philosophy to find and contemplate its objects which, with God as the greatest among them, cannot be reduced to thought. Clearly, it would be absurd to maintain that systematic knowledge of God, which certainly pertains to philosophy, deals only with human thought.

(16) The third mistaken definition is that of the Platonists whose error, contrary to the other two, sins by excess. For them, ideas alone are the object of philosophy; the only duty of the philosopher is to contemplate the *idea of ens*, τῇ τοῦ ὄντος ἰδέα.[9] But this is not correct. In fact, the idea of ens has to guide the human mind in finding the totally real and absolute ens. All intellectual speculation finishes here, not by way of the idea, but by way of affirmation and intuition.

Wolff's definition is reducible to that of the Platonists. For him, philosophy is 'systematic knowledge of possible things'. If, according to this definition, God is to be amongst the objects of philosophy, we are forced to maintain that philosophy deals only with the intrinsic possibility of God. This again is certainly not true: philosophy deals with the divine being, not with the mere possibility of this being. Moreover, possibilities do not constitute the reasons of things in their entirety, but are an element of these very reasons; contingent beings, we say, do not

---

[8] *Lezioni di Logica e di Metafisica, Lez.* 2. Here Galluppi says: 'After Descartes, philosophers have normally called *thought* any act and modification of the human soul, that is, modification which consists in *feeling*, knowing, desiring and willing.' This affirmation is false. If it were true, all philosophers from Descartes onward would be sensists and subjectivists. What we should say, to the honour of modern philosophy, is that some philosophers have been able to distinguish *thought* from *feeling*, and the objects of thought from thought itself.

[9] Plato, *Soph.*, p. 254 (Bipont.).

exist solely because they are possible but because, being possible, a first real cause has created them.

(17) Let us go back to metaphysics. Having fixed the meaning that we intend to give to this word, let us consider the special sciences into which it is divided.

Philosophical sciences can be ordered in various ways according to the aspects under which they are considered and from which they accept the norm governing their distribution. I have provided examples of the different ways in which philosophy can suitably be divided.[10]

One of these divisions distinguished three groups of philosophical sciences — the *sciences of intuition, of perception and of reasoning*, as I have called them.[11] By this, I do not mean that there are some philosophical sciences bereft of reasoning. Rather the name is drawn from the act of the spirit through which these sciences receive their object. Some philosophical sciences receive their object from intuition alone, some from intellective perception, and others finally from reasoning. The first, which require only *intuition* as the act of the spirit in order to possess their object, are the ideological sciences. Metaphysics, therefore, belongs to the sciences of perception and of reasoning. But does it embrace them all?

(18) It does not. Metaphysics, as philosophical teaching about real ens, can extend only to the branch of *ontological* sciences which deal with real ens as it is. It does not embrace the branch called deontological sciences (δέον, what is suitable, what is necessary) which deal with real ens as it must be. It is not without good reason that some authors have taken the word 'metaphysics' as synonymous with ontology.[12]

(19) Nevertheless, there exists a very intimate relationship between metaphysics and the deontological sciences; the teaching which shows what ens is, is the foundation of the teaching which investigates what ens must be if it is to be perfect. The apex of deontology is ethics, or δικαιοσύνη or hosiology or

[10] Cf. Ab. Antonio Fontana, *Manuale per l'Educazione umana*, vol. 3, c. 8, Milan 1834 [This chapter was written by Rosmini and inserted in the book written by his friend, Fontana. Cf. *Epistolario Completo*, vol. 4, letter 1991].

[11] *Sistema filosofico*, nn. 108, 128–129.

[12] Cf. Baldinotti, *Metaphysica Generalis Praef.*

whatever else we call it, because real ens is not complete unless it contains in its depths the moral form that completes and perfects ens.[13] Ethics, the science which shows what moral ens is to be, is deontology's last word and, therefore, the most philosophical of all sciences.

(20) We are now in a position to express more explicitly the group of sciences covered by the word 'metaphysics' and standing in contradistinction to other groups.

From what has been said, the whole of philosophy can be distributed into three groups, that is, *ideological, metaphysical* and *deontological* sciences. According to this division, the ideological sciences have intuition alone as their object; the metaphysical sciences include the sciences of perception and the first branch of the sciences of reason, that is, the metaphysical sciences; finally, the group of deontological sciences includes the other branch of sciences of reasoning.

(21) At this point, we see clearly both the position occupied by metaphysics in the broad spread of philosophy and the appropriate distinction between its various members. As we said, the sciences of perception are psychology and cosmology, while the first branch of the sciences of reasoning extends to *ontology in the strict sense* and to *natural theology*. These four constitute the group of metaphysical sciences.

(22) Although this seems a natural, elegant division, I have thought it more in keeping with my aim to change it slightly and reduce the final three to a single science which I have called *theosophy*. This would seem more helpful to scholarly understanding, and render the argument more comprehensive and magnificent by lightening the process and assisting minds to grapple with abstractions. Experience shows me that abstraction is a very difficult task for many intellects. This great synthesis is not arbitrary, however, but proffered by the nature of the case.

(23) Cosmology, for example, which teaches us about the world, can be dealt with in two ways, that is, physically or metaphysically — two ways which have been confused so far by authors who have written about cosmology. In fact, the description of the world of phenomena and its laws pertains to

[13] *Teodicea*, Milan, 1845, nn. 384–394.

the group of physical, not philosophical sciences. If teaching about the world is to belong to the philosophical sciences, it has to be considered in its final reasons, which can be sought either in the world or in its cause, that is, in Almighty God, the Creator. Considering the world in itself, we see that it is composed of matter, of sensitive souls and of intelligences. Matter, however, is only the term of the sensitive soul, from which it cannot be really divided without annihilation. In order to conceive of matter as it is, we have to consider it as joined to the soul which feels it. This we do in psychology. Moreover, as matter needs a sentient principle whose term it is if its concept is not to perish, so the sentient soul needs matter of which it is the principle if its concept, too, is not to perish. The sentient soul is not an ens, therefore, unless its act terminates in material or corporeal extension. And this is how psychology considers it. If we were to separate matter entirely from the feeling to which it refers, nothing would remain except a pure abstraction, an incipient ens which does not subsist — what the ancients rightly called a non-ens. This will be made clear in the treatise on psychology. Teaching about the world, in so far as it investigates the final reason of the world's existence in itself, that is, the reason which constitutes it as a conceivable ens, goes hand in hand inseparably with the science of the soul. In so far as it investigates the final reason of the world in its cause, which is different from the world, it obviously pertains to the science that has God, the sole cause of what is created, as its object.

(24) The part of cosmology which describes the phenomena offered to the senses by matter, and their laws, pertains, therefore, to the physicist; the other part, which seeks the reasons of the universe and which alone is truly philosophical, belongs partly to psychology and partly to natural theology.

(25) Ontology, properly speaking, deals with ens in its entirety and completion. The mind can, however, speculate in two ways when considering ens in this universality. It can either take the way of abstraction or that of ideal-negative reasoning. The latter leads the mind to supreme Being, absolute, totally real and complete Being. Abstract reasoning, on the other hand, brings the mind to an abstract theory of being, a theory applicable to every ens, contingent or necessary. This work of abstraction aims to know the conditions, qualities and common characteristics of

every ens which otherwise cannot receive the name and concept of ens — a name and concept which diminish as these conditions, qualities and common characteristics diminish. This highly abstract teaching does not have a real ens as its object, and cannot therefore constitute any metaphysical science, according to the definition we have given. What then is the value and aim of this teaching? Its sole purpose is to provide a way which makes possible for the understanding to ascend finally to knowledge of the absolute ens, that is, the ens in which all conditions of ens are fully and completely verified and from which the understanding can distinguish relative entia that share in only some of those conditions, none of which the understanding possesses as its own. In a word, ontology considered from this point of view is simply an immense preface to the treatise on God to which we intend to join it, and from which alone it receives its fullness and attains its purpose.

(26) In this way two real entia, known by us according to their condition, remain as objects of metaphysics, the *finite spirit* and the *infinite Spirit*, which give rise to the philosophical sciences we have called *pneumatology* and *natural theology*.

(27) I will not treat *pneumatology* in all its extension. The word, which expresses the science about spirits in general, deals with every kind of spirit and embraces the human soul as well as separate intelligences. I shall limit myself to a treatise on the soul, and deal with psychology for the following reasons.

(28) Only the human spirit falls under our experience. The philosopher can therefore deal with angels only by way of mere reasoning, devoid of perception. With such reasoning he can propose three questions to himself: do separate intelligences exist? what is their origin? what is their nature? The existence, cause and knowable essence are the three parts of angelology. But the existence of separate intelligences can be proved only by arguing from their suitability to the attributes of the Creator, that is, of their cause. Their knowable essence can be induced only by analogy with what is known of the soul that falls under our experience. We cannot speak of the nature of separate intelligences unless we have first known what experience tells us about the human spirit, that is, until we have dealt with psychology. I do not think that teaching about angels can by itself constitute a complete philosophical science. I shall,

therefore, expound it, together with the teaching about the world of which the angels are a part, when I speak of the supreme Being.

(29) In this way, teaching about the supreme Being is presented in three treatises or three distinct, but intimately connected parts. The first part is a kind of very broad introduction which reasons about being in general as the human mind conceives it by way of abstraction. This is the science commonly called *ontology*. The second party deals with absolute being by way of ideal-negative reasoning and corresponds to *natural theology*; the third is a kind of very broad appendix which deals with the things produced by the absolute Being, and corresponds to cosmology. The complex of all this teaching I call the*osophy*. But I do not wish to oblige myself to keep the three parts rigorously separate. I would prefer to follow the *didactic method*, and set out the information in a way better suited to every reader. In other words, I will not insist in any way on the ontological, theological or cosmological status of what comes first, provided that what precedes throws light on what follows. Science itself will draw greater unity from this way of doing things.

(30) Finally, I shall add, as the crown and apex of all metaphysics, a separate treatise about the best and wisest government of the world. This I shall call *Theodicy*, which I shall use as a link intimately joining the philosophical sciences with the science of revealed truth and in particular with *Supernatural Anthropology*.

PSYCHOLOGY

INTRODUCTION

I
Classification of the sciences:
complete and incomplete sciences

1. The human mind, by its acts, knows but does not constitute an entity; moreover, it knows the entity only in the part and from the point of view to which it limits its glance, or *attention*. Consequently it even divides what in the entity is undivided. The laws of attention, therefore, sever and limit the ens that is its object, but do not sever and limit the ens in itself. If the ens were to lose its unity, it would no longer be. These limited objects of attention, which are also called *mental entia*, are indeed portions of the object of a science, but are not its complete object. The object of a science must therefore be an ens, intelligible[1] in

---

[1] Entia are objects of science in so far as they are *per* se intelligible. Hence the distinction between *science* and *history*. Because *intelligibility* consists in *universal being*, *science* always considers entia in their essence, never in their blind reality. *History*, however, while presupposing *ideal* things in the mind, is content to affirm their subsistence while presupposing essence, and tells us only about *real things*. Theology alone considers its object as *real* because Almighty God is essentially real, and his very reality *intelligible*. All other contingent realities are not *per se* intelligible, but become so through universal being, or the idea, which does not enter as an element into the nature of contingent things but pertains to the divine nature. What, therefore, is the object of science? — Let me repeat: it is *intelligible being*. If we are dealing

its unity. One of the greatest founts of error is to be sought in
the division of the sciences according to *mental entia*[2] without
regard to the unity of entia in themselves. This gives flesh to
abstractions, by positing division in the nature of things which
of themselves are undivided, and thereby creating a great
number of chimeras. Every time a mental being is taken for a
complete being, the mind has fabricated a chimera.

2. *Complete sciences* must therefore be distinguished from
incomplete. The former have as their object an entire ens
considered in its species, and are divided in the same way as
entia themselves; the latter have as their objects particular ways
of viewing a being, that is, various *mental entia*.

3. The great synthesisation of knowledge, for which so many
have thirsted without finding a way of satisfying their desire,
pertains to the first division of the sciences. The second division
lays claim to analysis which, by detailing human knowledge,
throws such great light on it. But analysis easily becomes dangerous. Clever people who follow this way exclusively neglect
synthesis, and thus dismember and deprive of life the living
body formed by all that is knowable. Their imagination then
leads them to see perfect bodies in the dead members, which in
their view become objects of a perfect science. In fact, it is a ter-
minally sick, cadaveric science.

4. This is the fault not of *analysis*, but of its abuse, just as it is
the abuse of synthesis which induces the obscurity and frequent
confusion of ideas to be found in the works of philosophers
who are either ignorant of the analytical method or, in their
systematic opposition to it, speak in such a complicated,

with contingent entia, science has as its object *real species* or *genera* (which
are a kind of species themselves) because they render entia (not merely the
abstract parts of entia) intelligible (cf. *NE*, vol. 2, 646–659). If we are dealing
with *necessary ens*, the object of science is being itself in its essence. — Is
ideology, therefore, not a science? It is, because it deals with the essence of
being, and not with any part of its extremely simple essence. Nevertheless, it
is necessarily an elementary science because in the order of nature the essence
of being is communicated to us only as a universal means of knowledge.

[2] *Mental being* is not to be confused with *ideal being*. The former is the
work of the mind in that the mind, with its limiting attention, puts arbitrary
boundaries to being; but the latter, because the mind simply intuits being, is
not the work of the mind. In a word, mental beings are ideal beings, divided
and limited by the laws of attention.

[2–4]

all-embracing fashion that their words are like hard ground unbroken by plough or harrow.[3]

5. All danger in the classification of sciences will be avoided, therefore, if *incomplete* sciences are consistently regarded for what they are, branches only of *complete* sciences. In this case, a person dealing with an incomplete science will not claim to be developing one that is complete, but will work at some particular part without taking his eye off the entire body of the science.[4]

II
Unity of the science dealing with the human being — subsidiary sciences

6. Man is one. Consequently, the science that deals with man is also one. But man has been split up by abstraction, and many sciences have been constituted to deal with such divisions. No damage would have resulted if scholars had recognised these sciences as incomplete and kept before their eyes the unity of man. Provided, that is, someone had then come along to re-group the parts and indicate human unity by offering a theory proper to the complete science about man. I cannot see that this has happened yet, at least not amongst modern authors.

7. Physiologists[5] and psychologists have cut man in two without mercy, although both sides think they possess the whole man. Often, the physiologists have made him a brute; the psychologists an angel. I want to reunite our poor, miserably divided man.

---

[3] This is the immense defect of German philosophers; French philosophers tend to abuse analysis.

[4] I have indicated the dangers of the abuse of analysis, and the errors resulting from it, in several places. Cf. *Anthropology as an Aid to Moral Science*, 7; *The Philosophy of Politics*, vol. 2, *Society and its Purpose*, 830–838.

[5] *Pathology*, that is, the science of the sick human being is properly speaking only a continuation of *physiology*. It has already been shown that the laws governing illnesses proceed from the universal laws of life. These laws, given different conditions, produce different phenomena, that is, the phenomena of the healthy human being, and the phenomena of the sick human being.

8. I have nothing to say about students of anatomy, which is not even an incomplete science about man. A cadaver is not part of man. Anatomy belongs to an altogether different group of sciences and can only aspire to be subsidiary to sciences which have man for their object.

9. The *history of mankind* is not properly speaking science. It is history. Nevertheless, it adds a great number of precious facts to the theory of human nature. It, too, belongs to sciences subsidiary to the science about man.

III
Anthropology — Psychology

10. What is the most suitable name for the science about man? I have already called it *anthropology*, a word justified by its etymology. But in this case, what kind of science is *psychology*?

From the etymological point of view, the word indicates the science of the soul (ψυχή, soul). The soul, however, is not the whole of man if by *man* we understand human nature, or if we consider the soul divided from the body. In this case, psychology is an incomplete science in the sense I have explained (cf. 2, 7–9). Thus I have sometimes stated that psychology has to be a part of anthropology, just as the soul is part of the human being.

Nevertheless, if we consider the soul united with the body, in all its relationships with the body, and take the word 'man' to mean the *human subject*, we can say that the soul is the whole man because it is the subject. We can certainly say in every sense that the whole man is contained in the soul united with the body. Extension[6] falls within human feeling (if feeling pertains to the soul) as its term and matter, so that it is impossible to speak fully of the soul as the principle of feeling without speaking about man as a whole. That which is entirely outside the soul is outside the human being; the body pertains to the human being only in so far as it is in the soul.[7] The distinction

---

[6] St. Thomas asserts that *illud quod est totius compositi, est etiam ipsius animae* [that which pertains to the whole of this composite being pertains also to the soul] (*S.T.*, I, q. 56, art. 1, ad 5).

[7] Cf. *NE*, vol. 2, 983–1019.

between psychology and anthropology seems, therefore, to lack scientific utility and I have no hesitation in assigning the same place to both in the tree of philosophical sciences. I consider them as two names for the same science about the human being rather than as different sciences.

11. This treatise entitled *Psychology* will, therefore, be simply a continuation of the *Anthropology* which I have already published, but in which I deliberately left many gaps in my desire to deal solely with the anthropological or psychological information which seemed necessary as an aid to the moral sciences.

IV
Ideology and psychology — they provide the rudiments of everything that can be known

12. But what is the relationship between psychology and ideology? The rudiments of all human cognitions are *feeling* and *intuited being*. By first rudiments I mean all that is found in any cognition, through the attention of the mind, to be of such a character that it cannot be deducted by way of reasoning from preceding information, but is given directly by nature.

13. Feeling and idea are data given directly by nature.

The *feeling* given in human nature is neither deducted nor deducible through reasoning from any preceding cognition. In fact, it is not even cognition but becomes the matter of cognition when the understanding turns to it, grasps it with its intellective act and thus renders it its object.

The *idea*, that is, being in so far as it is the object of mental intuition, is also given to man by nature because it cannot be deduced by any reasoning, nor by any abstraction. It is presupposed by every reasoning and every act of abstraction.

Feeling has a subjective nature; intuited being, which is essentially object, cannot be given, except as *object*, to any subject. Otherwise it would cease to be what it is; it would no longer be intuited being because being given to a subject (for example, to the human subject) as object is equivalent to being intuited. Such intuition creates intelligence which is simply the intuition of being, the union of *object* with *subject* — a union in which object necessarily remains distinct from subject.[8] It follows that being, which is essentially object [*App.*, no. 1], is the form of every intelligence, the first cognition, the formal part of cognition.

This is why we said that everything humanly knowable starts from two *postulates*: 1. 'being is known'; 2. 'experience of the feeling about which one reasons is a datum'.[9]

14. It also follows that everything known or able to be known by man is divided into two parts: 1. that which is given to human beings by nature; 2. that which we can draw out and deduce with reasoning from what is given to us by nature.

15. The *reasoning* which we employ cannot in fact be applied to anything totally outside ourselves, but only to that which is within us. And, as we said, there is nothing in us except through reasoning or through nature. It remains, therefore, that reasoning draws its final consequences only from what is given to us by nature. But nothing is given to human beings by nature except *feeling* and the *intuition of being*. All cognitions are only the development of these two principles, which themselves are the materials making up the edifice of what is knowable. What is not contained in these principles cannot be developed from them. They contain in germ all human cognitions without exception and indistinctly. Reasoning distinguishes them, seemingly creating them before the eyes of the mind. *Being*, therefore, as object of the mind, and *feeling* are the two rudiments (cf. 12) of all human cognitions without exception.

16. *Ideology* deals with being as the object of the mind; *psychology* deals with the soul, the principle of human feeling. These two sciences, therefore, provide the rudiments of all other sciences which finally are resolved into them. When we ask of man: 'What is the source of your affirmation about this or that, how do you come to know it?', he will be able to reply: 'I affirm it, I know it, because I have deduced it by reasoning from

---

[8] Cf. *AMS*, 812–831.

[9] *AMS*, *Postulates*, 10–20. These two postulates are not *arbitrary*, but *necessary*. In other words, they must be reasonably conceded or, as I would prefer to say, they are posited, conceded, to man of themselves. They in no way weaken human cognitions, as we have shown elsewhere.

something else.' If we insist: 'How do you know this something else?', he can still say: 'By reasoning from something else again,' and so on. Finally, however, he will be forced to come to the primal data of nature, that is, the ultimately known thing to which he will appeal. This is necessarily either being intuited by the mind, or feeling. Having reached these extremes, no more deduction is possible. When asked: 'What is the source of your knowledge of being?' or 'What is the source of your feeling?', human beings can only reply: 'I intuit being; I do not deduce it. I feel; feeling is not the consequence of any reasoning, nor indeed of any cognition.'

17. It is in these final two rudiments of all human information, therefore, that we have to seek the justification and certainty of what we know. If these primal data are certain, other information found in them through reasoning is also certain because the very principles of reasoning are contained in the idea. We have shown the certainty of all the rest of what is humanly knowable from the certainty of its two unshakeable foundations. We have shown that in them no error is possible; that man, relative to them, is infallible because they do not depend on his will, but on his nature.[10]

18. — If what you say is true, we would know nothing of the real things that do not fall under our senses. Real things are not comprised in being intuited by the mind nor, according to your supposition, are they found in feeling — .

We have to distinguish the *essence*[11] of real things from their *reality*. As far as their essence is concerned, all real things, even those which do not fall under the senses, agree in *entity*. If they were not entia in one way or another, if they possessed no entity, they would be nothing; they would be neither things nor real things. But we know through nature what being is, and from being we attain some information about the essence of all things, precisely because the essence of being is to some degree and in some way common to all things. But we certainly cannot

---

[10] *NE*, vol. 3, 1245–1246.

[11] *Essence* is what is known in the *idea* (*NE*, vol. 2, 647).

Essence therefore pertains to *being*, while the word *idea* expresses a *mode of being*, that is, it indicates being *in so far as it is intelligible* (*Rinnovamento* etc., bk. 3, c. 3–51 [433 ss; 522]).

know anything in reality, that is, we cannot affirm that a thing subsists, unless we have some indication pointing to this. For example, the testimony of a person who has seen or heard some subsistent thing. The testimony can only be communicated to human beings by way of a feeling such as a word or, if we want to appeal to a miracle, through an interior revelation from God which again is reduced to a feeling. But leaving aside interior revelation (to which however the same reasoning could be applied), and confining ourselves to the example of the word by which someone attests to us the existence of an ens that does not fall under our senses, I grant, of course, that the sensation of the voice I hear is in no way a feeling of the real thing whose subsistence is made known to me. Nevertheless, it is a *feeling* which assures us that the person speaking knows that the thing exists. In turn, the knowledge that we have of the person's truthfulness provides sure proof that what he says is true, and that the thing he affirms does indeed subsist. Our knowledge itself of his truthfulness depends on other feelings, that is, on our sense experience which is either direct or mediated through other signs and indications. We have to conclude, therefore, that we can indeed know the subsistence of an ens that does not fall under our senses, but that we cannot know it without some feeling which serves as an indication and proof of its subsistence.

19. — I will not ask you how these indications or signs of things can be given, because I know what you will say. You will tell me that these things are connected with one another, and that we already understand in *being* itself the connections between things. This knowledge, which is natural to us because we draw it from being, is the means through which we integrate our cognitions by adding, as a necessary condition to what we know, that which we do not yet know.[12] I grant you all this; I grant that you have explained the way in which a person can use something known or some sensation as a sign and indication leading him to something else. Moreover, even if I did not understand the explanation you have given, I could not deny the fact; I could not deny that we do indeed use signs and indications and thus come to know that some entities subsist which

[12] *NE*, vol. 2, 558–575; vol. 3, 1044–1054.

are not revealed by our senses. However, I have another objection. A sign, a feelable indication, tells me that an ens subsists, but it does not tell me what it is. Nevertheless, I know, even about entia which have never fallen under my senses, what they are. Sometimes I know them as well and better than things I have seen and felt for myself. For example, I have never been to Constantinople, but I have heard about it and read so much about it that I know it better than Rome, which I have experienced through my senses, although only in passing. There must be, therefore, outside the senses some other way of knowing the objects of human cognitions. It is impossible that everything be reduced to those two rudiments, that which is *sensible* and the *being* known to us by nature, which you have established — .

It was precisely to help you with this difficulty that I distinguished from the beginning between knowing the *essence* of something and knowing its *subsistence* or reality. Now, you grant me that in order to know subsistence (I cannot induce it unless it is known to me through nature, or by that which is known to me through nature), I need a feeling, or at least a sensible sign indicating it to me. This sign, in so far as it is sensible, is given by nature, not by reasoning. Your difficulty, therefore, is concerned with the essence of the thing. So: distinguish between things similar to others which have fallen under our senses, such as Constantinople in your example, and things which have never fallen under our internal or external sense, such as colours for a person born blind. If we are dealing with things similar to those which have fallen under our senses, we know their essence by applying to them the knowledge of things we have perceived at other times. In this case, we are dependent upon the feeling given to us by nature. In fact, you have seen other cities and everything contained in a city so that, when someone tells you about a city you have not seen, your imagination uses this information to fill out the subsistence of, say, Constantinople. You mentally construct Constantinople, guided by the accounts given by travellers, through the species of cities you have already perceived with your senses, or in the model provided by your imagination. Surely it is the case that you are seeking the materials for your knowledge of Constantinople from feeling?

If, on the other hand, we are dealing with the kinds of things that have never fallen under our feeling, as in the case of colours relative to a person born blind, my answer is the same as before: 'You can have no cognition of the *essence* of the thing whose subsistence is attested except that drawn by your thought from the common entity known to you by nature, and from the subsistence indicated by some witness, and from the relationships between subsistence, entity and other beings known through feeling, whether these relationships are provided for you by witnesses or discovered by reflection.' This is the sum total of cognition which is possible for you.

20. Note, however, that this cognition is not as impoverished as it appears. The testimony given to you relative to that thing is capable of letting you know 1. its subsistence; 2. the determination, limitation and other ontological relationships it has with being and other known things, such as the relationship of cause, etc. and finally, 3. that which it is not.

21. Referring the various real things we have perceived with our understanding to being, intuited by the mind, we easily come to know the following.

1. There are some equal, indispensable properties to be found in entia which do not fall within our feeling and whose subsistence is known only through testimony. Their indispensable necessity is made known to us through information which comes to us naturally through *ens*. Granted that we know what *ens* means, we immediately understand that the things testified to us could not have been and would not be entia, unless they possessed those properties. These properties, common to entia known to us through feeling and common to entia attested to us, constitute the foundation of *analogy*. We know things we have not perceived, therefore, by their *analogy* with those we have perceived.

2. Some properties present in entia perceived by us through feeling must be absolutely excluded from entia we have not perceived. This provides, through *exclusion*, some kind of negative cognition.

3. If we add to these two ways the other two, that is, subsistence known through attestation and through ontological relationships attested to us, we can conclude:

We compose for ourselves the essence, knowable to us, of entia which do not fall within our feeling and to which nothing similar has occurred in our experience a) through the *sensible witness* given by other people which indicates subsistence or even shows us certain ontological relationships with entia known to us through feeling, certain analogies and certain negations; b) through *ontological relationships* with the same entia (relationships found by ourselves by means of reflection); c) through *analogies* with the same entia (analogies found by ourselves); d) through *exclusion*, again found by ourselves through reflection.

22. As an example of cognition that our feeling cannot reach, let us take the teaching about God, which we can have through reason.

We know of God's subsistence by means of ontological relationships with that which we know through feeling. These are relationships with the world. We realise that the world must have a cause because it is, and would not be if it had no cause. *Being* known to us through nature tells us all this; it is to *being* that we refer the world given us by *feeling*.[13]

In the same way, *infinity, necessity, simplicity* and so on are *ontological relationships* pertaining to the cause of the world. The cause of the world subsists, but it *could* not subsist without these determinations. Therefore it has them. We know that it *could* not *subsist*, that is, could not in these circumstances be *ens*, precisely because we know what ens is and hence what is needed for it to be ens, and to be this kind of ens.

What kind of concept is the concept of an infinite ens? There is no doubt that it must have all degrees of being; it must not be dead, but have feeling and intelligence to the highest degree. But how do we know the essence of feeling and intelligence? We know it through experience of what happens in ourselves, through our own proper *feeling*. How then can we know the feeling and intelligence of God? Only *through analogy* between what must be present in him and the feeling and intelligence which are present in us.

Likewise we understand, through *analogy* between the supreme being and all entia seen in the light of being known to us through nature, that the supreme being cannot lack *reality, ideality* or *morality*.

[13] *NE*, vol. 3, 1264–1273.

But we understand (knowing being) that it would not be absolute being unless it were being itself in its three forms. Thus, the concept of infinite, absolute being — already illustrated by means of the analogies we have mentioned and referred to the idea of being we have through nature — is transformed for us into the very being which subsists undivided in the three forms. This seems to me to be the highest concept that human intelligence can make for itself about God without reference to revelation.

This is how the whole of natural theology is reduced finally to its first rudiments, that is, to *being* which is known through nature, and to *feeling*.

23. Ideology (and logic, its continuation) deals with *being known through nature*; psychology studies *feeling*. All sciences, therefore, have to come to these first two for their materials. Everything given by the other sciences as *positive cognition*, that is, as cognition of real entia, has to be reduced to ideology and psychology, the origin of all other sciences and the basis of their certainty. The teaching of other sciences is certain if it is reduced almost mathematically to other *per se* certain teachings which have no need of reasoned demonstration.

V
Psychology — Cosmology

24. One difficulty remains. It would seem that the science of the world is itself the product of perception and observation. This science itself seems to provide primal data and the rudiments of what is knowable.

This science of the world, or cosmology, is indubitably a science of perception and observation. Moreover, if by 'world' we understand the whole of creation, psychology itself becomes a material part of cosmology because human beings are ultimately members of the world.

But it is one thing to consider sciences according to the matter they contain, and another according to the source from which they derive.

If cosmology is considered from the point of view of the source from which human beings produce it, we can easily see that it arises from psychology itself precisely because cosmology is a science of perception and observation.

There is no doubt that it is man, the soul, who perceives the external things which make up the world.

There is a duality in the feeling which is the soul, that is, a subjective and an extrasubjective element which on reflection are changed into *myself* and *not-myself*. We distinguish these two elements in all perceptions of corporeal things. We feel and perceive these elements contemporaneously, and in mutual opposition, as mutual limits.

The feeling which is the soul, therefore, brings us to know the corporeal part of the universe which is perceived only as something heterogeneous falling within feeling. This explains (I repeat) why the body is in the soul, not the soul in the body.

25. If, however, the world is perceived in so far as it is received in feeling, our cognition of the world, although certain, is partly phenomenal, partly absolute. In other words, the corporeal world as we have it in perception is a composite both of elements that we ourselves posit and of elements which are given to us. Separating one group from the other is the work of reasoning through which alone we discover the extrasubjective part, independent of ourselves. Such is the positive cognition we can have of the essences of things.[14]

26. The world, however, consists of spirits as well as bodies. But even for spirits we have to turn to psychology because we cannot form any positive cognition of other spirits except by starting from the feeling of ourselves. Spirit is feeling. We begin, therefore, from the feeling of ourselves, and with this positive cognition conceive other feelings, other spirits. Only reasoning enables us to put them together in various ways.

Psychology, therefore, provides even cosmology with its primal rudiments. Cosmology comes to birth in the womb of psychology just as the world we know is in the womb of the soul.[15]

---

[14] *NE*, vol. 3, 1210; vol. 2, 878–906.

[15] *Preface to the Metaphysical Works,* (28).

VI
The method to be used in psychological research

27. Knowing that *psychology* is the science that provides the *real rudiment* of human cognitions to all other sciences, just as ideology provides the *ideal rudiment*, we are in a position to deduce the method necessary to these primal sciences.

28. The *method* must be one of *observation*. It must bring facts to light with great precision, distinguish their parts, compare them and finally deduce conclusions from them. In all this, the eye of the mind must be continually fixed on facts in order to see clearly. During our observation, imagination must not be allowed to add, obscure or detract anything whatsoever. The aim is to attest to facts with the greatest fidelity, precision and sagacity, and to provide a description of them corresponding totally to the truth of what is before us.

What are we to make, therefore, of Christian Wolff's distinction of psychology into two sciences, *empirical* and *rational*, the former working through observation, the latter through reasoning?

VII
Christian Wolff's division of psychology into two sciences, one called *empirical*, the other *rational psychology*, is excluded

29. Wolff's division was embraced with admirable consent by Germany, and followed religiously by German philosophers. Nevertheless, it seems to me arbitrary and, moreover, suggested by erroneous opinions, especially about the nature of *observation* and *reasoning*.

30. *Observation*, it would seem, could be totally divided from *reasoning* and considered as a truly separate way of knowing. Reasoning would be another way, without need of observation.

Moreover, a different degree of certainty was predicated about these two separate and independent ways of knowing. Observation, it was claimed, induced full, undeniable certainty.

This was not the case with reasoning. Wolff himself noted that he had separated *empirical* from *rational psychology* in order to base moral and political truths on the former which, as containing teaching demonstrated through experience, is non-controversial.[16]

31. Both of these are sensistic errors and their prolonged presence in German philosophy shows the defect of this philosophy. It has a highly speculative, abstract (or rather mysterious) appearance, but its hidden depths contain corrosive sensism.[17]

In fact, only sensists are able to believe that observation can cause us to know truth by way of sensation without the use of reason, or (and this is worse) that the truths coming to us from this kind of observation are alone secure and non-controversial.

32. Nevertheless, it is a fact that no observation or experience of any sort exists unmixed with rational activity, although this is sometimes difficult to notice. Condillac himself was already aware that our sensations are mixed with inadverted judgments — this is the most beautiful thing he said. From Condillac to Lord Brougham's recent work on natural theology,[18] philosophers

[16] 'Practical philosophy is of the greatest importance. But matters of the greatest importance are not to be constructed on the basis of disputed principles. For this reason, we construct the truths of practical philosophy only on principles which are clearly established in empirical psychology' (*Discursus prael. de philosophia in genere*, §112). — But is it possible, I would ask, to establish ethics on a solid basis without presupposing a simple, immortal soul, or at least, if this is possible, to establish it while supposing the soul to be material and mortal? I believe it altogether impossible to demonstrate moral obligation while supposing the soul to be mortal. But, granted that moral obligation can be established prior to knowledge about the immortality of the soul, and without denying it, I think it obvious that morality itself leads us to conclude to the immortality of the soul as its consequence (this was the moral way of demonstrating immortality from Plato to Kant) and, as a result of this, to illustrate and develop ethics. Although ethics may, therefore, begin while prescinding from the immortality of the soul, it certainly cannot develop and reach perfection without the assistance of this truth. Wolff, however, demonstrates the simplicity and immortality of the soul in *rational psychology*, not in *empirical psychology*. It is, therefore, on rational, much more than on empirical psychology that ethics must be founded. This gives the lie to the reason he adduces for justifying his division of psychology into *empirical* and *rational*.

[17] *Teodicea*, 144–147.

[18] Translated into French under the title: *Discours sur la Théologie*

have become ever more aware of the multiplicity of judgments and reasoning which, mingling with our sensations, provides us with such knowledge of many truths (knowledge that we then erroneously attribute to sensations alone). Sensism would have fallen of itself if, continuing on this path, philosophers had adverted to and noted carefully all the hurried, almost furtive judgments accompanying feelings. I have tried to do this myself; the result has been the kind of certainty unavailable to merely sensible observation. In other words, sensations, devoid of an act of understanding to accompany them, offer us no knowledge of any kind. They are facts which terminate within themselves, of which we are unaware. Consciousness of sensation itself requires 1. that we turn our intellective attention to what passes in our feeling, and 2. a consequent affirmation through which we say to ourselves, 'Now I am experiencing some passion, some feeling.' This is clearly a judgment, but so spontaneous and so continuous with feeling that it escapes our attention. What we have at heart is not to gain knowledge of this judgment, but through it to know the feeling of which we have become conscious. This judgment, intimately united to feeling, constitutes *intellective perception of sensation*,[19] that is, knowledge.

What is the justification for the interior word that we speak to ourselves on the occasion of sensations when we say: 'I undergo something'? What demonstrates the certainty of this statement? I have no doubt, of course, that our *persuasion* of certainty about the word is natural, and that most people find this sufficient to exclude doubt about it. But if we want a demonstration that the persuasion does not deceive us, we have to analyse it to see how it is formed and what supports it. This analysis leads us to *being*, which we intuit through nature, where every reasoning becomes evident. Once our possession of ens has been verified in our cognition — in other words 'we know that what we

Naturelle indiquant la nature de son évidence et les avantages de ses études par Henry Lord Brougham etc. traduit de l'anglais, sous les yeux de l'Auteur par S. C. Tarrer etc., II, Dumant, Bruxelles, 1836.

[19] *Intellective perception of sensation* is not the first perception. It is preceded in the logical order, and accompanied in the chronological order, by the *intellective perception of real ens*, to which the feelable quality pertains, as I have shown in *NE*.

[32]

are affirming, is' — we can no longer doubt whether 'what we affirm is'. It is true, therefore, because 'being true' simply means 'being that which we affirm'.[20]

33. From this we can conclude that the certainty and demonstration of our sensible observations lies only in the force of the secret reasoning that we always carry out on them. Thus, in all sciences alike it is necessary to recur to the authority of reason, that is, of the idea of being, the final seat of evidence where we ascertain truths of both observation and of induction and consequence. The act of reasoning is in every case the organ with which we fashion sciences. We can never do without it.

No specific difference of method is present, therefore, between empirical and rational psychology. The difference is solely one of degree. What we have to demonstrate in empirical psychology is the fruit of shorter reasoning; what we have to demonstrate in rational psychology is again the fruit of reasoning, but of prolonged reasoning which allows deduction of new truths from preceding truths. This difference of degree does not give rise to two sciences, just as Euclid's division of his geometry into different books does not give rise to different geometries. His books are certainly not different sciences, but degrees of the same science.

VIII
The *synthesism* inherent to method and distribution in the philosophical sciences

34. From this truth (that reason is always the organ with which we compose the sciences both of observation and of induction[21]), we want to draw an important consequence destined

---

[20] *NE*, vol. 3, 1062–1064.

[21] It will be objected that the intuition of being is a cognition which has no need of reasoning. This is true, but no science is formed by this alone. Every science is a witness to our consciousness. Even the intuition of being does not enter the field of science unless we carry out an intellective act by which we tell ourselves that we possess the intuition of being. But this is impossible unless we reflect upon what is present in our spirit; telling ourselves that such is the case already means that we pronounce some *judgment*. But we cannot *demonstrate* the certainty of this judgment without making a

to clarify the method to be followed in the explanation and distribution of the philosophical sciences.

Merely *to feel* is not *to observe*. Observation implies an act of the mind that makes a feeling its object and concludes in a judgment. This act of the mind, either a judgment or an act of reasoning, is in the last analysis the application of ideal being to the feeling on which the mind fixes its attention. Every reasoning, therefore, necessarily includes two elements: 1. ideal being; and 2. the feeling to which ideal being is applied. The information obtained by way of reasoning about one of these two things cannot be had without information about the other. The two pieces of information are therefore posited in us contemporaneously. This is what I call *synthesism*.

35. Indeed, this twofold information that we want to gain for ourselves by reasoning (which alone gives rise within us to consciousness and the development of the sciences) must have from the beginning three objects: 1. our bodily feelings or their bodily terms; 2. ourselves, that is, our interior feelings; 3. the idea of being. If the first two are the objects of reasoning, it is clear that reasoning is made up contemporaneously of feelings and the idea of being (feelings cannot be the objects of thought without the idea of being). If, however, we suppose that the object of reasoning is the idea of being alone, either the supposition is understood strictly in which case it is absurd, or it is not understood strictly and a feeling enters to make reasoning possible.

I say that it is absurd to suppose some reasoning through the idea of being alone without the addition of some sensible element because the person who says something about this idea either predicates something about it, or predicates something about his intuition of it. He could, for example, affirm that he has this intuition. If he predicates something about the intuition of the idea, the feeling of himself becomes an element of his judgment or of his reasoning. He cannot say: 'I

further reflection upon it, that is, an act of *reasoning* which takes the form: 'We intuit being. But being is that which is. Therefore we intuit that which is. But that which is, is the truth. Therefore we intuit the truth. Therefore the intuition of being cannot mislead us; being which we intuit cannot be an appearance. If it were, the appearance would be the truth, which is a contradiction.' We need some reasoning, therefore, to make the very intuition of being an object of science.

have the intuition of being', unless he knows the self (the 'I') that he nominates — this self is a substantial feeling, a complex of feelings elaborated, as it were, by the understanding itself. If, however, he speaks not of the *intuition*, but of *being* as intuited, he can say nothing without first comparing it with subsistent things and, from this comparison, inducing that it is different from them. He may perhaps invent the word 'ideal' to mark this diversity. All this, however, supposes some information about feelings. He cannot say 'intuited being is ideal' prior to such a comparison. The word 'ideal' achieves nothing except the exclusion of the reality of substances or efficient causes. Nor can he even say to himself: 'Being is'. This is not an interior word but a linguistic phrase without meaning which adds nothing to *being*. Language can of course construct judgments if it discovers an apparent predicate; the mind cannot.

Synthesism, therefore, is inherent in every reasoning.

36. I conclude that the two elements of reasoning which synthesise, that is, which adhere inseparably to one another, cannot constitute two entirely and exactly separate sciences. Each must be constructed along with the other; each must explain the other; each must be understood by the same act of the spirit.

37. As we said, the sciences that deal with the first two elements of reasoning are *ideology* and *psychology*. Each needs the other. Theory about idea (which is reflective teaching dependent on reasoning) cannot be understood without theory about soul informed by idea. Equally, theory about soul is unknown until it is joined and illuminated by the theory about idea. This explains why I include in *ideology* a great number of things pertaining to psychology, and why I shall have to make continual use of ideological information in psychology.

38. Quite a number of doubts and questions arise here. If one of these two things cannot be understood without the other, which will come first? Can they be called simultaneous? If the truth of both has to be demonstrated, which is to be proved first? How can the truth of one be shown if the truth of the other, which has to be brought into the reasoning, has not been demonstrated?

I do not want to hide the importance of these problems nor the difficulty of answering them adequately. The reader knows,

[36–38]

however, that I regard every serious and apparently insoluble difficulty as an advance in science because it contains a precious secret. And this seems to me to be the case with these questions. My answer, therefore, runs as follows.

There are certainly some things of which we have to say that one cannot be understood without the other. All relative concepts, such as that of cause and effect, are an example. They are understood contemporaneously with a single act of understanding. However, they seem to separate and divide when verbalised because of the imperfection of the words used to indicate them. Nevertheless, the understanding itself supplies for the verbal defect by conceiving the thing as a whole, as soon as a word is used to indicate it. Thus, if we use the single word *effect* or the single word *cause*, the understanding immediately conceives what is expressed. Because the understanding cannot conceive effect without cause, or cause without effect, one of these words is sufficient to draw attention to both concepts (although not equal attention) which, bound together by nature, are a single thing, a sole relationship, for the mind.

39. The following principle has to be established if we wish to show the certainty of correlative teachings and the way of demonstrating them: 'Certainty arises from the same source as knowledge.' *To know*, and *to know the truth* is the same thing. The person who does not know the truth, does not know.[22]

40. It follows, when dealing with correlative teachings known simultaneously by the same act of the intellect because they provide the mind with a single complex concept, that it is impossible for one to be proved or ascertained before the other. They receive their certainty together from the light of truth common to them both.

41. This reply is valid for concepts and their correlative teachings. However, the case is slightly different when the synthesis takes place not between two concepts or cognitions, but

---

[22] *Rinnovamento* etc., bk. 1, c. 10 ss. — Note that even in errors there is always some part of truth. This explains why a person who errs seems to know, and indeed does know truly, but not in so far as he errs. If a person's mind were completely empty, he would not even be able to err. In a word, without truth there is no intellective act, either correct or incorrect, either leading to truth or leading to falsity.

between the form and matter of the same cognition. One example of this is found in intellective perception where a *feeling* is united with *being* intuited by the mind, and a single judgment is pronounced: 'An ens subsists.' In this perception, being is known to the mind beforehand; it is *per se* cognition, essential cognition, and has no need of feeling to be such. Feeling, however, or rather the *real ens characterised by feeling*, becomes known through being which provides both information about ens and the source of our certainty and proof in its regard. The proof can be set out in this way: consciousness attests that a feeling is present. But could not consciousness deceive us? Let us see. What is the meaning of 'consciousness attests the presence of a feeling'? It means that we know, that we affirm the presence of a feeling. But this affirmation: 'There IS a feeling' is reduced to affirming the identity between being and feeling. Saying this means simply that feeling is not nothing; the opposite of being is nothing. If we apply the two concepts of *nothing* and *feeling* to the words, the concepts are clearly contrary to one another, just as they are identical if joined to the words *being* and *feeling* (except that the former, containing more than the latter, is restricted by the affirmation to feeling and thus identified with it). If we do not attach the concepts to these two words, thought is eliminated. If thought is eliminated, even error is impossible. There can be no mistake in the proposition 'Identity is present (in the way explained) between feeling and being', or its equivalent 'There is a feeling'.

This demonstration is founded entirely on information about *being*: the soul, intuiting being, sees that everything is identified with being from which it acquires the truth and certainty of being itself.

42. Truth, certainty, the evidence of the witness of consciousness, take their origin from *being* which informs them, and without which neither consciousness nor any intellective act would be possible. Just as the spirit sees being, so with the same glance it sees the identity of real things with being. This vision, when reflective and concerned with something united to ourselves, is called *consciousness*.[23]

---

[23] Cf. the definition of consciousness applied to moral matters in *Conscience*, 9–17.

43. We have to be careful here. The intuition of being is a fact (the fact of knowledge) posited by nature. This fact of knowledge needs no demonstration; demonstration means 'the reduction of what we *believe* we know to the fact of knowledge.' When what we *believe* we know is reduced to the fact of knowledge, we no longer believe we know, but know. Nevertheless, persons who have not yet thought about themselves do not know that this is the case. Ideology and logic show them that every demonstration is reduced to this.

But, it may be objected, ideology and its continuation, logic, cannot be expounded without introducing perceptions, the witness of consciousness, and so on. Isn't this begging the question? — Definitely not. All that these sciences do is simply direct the attention of the mind to the *observation* of perceptions, and so on. It is not at all necessary to employ some previously demonstrated truth to direct the attention. Any stimulus whatsoever can be suitable for this, even a blind stimulus, even an error. For example, if someone, by lying, causes me to look at an object, I see the object just as well as if I were drawn to look at it by a truth. Once the mind has observed *perceptions* without exiting from observation itself, perceptions are ascertained because they are nothing more than 'the identity, shown to the human being, between feeling and being.' Perception identified with the fact of knowledge is no longer a belief that we know, but knowledge itself.

44. Hence, despite the synthesism between certain ideological and psychological teachings, both are furnished with certainty and demonstrated most rigorously without begging any question.

IX
The division of psychology

45. As we come now to speak of psychology, we have to ask about its starting point and about its sphere. As we said, the attention of our understanding is fixed on the soul by new, particular feelings formed in the soul by its passage from not feeling to feeling, that is, from not having a given sensation to having it. These changes, which take place in the soul, attract

its attention, causing it to turn in on itself. They produce consciousness which reveals to the philosopher teachings about the soul. *Consciousness*, therefore, is the proximate source of psychology.

46. But philosophers are not at all satisfied with the first testimonies of consciousness, from which they grasp what takes place in themselves. They want to go on to connect the feelings and operations of the soul and from them rise to know the soul itself, which is their subject and, in great part, their cause. Philosophers want to form for themselves the concept of soul which provides its *knowable essence*, and enables them to distinguish its nature. When they have succeeded in fixing the essence of the thing they are examining, they have found its ultimate, intrinsic reason and the principle of all the reasoning they can make about it. Philosophising means precisely this: finding the final reason in the genus of which one is speaking, that is, finding the principle of the discussion and, by means of it, ordering systematically the teachings which flow from and depend upon that principle.

47. Once the mind has risen to the essence of anything, it descends from it according to the course of operations proceeding from it. Philosophers, once they know the essence of the soul, and hence its substance, can mentally follow it in its development and note the laws which this substance follows in its operation and development.

48. Finally, having noted the modifications that arise in the soul as effects of its actions and passions, and either ameliorate or worsen it, the mind can study the stages by which the soul is degraded or ascends to the height of the perfection for which it is made. Philosophical meditation, following the soul itself in its journey to the twofold extremes of good and evil, comes to form the *ideal* of the soul[24] and to contemplate it in all its perfection, or at least to solve the problem about the indefinite perfection of the soul.

49. These considerations enable us to say that all the entire

[24] I call the *complete species* the *archetype* (*NE*, vol. 2, 648–652); the *ideal* is the state of maximum perfection attainable by an individual with its own activity. The archetype, therefore, is the perfection of something in its *nature*; the ideal is the perfection of something produced by its *activity*.

teaching making up psychology can fittingly be divided into three parts dealing with the nature, development and destinies of the soul. Here we find the *principle*, the *means* and the *end* of the human soul, and of humanity itself. This is the perfect schema of psychology. But because the destinies of the soul transcend in fact all limits of nature, I shall speak about them in the *Supernatural Anthropology*. My present work will be limited to the first two parts: the nature of the soul and its development.

DEFINITIONS

50. I presume that the definitions given at the beginning of the three books on anthropology are known to the reader. What follows has to be added to them if we wish to understand the following books on psychology, which are a continuation of those on anthropology.

I
Psychology (ψυχολογία) is the science of the human soul.

II
Soul is the principle of a active-substantial feeling which has as its term space and a body.

III
51. *Body* is a force diffused in extension, that is, in space.

IV
Force is that which produces what is undergone in feeling or in the extended term of feeling.

COMMENT — It may be objected that by defining force in this way, we neglect the effect of bodily force through which brute bodies mutually modify one another. The difficulty vanishes, however, if the reader keeps in mind what I have said elsewhere about this.[25]

V
52. 1st definition: *Substance* is the first act constituting an ens, through which the ens is mentally conceived without its having to be collocated in some other entity.[26]

COROLLARY — Hence the common definition of substance, 'that which exists *per se*', has to be understood in such a way that '*per se*' is taken not universally, but restrictively, that is, in

[25] *NE*, vol. 2, 672–691.
[26] *NE*, vol. 2, 612–613.

relationship to the entity of which it has no need in order to be mentally conceived.

2nd definition: *Substance* is the act by which an essence[27] subsists, whether this act is considered as realised or simply as able to be realised (in the idea).

COROLLARY — There are, therefore, two kinds of substances, as there are two kinds of substantial essences. Certain substantial essences posit a single, indivisible entity, others posit several entities in a complex being, one of which is the principal and constitutes the subject. The minor entity separated from the principal, that is, having lost its identity, is said to be another substance, and properly speaking another *substantial form*. Take, for example, the human soul, which is an essence resulting from a supreme, intellective principle and a sensitive-animal principle, of which the intellective principle is the principal entity constituting the subject. The sensitive principle is a divisible entity and can stand on its own, as we see in beasts. But the sensitive principle in man and in brute animals is not identical because although considered as substance in beasts, in man it receives another *substantial form* from its union with the intellective principle. It is not the substance it once was, therefore, but part of another substance.

VI

Accident is an entity which cannot be mentally conceived except in some other entity through which it exists and to which it pertains.

COMMENT — Although an accident can be conceived by way of abstraction as separate from substance, the mind cannot carry out this abstraction unless it has first conceived an accident as united with its substance.[28] Afterwards, when considering the matter abstractly, the mind itself is forced either to retain the information about the substance to which the accident is united, or to suppose the existence of a generic substance to which the accident may adhere.

[27] *NE,* vol. 2, 657–659.
[28] *NE,* vol. 2, 612–614.

COROLLARY — Hence the force through which alone body is mentally conceived makes us know body as a substance.

VII

53. *Human soul* is the principle of an active, substantial feeling which, identically the same, has as its terms 1. extension (and in it a body) and 2. being. It is therefore at one and the same time sensitive and intellective (rational).

VIII

Intuition is a (receptive) act of the soul through which the soul receives the communication of intelligible or ideal *being*.

COMMENT 1. This act is called *intelligence* by Aristotle. He says: 'Intelligence is concerned with indivisible things'.[29] For him, the 'indivisible' are the *essences* of things seen in ideas. For the Scholastics, therefore, *cognitio simplicis intelligentiae* [knowledge proper to simple intelligence] is equivalent to 'knowledge of possible things'.

2. Kant perverted philosophical language when he usurped the word *intuition* to mean *sensitive perception*. Such an alteration in the meaning of the word is another indication of the sensism that lies at the heart of his system; he provides sense with the act proper to the intellect.

IX

Sensitive perception is the act of feeling which receives in itself an extrasubjective force apt to modify feeling.

X

Intellective perception is the act with which the rational soul affirms (habitually or actually) a felt reality. I shall call the corresponding faculty *percipience*.

COMMENT — This explains St. Thomas' extremely appropriate definition of the word: *perceptio experimentalem quandam notitiam significat*[30] [perception means some kind of experimental information].

---

[29] *De Anim.*, bk. 3, tr. 20, 21.
[30] *S.T.*, I, q. 43, art. 5, ad 2.

XI

54. The *reality of being* is being in so far as it is feeling or possesses the force to produce or modify feeling.

COROLLARY — Perception, therefore, is communication between two realities, one sentient, the other sensiferous.

XII

Subsistence is the act proper to real being, that is, the act by which a being is real.

COMMENT — This and the preceding definitions indicate meanings given to words which have been defined by common, consistent use throughout the ages. They are not arbitrary meanings of my own. I have simply attempted to remove the *improprieties* into which individuals who have used them, and still use them, are apt to fall. This is not the case with the general mass of speakers and writers. Antiquity, for example, formulated the question of universals in the following way, which Porphyry repeats in his introduction to Aristotle's *predicamenta*: 'Do universals SUBSIST or are they posited in simple intellectual matters alone?', where *subsist* is obviously taken to indicate the act through which a being is *real*, in contradistinction to the act in which a being is merely *ideal*. Ideal being is not nothing, as materialists force themselves to believe. It is rather a *manner of being*, different however from that which we call 'real'. The question reproposed by Porphyry was argued by all the schools in precisely those terms. In other words, *subsisting* is used in contradistinction to *being ideally* or even mentally.

In the same way, my definition of the words *real* and *reality* expresses the propriety found in ancient philosophical language and faithfully retained by the Scholastics. One example can be found at the very beginnings of Scholasticism in a little work by Gerbert (d. 1003) on the question proposed by the Emperor Otto III: can we say that *making use of reason* is, as Porphyry maintains, an attribute of the *rational ens* (*De rationale et ratione uti, libellus*)?[30] Gerbert sets out Aristotle's opinion on

[30] It was published by Pez, *Thesaurus novissimus Anecdotorum*, vol. 1, p. 2, col. 147.

[54]

the distinction between *possible* and *real* by saying that this philosopher admits *possibilities* which can be unaccompanied by *reality*, and other *possibilities* which cannot be unaccompanied by *reality*, and finally some *possibilities* which can never be *in reality*. The last are *abstract possibilities*. This whole manner of speaking, maintained by the Schools, and indeed by all philosophers to the present day, shows that they took 'possible' or 'ideal', and 'real' in the sense attributed to these words. It never entered their heads to confuse what is *possible* with *nothing*. What is *possible* or *ideal*, therefore, and what is *real* are two primordial modes of being which have to be kept quite distinct. I also noted that the word *possible* does not, properly speaking, express pure *idea*, but idea accompanied by a *relationship* posited by the mind in comparing idea with what is real.[31]

XIII

55. *Myself* is an active principle in a given nature in so far as this principle is conscious of itself and enunciates its own act.

COMMENT — In the definition given in *Anthropology* (cf. 768), I defined *myself* as a *supreme*, active principle. Here we have to note that *supreme* means supremacy within the sphere of human nature. The quality of *universal principle* could also be added to the definition of *myself* provided it is clear that the principle is not always universal as *active principle*, but only as principle, whether passive or active. In fact, when someone says: 'I undergo pain or pleasure', he expresses a principle of passion which undergoes some experience, not a principle of action. And although a principle has a certain activity even in undergoing experience, this species of activity must not be confused with activity properly so-called which does something rather than undergo something.

XIV

56. *Nature* is everything that contributes to the constitution of an ens and places it in act.

---

[31] *NE*, vol. 2, 540–542.

COROLLARY — Here we can note the difference between *substance, nature* and *subject*. Substance is the first act through which an essence subsists (cf. 52). Nature, however, includes more than is necessary for the subsistence of a subject: it includes the necessary term of the act by which the subject subsists. For example, the act which gives subsistence to a brute body is force; this is the body's *substance*. But the *nature* of this body also includes the extension in which the act called 'force' must be able to diffuse itself. *Nature* also embraces all accidents, although not taken individually (some accidents can be absent), but as a whole (not all accidents can be lacking). For example, because a body can exist without its having a round shape, this accident does not constitute part of its nature. But the same body cannot exist without some shape. Shape in general, therefore, enters into the *nature* of body without pertaining to its substance. *Subject* is the principle of the sentient substance. For a substance to be called subject, it is necessary for it 1. to be feeling; and 2. to be considered in so far as it is principle. This second characteristic distinguishes *subject* from *sensitive nature*, which also embraces *what is felt*, a necessary element for the existence of a substantial feeling. *Subject*, however, is only *that which feels* because only that which feels has the notion of principle.

Part One

ESSENCE
OF THE
HUMAN SOUL

Book 1

The source and principle of psychology

CHAPTER 1

A concept of soul must be sought free from everything that operations of the mind may have added when composing it

57. One of the principal causes rendering philosophical questions difficult and almost inextricable is the fact that, in trying to understand something about an object, we are obliged to receive it as it has been conceived by our own mind (if it had not been conceived, we could not have considered it at all). We receive it in the greatest good faith, not doubting that we possess it just as it is in nature. This happens either because we do not reflect that it is the mind, not nature, which gives it to us, or because we are already under the preconceived opinion that the mind is as faithful in giving it to us as nature would be if she presented it to us with her own hands.

58. Nevertheless, there is no doubt that the mind, in placing things before our thought, does not offer them just as they are outside the mind, but as the mind itself has made them through the subjective laws of its own being and activity. At one and the same time, the mind has, as its first object, truth which never deceives, and its own proper nature which imposes certain laws. These laws certainly do not deprive the mind of its possession of truth, but they act as a brake holding it back from total sincerity in pursuing the truth which it attains only when, with the help of the objective light shining in it, it discerns within its thoughts its own work and what remains when its own work has been removed.

59. One of the most careful philosophical investigations, which calls for the greatest watchfulness and sharpness, must consist in first separating from every object about which we want to philosophise, all that pertains to our own mental activity and that which pertains to the naked object itself as it comes forth free from all the enfolding veils in which the mind itself has enmeshed it. All philosophers must begin willy-nilly from

the intellectual state in which they find themselves;[33] and they have to receive the object, as we said, just as it is in the mind when they begin to philosophise.

60. This, of course, applies to ourselves as well, as we start to expound the teaching about the human soul. We cannot but begin from the concept we possess of the soul. First, therefore, we have to see if the soul, as we conceive it, is truly the soul as it is in itself without any conception of our own, without anything that our mind may have added when conceiving it.

CHAPTER 2

Myself does not express the pure concept of the soul

61. I cannot doubt that I who feel, think, speak, am the soul. The soul, therefore, as I presently conceive it, is that being which I intend to express when I use the word *myself*.

62. But does this *myself* express the soul properly without any addition grafted upon it by the activity of my mind? This question cannot be answered without a prior analysis of the concept expressing *myself*. I have already undertaken this and found that *myself* expresses not only the *soul*, but the soul united with many relationships resulting from various mental acts that have to be undertaken before I can enunciate *myself*. I refer the reader to this analysis,[34] and add here some comments which will serve to confirm and perfect it.

63. The person who says *myself* (understanding what he says) performs an interior act by which he enunciates his own soul. *Myself*, therefore, is 'the vocal sign enunciated by an intellective soul (or more generally by an intellective subject) of his own act when he turns attention internally to himself and perceives himself.'

64. Let us stop here. Already the following is clear.

[33] *NE*, vol. 3, 1466–1467.
[34] *AMS*, 805–811.

1. The soul enunciating *myself* is a real soul. — *Myself*, therefore, does not express a pure idea. It does not express simply the *concept*, but also the *perception* of the soul. That word adds perceived reality to the noun *soul* (that is, to the idea, the essence of the soul).

65. 2. *Myself* is not the perception of any soul whatsoever, but of my own soul. — Here, the *relationship of the soul with itself*, a relationship of identity, is added to the general concept of soul by the word *myself*. It contains a second element distinct from the concept of the soul; it is a soul which perceives itself.

66. 3. The soul does not turn back on itself, nor perceive itself, unless it is stimulated and drawn to do so by some new, particular feeling, passive or active, arising within itself. The substantial feeling of the soul, because natural and uniform, is not suitable for arousing the attention of the soul itself. This attention is a new, particular act and, as such, requires as its sufficient cause a new, particular stimulus to arouse it. The soul which says *myself* does not enunciate itself in its primal state, but as found in a state already overlaid with activity. It enunciates itself as modified, experiencing, active. *Myself*, therefore, expresses the *soul* with the addition of a third element, that is, some modification which has come about as the result of passion or action. In general, *myself* expresses 'the soul which has moved to second acts'; it does not express the soul in its potentiality, as it is found initially, but in its actuality. In fact, experience shows that when we begin to enunciate *myself*, we do not enunciate it by itself but in union with a verb that expresses our action: for example, 'I, that is, myself, feel, will, think, work, and so on'. Only by abstraction and analysis do I later come to separate 'I (myself)' from its verb by considering what *myself* expresses on its own, cut off from its context, without which, however, it is never found in fact. I have to conclude, therefore, that it expresses the principle of the soul's activity, that is, the soul in so far as it is the principle of its various actions.

67. 4. Again if, in enunciating *myself*, the soul expresses itself as operating — if it means 'that which does something', that which for example, wills — the expression includes a fourth element and can be translated as follows: 'The person who wills is the same principle who perceives himself and as a consequence

says *myself.' Myself* therefore includes another reflection, and through it another relationship of identity, by which the person who speaks and enunciates *myself*, understands that he who perceives himself as operating is an identical being with the self who operates.[35]

68. Summing up all the differences that can be found between the meaning of *human soul* and the word *myself*, we make the following synthesis:

1. *Human soul* expresses a simple, general *concept* of the soul, the *essence* of the soul;

2. *Myself* expresses:

a) an *intellective perception* of the soul in which, as in every other perception, there is, in addition to the general concept of the thing, the affirmation of the *reality* given by feeling;

b) not every intellective perception of the soul, but the perception that a soul produces about itself when it contemplates the feeling that constitutes it in being, and hence knows itself as an ens;

c) a perception of itself in a state of activity, not in the primal state where special potencies are still not granted it; it expresses a soul that perceives;

d) finally, it expresses the soul as conscious of the identity proper to itself as perceiving itself and activating itself, or as prepared for action.

[35] Others have observed that the formation of *myself* includes a reflection by the soul. Abbé Feller started from this observation in his confutation of Buffon who attributed *myself* even to beasts: 'The learned naturalist', he says, 'has fallen into this error because he supposes that *myself* is made up only of sensation and memory (t. 4, p. 52). But *myself* is purely *intellectual* and the result of *reflection*; it is the fruit and enjoyment of thought. It is clear, therefore, that it cannot be found in beasts, granted the principles which he himself, the naturalist, has established about the nature of human beings and animals' (*Catechismo Filos.*, n. 147).

CHAPTER 3

The pure notion of the soul can only be attained from *myself* by stripping *myself* of all that is foreign to this notion

69. Nevertheless, there is no other way of reaching knowledge of the soul except by beginning from *myself*. It is in consciousness of our own soul that we can discover what the soul is in general; *consciousness* of ourselves provides *information about the feeling of the soul*, which is one of the first rudiments of our cognitions (cf. 12–15). Indeed, if we did not feel the soul in ourselves, we would not perceive it; and if we did not perceive it, we would have no source of positive knowledge about it. Words, the signs with which a master might perhaps want to communicate information, would have no meaning for us except to provide the merely negative cognition which we have described (cf. 18–20).

70. To acquire a true, pure concept of the human soul, we have to meditate on *myself*, where we find awareness of our own soul, and strip our perception, expressed by *myself*, of everything foreign to the general concept of soul until we have isolated the net concept that we are seeking. Let us do that.

CHAPTER 4

A start to expropriating *myself* of everything not pertaining to the pure notion of soul

71. In the first place, when the soul says: 'I act', it affirms itself as acting. This affirmation comes about through thought; to affirm is *to think*. But because the soul thinks itself in this activity, its affirmation about its activity involves a *reflection* of the

soul on itself. If the soul did not reflect in this way, it would not think of itself at all; it would not know itself, that is, it would have no consciousness of itself. But is consciousness of self essential to the soul? To answer this question, we have to see if the soul's reflective thought about itself is of the essence of the soul.

It is certain that *reflective thought* about the human soul is not essential to it; it is certain that consciousness is not born with the soul, has not begun with it and that there was a time when the soul did not know itself or have any awareness of itself. Only later, after thought had had exterior things different from itself as objects, did the soul begin to turn its thought upon itself.

72. We must not confuse the soul with its consciousness. Still less should we confuse the soul with the act by which the soul says: *myself*. Again, *reflection* by the soul is not to be confused with the soul itself. Consciousness, enunciation of *myself* and reflection are all accidents of the soul; they are not its substance, which in reality is prior to all these accidental modifications. Confusing the soul with these things is the source of immense mistakes and of the delirium in which the Germanic school has been and is lost. After Reinhold proposed the principle of consciousness, Fichte reduced the soul to consciousness itself, thus converting the soul into a reflection which, however — because reflection is an accident — banished substance from his philosophy. Nothing remained except pure accidents. At the end of his arguments, Fichte himself concluded: 'No being exists, only images; all reality is a dream, and thought is the dream of that dream.' German philosophy never emerged from this maze.

73. Fichte began from this proposition, which contains the error I have indicated: '*Myself* posits itself.' The proposition is obviously absurd because it supposes that *myself* begins to act prior to existing. But no being can posit or create itself. He should have said: 'The soul posits *myself*.' This proposition would mean: 'The soul affirms itself and thus changes into a *myself* because *myself* is the soul affirmed by itself.' The distinction between *myself* and the soul lies here: *myself* is the soul clothed with the reflection by which it affirms itself. There is nothing odd in the soul's producing this reflection, but it is extremely odd that the soul should be *myself*, that is, that it

should be the soul as reflected upon even before it has made this reflection.

74. Nevertheless, the person who philosophises is already a fully formed *myself*, who will find it very difficult to somehow disentangle and persuade himself that his *myself* is man-made, that is, an accidental, non-essential state of his soul or, better still, his very soul constituted in accidental conditions.

Our philosopher will find it easy to argue that the soul which says *myself* is affirming its very own soul, not any soul — which means that it is *myself* which affirms itself. It cannot be denied, of course, that there is an identity of substance between *myself* and its own soul; at the same time, there is certainly diversity on an accidental level where the union of this accident with the soul is indicated by the word *myself*. On the other hand, if this were not the case, reasoning would be extremely awkward. If *myself* affirms its very self, it affirms a *myself*; if it affirms a *myself*, this *myself* is already formed before its affirmation. We are going round in a circle.

The difficulty can be put in another way: if *myself* is formed by affirming itself, how can it be affirmed before it actually is? How does it know that what it is affirming is itself? To know this, it would have to have affirmed the affirming *myself* along with the affirmed *myself* and discovered the identity between the two. But it cannot compare the affirming *myself* with the affirmed unless it has perceived the former as well; to have perceived what affirms is the same as affirming the affirming self. This leads to an infinite series of affirmations because the same argument can always be made about the object of such a judgment which becomes the affirming self. This cannot be the way to explain the peculiar fact of the reflection with which the soul thinks and affirms itself. — If, however, we grasp that the word *myself* is suitable for the soul only after it has affirmed itself and brought itself to consciousness, not before, the difficulty, which appears extremely serious, vanishes completely. But we still have to explain how the soul succeeds in perceiving itself.

75. To do this, we have to return to the theory of intellective perception which we have explained in the book on ideology and in other places. This theory describes perception as an act of the subject who, in intuiting the essence of being, sees this essence realised in feeling. It is impossible to notice being in

feeling unless we first know what being is, that is, unless we first intuit its essence. But granted that a subject has this intuition of being, it is no longer difficult to understand that the subject sees, or rather notices being wherever it is, under every form, and therefore also under the form of feeling, which is one of the three forms in which being is. Granted this, we can understand how the human being as subject perceives himself intellectually; he recognises that this *himself* is nothing more than a feeling-substance. Just as he perceives all other feelings, so he perceives the feeling that is called *himself.*

The difficulty remains: how does the subject know that the feeling which he perceives in this case is himself, that is, how does he know the identity of the perceiving *self* and the perceived *self?* If this identity can only be known by a comparison between the perceiving *self* and the perceived *self*, the perception of ourselves cannot be explained in any way. We have to deny, therefore, that we know this identity by way of comparison between a perceiving and perceived self.

How then is the identity known? It is known directly in the very perception of self. If the subject sees the essence of being in his own feeling in such a way that he judges his own feeling to be an ens, this perception, like all others, contains the feeling that determines what is perceived to be this ens rather than some other. To achieve this, the feeling must be perceived as it is; it is not altered by the perception. It is, therefore, the variety of substantial feelings which gives rise to the variety of beings. The known characteristic, which distinguishes one's own feeling from all others not one's own, must be found in the nature of the feeling.

But what is this known characteristic which enables a person to distinguish his own feeling from all others? As we said before, it must certainly be something, a *quid*, perceived directly in the feeling itself. This *quid*, which is in one's own feeling and forms part of one's own feeling, distinguishing it from all others, is precisely that which is incommunicable in the feeling and which gives rise to the title: one's own. If we wish to express this with a general, abstract word we can aptly call it: *itselfness.* If we then want another word to enunciate the itselfness of the person who speaks and reasons rather than of any person whatsoever, I would propose enriching our philosophical vocabulary with the word: *myselfness* which corresponds to the much-used German *Icheit*. Oneselfness, itselfness, myselfness is indeed a *quid* of feeling, and is felt like all the other parts of feeling and like all other feelings, through the essence of being which is recognised in it. This feelable *quid* is the principle of individuation.[36] It also becomes the principle of personship, which too exists before being perceived. Granted this, it is clear that in the perception of our own feeling we perceive ourselves, provided the word *ourselves*, is taken to indicate the ownership of the feeling, that is, the itselfness which is the characteristic note of such feeling.

76. But when we say *ourselves* are we not perhaps asserting that we have already perceived ourselves? Are we not going round in a circle when we say 'perception of ourselves', which can be translated as 'perception of that which is already perceived'? — The comment is correct, and it reveals language's incapacity to follow the mind faithfully in its operations. Language was invented, in fact, by developed people to express the product of our mental activities, not to follow the operations as they were produced. I beg the reader to give all his attention to this matter, which I shall do my best to explain more at length.

The defect noticed in the phrase 'perception of ourselves' can equally be noticed in the same phrase referred to any other perception whatsoever. When I say 'perception of something, perception of an ens, perception of an object', I make use, and cannot do otherwise, of the words: *thing, ens, object*. But *thing, ens, object* already indicate a perceived *quid*, not a *quid* waiting to be perceived. Indeed, a *quid* not yet perceived cannot be called a *thing*, an *ens*, an *object*, because these words cannot be imposed by us on something of whose existence we know nothing. *Thing, ens, object* indicate that which is in some way. *Nothing* cannot be called a *thing*, an *ens*, an *object*. Nor can it even be called *nothing* unless we want to negate *things, entia, objects*. The word *nothing* cannot be invented or used except by a person who already knows something. But if the three words we have indicated mean that which persons have already perceived, not that which is still to be perceived, the phrase 'to

[36] *AMS*, 784.

perceive some thing, to perceive an ens, to perceive an object' is as defective as the phrase 'to perceive oneself'. Both beg the question; both mean 'to perceive what has been perceived.'

77. Does this mean that the activity called perception cannot be expressed in words? — It can be expressed, but only by indirect words, as we have tried to express and describe it. The activity itself however cannot be translated into words because everything that we express must be already perceived; otherwise it could not be expressed. We certainly could not give a name to that which is still not perceived. Perception, if it is to be expressed exactly, must be indicated with the words: 'that action through which the spirit acquires a real object'. This activity can also be called judgment and affirmation because the spirit has not acquired any real object until it has affirmed it, that is, until it has enunciated to itself the interior word: 'It is.' As I said elsewhere, *real objects* are formed (as objects) by the spirit as it perceives them [*App.*, no. 2].

78. — But if the real object is not present and cannot be named before the spirit has perceived it, what is it prior to perception? — It is a feeling, something felt, but never something understood. It is the matter of some future object of understanding, but it is not yet object; it is ens moving towards formation in the mind, but not yet formed ens. It has no intellective light in itself; it cannot even be named as *objects* are named. Feeling can only produce interjections, inarticulate sounds or, if you wish, articulate sounds, but not those imposed upon it by the mind, that is, by the mind as it imposes signs upon its objects. The sounds are only natural effects of an efficient, instinctive cause. They are like the wind moaning amidst rocks or sighing amidst plants, but never speaking and never intending to offer some sign to itself or to thoughts that it does not yet have. In the same way, various pleasant or painful sensations of brute animals are the efficient, necessary causes of the different sounds they emit. But these sounds are not words; they are not imposed as arbitrary signs intended to signify objects of the mind.

That which is not perceived in nature remains, therefore, unnamed, just as it is unknown. Nor can it be called a thing, an ens, an object. If we do speak of it, we speak indirectly, as I said. We do this by dissecting the ens, the thing, the object, that is, by removing the perception from what has been perceived. This is the way we come to realise that, by removing the perception, we do not remove the whole of the ens, or thing, or object, but are left with the material element, no longer understood by us, but felt. In other words, we are left with the obscure, altogether unknown feeling.

Applying what has been said to the perception of *myself*, I maintain that the word *myself* indicates the entire, totally formed perception. In the object expressed with such a word we perceive a feeling and in it the known characteristic — ownership, myselfness — which distinguishes it from all other feelings.

79. But how, then, can the soul which perceives itself know the identity between itself as perceiving and itself as perceived? This, you remember, is what you yourself maintained must be done when the soul enunciates itself with the word *myself*. How can it perceive this identity except by comparing itself with itself? — The answer is found in what has been said, but I shall do my best to clarify further this fact by showing that the identity between perceiving and perceived is already present in the perception of selfness.

The term of intellective perception is feeling; anything that cannot be felt cannot be perceived. We could not even perceive our own soul if it were not a feeling, and the term of perception. But we also perceive our operations, which therefore must also be accompanied by feeling. Thus we perceive our very own feeling (our very own soul) with all those activities and operations that modify and unfold it. Now the act with which we perceive the feeling constituting our soul, and which we later express with the word *myself* or *ourselves*, is also accompanied by feeling, and it too modifies and actuates our substantial feeling. When we perceive this feeling of our own which is the soul, and we perceive it with all its actualities (because they are all sensible by nature), we must also perceive it with the actuality of the perception of self because it has this actuality in the act of perception and in the feeling concomitant with the actuality. Our soul, therefore, does in a certain implicit way perceive itself perceiving. The act of self-perception can therefore be considered under a twofold respect, that is, as cause of perception or as feeling.

Under the first aspect, it produces perception; under the

second, it is the term of perception and is present in the perception itself. Nor should we be surprised that the same act can be both principle and term of perception if we consider that in every perception the term (feeling) is not posterior chronologically to its principle (the perceiving act). Principle and term must be contemporaneous if perception is to arise, because perception is simply the union of the principle and term from which it results. In other words, the soul, in moving itself to perceive itself, finds that, having reached itself with its act, it has already moved to such perception; the principle of the act of perception is embraced by the finalised, perfect perception. Hence the identity of the soul as self-perceiving and as perceived by itself is provided in human beings by the nature of perception. In other words, it is impossible for the perception expressed by the word *myself* to arise without this identity being included in it.[37]

80. — But why then did you tell us that in order to know the identity between what perceives and what is perceived a second reflection is necessary by means of which we compare ourselves as perceiving with ourselves as perceived and find ourselves identical? — You must note that when I said that, I was analysing *myself* as we have it present to ourselves, as consciousness gives it to the developed human being. Now it is certain that the philosopher who says: '*Myself* perceiving is *myself* perceived', makes a second reflection (and perhaps one of a higher order again) with which he compares himself to himself. Only of this mental operation made by the philosopher can we use correctly the expression that we previously reproved: 'perception of

---

[37] This truth was overlooked by Aristotle who also did not see that the first object of the intellective soul is *being in general*. This led him to say that 'intelligence was intelligence of intelligence' (Καί ἐστιν ἡ νόησις νοήσεος νόησις, *Metaph.*, final ch.). This way of speaking is absurd because the intelligence, if it understands itself, already exists and the definition provided begs the question. Nevertheless, Aristotle starts from a true principle when, in seeking the object of the first intellect, he says: 'It is clear that it understands what is most divine and honourable'. But in wishing to define what this is, he halts at *intellection* itself. He does not attain to *being in general* and as a result is constrained to define primal intellection as 'the intellection of intellection'. This circle, the same as that which entrapped Fichte, can only be avoided in the system I have proposed.

ourselves' or the other: '*myself* perceives *myself*'. The philosopher does, in fact, perceive the already formed *myself*. He meditates upon *himself*, that is, upon what he has previously perceived. As we said, it is the mind which presents to the philosopher the object of his meditation (cf. 57, 60). Fichte, precisely because he did not grasp the distinction between the *reflective myself* of the philosopher and the *myself of first formation*, lost himself in an interminable forest of errors. He knew only the *myself* which is the work of the mind itself, not the naked rudiment given by nature from the beginning to the human spirit. Moreover, this is the path we prefer to follow in order to justify common sense, which gives rise to languages and their different characteristics and expressions, which are always accurate provided they are understood in their original meaning. They become defective and fallible through the fault of individuals who want to use them for some other purpose. Thus if the phrase 'perception of ourselves' is taken to indicate the first perception that we have of our own feeling, it becomes unsuitable and fallacious. It was not designed for this. But if we take it to mean the reflective perception of an already developed human being, it fits exactly, and is true.

CHAPTER 5

The human soul is a substantial feeling which expresses itself through the word *myself*

81. The soul, therefore, is expressed by the word *myself*. If, however, we are to know its primal, essential state, it is necessary to remember that the word expresses, in addition to the concept of the essence of the soul, different relationships with which the mind itself clothes this state through the operations it carries out on it.

Having removed the veils of these relationships, we have found in the depth of *myself* a *feeling* which, anterior to *consciousness*, constitutes properly speaking the pure substance of the soul. We now have to meditate on this feeling, defend its existence and describe its nature.

[81]

CHAPTER 6
Opinions of philosophers

Article 1
Philosophers who did not know where to seek
the essence of the soul

82. We have to insist upon this because many philosophers did not realise that the essence of the soul had to be sought in a first feeling.[38] They strayed because their mind was infected by limited, fallacious principles drawn solely from the sensible conditions of matter and hence applicable only to matter apparent to the senses, not to all entia. These principles, although never truly ontological, were gratuitously taken as such.

83. The greatest obstacle to progress in philosophy is the immense facility people have for assuming that what we perceive with our exterior senses is the only mark of all entia. Actions and passions, they maintain, have to be similar and follow the same laws. Nothing is permitted which is in any way dissimilar from that administered by the senses; nothing must escape the rules of judgment valid for bodies. But the wings of the mind cannot take flight towards the regions of being unless we first realise that everything we perceive through the senses is only a tiny part of

---

[38] Sensists would have discovered the essence of the *sensitive soul* if, instead of allowing themselves to be waylaid by *transitory sensations*, they had risen to the fundamental feeling. But they would have been unable to arrive at the intellective soul without abandoning their system. Condillac did admit the fundamental feeling to some extent, although the hypothesis of the statue led him to the absurdity of making this feeling arise from sensations. Let me offer the following exceptional quotation from Destutt-Tracy which will confirm what I have said (I am always glad to find my opinions confirmed by others): 'Feeling is a phenomenon of our existence, it is our very existence. A being which feels nothing can indeed exist for other beings if they feel it, but certainly cannot exist for itself *because it does not know it.*' The final words betray the sensist who confuses *knowing* with *feeling*, but the preceding words testify to the teaching I have expounded.

being. The senses put us in touch with incipient entities that are relative only to us. Completed ens goes way beyond that, and teaching about it extends to altogether different principles.

84. Nevertheless, we cannot come to a halt before the merely sensible qualities of external bodies. Human beings, dependent on the law of perception,[39] have to suppose the existence of something else, of an act through which bodies exist. We are assisted in this by the imagination, and suppose that the other thing necessary for the subsistence of sensible qualities has its own place located under the sensible, superficial qualities. We call it 'substance' *(sub-stans)* without realising that if the substance of bodies lies under their surfaces, we could find it by breaking the bodies and searching around inside them — something that cannot be done.[40] Such an entity created by the imaginative faculty is necessarily a mysterious, inexplicable *quid*. Hence the sensistic conclusion that the substances of things are totally unknown.[41]

85. But if we silence the imagination and pay attention to reason, which is the only true guide in philosophical investigations, we shall easily see that the *act* through which the sensible qualities exist is simply the *sensiferous force*[42] manifested in our animal feeling as something *extrasubjective* when our animal feeling is modified. This is the first thing we understand in bodies, and it alone (determined by its effects, that is, by sensations) is sufficient to make us mentally conceive bodies. It is, therefore, *substance* (cf. 52), and it is that for which common sense provides the word 'body'.

86. Later, *reasoning* may find that the *sensiferous force* given by *perception*,[43] in order to exist, requires something more than what is included in the perception of bodies. This proximate

---

[39] *Sistema filosofico*, 30–31, 88–94; *NE*, vol. 2, 583–629.

[40] The essence of the soul is simply the *idea of the substance of the soul*. Searching for that which makes up the essence of the soul, therefore, is the same as searching for that which makes up its substance. *Substance* means simply *substantial essence*.

[41] *NE*, vol. 1, 47–65.

[42] *AMS*, 230–245; *NE*, vol. 2, 632–681.

[43] *Sistema filosofico*, 88–99.

cause of the force, although called *corporeal principle*,[44] always remains outside the concept of body, a concept given to us by perception alone.

87. Philosophers who located the substance of bodies in an unknown *quid*, not discovered with their reason but supposed by their imagination, continued along the same lines when they undertook to resolve the question: 'What does the essence of the soul consist in?'

First, they generalised their teaching about the substance of bodies. According to them, 'The substance of bodies is an unknown *quid* that gives existence to the sensible qualities overlaying it. The same is true, therefore, about every substance.' Persuaded that every substance has to be conceived or coined in the image of bodily substance, they took the substance of the soul as a support or substratum (*sub-stratum*) lying under the accidents of the soul but totally unknown.

88. It is obvious that this way of reasoning is quite arbitrary. We must abandon this *learned philosophy*,[45] for the sake of following common sense which wishes to indicate substances with nouns that grammarians call *substantives*. These are imposed on all the entia we perceive. According to common sense, perceived ens is substance. But if the substances of things named with words are perceived, they are not unknown; perception is a way of knowing. We should not create *substances* for ourselves with the imagination, but find them in perception itself whenever this is possible.

89. The entia perceived by us are bodies and our own soul (cf. 12–17). If we wish to discover the substance of bodies and the substance of soul, we have to look for it in *perception*. We did this when we dealt with the substance of bodies; we must do the same when dealing with the substance of the soul.

90. Note that we cannot in any way perceive that which we do not feel. Perception is experienced cognition (cf. 53), and without feeling there is no experience. We found the substance of body in feeling; and in feeling we must find the substance of the soul.

---

[44] *NE*, vol. 2, 855–857.
[45] *NE*, vol. 1, 29–34.

91. But not every feeling is substance. Some feelings cannot be conceived by themselves alone; they presuppose some other feeling prior to themselves, of which they are modifications. We have to go back to the first feeling through which and in which lie all the others, and prior to which no other feeling is experienced. A first, stable feeling, therefore which makes up the substance of the soul must be present (cf. 52). This is what I have called *fundamental feeling*.

Article 2
Philosophers who remain unaware of the fundamental feeling

92. It is extremely easy to perceive the fundamental feeling joined to its modifications, and to grasp it through a first reflection (this explains why common sense calls its principle, *soul*). But it is equally difficult to distinguish it, by way of new reflections, from its modifications and to recognise that it is the first, the principle of all other particular and accidental feelings.

93. Condillac supposes that sensible life begins as soon as his statue smells a rose.[46] In that first act, presupposed by our philosopher, the statue only senses the scent of a rose; *it knows nothing of itself*. However, we can give a benign interpretation to Condillac's way of expressing himself. He says that the statue, when smelling the rose, must believe itself to be the scent of the rose. If it has to believe that it is the scent of the rose, the statue must already sense itself because it predicates that scent of itself.

94. Dégerando and others said that only sensations of touch accompany the feeling of ourselves. This is another obviously false opinion when taken in its strict meaning. Benignly interpreted it becomes true; it is true if you mean that the sensation of touch is that which helps us more than any other to *distinguish myself* from accidental modification.

[46] *'Myself,'* says Condillac, 'is a collection of sensations.' This definition lacks whatever gives unity to sensations. It is a definition of *myself* in which *myself* is lacking. The same error can be found in his definition of body 'as a collection of qualities which you touch, see, and so on'. Obviously, body is missing from this definition.

[91–94]

95. Galluppi is right when he maintains that no sensation is possible unless it is accompanied by our own substantial feeling. As he says: 'Perceiving a sensation means feeling oneself to be modified; it means feeling oneself, having the feeling of *myself*.'[47] But he concludes erroneously: 'Even from the first sensation we have a perception of *myself*.'[48] and 'Our sensible life begins with the perception of *myself* and its sensations.'[49] He does not go back to the fundamental feeling which lies beyond acquired sensations, nor does he succeed in understanding how there is a feeling anterior to intellective perception and consciousness. Finally, because he is ignorant of the teaching about *object*, he uses this word to indicate the term of sensation. This hurls him into sensism as he struggles to avoid it.

CHAPTER 7
Proofs of the fundamental feeling

96. Having already shown that this feeling indubitably exists,[50] I simply wanted to direct the reader to those demonstrations, but I now find that I have at hand a note written in 1821, when I outlined some reasons suitable for proving the existence of this feeling. I think it useful to put this before the eyes of the reader, changing the word 'consciousness', which I used improperly, to 'feeling'.

97. A fundamental feeling exists in human beings.

First proof — In my present state, I find I have a great number of sensations, including those which have their source in the body, and the memory of previous sensations. Moreover, I have many cognitions and think many thoughts. But I find that all my sensations, present and past, and all my thoughts are distinct from one another. In fact, if two sensations or two thoughts

[47] *Elementi della Psicologia*, §7.
[48] *Ibid*, §8.
[49] *Ibid*, §10.
[50] *NE*, vol. 2, 692–721.

were not distinguished from one another in some way, they would not be two, but one. On the other hand, I see that I am always the same. It is I *myself* who think, perceive and do all these things. If it were not I, the same *myself*, who carries them out, I could not compare two sensations or two thoughts and come to know their diversity. This *myself*, therefore, is not the sensations and the thoughts. These differ; *myself*, on the other hand, is one. *Myself* is the subject who possesses the sensations and the thoughts. *Myself* considered in its own proper nature, is independent of sensations and thoughts which are accidental and vary continually, without however being able to make *myself* vary.

If I now begin to remove mentally some particular thought or sensation, I soon realise that I am not destroying *myself*; I feel that *myself* remains. If, therefore, *myself* remains identical when I take away from it any particular sensation and thought, it is clear that even if I were to remove all accidental sensations and thoughts one by one, I would not have taken away *myself*, the essence of which suffers in no way from being deprived of its accidental sensations and thoughts. *Myself* remains, even when deprived of all modifications. In this way, I come to form for myself the idea of the feeling which I express by the word *myself*, pure and simple.

98. *Second proof* — Words, which offer a faithful portrayal of ideas, confirm this. In fact, when I want to express the act of feeling, I say: 'I (*MYSELF*) FEEL'. Let us cancel the FEEL. Have I cancelled *myself* along with the feeling? Certainly not. But what if I cancel I (*myself*), and am left with FEEL alone? In this case, either I suppose *myself* in FEEL or, if I want to prescind absolutely from *myself*, FEEL has no meaning. In other words, the feeling expressed in the word *myself* exists independently of any particular sensation; on the other hand, the particular sensation, if it is to exist, needs the fundamental feeling in the same way that an accident cannot exist without substance, nor what is made without a maker — although there can be both substance without accident and maker without what he produces.

99. *Third proof* — Again, all my sensations only produce states or modes of existence of my soul which feels the given mode of its being provided by some particular sensation. But

how could it feel its modes of being if it did not feel itself essentially? What does 'feeling one's mode of being' or 'one's existing' mean except feeling the relationship of a given modification with oneself? If the soul is to feel this relationship, it has to feel itself because that modification is referred precisely to itself. If the soul were not to feel itself prior to sensation, sensation would be nothing for the soul. In such a case, sensation would be an action on a being that does not feel itself and cannot, therefore, feel anything else.

100. *Fourth proof* — We could also reason as follows: either this action is done in the soul or outside the soul. If outside, the soul feels nothing; if in the soul, the soul is an ens which either feels itself or does not. In the first case, the fundamental feeling is present; in the second, even the possibility of sensation vanishes. If the soul does not feel itself, how can it feel that which is in it? It would be like a person denying that he sees a table, but affirming that he sees its shape or its colour. The modification of what is sensible is sensible, but the modification of what is not sensible, is not sensible.

101. *Fifth proof* — Again, the argument can be expounded as follows: why does the soul feel the various modes of its existence produced by sensations? Doubtless, because it has the faculty of feeling the modes of its own existence. But isn't the first feeling, anterior to every acquired modification, a mode of existence? If it is, why remove it from the faculty to which all other modes are subject? Until we find some sufficient reason for the contrary, we must say that an ens which feels the modes of its own existence must also feel its first mode, which precedes all other particular changes.

102. *Sixth proof* — How does it come about that the soul, given that it is not felt through itself, can then come to feel itself by means of the modifications it receives? I grant that such modifications can move the soul to reflect on its own feelings, and compare its various states. It thus moves from its natural quiet to perceive its own feeling and come to a more distinct and satisfying idea of itself. But here we are talking about simple feeling, not of comparison between several feelings. I maintain, therefore, that actions carried out on the soul could never, however strong they were, bring the soul to feel itself if it did not already feel itself by nature from the very beginning. In fact,

these acquired sensations may be considered either before they have modified the soul or in the act of modifying it. Before they enter the soul they are still not sensations; in the act of acting on the soul neither the agents nor their operations can give the soul feeling because they themselves do not possess it and, even if they did, could not communicate it (feeling is incommunicable). On the contrary, it is the soul which makes sensations of the impulses it receives from agents different from itself. The soul, therefore, possesses feeling before the impulses were given to it, and independently of the impulses. It does not receive feeling from them, but gives it to them.

103. *Seventh proof* — No one denies that the soul at its origin and through its nature has the faculty of feeling. Not all will grant, however, that it also possesses the act of feeling. They say that the act is one thing, the faculty another. It is, of course, true that a particular act is very different from the faculty that produces all the acts. But what we need here is a clear idea of 'faculty'. This is how I understand it.

Certain conditions are necessary if a faculty is to operate. Given these conditions, the faculty operates, that is, it becomes a particular act (a faculty, in so far as it is act, ceases to be a faculty). Thus the faculty of sight needs light, that of hearing needs undulations from aeriform fluid, that of taste some tasty substance, and so on. Given these conditions, any faculty whatsoever activates itself. I also note that such action depends upon the faculty as a true efficient *cause*; other conditions influence the actions only as occasions, stimuli and so on. For example, although the balcony window must be open if the sun is to illuminate a room, it is not the balcony window but the rays of the sun which illuminate the room. There is a great difference, therefore, between the merely necessary condition and the cause. Equally, although a movement of air is necessary for me to hear some sound, it is my organ, my faculty of hearing, that hears, not the air. Let us grant, therefore, that the occasion of sensation is altogether different from the cause, and that this cause is the subject or faculty which feels. If the cause of feeling is the faculty, and this operates necessarily, granted certain conditions, the faculty carries out its act in virtue of its own activity, not in virtue of external things. It must, therefore, of itself always be in a certain act. If it did not possess a first act of

[103]

its own, there would be no way of understanding how it could pass from potency to act. There would be no sufficient reason for such a passage. As we said, no action of the body on the soul has power to draw the soul to act; the body can only offer an occasion for the soul's activity. The correct idea of faculty, therefore, is that which makes it consist in a *universal act* preceding all *particular acts*. This universal act is then particularised and specified when some individual matter is provided to which the faculty can apply and restrict its activity. Thus, different objects placed successively under an enormous mass of iron are crushed one by one, not because the mass begins to be activated each time, but because it operates, that is, weighs heavily, even if it is not crushing any particular object. If, therefore, the universal faculty of feeling present in the soul is already in act independently of external, particular impulses, the soul feels itself. This proposition is equivalent to saying that, after analysing the ideas we have of the soul, we declare it to be a sentient ens. Everyone grants us this.[51]

CHAPTER 8

The essence of the soul is in the fundamental feeling in so far as this feeling is substance and subject

104. The proofs, given in *A New Essay* for the existence of the fundamental feeling which constitutes the human being,

---

[51] Aristotle's definition of the soul, 'The soul is that by which first we live and feel and understand', (*De Anima*, bk. 2, c. 1) shows that human beings, as soon as they are animated, possess the act of life, of feeling and of intelligence precisely because they have in themselves that with which they 'first live and feel and understand'. In fact, if the soul is that with which one feels, that with which one feels is not present as long as one feels nothing. But the soul is always in human beings because it is the *substantial form* of its body, as we shall see. Hence, there must always be some feeling present. The same must be said about the understanding.

One can argue in the same way from Aristotle's other definition, 'Soul is the first substantial act of a physical, organic body; it is the power of that which has life' (*De Anima*, bk. 2, c. 1 and 2). And this is true whatever the philosopher's state of mind when he wrote these words.

are concerned with that part of the fundamental feeling which has as its term body and space. The proofs expounded in the preceding chapter demonstrate the existence of a feeling that extends to everything that can be understood as signified by the word *myself*. We need, therefore, to seek the substantial essence of the soul in the feeling that lies deep within *myself*.

105. From what has been said, we can already bring together certain information about the nature of such a feeling. That is:

1. When a human being enunciates *myself*, he does not intend to enunciate a fleeting and accidental modification, but a true, subsistent being. In other words, a substance.

2. A human being knows nothing of himself before affirming his own soul. In affirming it, he has perceived a subsistent being which is not in any other being as modification or as accident. In other words, he has perceived a substance.

106. 3. This subsistent being, this substance affirmed and expressed with the word *myself*, is a feeling-substance. An active, sentient and operating principle is present in this feeling. In other words, *myself* is a subject.

CHAPTER 9

The principle of psychology

107. The principle of every science is the definition of the object with which it deals. This definition expresses the essence of the thing; the *essence* of the thing under discussion is the principle of every reasoning about the thing. The extent of this reasoning depends upon the extent to which the *knowable essence* is complete relative to the being of the thing.

108. The knowable essence is positive when attained by way of perception (cf. 19–21). Hence, the sciences of perception, as I have called them (cf. 17–21), receive their principle from the perception of the ens which constitutes their object.

109. Perception, therefore, enables us to know the substance of the being positively. Consequently, the *substance* known positively in perception is the principle of such sciences. Let us apply these logical notions to psychology.

110. The principle of this science must be acknowledged

in the very perception of the soul. In other words, all the reasoning we can carry out about the soul must begin from what we know of our soul in our perception of it. But what we first perceive in our soul is its substance. The *substantial essence*, therefore, which is simply the substance itself intuited as possible in the idea, corresponds to the substance of the perceived soul.

111. Nevertheless, it must be noted that we perceive our soul only as a subject. The soul perceived and enunciated in *myself* is subsistent; it is not some possible *myself*. Subsistence is essential to *myself* as affirmed. A twofold operation is necessary, therefore, if we are to conceive mentally a *possible myself*, that is, the *idea of myself* cut off from perception. Through this operation, we carry over into the idea not only *myself* as perceived, but *myself* as perceiving. In other words, *myself* as possible is only the general possibility 'of a soul perceiving and enunciating itself' as I perceive and enunciate myself. When I affirm *myself* (that is, say 'I') I express: 1. a particular *myselfness*; 2. my own proper, particular *myselfness*. Myselfness, although always particular because it is of its essence a feeling proper to someone, can have a relationship of identity with *myself* who enunciates it *here and now*, or with another subject who also enunciates it. It is this relationship that can be universalised when we conceive that which is essentially proper and particular as possibly having *relationships of identity* with *myself* who is actually enunciating it, or with others whom I think as enunciating it. This is the way in which *myself*, which is particular of its essence, is universalised. It cannot, therefore, be universalised in itself but, as I said, in the relationship of identity between the perceived self and the perceiving, enunciating self.

112. The *proximate* principle of psychology, therefore, is what we know of our soul in the perception of ourselves. It is also the *remote* principle of the sciences which deal with spirits in general, and in particular of those spirits which do not fall under our experience. I say 'remote' because reasoning must intervene in the formation of these sciences.

113. This direct and truly logical way of scientific procedure was seen, followed and pointed out by St. Augustine and by St. Thomas, the greatest philosopher of our nation.

St. Augustine notes expressly that the human mind could not

know any other mind if it did not first know itself. 'How can the mind know any mind if it does not know itself?'[52] In other words, the human spirit would be unable to form the concept of any other spirit if it did not first perceive itself. It would have no example on which to base its concept. In the order of cognitions, therefore, knowledge of one's own soul is prior to knowledge of other souls and intelligences. These come to be known through reasoning based on the perception that the soul has of itself. The holy Doctor continues on the same path. 'The soul', he says, 'knows itself through itself.'[53] These words were abused and taken to mean that the human soul was known to itself through its own essence, as though it needed no other light to know itself. But St. Augustine repeats continually that neither the human being nor his mind is *light* to himself. However, granted the light communicated to the mind from on high, the human being does not know self by reasoning, which begins from something more known than self, but directly, that is, by way of perception. Hence he explains that as the mind knows bodies through the feeling which they produce by their action on the sense organs, so it knows spirits through itself, that is, through its own feeling which is the object of its perception.[54]

114. St. Thomas clarifies St. Augustine as follows. He shows that when St. Augustine says that the mind knows itself through itself, he does not in any way intend that it is knowable through its own essence. This is proper to God alone. But the mind knows itself through its act, that is, through perception of self, without needing to use any other inductive reasoning.[55] He says: 'Our intellect does not know itself through its essence, but

---

[52] *De Trinit.*, 9, 3.

[53] *Ibid.*

[54] *Mens ipsa sicut corporearum rerum notitiam per sensus corporis colligit, sic incorporearum per semetipsam* [As the mind itself gathers information about bodily things through the senses proper to the body, so through itself it gathers information about incorporeal things] (*De Trinit.*, 9, 3). The word *colligit* [gathers] is properly used to distinguish the operation of the intelligence which has to intervene to gather the information provided by sensations.

[55] *S.T.*, I, q. 88, art. 1.

by means of its act. This comes about in two ways: in a particular way when Socrates or Plato PERCEIVES that he has an intellective soul by perceiving his understanding.'[56] Here St. Thomas teaches that the human being knows his own intellect because he is conscious of understanding. He refers to the act of understanding because it is this which draws our reflection to ourselves. In other words, St. Thomas is explaining the reflective knowledge we have of ourselves, not the direct perception. But if we consider that reflection, the cause of our consciousness, could not take place unless perception had taken place, we can easily see that Aquinas' teaching about the reflective knowledge that the soul acquires about itself presupposes direct perception. He continues: 'And in a universal way by which, moving from the act of the intellect, we consider the nature of the human soul.' This is precisely what we have said takes place in those operations we call *objectivisation* and *universalisation*.

St. Thomas, therefore, establishes with Aristotle that the science of our own soul is the PRINCIPLE of all cognitions that we can have about pure spirits. 'Knowledge of the soul is a kind of principle enabling us to know separate substances. Our soul's knowledge of self enters whatever knowledge we can have of incorporeal substances.'[57]

CHAPTER 10

How to apply the principle of psychology to deduce the special information that forms the science of the soul

115. The substance of the soul, therefore, is *perceptible* to the soul itself, but could not be perceptible unless it consisted in a first, fundamental feeling. That which does not feel itself in any way does not perceive itself in any way. This explains how St. Augustine was able to write, with equal truth and acuteness: 'Rightly, nothing is said to be known if there is no knowledge of

[56] *Ibid.*

[57] *S.T.*, I, q. 88, art. 1. — Readers wishing to see a more extensive exposition of St. Thomas' mind on the knowledge the soul has of itself may consult *NE*, vol. 2, appendix no. 8.

its substance. When the mind knows itself, therefore, IT KNOWS ITS SUBSTANCE; and when it is certain of itself, it is certain of its substance.'[58]

116. However, several things have to be kept in mind if we are to apply this principle suitably in deducing the special information making up the science of the soul.

1. Sciences are not composed of *direct*, but of *reflective cognitions* acquired only when the mind turns back on its direct cognitions. Note that it is direct, perceptive cognition which affirms substances directly, not reflective cognition. But in seeking to know the *substance* of the soul and make this teaching *scientific*, we have to make use of reflection. After this, our next step is to make use of one or more acts of reflection to separate the elements posited by reflection, as we said. These elements do not belong to the naked substance of the soul, but to the reflective concept we have formed of it. If we omit this step, we shall take things pertaining to reflection for those pertaining to substance.

2. It is far easier to *reflect* on the acts of the soul than on the soul itself as it is given in perception. And our acts are necessary as stimuli to reflection. But it would be a mistake to conclude that every cognition, including the primal cognition of the soul, is drawn from its acts in such a way that we know it only from its effects (as though we were dealing with something foreign to ourselves, and our soul were not ourselves). At one and the same time, we reflect on the soul and on its acts. In fact, we would never be able to know that our perceived acts belonged to *ourselves* rather than some other subject if we did not perceive, together with our acts, *ourselves* as cause and subject of such acts. To have pure information about the soul, we have to employ a new reflection and separate the soul's acts from the soul itself, even though with prior reflection we have simultaneously turned our attention to both the acts of the soul and the soul itself.

117. 3. Finally, we need to notice that in objectivising the feeling of our soul which lies within the perception of ourselves, and thus universalising the information we have about it, we have formed a specific concept which we can now analyse with

[58] *De Trinit*, 10: 16.

further reflections. This enables us to compare the soul with other things known by us, such as bodies, and see their similarities and dissimilarities. The guiding rule we have to use in this analysis and comparison to avoid errors is this: 'Without the arbitrary addition of anything whatsoever, we must retain the concept of soul as given by the perception of itself and of the acts accompanying it.' This rule is a consequence of what we have said: perception is the principle of the science of the soul. No science can have more than that which is contained in its principle; no universal, objective concept of the soul can contain more than is present in the perception of the soul itself from which we have separated the concept. Any arbitrary addition is a mistake. Nevertheless, we easily make arbitrary additions to the concepts of things. This arbitrary faculty of affirmation is precisely the faculty of error. Normally, it is imagination which, intervening in place of reason, moves our faculty of affirmation or persuasion to state that our concept of something contains that which is not actually present and thus to define the thing badly by attributing to it a nature which is not its own. This is the source of false systems about the human soul, all of which are excluded and rejected at their very beginning by the logical rule we have explained which relates the concept of the soul to perception, and notes carefully whether what we have posited in that concept is found in perception. 'If it is found there, it is a legitimate element of the concept; if it is not, it is illegitimate and to be removed from the concept.' This extremely simple and beautiful rule was provided for me by St. Augustine, one of my two great masters in philosophical as well as theological speculation. I have only translated what he said into modern language.

118. St. Augustine distinguishes between the soul's *knowing itself* and its *thinking* of itself. To know itself, the soul needs only *to perceive itself*; but to think about itself, it must reflect.[59] Through perception, the soul knows itself as *present*; through reflection it seeks itself as *absent* because the scientific reflection

---

[59] *Ita cum aliud sit non se nosse, aliud non se cogitare, neque enim multarum doctrinarum peritum ignorare grammaticam dicimus, cum eam non cogitat, quia de mediocri arte tunc cogitat, etc.* (*De Trinit.*, 10: 7).

of which we are speaking deals with the universal, objective concept of the soul. However, says St. Augustine, mistakes do not arise in *perception*, but through the work of *reflection*; they do not come about through simple self-knowledge, but as a result of thought about oneself. He warns that the soul should think of itself as present if it is to avoid errors; it should not seek itself as though it were absent. In other words, pay attention to what perception of self provides, and do not abandon this for what reflection affirms about the soul,[60] as if the soul were an object alien to itself: *non igitur velut absentem se quaerat cernere, sed* PRESENTEM *se curet discernere.*[61] We should not reason about our own soul as though it were some third, unknown thing; we should not presuppose ignorance of ourselves. On the contrary, we should realise that knowing ourselves already, all we have to do is distinguish the SELF that knows from other things: *Nec* SE *quasi non novit, cognoscat, sed ab eo quod alterum novit, dignoscat.*[62]

119. The characteristic of perception according to St. Augustine is certainty; we cannot doubt about that which perception tells us of the soul. Perception, therefore, becomes a kind of spy, telling us what we know of the soul through perception and what we ourselves have added arbitrarily through reflection, about which we normally doubt. So, for example, no one has any doubt that the soul is the principle of feeling and understanding. This shows that the information is found in perception. But that the soul is air, fire or some other body is doubtful and not accepted by all. We can conclude, therefore, that it is an arbitrary addition and an error of reflection which has no validity. If it were present truly in perception, no one would doubt it.[63] This argument annihilates materialism.

120. St. Augustine adds another excellent indication for

---

[60] I have already shown that *direct cognition* is the criterion of *reflective cognition*. Cf. *NE*, vol. 3, 1112–1157.

[61] *De Trinit.*, 10: 12.

[62] *Ibid.*

[63] *Certa est autem de se* (anima) *sicut convincunt ea quae supra dicta sunt. Nec omnino certa est utrum aer, an ignis sit, an aliquod corpus, vel aliquid corporis. Non est igitur aliquid eorum* (*De Trinit.*, 10: 16).

knowing what does not come from *perception*, the faithful principle of knowledge of the soul and consequently the *criterion*
for knowing true and false teaching about the soul. He says that
when we doubt if a given nature — water, say — is the soul, we
should note whether we think about that nature in the same
way that we think about another nature which is definitely not
the soul. If we think about it in the same way, we can say that it
is not our soul. If it were, we would think of that nature in a way
totally different from all other natures. In other words, we
would think about it as present and as our own; we think about
other natures only as foreign to us and absent.[64]

121. St. Thomas, too, distinguishes direct cognition of the
soul, obtained by way of perception, from reflective cognition.
He says that the former is easy and admits no error; the second
is difficult because reflection has to be reined within the limits
of things contained in perception itself. Exceeding these limits
was the cause of the errors made by philosophers about the
nature of the soul.[65]

122. We conclude that scientific research about the substance
of the soul must be purged from three heterogeneous adjuncts
mixed in with it:

[64] *Si quid autem horum esset* (anima) *aliter id quam cetera cogitaret, non
scilicet per imaginale figmentum, sicut cogitantur absentia, quae sensu
corporis tacta sunt, sine omnino ipsa, sine eiusdem generis aliqua; sed
QUADAM INTERIORE, NON SIMULATA, SED VERA PRAESENTIA* (non enim
quidquam illi est se ipsa praesentius for the feeling) *sicut cogitat vivere se et
meminisse et intelligere et velle. Novit enim haec in se* (that is, through
intimate perception) *nec imaginatur quasi extra se illa sensu tetigerit, sicut
corporalia quaeque tanguntur. Ex quorum cogitationibus si nihil sibi attingat,
ut tale aliquid esse se putet, QUAEQUE EI DE SE REMANET, HOC SOLUM IPSA EST*
(*De Trinit.*, 10: 16).

[65] 'There is a difference between these two cognitions. The presence itself
of the mind is sufficient for the first cognition of the mind. This presence is
the principle of the act by which THE MIND PERCEIVES ITSELF. This explains
why the mind is said to know itself through its own presence. But for the
mind's second cognition, presence of the mind is not sufficient. A careful,
searching investigation is required, (that is, scientific, reflective cognition).
'For this reason, many people are ignorant of the nature of the soul and many
have erred about it.' He adds that the second cognition consists in 'knowing
its [the soul's] difference from other things, which means knowing its quality
and nature' (*S.T.*, I, q. 87, art. 1).

1. From all those substances or qualities not found in the *perception of our soul*, but added arbitrarily by human beings to its concept. This excludes all errors on the part of those who claimed that the soul was fire, air, a collection of atoms, and in general all materialists.

2. From all actual relationships with our reflection itself; for example, from self-consciousness, which is the work of reflection. This excludes all errors of ideologists who draw ideas from the soul itself (subjectivists), or who suppose that the first cognition needs no explanation because given with the soul, or that the soul is cognition, or knowable through its own essence.

3. From all that is perceived along with the soul, that is, from the acts of its potencies. These are accidents joined to the soul, not the soul itself although, as we said, they are perceived with the soul. In fact, we are moved to turn our attention on ourselves and thus perceive ourselves only through our accidental acts which at first are the sensitive acts determined by the action of external bodies. Although we have to separate the soul's accidental acts from itself in order to have pure information about the substance of the soul, we also have to separate from the soul the act of perception itself. Self-perception is not the soul; it is a mere operation of the soul with which it acquires its first information it has of itself. When we have separated the intellective perception of itself from the concept of the soul, we are left simply with the fundamental feeling, the object of the succeeding perception. It is the fundamental feeling which constitutes the pure substance of the soul. This excludes the error of those who claim that the soul is a totally unknown and unfelt *quid*, or who suppose that there must be, under the phenomenal *myself*, another substantial *myself*. I have refuted this error elsewhere.[66]

123. Finally, this method of philosophising about the soul brings us to know two things, two genera, as it were, to which all other psychological information is reduced. That is, we come to know and determine:

---

[66] *Rinnovamento*, bk. 2, cc. 13–17 [This reference probably refers to 283–285].

I. What the soul is. It is everything found in the consciousness of ourselves, in *myself*, but without the three adjuncts of which we have spoken. And

II. What the soul is not. It is not that which falls outside consciousness of ourselves, nor one or other of the three adjuncts that we ourselves have interposed and added with our imagination, or reflection or perception.

We now have to meditate on this substantial feeling as it lies in the depths of *myself* and distinguish its properties. Finally we shall analyse it more accurately.

Book 2

Some properties of the
essence of the soul

[INTRODUCTION]

124. In the preceding book, I indicated consciousness of ourselves as the source from which psychological teachings have to be drawn. At the same time, I established the PRINCIPLE OF PSYCHOLOGY, which lies in the *essence of the soul*. This consists, I said, in a *first, immanent and wholly substantial feeling*. The present book and the three following are dedicated to explaining (through meditation on that feeling) and revealing (by careful analysis) the elements, characteristics and attributes of the essence of the soul, and excluding those which have been falsely attached to it. Our teaching, therefore, will be partly negative and partly positive. In other words, I shall say what the soul is not, and what separates it from other substances; and I shall also indicate what it is in itself. I shall do all this as far as I can; I begin with the negative characteristic of unity.

CHAPTER 1

The unity of the soul in each human being

125. We have to draw all our positive teaching about the soul from meditation on *myself*. I shall begin immediately by showing that the soul is one in each human being because each is never more than one *myself*.

126. This direct, clear demonstration of the unity of the soul disposes of the error requiring simultaneously three souls, animal, sensitive and intellective, which certain authors have endeavoured to posit in human beings. A similar mistake is made by those who posited two souls, one sensitive, one intellective. The source of the errors is clear; these philosophers have always sought the kind of soul present in *myself*, but not where it actually is. Even granted the existence in human beings of a principle of vegetation and sensation distinct from *myself* (which could easily be the case), this principle would not be the human soul, but something different from it. It is indeed

obvious that the soul is one — as obvious as it is to each person that he is a single human being, not two or more. This is evident because consciousness tells him so, and consciousness is precisely the perception of the soul, or includes it. It is, therefore, a unique witness worthy of faith, and infallible in this argument. Later, I shall answer several objections which could be made against this truth.

CHAPTER 2

The substance of the soul is the sole principle of all operations

127. But despite the unicity of the soul, directly attested by consciousness, the operations of the soul, both contemporary and successive, are multiple and diverse. The relationship between the soul and its operations is the same as that which exists between *myself* and that which *myself* suffers or carries out.

128. When human beings say: 'I feel, I understand, I will, I move,' they declare themselves to be cause and subject of all these actions, both passive and active. *Myself*, therefore, is the sole principle and subject of all the passions and operations of the soul. But *myself* is the soul itself, that is, its substance perceived and affirmed by us. I conclude: 'the substance of the soul is the sole principle of all its different operations.'

129. Moreover, this principle is capable of feeling because *myself* feels itself; it is a first, original, substantial feeling because *myself* is felt by us as such. Hence

> soul is an original, stable, sole principle; the sole subject of all other feelings and of all human operations.

130. Describing accurately this first feeling principle by separating it from all inferior active principles means describing in a proper sense the essence of the human soul. We shall see, therefore, how all the soul's operations, all the elements added afterwards as it develops, are contained in the soul as in their

principle, and how the soul is first act in comparison with all second acts which are contained virtually in the first act.[67]

CHAPTER 3

The spirituality of the soul is proved directly through consciousness

131. Difficulties in consenting to this affirmation spring from the prejudice, 'There can be no feeling other than corporeal feeling.' This, as I said, is a prejudice. The species is taken for the genus. Because corporeal feeling is easily known, we arbitrarily conclude that every feeling must be corporeal. There is here a huge leap from the particular to the general. But to a careful observer of nature it is clear that feelings exist which are totally different from those produced by our own body or other bodies. On the other hand, no one can demonstrate that spiritual feelings, that is, feelings which do not terminate in any extension or matter, are absurd.

132. Direct meditation on *myself* shows without difficulty that there is such a feeling. The word *myself* does in fact express a feeling altogether different from every corporeal fantasy; *myself* offers neither extension, shape, colour nor anything else proper to any body whatsoever. The substance of the soul expressed by the word *myself* is, therefore, incorporeal and altogether immaterial. Every time we add something corporeal or material to it, we simply add to *myself* with the imagination that which is not present in it, but is the term of its acts. As we have already seen, the soul is neither its acts nor the term of its

---

[67] This again is a fact to be observed, not deduced through reasoning, or wilfully disputed. The great philosophers of antiquity had noticed this fact. St. Thomas, sharing their views, wrote: *Primus actus est universale principium actuum, quia est infinitum virtualiter,* IN SE OMNIA PRAEHABENS, ut dicit Dionysius (*De div. nom.,* c. 5) [The first act is the universal principle of all acts because it is virtually infinite, POSSESSING ALL THINGS IN ITSELF, as Dionysius says (*De div. nom.,* c. 5)] (*S. T.,* I, q. 75, art 5, ad 1). This is true in an absolute sense of God, and comparatively of all other first acts.

acts; all these things have to be separated from it if we are to reach the soul itself.

133. But a substance which has no bodily or material property is called 'spiritual' or *spirit*. The human soul, therefore, is a spirit.

CHAPTER 4

The immortality of the soul proved directly from consciousness

134. If the soul is a substance altogether different from the body, we cannot infer the death of the soul from the death of the body.

135. Moreover, the word 'death' means only the cessation in a body of acts of life and animation. The word 'death', therefore, refers only to the body, and it would be absurd to attribute it to what is not body. But spirit means a substance that is not body; spirit, therefore, is not subject to death. But the soul is spirit (cf. 133). Therefore the soul is immortal.

136. Nevertheless, a person who has not thoroughly grasped the efficacy or connection of the preceding propositions may be doubtful whether an individual retains any feeling of his own when deprived of all corporeal feelings and stripped of his own body. The doubt arises from observing that almost all operations of thought need images or other bodily feelings. It seems that those cognitions are accompanied by a bodily feeling in the way that other feelings, sensible of themselves, are not.

My own position is that intellective operations are sensible of their essence. I believe that the essence itself of a human being consists in feeling, as I said. If the actualised human essence were not sensible, it would not be a human being, nor could a human being perceive himself.

137. The objection is further resolved when we observe that if intellective operations were not in their own way sensible, they could never become such through the addition of animal feelings. Animal sensibility presents only itself to our perception, and we know perfectly well how to distinguish what animal

[133–137]

sensibility, tied to space, presents to us from what is presented by merely intellective operations totally immune from space. To put it briefly, we reason about our intellective operations: for example, about reasoning itself. We find in them properties totally contrary to the laws of matter such as 1. the indwelling of consequences in their principles, and the exclusion of space from consequences and principles; and 2. the simplicity of an act which, operating outside space, joins consequences to principles, and so on. All these are properties repugnant to animal feelings. But we would be unable to reason in this way about intellective operations, or find in them properties repugnant to animal feeling, if they themselves, with their immaterial objects, were not sensible. As we said, *feeling* is the first rudiment necessary for every discussion (cf. 12). Intellective operations, therefore, are also accompanied by their own sensibility. But, if this is the case, we have to say that the first amongst them, the immanent, essential action that we have called the 'intuition of being in general', is also sensible.

If the soul were deprived of all animal feelings, divested of the body and reduced to pure act intuiting being, it would still retain its own feeling. But we must be careful not to form a false, impure concept of this spiritual feeling.[68]

138. We must not add anything which pertains to the nature of bodily feeling. Moreover, we have to understand that the act of intuition is in no way extended outside its object (being). It is, as it were, a spiritual sense-experience which reveals only the object as its term, but which, as an activity, has a principle different from the object to which it adheres in a way essential to it and from which, therefore, it cannot be separated without lapsing into nothing. The sensibility proper to this intuitive act is consequent to the object intuited through the act. Without the intuition of the object, that act would not be sensible because it would not in any way be.[69] The sensibility of the primal intuition

[68] Cf. *Teodicea*, 848; and *Appendice*, 48–49 [Milan, 1845].

[69] When Cicero wrote: 'The mind itself is the source of the senses, and is ITSELF A SENSE' (Acad., 4: 10), he showed on the one hand that he was unable to distinguish sufficiently the difference between animal feeling and the mind. On the other hand, he understood that the mind itself was some kind of sense.

comes from the object referred to the subjective, sentient principle.[70]

139. We conclude, therefore, that the human soul, even separated from the body, retains *per se* a feeling of its own (although without reflection), and consequently its own essence, which consists in feeling. It is immortal. This is St. Augustine's extremely effective argument for the immortality of the soul.[71]

CHAPTER 5
The identity of the soul in its different modifications

Article 1
The difficulty explained

140. I feel in various ways, I think different thoughts, I undergo various experiences, I rejoice, I meditate, I work; it is always *myself*, the same 'I' who does all these things. On one hand, the feeling that lies within *myself* is identical; on the other, it changes continually. This would seem a contradiction, unless two feelings, one unchangeable, the other changeable, lie within *myself*. But in this case, how can the unchangeable feeling feel the changes of the other feeling without receiving them in itself? If, however, it does receive them, it is no longer unchangeable because they become its different sensations, modifications of itself. That is, if the various sensations have to fall within one single principle (otherwise there will be nothing to feel them, and feel them as successive and variable), it is useless to recur to two feelings, one of which changes, one of which does not. The same feeling which never changes must be that which feels changes. We return, therefore, to a single feeling.

---

[70] Cf. *AMS*, 258–268, where I showed that every feeling has essentially a *principle* and a *term*.

[71] Those who find that its (the soul's) substance is some kind of incorporeal life (that is, an incorporeal feeling) and that this substance is life animating and vivifying every living body, have tried as a consequence to prove, as anyone could, that it is immortal BECAUSE LIFE CANNOT LACK LIFE (*De Trinit.*, 10: 9).

But how? Are we to say that this single feeling is in part always the same, in part unequal? If so, we run into the same difficulty, and can ask whether the part that is always equal receives the various sensations which arise in the changeable part. If so, the same argument used in the hypothesis of the two feelings can be repeated: the unchangeable part becomes changeable as soon as it admits in itself the various sensations of the other part which it then feels. As a result it affirms them, and is modified when feeling and affirming them. It would seem that no unchangeable part remains in the feeling of *myself*. But in that case, how is it identical at different times and places? How is it subject to infinite sensations and infinite different thoughts?

141. The careful reader will be aware that this problem, one of the most difficult in psychology, has received wholly insufficient attention from philosophers. But if our principle is true — a grave difficulty in any science conceals a precious secret in nature; the secret once revealed allows for great progress in science — the mystery of identity which we have proposed is altogether worthy of our meditation.

142. Our consideration has to begin from what is evident. It is not right that we should abandon what is certain when we meet some apparently insoluble difficulty. But my own identity is evident; I am certain that in these different times and places it is always I who undergo experiences and carry out various things. This identity is found in my own feeling, in that part of it which I call *myselfness*. We said, however, that this feeling is perceived, not demonstrated, and does not permit of error. We have already established that consciousness of ourselves is the supreme, infallible criterion of psychology. Even if we do not understand, therefore, *how* the identical feeling can receive in itself various modifications without ceasing to be identical, its identity remains true. Let us see if we can find the way through the maze presented by this problem.

Article 2
A start to solving the problem

143. Right from the beginning, we note that when we say 'I experience and have experienced various sensations, I have carried out various actions', we always exercise the same form of intellective operation except for change in the term. This operation is called *affirmation*. I, that is, *myself*, affirm that at one moment I feel in one way, at another moment in another way; sometimes I am passive, I undergo something; sometimes I am acting; sometimes I operate in one way, sometimes in another. But I always *affirm*. Hence, if the operation is always identical in form but variable in its term, we have to conclude that there is a kind of identity which can be present along with a kind of variety, and that the operation carried out by *myself* in affirming my own feelings is one thing, while the affirmed sensations, the term of such an operation, is another.[72]

Myself who affirms is, therefore, different from the affirmed feelings. These are the object in which the operation of the affirming self terminates, but they are not *myself* who affirms. *Myself* in so far as it is an affirming activity can certainly remain unmodified even when the feelings it affirms change; these feelings are different from that activity.

But how can *myself* affirm these feelings if it is not affected by them? And if it is affected, how can it remain unchanged, unmodified? I answer: *myself* is certainly affected by the feelings it affirms, but our solution consists in separating *myself as affirming* from every other activity or possibility that can fall within *myself*. The fact that *myself* is affected constantly by new feelings does not cause *myself*, in so far as it affirms, to carry out some constantly changing operation. *Myself* as affirming is an activity that does not change whatever the feelings affirmed; *myself* as affirming is not modified by these feelings but remains its affirming self. In fact, it is necessary for *myself* to be affected

---

[72] Note that the expression 'affirmed sensations' also includes 'the operations of the spirit'. As we said (cf. 136–137), these also are sensible. Only as such, that is, as feelings, can they be objects of affirmation. Nothing that takes place within us can be affirmed unless it is felt in some way. Cf. *Teodicea*, 153.

by various feelings if its consistently even activity of affirmation is to repeat its acts. *Myself*, therefore, as *affirming activity* is the same for any of the many, varied feelings aroused in it.

Consequently, our observation tells us that feelings as objects of affirmation have no power to change the *affirming activity*. This remains what it is, although the feelings within it change.

144. The *affirming activity* rises from the depths of *myself* to stand over the *feelings* which take place in *myself*. This activity affirms the feelings, although the feelings can cause no change in it because the *affirming activity* is different from its objects. However, the complete explanation of the identity of *myself* requires further explanation, principally about the way in which the identical *myself* can be the principle of different activities, that is, of the activity of feeling and of affirming. Either the different activities have to be reduced to one, or *myself* has to be split in two. In fact, *myself* as affirming is the affirming activity; *myself* as feeling is the sentient activity. If, therefore, there are two activities totally different from one another, we have to say that *myself* is not one, but two; one affirming and the other sentient. In this case, we return to the first difficulty, which renders affirmation impossible.

Article 3
Continuation

145. I shall first show that the unicity and identity of a subject is not put in jeopardy by the fact that feeling and intellection are each composed of two elements (principle and term). I shall do this by recapitulating my entire reasoning in a series of lemmata which will gradually lead to the demonstration of the general theory that the multiplicity of feelings and operations pertaining to myself does not endanger the unicity and identity of *myself*. The need for careful distinctions in such a subtle argument is accentuated by the necessity of deriving many concepts from the depth of *ontology*, which I still have to publish. This means that often I cannot simply point to things already demonstrated, but have to investigate them with the reader.

[144–145]

Lemma 1

146. Two opposite elements are distinguished in every feeling: that which feels and that which is felt. This was demonstrated in *Anthropology*[73] by analysing feeling.

Lemma 2

147. Every feeling is one and simple. This means that what feels and what is felt, which are distinguished in the feeling, do not constitute two feelings, but a single, individual feeling. I also showed in *Anthropology*[74] (and it is self-evident) that a sentient principle does not exist without something felt, nor that which is felt without something that feels. These two conditions, therefore, give rise to a single feeling.

148. COROLLARY 1 — That which feels and that which is felt are, therefore, mutually dependent conditions. The law of synthesism is verified in them because, given both, one is distinguished from the other conceptually; given only one, it neither subsists nor endures conceptually.

149. COROLLARY 2 — It is clear that, if one element does not subsist without the other, and the concept of one cannot be had without the concept of the other to which it is related, both must constitute a single feeling and be found in an individual feeling. That feeling is precisely their union in act. The law of synthesism which binds the felt with the sentient is a new, speculative proof of the simplicity and unicity of the feeling that results from the bond.

150. COROLLARY 3 — We can deduce two general propositions from this fact of feeling: 1. 'it is not absurd that there are even in nature individuals which result from several different elements distinct in concept, and do so without loss of their simplicity and unicity as a result of the multiplicity of the elements'; 2. 'together the elements form an individual only when they do not exist outside the individual, and the individual results from the act of their union.'

[73] *AMS*, 230–322.
[74] *Ibid.*

Lemma 3

151. In every intellection we have to distinguish two opposite elements: that which understands and that which is understood. This proposition was also demonstrated by analysis in *Anthropology*.[75] Similar corollaries to those drawn in the preceding lemmata can be posited here.

Lemma 4

152. In the order of feeling, the agent is that which feels; the term of this action is that which is felt.

EXPLANATION — I have pointed out many times that to feel is to undergo some experience. How then can I say that in the order of feeling the agent is that which feels? — We have to pay great attention to the clause 'in the order of feeling'. Activity and passivity often intercept and intertwine in the same ens.[76]

---

[75] 505–509. — Duality of thought was clearly indicated in the last century by Abraham Kaan Boerhaave, a philosopher and medical doctor, in a book entitled: *Impetum faciens dictum Hippocrati per corpus consentiens philologice et physiologice illustratum, etc.* (Lyons, 1745). It deserves to be read. He says: 'Mind is said to be that which thinks. This is the first proposition that mortals know about the mind. Does this mean that thinking is the mind itself?' Here we recognise the Cartesian school which acknowledges that an act of thought is necessary for the mind to exist. He continues shortly after: 'This thought contains two things, namely THAT WHICH THINKS and THAT WHICH IS THOUGHT' (9–10). But the imperfection of Descartes' theory soon becomes apparent. After having said that the mind is 'thought itself' because it is the first property of the mind manifested to mortals, Boerhaave says that 'thought cannot be known or defined.' Here we find 1. a manifest contradiction between saying that *thought* is what is first known and saying that it is not known and cannot be defined; 2. that the door is opened to scepticism if the whole edifice of human thought is founded upon that which *cannot be known and cannot be defined.* — I say that thought or the mind knows and defines itself. It does not deceive itself in doing this because the truth of cognition is not a creation of its act of knowledge (which would make it subjective), but is given to it by the *ens* which it intuits, that is, by what is truly the first known.

[76] For an example of these different actions and passions whose conflict, so to speak, results in an ens, cf. *NE*, vol. 2, 1005–1019, where I show that the

As a result, several passive and active elements are distinguished in the ens. These elements alternate and mingle according to the various aspects under which they are considered; they pertain to the intrinsic order of the ens. There is no doubt, therefore, that the principle which feels is passive relative to what is felt, in so far as what is felt actuates the principle to feel in a specific way. At the same time, it is also certain that the principle alone feels; that which is felt does not feel. This explains why I said that 'in the order of feeling' that which feels is active. That which is felt, in so far as it is felt, feels nothing. Indeed it is opposed to the act of feeling because it is the term in which that act comes to rest.

153. COMMENT 1. — Hence that which feels is said to be the principle of feeling, that is, its active part; *that which is felt* is said to be the *term*, that is, the part which in the order of feeling is not active, but equally cannot be called passive.[77] In fact, *that which is felt*, as felt, has no sensitive activity, nor does it experience anything from that which feels.

154. COMMENT 2. — The *principle* of feeling is also normally called *subject* or *subjectum*.[78]

Lemma 5

155. In the order of understanding, the agent is that which understands; that which is understood is the term of the agent's action.

156. COMMENT 1. — Hence, that which understands is called the principle of understanding (cf. 153).

human individual results from actions and passions which take place between soul and body.

[77] I have shown that the saying 'There is no action without corresponding passion' is contrary to philosophical observation of different entia and contains a materialistic prejudice (*Rinnovamento*, bk. 3, c. 47).

[78] It would be desirable to note always the distinction I make in several places when using these two words. I take the first to indicate a principle which feels or acts when the principle is a substance, and the second to indicate any special principle which feels or acts when it is a simple faculty. The two words, which distinguish our two operative *principles*, are often useful for abbreviating and clarifying philosophical argument. Cf. *The Philosophy of Right*, vol. 1, *The Essence of Right*, 239.

157. COMMENT 2. — The term of understanding is not totally passive. It is simply not active in the order of understanding because it is not that which understands. Nevertheless, in a superior order it is active in its own way because it is that which makes the intelligent being understand.

158. COMMENT 3. — The way in which the term of understanding makes that which understands understand is not such that it *changes* that which understands. It does not act like a body which collides with some other yielding body and changes its shape (as though that which understands were prior to that which makes it understand). We are dealing here with a *creative* action to which nothing corresponds on the other side of the relationship. Again, we see, by carefully observing what happens, that what is understood is in what understands but preserves its own essence distinct from that which understands. Consequently its mode of acting can be called *self-communication* to which there is no corresponding *passivity*, but a concept of *receptivity* and first potency.

159. COMMENT 4. — The principle of understanding is also called *subject or subjectum*.

Conclusion

160. If that which is felt does not act in any way in the order of feeling, and that which is understood does nothing in the order of understanding; if, moreover, the agent alone is the principle which feels and understands, and is alone called subject, it is clear that the duality (principle and term) found in feeling does not detract from the simplicity and unicity of the feeling and understanding subject.

Article 4
Continuation — The feeling and intelligent subject remains
the same whatever change takes place in the terms of
its actions, or in the actions themselves

161. I will now demonstrate a second thesis: the feeling or intelligent subject remains the same whatever change takes

place in their terms. The terms in question are first, that which is felt (term of the feeling subject) and second, that which is understood (term of the intelligent subject).

The following difficulty requires the demonstration of this thesis. Although it appears clear from what has been said that what is felt and what is understood are outside the feeling and intelligent nature which constitutes the subject, and by adhering to the subject neither multiply it nor remove its unicity, it is also true that they are conditions determining its activity. As a result, it seems that changes in these conditions must cause the sentient or intelligent principle to undergo some modification. In fact, feeling in one way or feeling in another, or understanding one thing or another to varying degrees, are accidents that change the action of feeling or the action of understanding.

162. First, we have to clarify the question by determining its various parts. The following observations enable us to do this.

First, it is certain that, given real individuals, they can conserve their identity despite the things which change in them.

163. To see how this is possible, we have to establish that not everything found in an individual *names* the individual and constitutes it as that individual, that subject. This is clear from the kind of analysis we have carried out on feeling and intellection which shows that what we call 'sentient subject' is not everything found in the feeling, but only the active principle of feeling; what we call 'intelligent subject' is not everything found in intellection, but only the active principle of understanding. This is sufficient for us to recognise that the solution of the thesis with which we are engaged has to depend upon an accurate determination of that which must remain unchangeable in a given subject, if the subject is to preserve its identity.

164. In dealing with the sentient subject and the intelligent subject, we have found that the immutability we are seeking cannot and must not be sought except in the principle of immutability. But granted changes in that which is felt or understood, it cannot be denied that the action of the sentient principle and the intelligent principle changes. In other words, this action is borne to other terms where its activity either increases or diminishes. We should note, however, that the *action* itself must be carefully distinguished from the *principle of the action*, and that there is nothing contradictory in affirming identity and

lack of change in the principle, together with change in the action.

165. It will be objected that the principle itself is subject to change if it acts differently. — But this shows that the distinction I made between principle of action and its action has not been thoroughly understood. The principle is united to the action, but is not the action; if the principle were the action, it would cease to be its principle. The word 'principle' indicates a first, simple and immutable point; anything added to this is no longer principle. It is true that the principle cannot be separated from its action, but it can and must be really distinguished from it. Here again we come face to face with the law of synthesism through which two things are inseparably united without being confused. The principle, therefore, is a simple point logically anterior to the action, which can be compared to a line proceeding from its point. In such a case, it is not absurd to imagine several different actions proceeding from the same point, just as it is not absurd for several lines to begin from the same point without any change in the point.

166. The principle of action can and must be separated by our thought from the action. We must acknowledge the immutability of the former and the mutability of the latter.

But if action arises through power of the principle, we have to say that all actions proceeding from a principle are contained in the power possessed by the principle. — This is certainly true, and is attested by the consent of mankind which drew from this kind of observation the concept of power, potency and first act distinct from second acts, that is, actions flowing from the first act. In the first principle, therefore, we find a certain activity from which, under given conditions, actions arise. This activity, *potency*, *virtuality* or *first act* (as it would be better called) always remains the same; it is unique, simple, anterior to all actions. It is called 'substance' by all mankind (a name which excludes all actions) and 'substantial subject'. Everyone agrees about separating the principle of actions from the actions themselves; everyone agrees about the importance of speaking of the principle separated from the actions.

167. This is also the way in which arose the common distinction between *substance* and *accidents*.

'Substance is that which the mind conceives in a being

without the mind's having to make use of anything else to form a first concept of the being.' It is clear that accidents cannot be conceived on their own; we have to fall back on the substance through which they subsist. In the same way, second actions cannot be conceived on their own. The mind, in order to have some concept of them, must fall back on the principle which produced them. Second actions cannot stand without their causal principle. When I have reached the first principle of actions in every given order of activity, I can go no further; I must stop. This first principle is conceived by the mind, therefore, without its having to ascend to some ulterior principle within the being under consideration. Here the mind comes to a halt and declares the principle to exist *in se*.[79]

168. Substance is also defined as: 'The act by which the specific essence subsists' (cf. 52). But in any subject whatsoever, the first principle of actions is precisely that first act in which all the actions subsist. Hence the first principle of feeling and the first principle of understanding are both substances, if separated from one another.

169. Because the first act of a being is that which constitutes its substance, and second acts are normally accidental, we usually add the concept of immutability and permanence to the concept of substance in *relationship to its actions*; immutability and transitoriness are normally attributed to the actions.

170. Another question arises here: 'What determines a first act (a substance) to have the power of extending itself to one, certain determined group of second actions rather than another?' Our reply about the possibility of these groups has to be found in the *intrinsic order of being*. This order excludes the possibility that certain actions may be found virtually comprised in a single potency, but allows others to be associated and fused in one potency.[80] The real subsistence of such substances

[79] It may be objected that the first principle itself is not conceived except in relation to its actions. — This is true, but the mind can abstract from the actions; it is sufficient that it conceive them as virtually contained in the principle. We have here two questions: 'How does the mind come to form the concept?' and 'Does this formed concept stand on its own without need of another?'

[80] Cf. *NE*, vol. 2, 648.

depends solely, however, on the will of the Creator who draws
to the act of subsistence some substances rather than others
from amongst those which do not involve contradiction.

171. One other observation must be made. All the activity of
the sentient principle is determined by that which is felt, and all
the activity of the intelligent principle by that which is understood. This results from the analysis we have already made of
the sentient and intelligent principle. As we saw, that which
feels does so only in so far as something felt is given to it, and
that which understands does so only in so far as something
understood is given to it. If, therefore, that which is felt determines the activity of that which feels, and that which is
understood the activity of that which understands, it follows
necessarily that what feels must, in order to remain identical,
have inherent to itself from the beginning of its existence,
something felt in which all future sensations are virtually contained. Equally, if that which is understood determines the
sphere of activity of that which understands, the latter cannot
remain identical in its successive acts of understanding unless it
has inherent to itself, from the first moment of its existence,
something understood in which are virtually comprehended all
the objects which can afterwards be represented to its understanding.

172. If we have a thorough grasp of this observation, we shall
find in it a new and very effective demonstration of my theory
about the fundamental feeling (cf. 96–104) and about universal
being naturally intuited by the human soul. Only in this theory
do we find verification of the fact that we, as sentient beings, feel
virtually from the first instance everything that we later come to
feel distinctly. Corporeal sensations are in fact simply modes of
the fundamental feeling itself.[81] Again, it is only in this theory
that we, as intelligent, understand virtually everything that we
later come to understand distinctly. The intelligible entity of all
things is reduced to the intuition of being in general.

173. If, then, we take as proven the simplicity and identity
of the feeling and intelligent principle in the various
sense-experiences of the former and the various intellections
of the latter, the truth of our system is also proved. If instead

[81] Cf. *NE*, vol. 2, 705–706.

we start from our system, that is, if we admit the truth of the fundamental feeling and of the intuition of being, the most subtle difficulties about the simplicity and identity of the sentient principle are solved; its simplicity and identity are a necessary consequence. The wise reader should pause here to consider the harmony of truth. The identity of the sentient and intelligent principle (which are not doubted by anybody) is a truth apparently very distinct from the truth of the existence of the fundamental feeling and of the intuition of being. Nevertheless, these truths agree and harmonise admirably, they sustain one another, and become proofs of each other because each contains the other deep within itself.

Article 5
The sentient subject and the intelligent subject in human beings are one subject, not two

174. A final difficulty remains, which can easily be solved after what has been said about the other problems. How can the sentient principle and the intelligent principle be one principle in human beings? To answer this we have to return to our teaching about *substance*.

175. We said that substance is the *first operative principle* of an ens from which flow its actions and passions, and consequently its different states. These actions and passions and different states are contained in this principle virtually, that is, in the power, activity or potency which is their efficient cause. We also said that we can conceive different groups of these actions, passions and states, although it is not possible *a priori* to demonstrate that every group is possible, that is, reducible to a first act, first power, first substantial principle.

176. Determining *a priori* which of these groups can be included virtually in a first substantial principle would require nothing less than total knowledge of the intrinsic order of being. But the intrinsic order of being is not known to us directly; it is brought together gradually from observation and experience. Only when observation or experience shows us the existence of a group of activities united in a single substantial

principle are we authorised to conclude that such a substantial principle is possible. *Ab esse ad posse datur consecutio* [From what actually is we can conclude to what is possible].

177. Internal observation witnesses that at one and the same time each of us is a single, sentient and intelligent principle. Every human being can say to himself: '*Myself* who feels am the same *myself* who understands. If I were not the same, I could not know that I feel nor that I reason about my sensations.'

On the other hand, there is no repugnance in a sensitive activity having the same principle as an intellective activity, if we consider that several actions can begin from the same principle, as we said, just as several lines can begin from the same point.

178. However, I have to admit that one extremely serious objection still remains. I said that constituting a sentient principle necessarily requires our mental conception of a primal felt thing which virtually comprises all the particular actions of feeling that we are later able to carry out. In human beings, this primal, fundamental felt thing is one's own body, sensible in space. We also said that constituting an intelligent principle necessarily requires our mental conception of a primal understood thing which virtually comprises all that we later understand. In human beings, this primal, understood thing is being in general.

Now if the sentient principle is constituted by what is felt bodily, and the intelligent principle by intelligible being, we have to say either that the extended bodily element and intelligible being are identical or that they constitute two different principles, never one.

179. Answering this extremely serious objection means noting that there is an entity in every thing that is felt because every act of any kind is an entity. But the felt entity certainly lacks intelligible light or knowability. In fact, the phrase *felt entity* does not include *understood entity*. Saying *felt* rather than *understood* is the same as excluding knowability from feeling. On the other hand, that which understands has for its object an *understood entity* because the understanding principle simply understands, and everything that it understands is necessarily entity. The term of the sentient principle and the term of the intelligent principle are, therefore, equally *entity*. Some identification is present in their terms.

[177-179]

180. But how are they distinguished? — They are distinguished by the different way in which the same entity adheres to the same principle. Entity is communicated to the sentient principle in entity's mode as felt. This is what I also call reality and activity. But entity is communicated to the intelligent principle in entity's mode as understood. This is what I also call ideality, intelligibility, knowability, light, and so on.

Granted this, it is clear that the sentient principle and the intelligent principle can co-penetrate to the extent of forming one and the same principle of operation. The same term is present in both principles, although it terminates in one of them by adhering to it in one mode and communicating itself in one of its forms, and in the other by adhering to it in another way and communicating itself in another of its forms. Two principles are present, therefore, if we consider the *form* in which entity is communicated; but only one if we consider *entity itself* which is communicated irrespective of its forms. We can say that two principles are present provided we recognise that in us they are not two first principles, but that above them there is a prior, single principle which holds them subordinated and joined to itself. This first principle has reference to *entity* and not to the *forms of entity*. It is the principle of synthesis in both the theoretical order (by manifesting itself in its characteristic as *reason*) and the practical order (by manifesting itself in its characteristic as *will*). This superior intellective principle is, as superior, the point from which the two activities, sensitive and intellective, spring. It is called the *rational principle*.

CHAPTER 6

The nouns 'substance' and 'subject' applied to the human soul

181. Our reasoning so far shows that the human soul is a *single*, *substantial subject*.

It is a subject because it is a first principle of actions endowed with feeling;[82] it is a *substance* because this principle is conceived

---

[82] *AMS*, 767.

by the mind as existing in itself and not in something anterior in the order of feeling and understanding.

182. We should note the difference between the noun *substance* and the phrase *substantial subject*. The word *subject*, which I use to express the active principle of a feeling, is employed as a name for *soul* in so far as it refers to the essence of the soul in all its simplicity (cf. 81). The word *substance*, which indicates the first act through which the whole being subsists, embraces all that the first act makes subsist; the 'substance' embraces the entire feeling both in its principle and in its term. The first feeling is, therefore, rightly called substance provided that it is seen from the point of view of principle rather than term. The act making feeling subsist is precisely the principle of the feeling.[83]

183. This distinction between substance and substantial subject shows that only a sensitive or intellective ens can be called 'substantial subject'. The word 'substance', however, is suitable for inanimate bodies in so far as our mind conceives them with their own act of subsistence.

---

[83] In his book *On the Soul*, St. Gregory Thaumaturgus proves the soul is substance because it remains identical under different modifications. He starts from the following definition of substance, which is equivalent to that which I have given: 'Substance is that which, while remaining one and the same in number, receives contrary things in itself.' He then goes on to demonstrate that this is precisely what occurs with the soul. Following the same path, I began by demonstrating the identity of the soul under various, contrary modifications. I then rose to investigate the first subject of these modifications, demonstrating that it must be a first principle of all consequent activities and actions, and contain them all virtually. In this principle all the activities and actions have their root, from which they draw their subsistence (their first act of subsistence). I then concluded that by calling this first principle 'soul', the human soul has all the conditions constituting a true substance. — St. Thomas acknowledges 'acting *per se*' as the known characteristic of substance: 'Nothing is able to act *per se* except that which subsists *per se*', and from this principle proves that the soul is a substance (*S.T.*, I, q. 75, art. 2). I say the same thing when I define the soul as 'a first principle of action'. However, I add 'in a given order of activity' to avoid confusing it with God (who is the universal first principle), and thus falling into pantheism.

A question about the invariability of the soul, and the changes to which it can be subject

184. So far, we have investigated the intimate constitution of the soul and found:

1. that it is a single, simple principle, sentient and intelligent at the same time;

2. that this principle is an activity in which are contained virtually all the second acts, sense-experiences, intellections, and so on;

3. that this sphere of activity is determined by that which is *first felt* and *first known*, that is, by the felt and the known which naturally adhere to the active principle. The fundamental felt virtually comprises all future sense-experiences, and the known comprises the objects of all future, distinct intellections.

These teachings give rise to a question necessary to complete our study on the identity of the soul. I ask: 'Would it be possible to change that which is first felt or understood by the soul? If a change did take place, would the soul preserve its identity?'

185. I reply that such a change would not involve any contradiction in its concept. However, we cannot say whether the identity of the soul would be preserved without first distinguishing the five conceivable changes in that which is felt or first understood. These are: removal of what is felt and what is understood, removal only of what is understood, removal only of what is felt, addition or change to what is felt, addition to what is understood. We shall look at these one by one.

Article 1
Removal of what is first felt and what is first understood

186. If what is felt and understood were entirely removed, the sentient, intelligent subject would be annihilated; the soul would no longer exist.

Article 2
Removal of what is understood

187. If what is first understood were taken away, the human soul would lose its identity. This is explained by the order present between the principle of feeling and the principle of understanding which in the human soul are united in a single principle. The order is this: the intelligent principle is superior to the feeling principle in such a way that the former is the proximate origin of the common principle of understanding and feeling.

188. We shall understand this truth if we note that only an intelligent principle says: 'I feel'. Saying 'I feel' is a thought that a human being has about his own sensations. Thought, however, pertains to an intelligent principle. The sentient principle, on the other hand, cannot say either 'I feel' or 'I understand'; it cannot say anything, but only feel.

189. It is true that there is a common principle, above the feeling, intellective activity, which renders us aware of our sense-experiences and intellections, and unites them. This principle, however, is formed directly by the intellective activity and called 'rational' because it is an intellective act bringing about union between sense-experiences and intellections. If what is first understood were removed, intelligence would cease and with it the first principle of the soul. But the soul's own essence resides in this first rational principle, as we said. Deprived of this, the soul would *ipso facto* lose its identity and cease to be the ens we now call 'human soul'.

Article 3
Removal of what is felt

190. The opposite would occur if what is first felt were removed from the soul, which would not lose its identity because the first principle constituting its essence would be preserved. Its proximate principle of feeling would indeed cease, but the intellective activity would, as the superior principle, always contain virtually the principle of feeling, although this could not be said to actually exist.

191. Nevertheless, the state of the soul deprived of the fundamental corporeal feeling would be immensely changed. All perception, every affirmation and hence all consciousness of self would be rendered impossible. The soul would retain its own feeling, but it would have no sufficient reason, no stimulus inducing it to turn its intellective activity back on this feeling and perceive it. It is a law of the human soul that it is first drawn to act by stimuli different from itself. Only later does it place some end before itself through which it operates independently of stimuli. If, therefore, its accidental, acquired sense-experiences were taken from it, together with the fundamental corporeal feeling, it would not have by nature any real good which it could desire to reach or propose as an end of its operations. Hence, it could not even reflect upon itself.[84]

Article 4
Addition or change to what is first felt

192. If something were added to what is first felt by the soul, the soul would certainly have received some *substantial* change. Its first active principle, however, where its essence resides, would not have changed; the soul would remain identical. But the activity of the primal principle would have been enlarged relative to the matter of its operations.

193. In this hypothetical case the soul, by preserving all that it first feels, would also keep its memory of self and of its preceding state. It would therefore be conscious of its own identity.

194. But what do we say if what is first felt is not preserved but totally changed into something else? In this supposition I maintain that the soul would preserve its own identity because it would preserve its first (intellective) principle. However, having lost its memory of its preceding state, it would not be conscious of its own identity. Memory and consciousness of this state are founded in previous perceptions, which would cease.

[84] In *NE*, vol. 2, 612–613, I have refrained from positing the characteristic of *substance* in immutability. Substances are said to be unchangeable *relative* only to accidents.

195. It might be thought that previously formed abstract ideas, which do not require any corporeal image, could remain. But if this were so, they would remain, I think, only as aptitudes. Even if they did remain in the depth of the soul, they could only be contemplated by it on condition that what was newly felt had some relationship, some law of association, with what was first felt. Abstract ideas, although without need of corporeal images, are nevertheless tied to sensations and images, or at least to traces of sensations and images, in such a way that, deprived of them, we cannot turn our attention to abstract ideas alone. On the one hand, we have no reason for doing so; on the other, our attention is deprived of a guide leading it to find abstract ideas and advert to them. Abstract ideas, even if present in human beings totally deprived of sense-experiences and images or vestiges referring to these ideas, would remain in the state in which they are when, bereft of consciousness, we do not think of them. But, as I said, it seems to me much more probable that such ideas would not be present in any way in human beings. They consist essentially in a relationship with what is real, but if we suppose that what is newly felt has no likeness to what was felt before, nothing real exists to which ideal being can be referred. In fact, even the substance of the soul presents no likeness of any sort with what has been felt previously.

Article 5
Addition to what is understood

196. There can be no hypothetical case of change in what is first understood, but only of addition to it. That which is first understood cannot change because it is of its nature unchangeable. Nor can it diminish; ideal being is totally simple in its concept. It can, however, increase in one of two ways: either by the determination of concepts within it, or through the realisation (actualisation) of essential being itself.

197. Concepts are positive or negative. Positive concepts are founded in some reality that we perceive. If concepts founded in realities perceived by us increase in the human mind, our being is not changed substantially. However these concepts increase in our understanding, they are already virtually comprised in what we have first felt and understood. If, however, we are

speaking of concepts referred to realities different from those contained virtually in what we first feel, there can be no question of these concepts being given to us prior to our perception of something felt which corresponds to those concepts. In this case, we are dealing with our previous hypothesis in which there is an increase in what is first felt by us.

198. Negative concepts are those with which we know an ens that is understood not in itself but only through its relationship with another known ens. These concepts have no power to change the soul substantially however many of them it acquires.

199. The case in which that which is first understood increases through the realisation of being, the essential object, requires extremely important consideration because it takes human beings from the natural to the supernatural order. At this point, essential being, in addition to its quality as light of the mind, also becomes what is felt by the mind. But, because real being in such a case is identical with ideal being, the principle which first intuited ideal being remains identical, although it feels the reality of being. The soul or substantial subject does not lose its identity, but acquires new, infinite dignity. It is the same intellect which intuits the ideality of being and contemporaneously perceives its reality.

What has changed is properly speaking that which is felt. In other words, an essentially different felt thing is added to what was previously felt. The former is infinitely greater than the latter; it is something felt, but pertaining to intellective sense. The first principle, uniting what is felt and what is understood, and the fount of reason and will, has not changed its nature but increased it infinitely. The addition of activity brought about in it is greater and more elevated than all its previous activity. A new principle of activity has been added, that is, a principle enabling the first principle to act supernaturally.

But the *first principle*, which brings together in itself all the inferior activities, is called *person* in so far as virtually it contains one *supreme activity* ruling all other activities. It retains its identity as *subject*, therefore, but becomes a new person in so far as it receives a new activity, far superior to that which it had previously.[85]

---

[85] *Opuscoli morali* (Pogliani, 1841).

CHAPTER 8

The difference between the human soul, pure intelligences and animal souls

200. Having discovered what constitutes the human soul and its principal properties, we still have to investigate the differences separating it from pure intelligences and other natures akin to it.

The human soul, as we said, is that first principle of feeling and understanding which, without ceasing to be one and to have a single radical activity, is constituted by something felt, extended and corporeal, and by something understood, that is, indeterminate being.

The soul is called *first principle* because it is a principle superior to the sensitive principle; it is a principle virtually containing within itself the sensitive principle in such a way that the actual existence of this principle pertains to human *nature* but not to the *essence* of the soul. It is sufficient for the essence of the soul that the principle of animal feeling be virtually contained in it.

201. At this point, we can illustrate the difference separating the human soul from pure intelligences[86] and from purely animal souls. The human soul stands as it were midway between angels and animal souls.

202. The angels lack that which is felt corporeally and are, therefore, devoid of the principle of animal feeling and of brute sense-experiences. They are not passive relative to bodies but

[86] Belief in the existence of pure spirits, or angels, goes back to the most ancient memories of the world. All Eastern traditions agree in affirming it. In the first Chinese sacred book, the Chou-King, Confucius collected, in 484 BC, passages from the most ancient histories and traditional precepts. He frequently mentions spirits. In chapter 2, we read about the Emperor Chow who, it is claimed, reigned more than twenty centuries before Christ: 'He carried out the *Loui* sacrifice to *Shang-ti*, and the ceremonies to the six *Tsong*, to the mountains, to the rivers, and in general in honour of all the spirits.'

The word 'Shang-ti' is used to denote the supreme being because it means 'that which is most worthy of respect'. To this being the great sacrifice, *Loui*, is made. *Tsong* is used of the greater spirit. It means 'that which is worthy of respect'. Then come the lesser spirits of the mountains, rivers, and so on.

active and, instead of animal feelings, possess the feeling of their own activities and terms. We shall explain this more at length, if God wills, in *Cosmology* or *Theosophy*.

203. Animal souls are simply principles of bodily feeling severed from intellectual activity. These principles, actually constituted because they are alone, are also first principles and, as first activities, cannot be denied the name of substantial principle or substances.

<h2 style="text-align:center">CHAPTER 9</h2>

<h3 style="text-align:center">Relationship between the substance of the soul and human nature</h3>

Article 1
The soul is the form of the human being

204. We can also see, therefore, the relationship between the human soul, that is, the substance of the soul, and the whole man,[87] that is, human nature, the composite resulting from soul and body personally united.

205. A single individual arises from this union, single because the individual has a single supreme principle which virtually brings together in itself all inferior activities. This supreme principle is the substance of the soul.

206. Because the substance of the human soul is the active principle, that is the principle which embraces virtually all other activities in man, it is normally called *form* of the human being. The word *form* has been understood from very ancient days as 'the first active power found in a given being, through which it is this being rather than another.'

207. A passage from St. Thomas helps to confirm this. Aquinas explains how the Aristotelians call the soul *act of the body*. He says: 'In the individual whose soul is called "act", the soul too

---

[87] Sometimes the word *man* is taken to mean *subject*. In this sense, man is reduced to soul, as we noted (cf. 10). Sometimes *man* means *human nature*, and in this sense the soul is only the form of man, as we shall explain in this chapter.

is included, in the sense that we speak of heat as the act of something hot, and light as the act of something bright, although it is not bright without light, but bright as a result of the light. Similarly, we say that the soul is the act of the body, and so on, because the body, as a result of the soul, is body, is organic and is a potency possessing life.'[88]

Article 2
How that which is first understood is the form of the intelligent principle

208. In man, however, there is, besides the activity constituting his substance, something else not pertaining to that activity, although it contributes to maintaining it. This is what is first understood; it is not the activity which understands, but that which renders this activity possible and subsistent. It is rightly called the *form of the intelligence* in so far as it adheres to the subjective principle and renders it intelligent.

209. It is an extrasubjective term of the intelligence, and properly speaking its *object*. In calling it the *object* of intelligence we mean that it is a term distinguishing itself from the intelligent principle in the very act communicated to that principle. It communicates itself without confusing itself; indeed, it distinguishes itself from the principle and from every subject (through intuition).

Article 3
How that which is *first felt* can and cannot be called the form of the sentient principle

210. In the same way, that which is *first felt* is not the sentient activity, but an extrasubjective element. This element, however, does not possess any *relationship of object* to subject because that which is sentient does not, as sentient, distinguish it from itself, but simply feels it. In fact, in every sense-experience the sentient principle is not felt in a manner distinct from its term. Only the intelligence distinguishes it. The term of the sense-experience together with that which feels constitute a single

[88] *S.T.*, I, q. 76, art. 4, ad 1.

feeling, and can never become two through any sensitive act because sensitivity does not reflect upon itself, but finishes simply in its own act. That which is felt can be called *term* but not *object* of that which feels.

211. Nevertheless, that which is felt can be called the *form of that which feels*, just as that which is first understood (object) can be called the form of that which understands. What is understood and what is felt are properly speaking the final perfection, the apex and, as we said, the term of the act of understanding and feeling. There is, however, an immense difference between these forms. The essential object is so necessary that, even if all human minds were wiped out, it would not cease to exist. It does, in fact, demand and presuppose an eternal mind where it can never cease to be.[89] On the other hand, what is felt bodily is obviously contingent and can be annihilated.

212. Elsewhere I have described what is *first felt* as *matter* of the potency of feeling.[90] I also said that *matter* is not what is first felt, but the force extraneous to feeling which changes feeling. This force is what I have called *sensiferous*.[91] Here it seems that I am developing a third opinion by affirming that *what is felt* is the form of what feels. These apparent contradictions now have to be reconciled.

213. The contradiction is indeed apparent, not real, and is caused by the complication of actions and passions produced in the interior of the sensitive being. The word *matter* means something relative, and changes its meaning as the precise terms of the relationship change.

214. Let us define matter. 'Matter is an element constituting a given entity, but extraneous to the activity of the given entity and subsisting in virtue of that activity.'[92]

215. Let us now examine carefully the sensitive ens. If we consider *sentient activity* within this ens, it is clear: 1. that what is

---

[89] Hence the *a priori* demonstration of the existence of God given in *NE*, vol. 3, 1456.

[90] *NE*, vol. 2, 1005–1019.

[91] *AMS*, 247–257.

[92] I shall speak more at length about matter in the second part of *Psychology*, where I shall show that its essence is to be *term*, never principle. Extremely important consequences derive from this.

first felt is an element constituting this activity because without the felt there is no act of feeling; but it is also clear 2. that this element is extraneous to the activity because what is felt is not that which feels, but its opposite; it is also clear 3. that by this activity, that is, by the act of feeling, that which is felt is posited in being because *that which is felt* would not be without the act of feeling of which it is contemporaneously the effect. Hence, *what is felt* is the matter of feeling, as I said in *A New Essay* where I observed, however, that this condition of *matter* pertains to the first, immanent felt thing, not to what is felt in acquired sensations. In fact, the sensitive ens is constituted by the former, not the latter. Consequently, I said that *what is first felt* is matter of the sensitive ens, and that what is *felt later* are terms of the *actions* of the sensitive ens. There is nothing, however, to prevent our calling these accidental felt things *matter* of accidental sensations.

This argument is entirely true as long as the *potency of feeling*, not its act, is under consideration. In other words, if we consider this act in its formation, not as already fully formed. It is certain that what is felt still does not exist as long as the primitive act of feeling is being formed. It exists only as soon as the act of feeling is totally formed. At the moment of formation, activity is present on the part of the operating principle, and passivity on the part of the effect (the felt) which is produced. At this moment, therefore, what is felt bears the characteristic of matter which is at it were invaded by the sentient act.

216. But if we consider the act of feeling at the moment when it is formed (when what is felt in it is not in potency, but is itself in act), it is certain that what feels in this moment feels in virtue of what is felt, precisely because what is felt is the final evolution and perfection of what feels. It is, as it were, the final outcome of what feels. At this moment in the existence of the sensitive ens, when it is fully developed, what is felt can be called its form not because the felt feels but because it is that through which what feels, feels. It is not form in so far as what is felt is the sentient activity, but in so far as the activity is not called 'sentient' until it has produced what is felt, although the activity, not yet sentient but on the way to become such, precedes what is felt. We can therefore distinguish two moments in the existence of a contingent sentient being: 1. when it is about to become sentient and

2. when it has already become sentient. In the first moment, what is felt, which does not yet exist but is about to be produced, takes on the concept of matter and of a certain passive term; in the second, when that which feels is completely activated, that which is felt takes on the concept of form because this act dwells as it were in what is felt and is complete as a result of what is felt. What is first felt is therefore matter of the still inactivated potency of feeling but form of the activated potency as potency. Although these are different aspects or views on the part of the understanding, they have their own value. If they are not kept distinct, the language formed on their basis becomes confused, and renders concepts false.

217. But is it then true to say, as I did in *Anthropology*, that *matter* is properly speaking not that which is felt, but the brute force which changes what is first felt (the force called *sensiferous*)? — In *Anthropology* I offered a distinction between *body* and *matter*. I said that something felt and extended was sufficient for the concept of body. In fact, what is felt and extended contains 'a force with power diffused in extension', which are the two elements constituting the concept of body.[93] But I also said that besides *what is felt*, there is in nature something anterior to the felt, a kind of substratum to the felt itself. It is a force that does not belong to the constitution of what is felt, but changes it. We know of its existence through the violence we feel done to us when one felt thing is taken away and another substituted in its place;[94] the same is true for extrasubjective perception. This force, which properly speaking causes that

---

[93] *NE*, vol. 2, 871.

[94] We can prove as follows that the material part is not an element of *what is felt* as such. 'The material particles of our body can be substituted by others without our feeling this substitution, provided it comes about naturally and without any change in the felt extension.' Consequently, it is impossible to notice the changes of particles which occur at every moment in the human body, as long as the body remains identical, because *the material part is not properly speaking constitutive of the human body*. It is true that the particles lost or acquired daily by the body can be connected with minimal sensations which, through their persistence and number, can be fused into certain general feelings — for example, that which accompanies digestion. But it is certain that if material particles of the same species and form were substituted in an instant, say by the power of God, there would be no sensation.

which is felt, is called *matter* in relationship to the felt itself, for which we reserve the name 'body' in the proper sense. We do not know the existence of this force anterior to what is felt and to the subjective body except through what it does in the felt itself, that is, through the violence with which it alters and changes the felt. The positive foundation of our concept of body, therefore, is *what is felt*, that is, what is felt is the first thing that we know about body. From it alone do we argue to the formation of the first, essential concept of body which, as a result, essentially involves the actual sensibility of body. But the force that subtracts or changes what is felt is not itself a felt extension. It does not possess, therefore, the actuality that characterises the concept of body. Nevertheless, although extraneous to bodily activity (which, according to us, consists in actual sensibility), that force is considered as an element necessary to the *material body* because the force operates in every point of what is felt as extended, and can withdraw every point of this felt extension from our sensitive principle, just as it can proffer some other sensible extension to this principle. In other words, this force, before being felt, operates in the soul to produce what is felt. As a result, it is considered in potency to be felt. It does not have, therefore, the act of being felt, but it is a previous, necessary condition of what is felt. This is the first characteristic of matter which, as we said, is an element constituting, but exterior to, the activity resulting from matter and form.

But where do we find the other element? Where do we find that it exists in virtue of the activity itself? It is found in the fact that the concept of force which produces or changes what is felt is known by us only through what is felt. All that we know of this force is its relationship with what is felt. Consequently, as potency is known through act, so the force producing what is felt is known only through and in what is felt. In this sense, it exists through what is felt because it is in this that we find the force actuated. Generally speaking, therefore, we call this force *matter*.

218. There is nothing to prevent our considering this force in two distinct moments, that in which it acts on the soul and is moving to produce what is felt, and that in which what is felt is already produced. In the former moment, this force is not the matter of what is felt (which does not yet exist), but rather the

action of the corporeal principle which is argued to, rather than perceived by, the human being. In the second moment, the force is conceived mentally to be the felt in potency. In this case, it is called the matter of what is felt, or the *matter of body*.

Article 4
The sense in which the body can be called
matter of the soul

219. In the *composite*, soul is the form, body the matter of the human being. But can we also say that body is the matter of the soul? This is possible provided we mean by body the *matter of body* which we have just defined.

220. To understand this, we first have to demonstrate that in our present state we conceive body and matter as a single ens manifesting two activities, the first of which consists in producing a feeling without itself being felt. From this point of view, we have what we call *matter* or *material body*. The second activity consists in being felt directly. From this point of view, we have what we call *body*.

We realise that these two activities pertain to one and the same ens by noting that the first activity, which moves towards the production of that which is felt, acts in the entire extension of what is felt, which it changes and alters. This shows that matter is extended and occupies the same identical extension as what is felt. As a result, we conceive matter as if it were what is felt in potency, the body in potency. But potency and act pertain to the same ens. We conclude, therefore, that matter and body are the same ens.

221. All bodies exterior to our own manifest only material activity. We call them 'body', however, precisely because we feel their force spread in the identical space in which the subjective sensation (that which is felt directly) is diffused.[95] Identity of

[95] Cf. *NE*, vol. 2, 842.

space enables us to understand that the *anatomic body*, as we have called it, is identical with our *subjective* body.[96]

Nevertheless, when we consider both these activities in the body, we call it *material body*. Thus we attribute material properties to the body as to their subject.

222. Granted this, we now want to explain how, in the composite human being, corporeal matter is suitably called 'matter of the soul'.

If we compare an animate[97] with an inanimate body, we can see many great differences between them. It is certain, therefore, that animation alters and modifies the body in so far as it is the object of our external observation and called by us the 'common' or 'anatomic' body.

223. From this, Aristotle induced that there is a certain act proper to the animate body but absent from the inanimate body. In this act he posits the essence of the soul. I cannot agree with this definition. As far as I am concerned, the soul is not an *act of the body*, but the *principle* which produces this act [*App.*, no. 3]. In a word, the *soul* produces *animation*, but is not animation itself.

224. Aristotle, I believe, erred because he considered only the phenomena of the common, anatomic body. These are in no way the essence of the body, but mere signs enabling us to induce its material activity. Moreover, he did not succeed in comprehending the body as given by the subjective feeling, in which the essence of body consists. The fact that Aristotle granted a soul to plants showed that he restricted his considerations to the external phenomena that the body produces on our organs. Aristotle's vegetative soul, lacking all feeling, is simply a principle assumed to explain the extrasubjective phenomena presented by the organisation, nutrition, growth,

---

[96] *AMS*, 135–261.

[97] Let us grant that a body in which no animal phenomenon were observed is nevertheless made up of animal elements, each of which is too small to be sensed by us. In this case only the composite body would fall under our senses. This would then be called, and actually be, an inanimate body because the composite body would in fact be inanimate. We can. therefore, allow the existence of brute bodies even in every possible hypothesis about the animation of the primal elements.

generation and germination of plants. There is nothing subject-ive in this, however. No feeling is attributed to plants; they lack the substantial subject which alone can be called 'soul'.[98] On the other hand, animation and soul are certainly present where this subjective or sensitive principle is found, as in animals. Is anima-tion, however, itself an effect of the soul's action in the body, or is it ultimately perhaps an effect of the mutual actions between body and soul?

I have already stated my opinion; I said that the material body, which has no power of itself to act on the soul, is first modified by the soul and drawn into a new act enabling it to act on the soul and there produce feeling. Aristotle himself, together with many of his followers, acknowledges this.[99]

This first modification received by the body from the soul, through which the body moves towards the production of feel-ing, is properly speaking that which constitutes animation. Through this animation the body is apt to produce externally the extrasubjective phenomena proper to animated bodies and equally apt to produce feeling in the soul. In so far as the body receives from the soul this act of animation, the body becomes matter for the operation of the soul itself.

225. Nevertheless, we still have to show that animation of the

[98] To be animated, plants must have a sensitive principle for their actions. If this principle were not sensitive, it would have only an extra subjective existence, which could never constitute a true, substantial subject such as the soul. Some philosophers, besides supposing a soul for plants, attributed indi-visibility to it. This was consistent. Amongst them were Nemesius (*De Anima hominis*, c. 2), Marsilio Ficino (*De Theol. Platonis*, bk. 1, c. 6–8), The Tianese [Apollonius of Tyana] (*De Anima*, bk. 2, text. 22), and Pomponazzi (*De nutriente et nutrito*, bk. 1, c. 10). — The Syrians mentioned by Gennadius distinguished two souls in the human being, a *sensitive* soul pres-ent in the blood and an *intellective* soul. Apparently they had recognised that there was no third, *vegetative* soul. Gennadius (AD 470) writes: 'Nor do we say, like James and other Syrian writers, that in a single human being there are two souls, an animal soul which animates the body and is mixed with the blood, and a spiritual soul which furnishes reason. We maintain that there is one and the same soul in man which vivifies his body by its society and disposes itself by its reason' (*De Eccles. dogmat.*, c. 13).

[99] Aristotle's words, 'There is nothing potentially alive which is void of soul; each living thing has a soul', clearly means that it is the soul which gives the body its aptitude for being animated.

body is first of all an act of the soul acting in the body rather than an act of the body acting in the soul.

To do this, we need to note that continuous extension, at least continuous subjective extension, which is essential to the body, is found only in an unextended principle.[100] In fact, all ways of conceiving the extension of the body are reduced to two, just as the concepts of extension formed by human beings are reduced to two; that is, we have a concept of material, extrasubjective extension and a concept of corporeal, subjective extension. The concept of extra subjective extension is that of a force which changes what is felt; the concept of subjective extension is that of the felt itself of which extension is the mode. The first of the two concepts, therefore, is reduced to the second so that, by analysing all we know about the extension of the body, we come to conclude that its essence is simply the *mode of what is felt* bodily and fundamentally.[101] But

---

[100] *AMS*, 94–103. The ancients had glimpsed this great truth, but expressed it in other words. They said, for example, that the body needs something simple to contain it. This manner of conceiving the body as contained in the simplicity of the soul can be found in Nemesius, who attributes it to the most ancient masters. He says: 'The things said by Ammonius, Plotinus' teacher, and Numenius Pythagoreus, are sufficient answer to all those who maintain that body is soul. The ancients say that bodies change of their nature; they are totally dispensable and infinitely divided. If, however, nothing unchangeable is left in them, they need SOMETHING TO CONTAIN and connect them, something to restrict and limit them. We call this *soul*. If, therefore, body is soul, even in the most tenuous fashion, what will CONTAIN IT? It has been shown that every body requires SOMETHING TO CONTAIN IT and so on *ad infinitum* until we come to something which is devoid of body' (*De nat. hominis*, c. 2). This passage receives its full light and efficacy if we are clear about what has already been shown, that is: 1. a continuum is necessary for the body; 2. the *extended continuum* can have its seat only in the unextended principle which is the soul.

[101] This is a suitable point for recalling the famous Scholastic question: does the soul inform *naked matter*, or does it inform *matter possessing the form of corporeity*? According to what I have said, the soul would inform naked matter, and Suarez' opinion, together with that of many of his predecessors, would be true: the soul provides matter with 'some degree of corporeity', although in another sense. St. Thomas agrees with this. After showing that in each species there can be only one *substantial form*, he writes: 'The soul is a substantial form because it constitutes the human being in a determined species of substance. Thus, there is no other substantial form between the soul and PRIME MATTER. Human beings are perfected by the

that which is felt fundamentally is the animate body. It is, therefore, through an action of the soul that the body is animated because the soul is that which gives the body its *subjective extension*, to which are connected all the extra-subjective phenomena of bodies called animate.[102]

Article 5
The sense in which the soul is said to be the form of the body

226. If the body is matter of the soul in the composite, it follows that the soul is the form of the body, that which gives the body animation, the act through which the body lives. This consists, as we saw, in the body's becoming subjectively extended, that is, being felt as extended in the fundamental feeling. This first, essential characteristic of animation is consistently coupled with extrasubjective phenomena, the *signs* of

rational soul according to different degrees of perfection, which make it BODY, ANIMATE BODY and RATIONAL SOUL' (*De Anima*, art. 9). This thesis (that *prime matter* receives from the soul its being even as *body*, not just its animate being) is taken very seriously by Aquinas who uses it to show that the soul according to its essence is in all the parts of the body, and to demonstrate other propositions of considerable import. But as far as I can see, there is no complete demonstration until we come to realise that the concept of body, as it appears from careful consideration of its origin, is the same as that of the *felt*, which involves an essential relationship with what feels. Only at this point is it clearly demonstrated that the *form* itself *of corporeity* depends on the soul. However, I cannot see that the Scholastics were clearly aware or even indicated a truth of which they did indeed feel the need. I cannot see that they clearly indicated the nature of *subjective extension* which becomes the proper form of the body. — For those wanting to know about this Scholastic controversy, cf. P. Suarez, *Metaphysicarum disputat.*, d. 15, sect. 10, n. 8–15; d. 13, lect. 3. — *Tract. de Anima*, bk. 1, c. 2).

[102] It is worth noting that the sentient principle which in brute animals is the soul does not exist without that which is felt, just as what is felt does not exist without the sentient principle. This explains why the ancients used the word 'soul' to express the result of the contact between two elements distinguished mentally in the composite, but not existing separately. Hence, the word 'soul' is sometimes used to indicate the *animating sensitive principle*, the cause of life in the body, and sometimes the *life* itself of the body, that is, Aristotle's *actus corporis*.

animation, but not animation itself. But is the form of the body the intellective soul or only the sensitive soul?

227. There is only one soul in the human being, the *rational soul*, which therefore is the form of the body.[103]

228. I said the *rational* rather than the intellective *soul* (although the word 'intellective' is normally used promiscuously for the word 'rational') because we have already seen that the intellective and sensitive principles depend in the human being on another principle which unifies them in itself and, being first principle of both, constitutes the human, substantial subject (cf. 180). This first principle (in which resides the substance of the soul) is called with greater propriety *rational*.[104] This is in accord with the definition we have given of *reason*, that is, 'the faculty which unites what is sensible with what is intelligible by enunciating what it feels through the idea, and acting according to what it enunciates.'

229. Nevertheless, the first principle, that is, the rational principle, is not *immersed* entirely in matter, as the Scholastics say,[105]

---

[103] The Council of Vienna, under Clement V (1311) defined the following: 'We reprove as erroneous and inimical to Catholic truth all teaching which asserts or doubts that the SUBSTANCE OF THE RATIONAL or intellective SOUL is not truly and *per se* the form of the human body. This is in accordance with what the said Council has approved' (*Clement.*, bk. 1, tit. 1). This teaching was confirmed in the 8th session of the Lateran Council under Leo X.

[104] Thus, St. Thomas writes: 'Indeed the soul is the form of the body ACCORDING TO THE ESSENCE of the intellectual soul, not ACCORDING TO ITS intellectual OPERATION' (*Q. de Anima*, art. 9, ad 2).

[105] The soul is of itself true and perfect; it is single, intelligent, in no way composed of crass matter, but mixed with this crass nature THROUGH THE SENSES' (St. Gregory of Nyssa, *De hominis opificio*, c. 14). — Feeling is the effect, term, complement of animation which can, therefore, be attributed to the soul in so far as it is sensitive. But the soul, in the same animation completed through *sensory life*, also produces *organic life*, as I explained in *Anthropology*, 367–498, to which I refer the reader. It was the consistent opinion of ecclesiastical writers that even organic life should be attributed to the soul itself. St. John Damascene will serve as an example for them all. He writes: 'The soul is a living, simple substance, devoid of body, of its nature hidden from bodily eyes, immortal, sharing in what is rational and intelligent, devoid of shape, using a bodily organ TO WHICH IT GIVES LIFE, GROWTH, SENSE, AND THE GENERATIVE FACULTY, having its mind undivided from itself because the mind is simply THE PUREST PART OF IT. What the eye is to the body, the mind is to the soul. The mind is furnished with free will, and

but only in so far as it is the principle of activity which perceives the body. Its purely intellective activity remains immune from matter. A mere intellective operation such as the intuition of being receives nothing from bodily sensation, and even rational operations, although receiving from sensation the matter on which they work, retain an altogether immaterial form throughout these operations.

230. Hence the ancients' distinction between *soul* and *spirit* (*anima* and *animus*). The word soul (*anima*) was attributed to the proximate principle of animation of the body, that is the sensitive principle, and the word spirit (*animus*) to the same substance in so far as it is intellective and immune from bodily contact.[106] The ancients were also accustomed to say that beasts have only a soul (*anima*), but that human beings have in addition a *spirit* (*animus*).[107]

CHAPTER 10
The reality of the soul

231. It is proper to all contingent, limited things that their nature consists in *reality*. *Ideality* enters their nature not as an element, but solely to render entia knowable to the understanding.[108] Only necessary, absolute being is of such a nature that its

with the faculty to will and act. In a word, it is changeable and as such subject to the alterations of the will, granted its created state' (*Della fede Ortodossa*, bk. 2, c. 12).

[106] 'One and the same spirit is called SPIRIT RELATIVE TO ITSELF and SOUL RELATIVE TO THE BODY. — Hence the human soul, because it has being IN THE BODY and OUTSIDE THE BODY, is called both SOUL and SPIRIT. It is called SOUL in so far as it is life of the body; SPIRIT in so far as it is a spiritual substance furnished with reason. In our present life the SOUL is dependent on the SPIRIT'S salvation' (Hugh of St. Victor, *Tract. super Magnif.*).

[107] 'How shall I divide living things? Let me say that some have a SPIRIT (*animus*), some have only a SOUL (*anima*)' (Seneca, *Ep.* 58). — 'Our common maker gave them only SOULS; to us he gave a SPIRIT as well' (Juvenal, *Sat.* 15: 148).

[108] This accords with something I have often said: the nature of contingent things cannot be found in *being* unless we have some feeling, that is, unless we have perceived their *reality*, or some *real likeness* of them (cf. 195).

complete reality lies essentially in the depths of ideality, and vice-versa, so that both real and ideal being pertain to the nature and constitution of infinite ens.

It is a fact worthy of the greatest attention but not easy to grasp, that the nature of the soul, like every other contingent ens, is not constituted by ideal being. The difficulties are two:

1. Without the use of ideal being we have no knowledge of our own soul or that of others or of any contingent being. It seems, therefore, that ideal being mingles with the soul and with all contingent beings.

2. The soul is intellective only by means of the intuition of ideal being. It seems, therefore, that ideal being pertains to the nature of the soul.

232. The first difficulty is overcome by noting that we cannot perceive our soul without making use of ideal being (from this perception we then derive the concept of every soul). Nevertheless, it is also true that to understand the soul purely in its nature, without any foreign addition, we have to subtract perception itself, and therefore ideal being (which is the means by which we perceive the soul), from our perception of the soul (cf. 69–70).

233. In answering the second difficulty I accept that the soul is intellective by reason of the intuition of being (there is no doubt whatsoever of this), but it does not follow that ideal being is an *intrinsic* element of its nature. This can be proved:

1. By having recourse to consciousness of ourselves, that is, to the principle of the science of the soul and the criterion enabling us to distinguish true from false in this discussion. Now we know very well, and understand clearly, that we are not ideal being. Ideal being is a universal, *myself* a particular; ideal being is not modifiable, *myself* is subject to modifications; ideal being is a means of knowledge common to all mankind, *myself* is not in other people, but exclusively in me. Other people do not use *myself* in order to know, but carry out their acts of knowledge without any information about me or even about my existence.

2. It is clear, that ideal being, granted its connection with the *subject* through intuition, is not the subject. Intuition of its nature distinguishes its term from itself, excludes it from itself, and posits it in counter-position to itself. Hence the word

objectum. For further clarification of this truth, I refer the reader to those places where I have shown that it is not absurd for one thing to in-exist in another without mixing with the other. This is what actually takes place by means of intuition in the union of ideal being with the subject.[109]

234. You object that, according to me, the act of intuition is created by virtue of the manifestation of being, and that consequently the very act of intuition is an effect of being. — This is true, but it does not give rise to difficulty. Although intuition and that which intuits are the effect of the manifestation of ideal being, it does not follow that they are an *act* of ideal being itself, but the very opposite. Cause is not effect. How this *manifestation* comes about, how it is a kind of *creation*, does not concern me here. This is an altogether higher, more sublime question. I simply maintain that what is intuited is not that which intuits, that is, the soul. And this is evident.

CHAPTER 11
The finiteness and infinity of the human soul

235. From our knowledge that ideal being is not an internal, constitutive element of the nature of the soul, and that this nature is merely *real*, it is easy to conclude that the human soul is a finite ens. The infinite is found in man only by having recourse to ideal being which, as we said, is not part of man himself.

236. This truth is given to us directly by consciousness of ourselves. Each one knows that he is finite. When he says *myself*, he affirms a reality which excludes innumerable other realities of equal and different condition; he affirms something finite.

237. At the same time the human soul, as intellective, is united

---

[109] *Rinnovamento*. Platonists saw the intimate union of ideas with the soul, but exaggerated it because 1. they spoke of a certain continuity between ideas and souls; 2. they then took ideas themselves as souls. Iamblichus writes: 'The very unity of the gods (these gods are the ideas) unites souls to themselves from eternity through their own unities according to the proper, efficacious proximity of souls. As a result, there seems to be a CONTINUITY' (*De Mysteriis*, 1).

with an infinite being, which the idea is. From this point of view, it shares in a certain infinity. Ideal being, in relationship with the mind, does in fact resemble an infinite, evenly-illuminated space relative to the eye. Hence, although real things known by us are always finite because the real thing (the soul) which perceives them is finite, the *means of knowing* (the idea of being) real things perceived by sense is never exhausted or rendered inefficacious. It is always sufficient for knowledge of other ral things which may be given to us in sensitive perception, even indefinite perception, and in the case of infinite reality.[110] St. Thomas says:

> Our intellect knows what is infinite to the extent that the intellect is virtually infinite. This virtual infinity is not determined by bodily matter (*I would say, 'by any finite reality whatsoever'*). Rather it is cognitive of what is universal (*the idea of being*), separate as it is from individual (*subsistent*) matter. The virtual infinity of the intellect does not terminate in some individual, but on its part extends to infinite individuals.[111]

238. An objection could arise here. — Ideal being is the form of the intellective soul; but form and matter are two constitutive elements of a nature; therefore ideal being is a true, constitutive element of the soul. But ideal being is infinite in its ideal condition. The human soul, therefore, is composed of finite and infinite. —

I reply by distinguishing the minor of this syllogism as follows. *Forms* are of two kinds, subjective and objective. Subjective forms pertain to the subject, which they constitute. Objective forms neither pertain to the subject nor constitute it, but draw the subject into act and can also be called, therefore, *immediate causes of the form* of the subject. Nevertheless, they are called *forms* with equal and perhaps greater propriety when they are considered as term of the act of intuition. Being in general, as the term of this act, is appropriated for the soul without ceasing to be universal in itself.[112] In fact, although it is true

110 *Teodicea*, 145, 151.

111 *S.T.*, I, q. 86, art. 2; and q. 89, art. 4, ad 1.

112 In this way, we resolve the objection (to calling ideal being 'form') which springs from the principle: 'It is impossible for there to be one form

that being in general is intuited in exactly the same way by all intellects, it is not the term of one intellect in so far as it is precisely the term of another. In this sense, we can say that the truth possessed by the human being is created. What we mean is that the proposition, 'The truth of the intellect is created' is equivalent to the other proposition: 'Eternal truth has become the term of a created intellect.'[113]

239. Here we need to consider that every action terminating in an entity different from the action presupposes a kind of contact with that entity. At the point of contact, communication is present between the thing which touches and that which is touched. But in the case of intuition, that which is touched, ideal being, cannot be changed or altered, or mixed with anything else.[114] Communication, therefore, produces no variation in ideal being, but in the subject alone. The variation occurring in the subject consists in placing the subject in possession of intelligence, or light. But that which is possessed is not to be confused with the possessor whom it enriches. Thus, the person possessing gold is not gold. Ideal being, as light and form of the intuiting subject, does not suffer any change or restriction in itself.

240. It would not be out of place here to consider the following question: 'Is the intelligible communicated in a limited or unlimited manner to human nature? If the former, what does this limitation consist in?'

I reply briefly. The intelligible is eternal, necessary being in which essence and subsistence are not distinguished but form a single, extremely simple ens. Essence shines in the idea, it is the intelligible. If human beings were intellectually to behold the intelligible fully, they would see the Almighty whose essence is his very subsistence. However, the intelligible cannot reveal itself in all its fullness to any created being without transporting this being to a supernatural order where it sees the Creator. Indeed, the Almighty is above created nature, and the only truly supernatural ens. Direct communication with the divine subsistence is that which forms the supernatural condition of intelligent creatures.

for a number of different things' (cf. *S.T.*, I, q. 76, art. 2).

[113] St. Thomas speaks of a created truth (*S.T.*, I, q. 16, art. 7 and 8).

[114] *Rinnovamento*, 433–443.

241. But could some subjects, without being granted perception of the divine subsistence, see the intelligible in a more perfect way than it is seen by human beings? I cannot let this important question pass.

The intuition of being can be considered from the point of view of the intuiting subject and from that of the intuited object.

In the first case, the intuition can be or appear more or less perfect. It would seem that this perfection can vary in three ways. 1. According to the *intensity* of the act. Here, ideal being produces a deeper impression in the subject, reveals more light and is seen more distinctly. 2. According to greater facility for *reflecting* on the idea and intuition. This is properly speaking a perfection of the faculty of reflection, not of intuition, although human beings seem to add light to intuition when they render themselves more easily and perfectly conscious of it. However, the intensity of the faculty of intuition does assist reflection. 3. According to greater facility in *applying* the idea. This renders perception and reasoning more prompt and perfect. Here, too, perfection resides in the operations of reason, not in intuition, although the opposite seems the case. The preceding perfections of *intuition* and *reflection* contribute considerably to the perfection of reasoning. This, of course, depends to a great extent on the perfect organisation of the cerebro-spinal system. These differences should be discussed in a treatise on the differences in mental capacity.

242. The question still has to be answered from the point of view of the object itself. The question is: can a subject be given more of the intelligible to intuit than is given to human nature without, however, the subject's being granted perception of the divine subsistence? I reply that this is impossible, for the following reasons.

No subsistence, other than the divine subsistence, is *per se* intelligible. The intelligible *is* the essence of ens, and only the divine subsistence is identified with that essence.[115] Amongst subsistences it pertains to God alone, therefore, to be intelligible. Nothing can be added to ideal being that is *per se* intelligible unless there is some passage to the supernatural, divine order.

---

[115] *Rinnovamento*, 433–443.

It may be objected that ideal being as intuited by us is totally indetermined and that it could contain many of its determinations without our having recourse to God to determine it. In fact, ideas of contingent entia are determinations of ideal being which could, therefore, be granted to the faculty of intuition in other minds in a more perfect (because more determined) way than in the human mind. —

This illusion arises through imperfect understanding of the origin of these determinations of ideal being, these special or generic ideas. They arise[116] through the relationship of real, subsistent entia with indetermined being in general. These entia are not properly speaking ideas, but relationships of subsistences or their vestiges with ideal being. The presupposition is that these subsistences are somehow known already. But contingent subsistences are not *per se* intelligible, and consequently add nothing to what is intelligible. Nothing is added through them relative to what is intelligible; they simply provide occasions for new acts by the intelligent subject. The increase in knowledge comes wholly from the side of matter, not form; from the side of the subject, not the object.

243. Intelligence, therefore, can be increased or reinforced without any increase in what is *per se* intelligible; intelligence increases every time a greater supply of subsistences or realities is furnished for it to perceive. Intelligences, restricted to the natural order, cannot differ therefore amongst themselves by reason of greater or lesser quantity on the part of the intelligible which is proposed to their faculty of intuition. They differ solely according to the greater or lesser quantity of perceived reality, or according to some reality of a differing nature. It is not the object itself of intuition which can increase, diminish or vary, but whatever falls within the sphere of feeling. This explains why I maintained that angelic nature differs from human nature according to the different, more suitable feeling with which it is endowed. The difference comes about not through different intuition, but through a different nature and a different quantity of things naturally perceived (*Teodicea*, 750–751).

244. — But isn't it possible to have ideas of contingent things

---

[116] *Rinnovamento*, 228–232.

without their first having to be perceived? Don't we ourselves have many ideas of which we have no perception? Can't things be known through their likenesses without our having experienced their action in ourselves? —

Drawing attention to what happens in human beings is excellent, but arbitrary use of our imagination is not recommended. We have to observe patiently what actually occurs. This is the only way to avoid error.

Now there is no doubt that the most accurate observation shows we have no *positive* idea of anything subsistent unless it is preceded by some perception to which we can refer it. Thus, a blind person has no positive idea of colours. The word 'colour' does not have the same meaning for him as for others. Indeed, he would never have invented the word if he had not heard it or perceived it from others. It is true that the idea of what a person has perceived in his feeling remains even when the perception has passed, but this occurs only because the perception never passes completely. We retain vestiges of it in our imagination which is a kind of interior perception, a reawakening of the external perception.[117] If the perception were to pass without leaving some trace or habit in the imagination, there would be no way in which to refer being to the feeling, in relationship to which the idea itself, as determined, consists. This is what happens in human beings. Let us see if something else could occur in some other being.

245. An intelligence, it is said, can know things by means of their *likenesses*. This is true, however, only in a certain sense, which needs careful definition. If a likeness is to be capable of making me know what it represents, I must compare the likeness and the thing itself. I have to become aware of how faithful and how different the likeness is to what it represents. Otherwise, I would not know that it is a likeness rather than the thing itself. But how can this comparison be made if I do not know the subsistent thing? A comparison can only be made through a comparison of terms. I cannot, therefore, know the subsistent thing by means of some likeness unless I already suppose that the subsistent thing is known to me. But it is known (if we are dealing with contingent things) not *per se*, but through

---

[117] *AMS*, 350–354.

perception. The likeness alone, without the perception to which it can be referred, is not sufficient to enable me know the subsistent thing.[118]

246. — But wouldn't it be possible, without previous perception, to know something indicated through its likeness provided some other being had revealed that this was its likeness?

I reply: 1. In this case, the thing would not be known through its likeness alone, but with the help of some revelation on the part of another being. The revelation itself presupposes some perception.

2. The likeness, if it were merely a vestige of the thing, would give us only a negative idea, that is, it would produce in us a persuasion of the thing's subsistence, but would not permit us to know its nature.

3. If it is a true likeness, it must be such that with it we perceive the nature of the thing. In this case, in so far as it is similar to the thing, its reality would have to be of the same nature as the thing. For example, a portrait enables me to know what a person looks like because in it I perceive the same colours and shape as those present in the person concerned. I do, therefore, perceive a reality which has the same characteristics. But because the portrait differs from the person in its lack of solid extension, flexibility in the flesh, and so on, I do not perceive the person: the likeness, to this extent, is no longer a likeness.

Note the question carefully: I asked if it were possible to have a *positive idea* of something without any perception of it, and I said 'No'. But this need for perception does not extend in any way to all equal or similar individuals. It is sufficient to perceive one of them to satisfy our condition and have a positive idea of all individuals equal to the one perceived. If we have perceived one individual, others are known through likeness or equality with that one. But I maintain that if we do not perceive one, we cannot know others because the first one, similar to them, is lacking. If, however, some perception is given us, we certainly have the likeness of other individuals perceivable in the same way. In this case, we know them through *likeness* without perceiving them.

[118] *NE*, vol. 1, 104–109.

It remains true that no reality is known without perception, and that there are no likenesses of real things without perception of their reality. Consequently, if we suppose that an intelligent subject is given likenesses capable of permitting knowledge of real things, we also suppose that he is given internal perceptions of real things. But the perceptions of real things, that is perceived feelings, however acquired or communicated, do not increase the intelligible, the object of intuition, if the things we are dealing with are contingent. The intelligible cannot be increased notwithstanding the determinations or concepts of contingent, finite things which may be added to it. It can, however, be increased in one single way — through the perception of God himself. As we said, the divine subsistence, alone amongst all subsistences, is *per se* intelligible. Different intelligences have to be distinguished, therefore, not through any diversity occurring in *ideal being* which informs them, but through the diversity found in *real being* which constitutes them and receives a different sphere of native or adventitious perceptions acquired by means of accidental acts.

This ends the second book of *Psychology*.

Book 3

The union and mutual influence of soul and body

[INTRODUCTION]

247. We may sum up what has been said about the essence of the soul as follows. We saw that it lies in the primal, *substantial* feeling we express when we say *myself* (cf. 69–70). Only by meditating on this feeling can we know with certainty the characteristics of the essence of the soul. Consequently I made feeling the *principle* and *criterion* of all psychological teaching.

I then investigated this intimate feeling and showed that in every human being the soul is one and the principle of all human actions, that it is simple, incorporeal and does not die. In fact, the word *death* simply means the experience undergone by the body when the soul ceases to vivify it. But the soul is active in the body's death, of which it is the negative cause through the cessation of its act, called animation.

Our next problem was the identity of the soul, complicated by an apparent triplicity in the soul's nature. We saw that there is first a principle and term, then a plurality of terms with many actions, and finally two active principles of very different character: feeling and intelligence. We showed however that the term is not an element intrinsic to the soul but simply its condition or *essential relationship*. The term cannot therefore duplicate the soul; the multiplicity of the term cannot be in the soul, which is purely *principle*. Also, different actions, because they are not the soul, do not multiply it. Finally we found that over and above the two active principles discernible in the soul, another principle governs them both, and that in this superior principle, which is the soul itself, the soul's identity is properly located.

Next, we examined the kind of changes the soul could undergo without losing its identity, and the kind that could cause this loss. This gave us a good opportunity to discuss the differences which separate the human soul from the souls of brute animals and from pure intelligences.

After this, I showed that the nature of the soul (as of all contingent things) is that of being simply real. Consequently, unless its reality is perceived, or there is some vestige of it to which its reality can be referred, we cannot conceive its essence positively. The essence of the soul is known by means of a *concept* which is determined and as it were outlined in ideal being by an act of the mind which considers the relationship between the real and the ideal.

Finally, I proved that the soul is finite precisely because it is real and in so far as it is real. But, because *being* is its object, the soul communicates with the infinite. *Being* is like an interminable space into which the soul can freely and infinitely extend itself.

248. The nature of the soul, therefore, and its limitation, consists in its reality (for this reason I placed its nature in feeling which is precisely what is real).[119] We must now investigate and analyse more fully the soul's limitation. To do this, we must consider the soul relative to the body it animates. Properly speaking, the soul is limited by extended, corporeal reality which also contributes to its actions. In this book therefore I will deal with the nexus between, and the mutual influence of, soul and body.

CHAPTER 1

The sensitive soul is united with the body by means of feeling

249. Consciousness tells us that of all the things different from the soul, body is the only reality sensible and perceptible by the human being. This direct proof is all that is necessary, and from it we can immediately draw a very important corollary: soul and body are joined by means of feeling.

250. Because it is precisely in feeling that I have placed reality, the union between soul and body is real. But we must not picture this union as similar to that of a body acting on another body, where the action of one is similar to the action of the other, the passive experience and re-action of one similar to the passive experience and re-action of the other (this is the origin

---

[119] When I say that the *essence* of the soul is in *feeling*, this means feeling considered in itself, as possible.

of the erroneous principle that 'action is equal to re-action'[120]), and hence the touch of one similar to the touch of the other. On the contrary, we are dealing with two entia of different nature, each acting on the other in its own way, that is, in a different way, each experiencing and re-acting differently. Now, the union of soul and body is clearly demonstrated by the fact of *feeling*, from which are excluded all mechanical laws applicable to the mutual action of bodies. I called this union of the soul and body and their mutual action a *relationship of sensility,* and have discussed its nature and laws extensively.[121]

251. I also showed that every feeling has, as it were, two extremes, called by me the *sentient* (the soul) and the *felt* (the body). Every feeling is composed of that which is felt and that which feels, and this feeling, as first and fundamental, is a single, indistinct ens. Consequently, not only must the body must be united to the soul, and the soul to the body, but the union must be that of form with matter.

252. I next directly refuted the hypothesis of pre-established harmony and of occasional causes. I argued on very clear grounds that these could not give any knowledge of the body, because all such knowledge comes down to this: the body is term of the soul's feeling. The very notion of body essentially involves a relationship of union with soul, and of the real action and passive experience between the two principles. In short, I found that physical influence was contained in the very definitions of soul and body.[122] If we remove the real union (the physical influence), neither soul nor body can be conceived or named.

253. We must not forget that, although the animal is a single feeling, this feeling contains the simple principle (the sentient) and the extended term (the felt). These two elements form one and the same feeling. The body, the term of the feeling, is not given to the animal in its first state, that is, isolated from the feeling principle to such an extent that it constitutes a separate feeling; on the contrary, one single feeling is configured in such

---

[120] *Rinnovamento,* bk. 3, c. 47 [497 ss.].

[121] *AMS,* 230–246.

[122] *NE,* vol. 2, 998–1002.

a way that under one aspect it is sentient, and under another, felt. Then, through the action of intelligence, the felt is divided from the sentient in the way I will now explain.

CHAPTER 2
The union of rational soul with body comes about by means of an immanent perception of animal feeling

254. It is easy enough to understand how the animal is an indivisible feeling in which the feeling principle, or soul, constitutes a single thing with the felt term or body and is thus the form of the body. It is not so easy to explain how the *rational* human soul is the form of the human body. How does a rational soul communicate with and inform a body?

Article 1
Rational activity contains sensitive activity

255. The question is largely answered by what has been said. We showed that the rational soul is a principle which virtually includes corporeal-sensitive activity.

St. Thomas had already written that 'the intellective soul virtually contains within itself all that is in the sensitive soul of brute animals and in the vegetative soul of plants.' He explained his concept by a fitting image:

> Just as a pentagon does not depend for its existence on a quadrilateral or another pentagon (recourse to a quadrilateral would be superfluous because already contained in a pentagon), so Socrates is not a human being by means of one soul and an animal by means of another. He is both through one and the same soul.[123]

[123] *S.T.*, I, q. 76, art. 3.

In another place, he re-affirms that

> the rational soul, although one in essence, is virtually multiple because of its perfection.[124]

This is undeniably difficult to understand. To explain it better, I will add some observations to what has already been said.

Article 2
Rational activity contains sensitive activity in a way proper to itself

256. At the outset we must rid ourselves of the prejudice that things are absolutely and exactly as they appear to our senses, and that generally speaking things perceived through sense have no other entity than that perceived in a given feeling.

257. It is true that if there is a stable way of feeling, and especially only one way, or only one way to which we give our exclusive attention, the thing perceived in our feeling becomes the foundation of our idea of the thing. We understand that its substance is precisely the entity we have perceived in our feeling; the name we give it indicates the substance.[125]

We can however feel a thing in two or more ways. If we consider these ways, we see immediately that the appearance of the thing differs according to the different ways of feeling. Thus, the same object, perceived with our eyes, is something coloured; perceived with the palate, it is something that has taste; perceived with the nose, it is something odorous, etc. But the difference is much greater when we consider our body perceived as something extrasubjective by our external organs, and perceived by our internal feeling as the term of

---

[124] *Ibid.*, art. 5, ad 3.

[125] Here, the reader must bear in mind what I said about the knowledge of essences in *NE*, vol. 3, 1213–1244, and about what is relative and subjective in our perception of bodies in *NE*, vol. 2, 878–905 and *Rinnovamento*, 497 ss., as well as in many other places, where I showed that that which feeling presents about things different from us always retains something subjective and relative. Only the intellect gives absolute knowledge.

our fundamental feeling. I have discussed all this at length in *Anthropology*.

258. Similarly, the terms of our sense-perception appear as different things if, besides considering them in relationship to ourselves as perceivers, we consider them relative to each other, in the way, for example, that we consider an external body relative to another external body. If we compare one external body with another we find relationships of extension, size, etc. However, if we compare an external body with our feeling principle, we no longer find these relationships but a totally different relationship which I have called relationship of *sensility*.[126] The term of the perception changes therefore according to the nature of the perceiving subject and the way in which it perceives. The character of the felt as felt is determined by the nature of both the term-entity and the sentient principle, and by the manner of feeling, etc. All these things have already been thoroughly explained.[127]

259. An entity relative to one feeling is therefore different relative to another feeling, that is, the entity manifests its activity differently according to the feelings whose term it is. Sense-perception takes perceived things according to their different activities relative to feeling. Consequently, that which a thing contributes to feeling contains a great deal that is relative.

260. On the other hand, all that is perceived by the understanding is perceived absolutely, not relatively. To perceive absolutely is to perceive the very *entity* of things; it is not the direct perception of their *sensility, extension* and other relative activities. Note however, that *sensility, extension* and other activities relative to different feelings are all understood in the *entity*, because relative activities have their source in the entity. Indeed, extension is an entity *sui generis*, as also is sensility. etc. But the understanding perceives these activities in so far as they are all reduced to entity; it perceives them, not precisely as such but because they share in entity. This is what is meant by understanding absolutely. Whether it is true or not that the thing is extended, coloured, etc., it is always true that it is an entity and that extension and the feelable qualities are also

[126] *AMS*, 230–233.

[127] *Rinnovamento*, 325 ss.

entities. The proper object of understanding therefore is always true because the understanding does not stop at anything relative but considers it in relationship to what is absolute in the understanding itself. Hence, while bodies have on the one hand a mutual relationship of extension, size, etc., and on the other a relationship of *sensility* with respect to the feeling principle, they also have a relationship of *entity* with respect to the understanding, a relationship which is absolute and necessary in contrast to other partial and variable relationships.

261. Nevertheless, although the understanding perceives everything given to it to perceive relative to absolute entity, it perceives only what feeling gives it. Indeed it cannot perceive what is not in any way felt. On the one hand, of itself understanding perceives things without altering, diminishing or modifying them; on the other, it is given things to perceive which are already modified or rather put together by the limited feeling which presents them to it. It is this which explains why knowledge of things is limited, not the fact that the understanding breaks them down, or composes or limits them.

262. It is clear therefore that if there were a feeling that could apprehend the whole real entity of things and not just a part or a particular activity, the thing would be presented to the understanding's perception without any limit or division whatsoever, and the understanding would have a totally absolute knowledge of it. This happens in the case of the substantial feeling which has an ens of its own. The same must also be the case when essential Being communicates itself in its real form to the human being. This Being, which is entirely simple and unchangeable, cannot communicate itself except as being. The feeling principle that perceives it must be such that it can perceive entity itself, which is the object of the intellect. Hence, this principle must be an intellective sense. The intellect, as intellective sense, feels real entity and, as intellect itself, feels ideal entity; it is a single ideal-real ens, a power that unites within itself two actions which in themselves are divided, namely, sense and intellect. God is perceived in this way.

263. The understanding always perceives *absolutely*, that is, has *absolute notions* of all the things it perceives, together with a complete perception of itself. But only in perception of God does it truly perceive the *absolute*, and have an *absolute*

knowledge.[128] However, we must add that it is possible on the one hand to have an *absolute knowledge of contingent things* when they are perceived as they are in God in the creating act; on the other hand, it is possible to have an *absolute but negative knowledge* of things when, through a higher reflection, we remove from *relative knowledge* that which in it is relative.

Article 3
It follows that the rational principle is united to the body through immanent perception of the animal feeling

264. From all that has been said we can conclude:

1. The rational principle does not communicate directly with things in so far as they are thought to subsist outside feeling, but with *felt things*, that is, with things given to it to perceive in feelings.

2. This communication takes place with felt things through their *relationship of entity* with the rational principle, not through their *relationship of sensility*.

3. The *relationship of entity*, because absolute, includes all other relative relationships including those of *sensility*.

4. The *rational soul* is united to the body in so far as it is united to the animal feeling because what is felt, besides having the relationship of *sensility*, also possesses the superior, absolute relationship *of entity*; the latter includes the former, as the greater includes the less. Although every felt thing is a determinate entity, this relationship of entity is manifested solely to the understanding which, having entity (essential being) as its object, extends to every entity.

5. The unity of the soul and of the human being lies in this rational principle which is able to *perceive* what is felt or corporeal, or any other nature given to the human being.

6. Finally, the unity of the human being consists in a single feeling proper to the rational principle, a feeling which includes both animal feeling and rational feeling in such a way that the latter contains the former, as the greater contains the less. Hence

[128] *PE*, 58–61.

the human being, in his first state, does not have two feelings, that is, an animal and a rational feeling, but a single, extremely simple feeling which has both a principle and a term. He has a principle, the rational principle itself; he has a term, the idea of being. In this being, he sees the animal feeling which he experiences. As I have said, a single ens, object of the single rational principle, is formed, by means of perception, from the subsistent felt thing and from being. This *primal, fundamental perception* of all that is felt (principle and term) is, so to speak, the marriage-bed where what is *real* (animal-spiritual feeling) together with the *essence* intuited in the idea form a single thing. This single thing is the human being.

Article 4
Distinction between the individual, fundamental feeling which constitutes the human being and the primal perception of the animal feeling where the nexus between soul and body is located

265. We must note that feeling includes the whole human being and constitutes his unity. *Rational perception* however extends only to the animal feeling. The perceiving principle can perceive itself only later, through reflection, when the need to distinguish itself from all else in its feeling arises on the occasion of external sensations. In the human being therefore, in his natural state at the first moment of life, there is 1. a single, constant-fundamental animal and spiritual feeling; 2. an immanent, rational perception of the animal feeling.

266. We must grant therefore that, in order to explain the union of soul and body, the rational soul has a primal, natural and continuous perception of the animal-fundamental feeling. Because the soul is rational, it can be joined to this feeling only by a rational act. The first of all rational acts, the act which communicates directly with the reality of an ens, is perception.

CHAPTER 3

The nature of the first perception by which the rational principle constantly perceives its own animal-fundamental feeling and thus unites itself to the body

267. We should not misunderstand the nature of this constant perception of the animal-fundamental feeling. Characteristics of this perception are:

1. By it the soul does not perceive the extrasubjective, anatomical body but the whole animal-fundamental feeling in itself, indivisible, continuous, harmonious, etc.

2. Consequently, the soul does not perceive the principle of feeling without its term because the principle cannot exist without its term.

3. Similarly, the soul does not perceive the subjective body (the term of the feeling) divided from its principle. This mental division of the term of animal feeling from its principle is carried out only later, through reflective analysis on the feeling. A felt body divided from its feeling principle cannot exist by itself. The primal, natural perception, which does not isolate the body from its principle, is insufficient to give us the pure notion of subjective body.

4. Much less does the soul perceive the parts of the body separate from the whole. On the contrary, it perceives the whole in its perfect simplicity and harmonious unity.

5. The soul perceives nothing extrasubjective, such as shapes, sizes, boundaries, etc.

6. We have no awareness of the perception in its initial state, because awareness arises from reflection on what happens in us. This perception is anterior to every reflection.

268. We must now investigate whether, in the *fundamental perception*, the soul enunciates an express affirmation.

The reader may think this is my opinion because I have consistently kept the concepts of affirmation and perception together. But I did this only for particular, transient perceptions to which an express assent of the spirit is always, or nearly always, united. Perception in general however is seen to have three degrees: 1st. apprehension, which is an implicit, habitual affirmation; 2nd. express or actual affirmation; 3rd. persuasion.

269. *Persuasion* can be implicit and habitual, or express and actual, depending upon whether it arises from *apprehension* or from implicit or express *affirmation*. These two degrees, affirmation and persuasion, rapidly follow one another and cannot exist without each other.

270. But could the first degree, *apprehension* or habitual affirmation, exist without *actual affirmation*? This is precisely what happens in the first perception through which the rational principle has a continuous union with the animal feeling.

Animal feeling, because it is one, and without distinguishable boundaries (the distinct boundaries of our body pertain to extrasubjective experience) is indistinguishable from other feelings, which do not yet exist. Moreover, it cannot attract attention because it is uniform, natural and, so far, the only thing perceived (the human being has not yet rationally perceived himself) (cf. 267). Again, the soul does not need to say anything to itself — it would not even know what to say. Nevertheless, despite all this, a kind of *implicit*, habitual assent, an indistinct affirmation of what comes later, is not excluded from apprehension.

271. It may seem more suitable to call simple apprehension *rational apprehension* rather than *perception*. If so, I would not disagree.

CHAPTER 4

How philosophical meditation, in analysing the animal feeling perceived by the soul, distinguishes the subjective body and recognises it as having the same nature as extrasubjective bodies

272. How do we separate and distinguish, in the primal perception of the fundamental feeling, the body which, as term of this feeling, is not separate from it? The answer demands much mental activity carried to a very high level of reflection, as follows:

273. *1st. level.* Through sense-experiences we first perceive external, extrasubjective bodies. They are presented spontaneously to us as something separate from our feeling principle. We are passive in their regard, perceiving them as a foreign energy, independent of the activity of our subjective, feeling principle. In other words, we perceive them precisely as extrasubjective bodies, that is, independent of the subject.[129]

2nd. level. Next, reflection shows us that in every sense-experience produced in us by an extended, extrasubjective energy there is something subjective, in addition to the foreign energy.

3rd. level. Meditation on the nature of this subjective element shows it to be a modification of our feeling, which now feels in a new, unaccustomed way

4th. level. From the concept of modification we reason that even before this sense-experience there was in us an ordinary mode of feeling, which has now been modified. This feeling is the fundamental feeling.

5th. level. Moreover, we notice that the modification, that is, our sense-experience, is extended in an extension equal to that of the foreign energy acting in our feeling. We conclude that subjective feeling itself has extension as its term.

6th. level. We also see that every feeling presupposes an agent and an energy different from the feeling principle, although indivisibly united with it and dependent on it in many ways. We conclude that the term of our animal-fundamental feeling is a body, because it has the two conditions constituting body: energy and extension.

7th. level. Next, by means of external sense-experiences, we discover the limits of this term.

8th. level. Finally, we find that the same body, the term of the fundamental feeling, falls under our extrasubjective experience just as every other foreign body does, and we conclude that the subjective body and the extrasubjective body have an

---

[129] The subject, in a state of mere feeling, has as yet no perception. The mind therefore does not need to deny feeling and distinguish it from bodies to be able to perceive it, as Fichte wanted. As I said, external bodies spontaneously present themselves as different to the attention of our understanding which attends to them alone.

identical nature, although only one depends on the principle of feeling.

This is my analysis of the *fundamental perception* and, I conclude that through it a body is united to our rational soul.

CHAPTER 5

Concerning Averroes' opinion that the body is united to the rational soul by means of the intelligible species

274. Averroes glimpsed something of the preceding teaching about the union of soul and body, but the imperfection of Aristotelian philosophy did not allow him to grasp the truth. Instead, he proposed a system rife with errors: according to him, the soul is united to the body by means of the *intelligible species*.[130]

275. This opinion demonstrates Averroes' clear awareness that only a rational act could unite the rational principle to the body; if the act of union were not itself rational, the union would have been brought about by a potency different from the rational principle.

Ignorant of the rational act and its nature (which unites soul and body), he declared that it came about by means of the *intelligible species*. This species, he said, was present both in the phantasms pertaining to the corporeal organ and in the possible intellect.

276. It is erroneous however to say that the intelligible species is present in phantasms. St. Thomas himself noted that phantasms are what is understood; the intellect is that which understands. Averroes' statement would not explain how a person who has phantasms in the corporeal organs is the same person who understands. Such a person would be like a wall that has colours which are not exclusively in the eye of the one who sees them. St. Thomas concluded correctly therefore that no system is suitable for explaining the union of soul and body unless it

---

[130] *De Anima*, bk. 3, text. 5 & 36.

[274–276]

can demonstrate that the soul by which the human being lives, feeds, feels, has phantasms, moves and understands, is the soul itself. In other words, the system necessary for explaining the nexus between soul and body must be able to demonstrate that the rational soul is joined to the body as intimately as form to matter.[131] However, after establishing this important truth that *ipsa anima, cuius* EST HAEC VIRTUS (intellectiva) *est corporis forma* [the soul, which HAS THIS (intellective) POWER, is the form of the body],[132] the Saint does not go on to propose the system. I want to take this valuable argument from St. Thomas and, if possible, develop it further. Let us look more carefully at the defects of the system proposed by the Arab commentator.

277. The deficiency in Averroes' thought was:

1. He did not advert to the nature of *perception*, which really joins perceived and perceiver into one. On the other hand, *species*, when defined as a likeness of phantasms (as the Aristotelians define it), is something entirely abstract and purely intellectual. It does not unite phantasms to itself and, still less, the corporal organs where the Aristotelians located phantasms.

278. 2. It is false that the *intelligible species* has two subjects, the possible intellect and phantasms, because the intelligible species is not in phantasms. But in the case of *perception*, the contrary is true: feeling exists not only in itself as feeling but in the idea as an *essential entity*. This juncture of idea with feeling gives rise to perception, to which the human being adds a more or less explicit affirmation, which is simply a disposition and movement of the rational principle itself.

279. 3. In the third place, Averroes did not see that phantasms are only *accidental* modifications of the fundamental feeling. Hence, they cannot be assumed to explain the *substantial* union of soul and body.

280. 4. Much less did he notice the two ways we perceive our body. Our body presents itself to us as two things of different nature, although they are not so. We called these two things *subjective body* and *extrasubjective body*. Averroes did not realise that the union of soul and body remains inexplicable if

---

[131] *S.T.*, I, q. 76, art. 1.

[132] *Ibid.*, ad 1.

we ignore the concept of extrasubjective body. This concept, instead of revealing the intimate nature of the body, presents mostly a phenomenal body relative to our faculty of external feeling. The greatest modern philosophers, such as Malebranche and Leibniz, ignorant of the subjective body, declared such a physical influence impossible and invented the hypothesis of occasional causes and pre-established harmony.

281. 5. Similarly, Averroes was unaware that the body, adhering to the soul from the very beginning, is not isolated. It adheres to the soul because included in the fundamental feeling, whose term it is. This feeling becomes object of the first perception through which the rational principle communicates with the body.

282. 6 Finally, the *intelligible species* is not itself an act but an object contemplated by the mind, as Aquinas notes. The rational soul must also be united to the body with its own act. Even if the object of its intuition were united, the soul itself would not be united, because the object it intuits does not itself intuit.

283. Averroes' error, that the intelligible species is the means of communication between soul and body, inevitably resulted in the strangest consequences.

Although the intelligible species is a pure idea, the Arab thinkers had made phantasms subject to it, and maintained that the soul, by means of this species, communicates with bodies. Consequently, they had to attribute to the intellect and imagination (which are subjects of the intelligible species) a extraordinary power over bodies. This power was not only over one's own body but over distant, foreign bodies which, although not actually perceived, were present through their phantasms. The Arabic school never gave up this absurdity. Such is the force of idolised false principle!

284. Avicenna,[133] for example, stated that the human soul could, with a strong imagination, alter both its own and foreign bodies, making them ill or healthy; it could produce hail, snow or wind, extract unusual powers from the stars, unhorse distant riders and hound them into the ground; it could grow plants without seed or generate human beings without use of the

---

[133] *Sen.*, 2, bk. 1; *Doct.*, 2. c. 14; *Natural.*, 4, 7; *Metaph.*, c. 6 & 9.

generative organs! The same prodigies were attributed to the Moorish philosopher, Avicembron, and to Al-Gazzali.[134]

285. The Platonists, taking another road, made the same extraordinary errors. They confused what is *real* with what is *ideal*, that is, they made ideas subsistences. Other philosophers mixed Platonism with Aristotelianism.[135] According to them, the intelligible species and phantasms worked marvels. This explains the prodigies of Apollonius of Tyana, and so many other marvels narrated by historians, a part of which were probably illusions resulting from induced sleepwalking.

CHAPTER 6

Descartes' teaching that thinking is essential to the human being

286. Here we can also say something in favour of Descartes. When he said, 'I think, therefore I am', he glimpsed a truth. The human soul in fact always thinks, because it has an immanent perception. Descartes deduced that the soul had always to think because the concept of human being is rooted in thinking, or rather, because thought is present in the concept of the human being. He should have spoken 1. about immanent thought, not transient acts of thought; these would prove only the existence of a subject who was as transient as the acts themselves; 2. about human thought, the kind that characterises humans and could not be the intuition of being, cut off from any nexus with the body; 3. about thought proper to the human subject, composed of soul and body. Immanent thought of this kind is simply the primal perception, the root of the nexus between the rational

---

[134] Al-Gazzali, *Phys.*, bk. 5, c. 9.

[135] Cf. Marsilio Ficino, *Theol. Plat.*, bk. 3, c. 1; Andrea Cattaneo da Imola, *Lib. 1 de intellectu et de causis mirabilium effectuum;* Pomponazzi, *L. de incantat.*; Paracelsus, *L. de signat. rerum*; Agrippa, *L. de occ. philos.*; Giacomo da Forlí, *Tech., 3, q. 11;* Coelius Rhodiginus [Ludovico Ricchieri of Rovigo], bk. 20, c. 15. — A rich source of learning in this matter can be found in *Prefazione storica* at the start of *Fatti relativi al mesmerismo e cure memeriche* by Drs. Cogevina and Orioli, Corfú, 1842.

soul and the body. He sensed the truth therefore but did not grasp it, nor find the words to explain it.

287. Hence, when Romagnosi and others substituted Descartes' reasoning with 'I feel, therefore I am', they did not understand the possible force of their formula. Indeed 'I feel, therefore I am' does not in any way prove the existence of the human being; at most, it proves the existence of a sensitive being. To prove the existence of the human being we must have recourse to an act proper to a being composed of intelligence and animality, that is, to an act of the rational principle. Existence of such a being requires proof that his essence is subsistent, which means recourse to immanent thought because essence does not change. Explained in this way, Descartes' statement acquires light, and his reasoning, force; it proves that the essence of the human being lies in an immanent act of thought, but does not say which thought! It certainly cannot be any kind of thought; it must be the kind I described and called primal, natural perception.

CHAPTER 7

The activity and passivity of the soul relative to the body to which it is united

Article 1
The relationship between formal and efficient cause

288. I have spoken about the nature of the rational soul as *formal cause* of the human being. I will now explain how the rational soul is the *efficient cause* of human actions. *Formal cause* posits and maintains an ens in being; *efficient cause* makes it act. The rational soul therefore, as formal cause, posits and maintains the human being in being; as efficient cause, it makes him act.

289. It is clear that the reason for the action of an ens must be sought in its form; form gives being, and everything acts according to its being, as the ancient saying states.[136] St. Thomas

---

[136] *Anima enim est forma, forma autem est principium agendi, non*

shows that the soul is the form of the composite, precisely because it is the proximate principle of all the composite's actions: *Quo aliquid est actu, eo agit* [A thing acts in so far as it is in act].

> Every thing acts with that which makes it what it is. The first thing by which the body lives is clearly the soul. Now, life reveals itself through various actions at different levels of living beings, and the first thing of all with which we do each of these vital actions is the soul. The soul is the first thing with which we feed ourselves, feel, move from place to place and likewise with which we understand. This principle therefore with which we first understand, whether we call it intellect or intellective soul (I call it *rational* soul), is the form of the body.[137]

290. Our task then is to find in the form of the human being the origin of the soul's actions and of the potencies to which the actions are reduced. However, I will discuss specification of the human potencies issuing from the form of the human being in the second part which deals with the development of the soul. Here, I simply have to complete the reasoning already begun concerning the nexus between soul and body. To do this I will first explain how the soul is united to the body as form of the body — this posits the composite human subject in being — and then explain the *commerce between the soul and the body*, that is, how the soul is the sole cause of all the movements the human being produces in his body.

Article 2
How the nexus between soul and body by means
of the primal perception explains the activity and passivity of
the rational soul relative to the body it informs

291. We have seen that the soul is united to the body not by

materia. Forma enim est actus et dat esse: OPERARI AUTEM REQUIRITUR ESSE [The soul is form. Form, not matter, is the principle of action. It is act and imparts being: BEING IS REQUIRED FOR ACTION], T. Fyens, *De viribus imaginationis*, q. 1.

[137] *S.T.*, I, q. 76, art. 1.

means of phantasms or intelligible species (these are not acts of the soul), but by a constant, total and fundamental perception of the fundamental feeling. Let us now see how this principle, as our starting point, helps to explain both the action of the rational soul on the body it informs and its passivity.

Perception of a substantial feeling means identification between what is real (a feeling) and the essence of being (intuited by the intellect). It is an act of the rational soul with which the soul apprehends reality in relationship with idea. In short, it is a perception of the ens itself under two forms simultaneously. The *ens* is identical under the ideal and the real forms; its mode alone varies. Only one potency therefore is necessary to perceive it; this potency is the rational principle, in which the unity of the human subject is located. Thus, the rational principle attains the ens under two forms, because it is the *faculty of ens* and consequently of ens under all the forms in which ens communicates itself. The rational principle cannot apprehend a feeling and nothing more, because feeling pure and simple cannot manifest *ens*, which is the proper object of reason. Feeling however, united to being (intuited by the mind), acquires the nature of ens, or certainly reveals itself as such, and thus becomes the proper object of reason.[138] *Feeling* must therefore be considered in two modes: either pure and simple, in which case it is outside the rational order and must be attributed to another potency or principle, the irrational sentient principle, or be considered united to the essence of being, and be in this essence by means of rational perception. United in this way to being, it has become ens for us and entered the rational order; it now pertains to reason.[139] There

---

[138] The animal-fundamental feeling and its modifications never become object of the rational principle through a *similitude* (that is, through the *intelligible species*), as the Scholastics taught. But the rational principle itself perceives real feeling united to ideal being.

[139] Although Aristotle saw this union, he did not see that it was operative solely in *perception*. This opened the way to the error proper to the Arabs. In fact, Aristotle wrote that *species intellecta calidi et frigidi talis existit qualis et rerum unaquaeque* [the intellectual species of what is heat and cold exists exactly as the things themselves] (*De motu animal.*, c. 6). He did not see that this is the case only in *perception*. He also wrote that *scientia quae est actu est idem quod res* [knowledge in act is the same as the thing] (*De Anim.*,

is definitely feeling in the rational order, but only on condition that feeling has become an ens, that is, is identified with the essence of ens seen in the idea.

292. We have found the mode and condition by which the fundamental feeling enters the rational principle as its subject. We can now explain how this principle is able to act in and passively undergo action from the body.

The rational principle is certainly endowed with activity. We must presuppose this, or rather believe it from undoubted experience. The difficulty lies in explaining how the object on which the principle's activity is exercised can be presented to the principle, which can act only on its own object. Once we have found the mode in which the animal feeling can be received in the rational principle, our greatest difficulty is overcome. This mode can be only in the *perception* of a substantial feeling. Every other nexus would be neither a *rational* nor a true physical bond, nor would it explain the real connection of the body with a rational soul. Note that perception is a real physical conjunction of the perceiver with what is perceived. The Scholastics' dictum applies here: *ex intellectu et intelligibili fit unum* [a single thing is formed from the intellect and the intelligible], which, reduced to an exact statement, becomes: *ex percipiente et percepto fit unum* [a single thing is formed out of the perceiver and what is perceived].

293. Although this contact of the two substances, called *contactus virtutis* [contact through power] by St. Thomas, differs naturally from the contact of bodies, it gives rise to a kind of continuation between the two substances, placing one within the other, that is, within the sphere of action of the other. For example, when I use my hand to lift a body and place it elsewhere, the body adheres to my hand and becomes a kind of continuation of it, with the result that my hand's movement is communicated to the body. The same happens in the primal fundamental perception relative to the substantial feeling.

bk. 3, c. 5); elsewhere he says that 'the intellect becomes intelligible by understanding'. Although he says this happens by means of similitude, he has no hesitation in adding that *species habent rerum virtutes* [species have the energies of things] (*De motu animalium*, c. 6) [701, 20–22], thereby always confusing *species* with *actual perception*. The error of the Arabs has its root in a truth unnoticed by Aristotle.

294. Let us now consider how this fundamental perception can explain the action of the rational soul on the body and vice versa.

The object of the perception we are discussing is the animal-fundamental feeling. This feeling has a *principle* (the sentient element) and a *term* (that which is felt). The term (the felt) is the subjective body; the sentient element is the principle on whose activity, when posited in being, the felt depends. The sentient element is active, the felt passive. In brute animals the principle producing the spontaneous modifications and changes in their bodies is the sentient element, which in animals is called sensitive soul.

If, therefore, by means of the perception under discussion, the rational human soul is really united with all the animal feeling, it is united with the sentient element as well as the felt, the two elements from which that feeling results.

295. But the sentient element has an active nature. If then the rational soul can exercise its activity on the sentient element without in way altering the nature of this element, it can begin to act on the felt precisely because it can act on the sentient element.

296. On the other hand, the felt by its nature has to be passive relative to the sentient element which places it in act as felt. In this case, because the rational soul can perceive the felt only as a passive term of the sentient element, it must receive it exactly as it is in itself and modify it only by moving the sentient element.

297. The fact that the rational soul is unable to modify the felt directly means that it can only apprehend the felt. This explains why the rational soul, when receiving feelings and all sense-experiences, shows itself passive, although it is not really so: sense-experiences can only be apprehended by the rational principle, not directly modified by it because they are passive relative to the sentient principle, and their nature consists in this passivity.

298. We conclude: the activity of the soul on its body and the passivity demonstrated by the soul relative to the body are explained *by means of the perception of the fundamental feeling*. This gives us the very important, simple formula: 'The rational soul is as active on its own body as it is active on the sensitive principle,' nothing more.

[294–298]

Article 3
The activity of the rational soul on the extrasubjective body

299. I have shown how the rational soul united to the subject-ive body can be active relative to the latter. From this we easily see how the soul can also be active relative to the extrasubjective body and produce in it the movements perceived extra-subjectively. Relative to this, we need only recall what was said in the *Anthropology* about the relationship between the two bodies and about the two series of phenomena presented by these bodies.

The two bodies are simply one single body perceived differ-ently. I have amply demonstrated their identity.[140]

300. I said there that I did not consider extrasubjective phenomena as effects of subjective phenomena, but solely as a parallel, harmonious series. This was sufficient for our discus-sion at the time, without further investigations. But although subjective phenomena are definitely not the cause of extra-subjective phenomena, the two series have a proximate cause in the sentient principle and a remote cause in the activity of the soul. Furthermore, the extrasubjective phenomena are partly the result of the body's relationships with the five special organs of exterior sensitivity.[141]

Article 4
Can the rational soul cause animal movements harmful
to the animal?

301. Ancient thinkers called the natural, radical activity of an ens *nature*, which, according to them, always tends to preserve and perfect itself, never to change and destroy itself.

302. The noble philosopher of Antwerp, Thomas Fyens, begins his discussion from this principle and shows that the soul

---

[140] *NE*, vol. 2, 842; *AMS*, 197–229.
[141] *AMS*, 227–228.

cannot directly move itself in a way harmful to itself: 'The soul is a nature. Nature is certainly a principle of movement in natural things but only of movement that fits nature, not of every movement. It is not therefore an active principle of change.'[142] Hence, the soul cannot change its own body.

Hippocrates founded medicine on this principle, that is, on the energy of nature which always tends to heal, not to harm: Νούσων φύσιες ίητροι.

303. This teaching seems to some extent contrary to what I said in the *Anthropology* where I distinguished *healing forces* from *disruptive forces* in the human being.[143] Note however that *disruptive forces* do not pertain solely to *animal nature* but to other causes acting in and disrupting this nature.

304. Human beings are not solely animal: they have intelligence, which takes them far beyond the sphere of animality and can itself cause changes in disordered animality.

305. Furthermore, because human beings are free, they have the power to misdirect themselves and thus harm their animality, and even destroy it. Free nature withdraws from the above-mentioned law according to which it is the principle of only preservative, useful movements. This law is valid solely for natures which act from necessity, not for those that act freely.

CHAPTER 8

Can the pure intellect act effectively on the body?

306. We have discovered the root and general source of all the different effects produced in the body by the acts of the rational soul. We found it in the immanent perception of the whole of the fundamental feeling which the human being has by nature, a perception which stably unites the rational soul with the body and makes them one single subject.

This is also the key which opens the secret of the mysterious efficacy of the partial, transient, second acts of the soul on the

---

[142] *De viribus imaginationis*, q. 6.
[143] *AMS*, 401–414.

body. We will not be wasting time if we discuss this, keeping to the facts given by experience.

307. I begin with a comment about the question, 'Does the pure intellect have any power over the body?'

The pure intellect differs from the rational principle in two ways: the rational principle is called 1. *intellect* in so far as it *intuits* ideal being, which exceeds every finite reality, and 2. *rational principle* in so far as it *perceives* some reality and consequently reasons.

We ask therefore whether the intellective principle can act effectively on the body, independently of acts of perception and reasoning.

308. It is easy to see that the intellective principle cannot exercise any action on the body directly, because its concept excludes all such communication. It is called intellect in so far as its object exceeds every finite reality given to its perception.

309. Nevertheless, the intuition of being also informs souls which are rational and in communication with the body. In this case, we can fittingly suppose, the intuition acts so that these souls are differently disposed from the state of souls without the intuition. And because the soul, as we shall see, governs the organisation, it seems certain that an intellective soul does not organise the body in the same way as a purely sensitive soul; it makes the body suitable for itself, acting always as form of the rational principle. The intellective principle has a perfect unity with the rational principle. It must therefore be capable of producing unity and harmony in the object of its perception and in the body included in this object.

310. Moreover, the intellect contributes to all those modifications of the rational principle, and consequently of the body, which are caused by cognitions and affections whose objects are things beyond the sensible, animal sphere.[144] Cognitions and affections of this kind contribute very powerfully to good and ill in the body. This is so true that suicide itself, which happens only in human beings, not in animals, must be attributed to this potency which exceeds animality. But because the *proximate*

---

[144] St. Augustine says: *Arbitror enim omnem motum animi aliquid facere in corpore* [I consider that every movement of the spirit does something in the body] (*Ep.*, 9).

cause of all these effects is ultimately the rational principle, I must now speak about it.

CHAPTER 9
The efficacy of the acts of the rational principle on the body

Article 1
General extension of this efficacy

311. The first question is: 'How great is the power of the rational principle over the body?'

312. I reply that the rational principle, which communicates directly with the sentient principle, has *per se* absolute power to produce in the body it informs all those movements which the feeling principle itself produces in the body.

I say *absolute power* because it is one thing for the rational principle to be able to produce these movements, considering its nature and its nexus with the sentient principle; it is another for it to produce them constantly without regard to circumstances.

313. Certainly, the power of the rational principle to move the different parts of the body cannot be activated unless certain conditions, about which I will speak later, are verified. In their absence, the rational soul is apparently powerless to cause such movements, or encounters different degrees of difficulty in accomplishing them.

Article 2
Efficacy of the special acts of the rational principle

314. I now wish to examine the efficacy exercised over the body by the rational principle with its special acts. I shall maintain that it changes the body through two kinds of activity: *intelligence* and *will*.

§1. *How the body is changed by the rational principle through acts of intelligence*

A

Perceptions, and an explanation of their spontaneity

315. The first act of the rational principle is special perception, which immediately presents an extraordinary fact. As soon as our senses are struck by some corporeal stimulus, the rational principle is moved to execute the act of perception. What is the origin of this immediate spontaneity of movement?

316. If the impression moved only the sense, the rational principle would not know that it had a sensation or a body to perceive, and consequently could not move itself to perceive it.

This fact becomes very clear when we consider the fundamental perception. If it is true that the rational soul, by means of a law of its nature, perceives continually the whole animal feeling, it is clear that it must also perceive both the changes which occur violently in the feeling and the force producing these changes, that is, the stimulating body.

317. There is also the other question: 'In perception, does the soul exercise some activity on the body?'

Let us first consider sensitive perception in brute animals, and then rational perception.

Sense-perception takes place naturally and spontaneously, as I have explained elsewhere. The fundamental feeling necessarily feels its own modifications.[145] Initially, when the animal is not yet developed, this action follows the same law of spontaneity by which the sense-principle pervades what is felt.[146]

Next, the sensitive principle acquires a habit which increases its activity. It does this in virtue of the same law of spontaneity, immersing itself more, as it were, into what it finds pleasant, and refusing to co-operate with what is painful.

We have seen that the level of intensity and activity of the sentient principle can vary in sensitive perception.[147] Nevertheless, this greater intensity of certain feelings produced by the

---

[145] *NE*, vol. 2, 677–686.
[146] *AMS*, 375–386.
[147] *Ibid.*, 426–494.

activity of the instinctive, sentient principle[148] does not appear to be a direct effect of the principle. On the contrary, it seems to be an effect obtained through intimate movements produced by the principle in the sensory organ, that is, through an action on the body.

318. In the case of the rational principle, we have seen that it has as much power over the body as the instinctive-sentient principle, which it perceives and controls (cf. 311). We shall have to say therefore that in perception the rational principle can modify the sensory organ by moving the sensitive principle to accept a more intense perception.

319. Furthermore, the rational principle perceives more intensely and distinctly when it increases its *rational attention*. This attention, which may not heighten the intensity of the perception as sensitive, does heighten it as rational. Even the different degrees of intensity in the attention of the intelligent spirit can probably produce certain minimum movements in the body for the reason given above (cf. 309).

B
Imagination

320. Images are internal sense-experiences reproduced from external sense-experiences.

Generally speaking, they receive from memory, or the faculty which retains previously experienced sensations, the aptitude to indicate an external body whose sensible picture, as it were, we seem to see in them.

Why is the arousal of our perception of external bodies restricted for the most part solely to sensations and not to phantasms, unless the latter are aided by the memory of sensations?

321. The aptitude of sense-experiences rather than phantasms to make us perceive external bodies is due to their two characteristics:

1. In sense-experiences we perceive a foreign body which violently stimulates and alters the external part of our sensory

---

[148] In *AMS* [371], I showed how instinct is simply the activity of the sentient principle.

organ. Images do not do this; they are not stimulated by any foreign body, but by internal stimuli and movements of our body. The stimuli and movements therefore are either felt subjectively, or not felt with the same constancy as external stimuli.

2. Granted the number of our different organs, many different sense-experiences can be repeated; we can experience the same foreign body through our various organs as often as we like. We thus recognise in our body a constant power to produce sensations; this power gives us the concept of a permanent corporeal substance. But these experiences are not present in phantasms.[149]

322. Nevertheless, when external sense-experiences have given us concepts of bodies, phantasms easily re-present these concepts to us as if they were the sense-experiences themselves renewed internally. We readily unite to them the concept of the body previously formed through the external experience.

323. However, we still need to explain how we acquire this inclination for adding the idea to the phantasm. For example, we add the idea of a stone to the phantasm of a stone, knowing that the stone whose phantasm we have is neither present nor perceptible. How do we explain this natural, spontaneous association between phantasms and corresponding ideas?[150]

324. The basic reason was given when I explained the spontaneity of the perceptions of external bodies (cf. 309). The rational principle, united to our animal-fundamental feeling through a natural, continuous perception, is always actuated to perceive intellectively every change it undergoes. However, perception of this change, which takes place in the fundamental feeling, is not sufficient in itself to explain how the idea of an external body is added to the change. The addition is explained by the *association* of the phantasms with the corresponding external sense-experiences and with the idea of the body formed through these experiences. This association becomes habitual and always ready to act. Thus, we must not presume that babies think of a body, for example, every time a phantasm is aroused in them; they have not yet formed ideas of external bodies nor associated phantasms with the ideas.

[149] *NE*, vol. 2, 876–877.
[150] *NE*, vol. 2, 519–520.

C
Memories

325. The rational principle is clearly more *active* on the body through the function by which it activates and composes *positive cognitions* habitually stored in it. *Positive cognitions* result from the two elements of *idea* and *feeling*, or the vestiges of feeling. In order to recall these cognitions to its attention, the rational soul must exercise an action on the *corporeal feeling*. If we suppose that this feeling pertains to phantasms, the soul can exert its power to arouse them, but must also renew the movement of the cerebral organ.[151]

326. Certain physiologists, who know very little about psychology, do not hesitate to call the brain 'organ of thought'. The truth however is that pure thought has no organ; the brain is simply the organ of *corporeal imagination*. Their error is caused by the soul's readiness to associate *idea* with *image*.

327. The re-memorising and composing of positive information is accomplished by the varying re-stimulation of the images. The movements in the nerves of the brain correspond, in the extrasubjective order, to this re-stimulation.

The power needed by the rational principle to arouse images, compose them into various groups and heighten their vividness (which depends on the strength of the intellective concept and on the feelings and passions moving the understanding) is well known and discussed by many authors. The thought of what is conceived as good conjures up joyful, bright images; what is conceived as evil, conjures up sad, frightening images. The former can induce great joy; the latter, extreme sadness.

328. The reason why we clothe our ideas with images analogous to our ideas is exactly the same as the reason why images arouse thoughts in our intelligence; in other words, it lies, as we said, in our association of images with sensations and of sensations with ideas. The image replaces the sensation to which the intellective perception of the external body is naturally united, and the positive idea is included in the intellective perception.

---

[151] *AMS*, 350–354.

As intellective-feeling beings, our thought is necessarily composed of *intuition* and *sense-experience*, and is incomplete unless it results from both these elements. This function, by which the concept calls up the image, and the image the concept, I call *human-synthetical force*.

All these facts are very easily explained by means of the fundamental perception.

D
Rational feelings

329. The objects we perceive cause feelings in us which are joyful if the object is perceived as good, or sad if perceived as bad. They are called *rational feelings* (or *intellectual*, if caused by the intuition of pure concepts) in contradistinction to *animal feelings* which, to exist, require only sense and instinct, but not the use of reason.

With internal observation as our guide once more, let us see what kind of activity rational feelings have in changing the subjective body and thus producing extrasubjective movements.

First of all, the object of the information that moves feeling can differ from the subject, but also be the subject itself when contemplated as object. These two classes of rational feelings can be called *objective* and *subjective-objective*.

330. Purely objective feeling arises in the rational subject whenever the subject apprehends any entity whatsoever, because every apprehended entity is a source of joy — this explains the saying of the Scholastics that ens and good are interchangeable.[152] The feeling therefore naturally increases in proportion to the entity, which, when the greatest, produces the greatest mental enjoyment.

331. Subjective-objective feeling arises whenever the subject perceives something that is good or bad for itself. We need to define what is good and bad for a subject, and strictly speaking for the human subject. In general, for the human subject, good is a pleasant state or action, and evil, a painful state or action.

---

[152] *The Essence of Right*, 108–112.

[329–331]

Pleasure and pain (I use these words in their widest sense) pertain to feeling. Hence, good and bad for a human subject are respectively pleasant and painful feelings. Among the pleasant and painful feelings of a rational subject, some are intellectual, such as those which arise, as we said, from every object of the mind; others are animal; many are a mixture of both. When the rational principle perceives some good proper to it, a feeling of rational joy is immediately produced; when it perceives some evil proper to it, a feeling of sadness (also rational) is produced. Furthermore, a subjective-objective feeling of joy and sadness arises in human beings not simply when they intellectively perceive something good or bad for themselves, but also when they perceive something with the power to cause, or to increase or diminish, this good or evil. Hence, a subjective-objective feeling is that which arises in the human being as a result of the information about his own good and evil, or of the cause of these.

332. We see therefore that subjective-objective feelings follow upon the *orders of reflection* so that the orders of subjective-objective feelings (pleasant or painful) correspond to the orders, indefinite in number, of reflection possible to a human being. Thus, after I have enjoyed the contemplation of an ens, I can, by reflecting upon myself, take pleasure in my enjoyment. If I then reflect upon this pleasure, it can itself be the cause of delight and satisfaction. I can say the same about this satisfaction, and so on *ad infinitum*.

333. All these objective or subjective-objective rational feelings can be considered in two ways, either apart from any possible influence of the will upon them, or as modified by the action of the will.

334. Considered in themselves apart from the influence of the will, they obey some necessary laws rooted in the nature of the object and subject, and can be reduced to the following.

The law governing *purely objective feelings* makes them as great as the contemplated ens which produces them. They constitute the universal, human faculty of *loving objectively*: by nature, we love every being, major entia more, minor entia less.

335. The laws governing *subjective-objective feelings* are more complex. These feelings originate from the good and bad we perceive rationally in ourselves or from their causes. This

good or bad in the human subject results from many elements: 1. from what is good and bad for the animal (animal feelings), 2. from intellectual good and evil (objective feelings and subjective-objective feelings), and 3. from moral good and evil.

The rational principle perceives all these kinds of good and evil, whose fusion produces the complex good and evil we rejoice in or suffer from.

The perfection of the perception of this complex good or evil (the perception is also itself a kind of fusion of many perceptions) depends on more or less perfect nature in human beings, and the extent to which they have reached perfection. It would take too long to describe how the perfection of this perception of the three kinds of subjective good and evil depends on the perfection of human nature in itself or the development of this perfection by means of its physical, intellectual and moral progress. I will omit such a long investigation and reduce to a single general formula the laws governing the natural formation of subjective-objective feelings: 'The human being receives joyful or sad feelings in proportion to the natural perception of what is good or bad for him. The degree of rectitude of this perception will depend on the degree to which intellectual light and moral feeling prevail over animal feeling or vice versa. The perception can also vary in vividness and efficacy.'

336. Granted this, let us see how the *rational principle*, with *its own* different *feelings*, influences *animal feeling* and, by means of this, produces certain *movements* in the body.

Rational feelings always proceed from some intellection. The intellections of the human mind can primarily be so cut off from space and time that they are immune from every corporeal image; they do not need to be formed by any corporal organ. At least the idea of being in general is an intellection of this kind. But can such a pure, immaterial thought cause feelings?

337. Let us distinguish the various accidents pertaining to this kind of thought.

First accident: the object of some thought is in itself pure from every corporeal image, but human beings, who tend naturally and habitually to represent everything by images, very easily associate with the act of thought another act with which they arouse in themselves images of varying refinement and subtlety. These images clothe the object and make it appear, they think, more intense, although in fact they falsify it. This role of the imagination has to be rejected because our question concerns a pure idea.

338. The second accident: human beings are multiple subjects, that is, principles of many faculties; they never (or with very great difficulty) move one faculty alone. When thinking reflectively of the object of intuition and not simply intuiting, they cannot move their reflection without activating some other faculty. I do not doubt therefore that the effort to contemplate a pure idea and, still more, the effort to silence every other activity within us, sets in motion the very powers we wish to subdue. We cannot turn again to a pure idea without some activity of the brain nerves; the brain must play a part because its modification follows upon that of the mind as an automatic sequel of the mind's action. We must also reject from our calculation the action of other faculties which *per accidens* accompany the pure act of the mind, because our question concerns only some sensed effect of a pure idea.

339. Ignoring every image-involvement and every consequent movement connected with it, I believe therefore that a pure idea causes a *merely objective* intellectual feeling of pleasure, and that the degree of this feeling corresponds to the degree of perfection and vividness of the intuition.

But does this feeling, foreign to the order of corporeal things, influence the animal feeling, and by means of this, cause movements in the body?

It is certain that this feeling pertains to some nature of totally immaterial things. We must however keep in mind the *identity* of the human subject, who is simultaneously principle of spiritual and corporeal feelings. When the spiritual affections of this subject modify his state, making him more perfect or imperfect, more or less happy, they necessarily produce some effects and modifications, even if indiscernible, in the animal life of which he is the principle. Indeed, experience shows that the human soul, when affected to any degree by a spiritual joy, becomes more active relative to the body, quickening the blood's circulation; sadness has the opposite effect.

340. If we consider the subjective effect, that is, the good and bad state of the soul, whatever its cause, we easily understand that it differs not in species but in degree, although the causes

responsible for joyful or sad states can vary specifically, generically and even categorically. Because the soul is simple, its manner of being, its state is simple. Although it has only one natural perfection, this perfection admits of indefinite degrees. This perfection is its happiness. The strength of the soul corresponds to the degree of its perfection and happiness, and as vital principle exercises on the body an energy proportionate to its perfection. Objective feelings are joyful in proportion to their perfection, and make the soul happier and more active.

341. It seems in fact that actual joy, when it passes a certain limit, can produce movements forceful and sudden enough to disorder the body and cause death. This phenomenon of the sensuous instinct however is not proper to human nature; on the contrary, its origin is in decadent nature, where weakened reason can no longer dominate the affections, which in this case are always man-made and unnatural.

342. What has been said about purely objective feelings applies to subjective-objective feelings. The latter modify animal feelings more closely than purely objective feelings. Objective feelings can modify animal feelings only by subjectivising themselves in such a way that they move the body by communicating their action, which they do by three links, as it were, or series of causes and effects: 1. objective feelings, 2. subjective-objective feelings, 3. animal feelings, 4. extrasubjective movements.

§2. *How the body is changed by the rational principle through acts of the will*

343. The rational feelings we are discussing are sometimes willed, sometimes unwilled. Unwilled feelings in the rational subject are those arising without the will's command; willed feelings, those arising through the will's direct or indirect command.

344. Can the will modify feelings which of their nature are unwilled? Only some, and with a limited action, as I have explained in *Anthropology*.

345. The action of the human will cannot alter the universal

feeling through which human beings tend to good. This feeling is natural, unwilled and superior to the will, which originates from it.

346. The universal feeling through which we tend to good, to every good, gives rise naturally to all objective feelings. These, according to the law governing them, are so proportioned to the greatness of the conceived ens that their natural gradation is the natural gradation of the entia. Ordered and graded in this way, they are natural and unwilled, that is, they naturally originate in us without an act of will. Indeed, we might prefer to say that they themselves initiate spontaneous, consenting acts of the will. The will, however, can influence them by altering their order; it can, by opposing nature and truth, increase the value of some, diminish the value of others. It does this with acts, particularly repeated acts, which leave traces and attitudes in the soul, generating arbitrary opinions, prejudicial habits, and habitual, immoral judgments and affections.

With its energy and free feelings, the will can also preserve the order of these objective feelings, and increase and enjoy their intensity.

347. Unwilled natural feelings of intelligent human nature[153] become *willed* in the measure that the will alters and increases them.

348. The will also acts swiftly in the body in another way, with such imperiousness that no feeling at all seems involved between its command and the corporeal movement. For example, if I want to move my arm I do so simply by an act of my will, and am unaware of experiencing any enjoyable or painful affection, any pleasant or unpleasant feeling.

349. Nevertheless, careful consideration shows that, in moving a member of the body, the command of the will does not communicate the movement without the intervention of some feeling, a feeling which differs from that of affections and passions. I have already distinguished animal feelings into shaped and unshaped feelings,[154] and the shaped feelings into external

---

[153] The matter of rational feelings can be animal feelings and animal good, which can both stimulate intellectual feelings whenever the understanding perceives them and JUDGES them as a good.

[154] *AMS*, 135–229.

feeling-experiences (sensations) and internal feeling-experiences (images). The will commands movement mostly by means of images; the proximate principle of the movement is the image of the movement that the will wishes to produce or of the final position the animal wishes to assume.[155]

350. I say *mostly* because I am speaking about human beings in a developed state where they freely act and command their movements through the image possessed by the extrasubjective forms of these movements. In undeveloped human beings the will can produce movement only with the internal feeling of their own activity and of movements subjectively felt beforehand, provided the feeling of these movements is pleasant or springs from needs. In this case, although we move our limbs with an act of our will, we do not know the extrasubjective form of the movement we produce; we do not have present the extrasubjective effect of our internal acts and consequently *do not will it*; the act of our will terminates directly in subjective, internal space. We neither choose nor command one extrasubjective movement from among many. The movement results from its relationship with the interior activity whose purpose was to improve the state of feeling.

CHAPTER 10

The conditions necessary for the rational principle if it is to produce the movements it wishes in its own body

351. The rational principle changes and causes movements in its own body by acting as *intelligence* and *will*. But it has *dominion* over its body solely through the action of its *will*.

352. The will's action, and hence its exercise of dominion over

---

[155] The animal movement which is small at the place of the image and then communicated to the limbs is not felt in any distinct way. Only the resulting large movement is felt because its production causes displacement of parts in the mode of extrasubjective bodies. Internal, subjective movements are often indistinct for the reason I have given elsewhere. Moreover, it cannot be denied that exertion and effort are felt, at least when they are notable.

the body, is subject to certain conditions, which we must now investigate.

We said that movement of the body can be produced by the will in two ways: with or without knowledge of the effect of what it commands (cf. 343–347), that is, without knowledge of the effect of the extrasubjective movement as it appears to the external senses in its relationships to the other parts of the body.

Whenever, for example, a baby wishes to move its hands, it does so either by instinct or by command of its will. But the will commanding the movement is ignorant of the harm the movement will do when a finger is poked in the baby's eyes. The baby knows neither the relative extrasubjective position of its hands and eyes, nor the external effect of the internal act with which it initiates the movement.

Suppose someone has never seen himself, nor made any movement whatsoever. With his will he decides to move a part of his body for the first time. He knows the part only internally and subjectively; the choice of the movement is totally internal. No external movement is chosen precisely because he knows none. Nevertheless his internal choice results in an external movement, which for him is something new and extraordinary, the revelation of a mystery.

353. When he carries out the internal act causing the movement, he neither foresees the external effect nor knows the relationship between the part he moves and the other parts of his body; the subjective and extrasubjective phenomena differ so much from each other that one cannot be argued from the other without prior experience. The extrasubjective phenomena of the movement are not known *a priori* but only through the experience of his external sense organs to which the phenomena pertain. Nor can he deduce the phenomena from the fundamental feeling or its internal, purely subjective modifications. Hence, as long as he does not experience the extrasubjective phenomena of his body movements, they remain unknown, and he cannot choose one in preference to the other or even will them in any way.

354. The first condition therefore making it possible for the will to exercise its locomotive power by commanding extrasubjective movements is the knowledge obtained through actual experience.

355. But this condition is not enough. We also need to know the nexus between the external movements of the body (movements perceived by our external sense organs) and the commanded internal acts which produce them. We need to know that a given external movement corresponds to the internal act; for example, we need to know to which internal act a given movement of our hand or leg corresponds. These internal acts which command external, extrasubjective movements are *active feelings.* In our practical cognition therefore we have to unite these *active feelings with their consequent external movements.* Our internal movements, which vary in proportion to the subsequent external movements, must become the object of some *perception*, not of speculative cognition. This *practical* cognition is 'the association of perceptions we form from our active feelings with the extrasubjective movements consequent upon these feelings'.

356. The *practical cognition* of a certain system of actions, when it has become habitual, is an art. This *art* must be learnt if we are to activate our faculty of producing in our body the extrasubjective movements we desire. Until it is learnt, we cannot practise it although we have the faculty to do so. We need to learn how to hold ourselves erect and balanced, to walk and in short to make all external movements.

357. Not everybody is equally good at moving his body. Skilful dancers, instrument players, fencers and many others differ from the unskilled only because the latter have not acquired the habit of executing a certain order of bodily movements with precision and agility. The will (the first cause of these movements) does not choose individual movements but various groups of possible movements, groups which the will already knows in a practical way together with their nexus with the internal, subjective acts producing them. If a single internal act is sufficient to produce an entire group or order of movements, the act is called *habit* or art.

358. Nevertheless, all human beings learn to do certain bodily movements necessary for life or suggested by the various circumstances in which they find themselves.

Most people, however, put little importance on acquiring the art of producing with their will movements not needed for their existence and well-being, or even contrary to their well-being. Their will is not interested and lets the vital and sense instincts act in their own way. This does not mean that we lack the faculty to produce these movements with our will, but simply that we do not activate the faculty and develop habits. This is so true that sometimes we use our *freedom* to oppose our *spontaneous will* even capriciously, and demonstrate our power to halt or modify instinctive, spontaneous movements. For example, eyelid flicker is certainly instinctive, and helps to protect the eyes against dust and other particles in the air as well as to give rest to our sensory system. Here, the will allows the instinct to act. Some individuals have used their power of freedom to do the opposite, and have learned to keep their eyelids open for as long as they liked. Similarly, closing our eyes when an object comes towards them is an instinctive movement; so too is contraction of the pupils against intense light and their dilation in darkness. Certain individuals, like William Porterfield and Felice Fontana, have freely trained themselves to do the opposite.

359. Although some modern authors attribute the contraction of the pupil struck by intense light to the influence of the blood, it is impossible to explain the influence of mechanical excitation caused by light without having recourse to the vital, sensitive principle. The contraction is evidently explained by the irksome sensation of excessive light. The sensation is a subjective phenomenon pertaining to the *feeling* principle, which is forced by the irritation to initiate the movements of the iris. These contract the opening of the pupil where the light enters and thus lessen the sensation. Granted that the sensitive principle obtains this effect by initiating the flow of blood, the influence it exercises on the circulation in the tiny vessels is evident. On the other hand, the free will, by doing the opposite, can prevent the pupil's dilation or contraction, in which case it affects the circulation by its influence on the sensitive principle.[156]

[156] Porterfield must be counted among those who were fully aware that animal phenomena had to be attributed to the soul. His observations *on the internal movements of the eye* are found in *Esperienze ed osservazioni mediche d'Edimburgo*, vol. 4. But even this author, like other animists, confuses the volitive, intellective principle with the instinctive, sensitive principle. In fact, to show that animal movements are produced by the will,

360. Townshend's famous example confirms the will's power over the circulation of the blood. This Englishman, shortly before his death and while on his back, could evidently control at will the movement of his heart and pulse.[157] I suspect that if his body had been dissected some peculiarity would have been found at the juncture between cerebral and ganglionic nervous systems. Because both these nervous systems are always in continuity with each other, it seems that the will's influence on the circulation cannot be absent, although individual physiology in people can vary the circulation.

361. Sleep is also an animal phenomenon which must certainly be attributed to the *sensitive principle*, although the *will*'s influence through its dominion over the sensitive principle certainly cannot be excluded. On the other hand, the influence of the *intellectual feeling* is obviously apparent if we consider how mental exercise, particularly some fixed, passionate thought, prevents sleep, or how mental inertia helps sleep, as in babies, daydreamers and the indolent.

362. But no observer of nature will deny that the intellective principle acts during sleep, although the effective command of the will varies.

The will, by suspending the action and effect of the sensitive principle, can contribute with its energy to blocking the principle as it is about to cause sleep. The will can also stimulate the principle to produce sleep, particularly in people of great nervous mobility.

It is true that when we want to sleep, we relax our body and reduce the action of our will; we refrain from acting on our understanding or co-operating with and directing its action. Consequently the action of our mind, stimulated and directed

---

he advances Lister's observation that the heartbeat of the snail is WILLED (*De cocleis et limacibus*, Londini 1694, p. 38). The snail certainly has no will, but Lister's observation is important and efficacious in showing that the heartbeat depends on the animal *sensitive principle*. Only in the human being is this principle subordinate to the will, which rules and modifies the human subject with different degrees of dominion. Lister's observation however will be of use to us later.

[157] Cf. George Cheyne, *Sulla malattia inglese* (London, 1733), p. 40. This doctor, together with others, maintains that the cause of all animal phenomena must be referred to the soul.

by our will, particularly our free will, has a greater role in preventing sleep.

But to show that the will can in fact act positively to produce sleep, I have no hesitation in calling on the phenomena of artificial somnambulism which others rather rashly call animal magnetism.[158] Somnambulism is a special state of sleep. I myself knew a certain Ricamboni who slept at will and when called in the middle of his sleep began to walk. This at first seemed so extraordinary that I thought it was a trick. Later, however, after comparing this fact with other facts and considering all the circumstances, I stopped doubting and accepted its truth. I was also present at experiments made on a girl who had the faculty of *artificial somnambulism*. The person doing the experiments used not only so-called magnetic movements but any sign or arbitrary act to make her fall asleep. When I asked her if she could will herself to sleep without the gestures which the doctor made before her eyes, she said quite ingenuously 'Yes' and assured me that she fell asleep at will.

363. The will also exercises its power over the organs of secretion by influencing the peristaltic movement of the intestines. And we all know how highly excitable people, like women, weep or stop weeping at will.

364. To sum up, the intellective principle, to which the will pertains, has natural dominion over the sensitive principle, provided: 1. it knows by experience extrasubjective movements, if indeed these are to be the object of its volitions, and 2. it has come to know in a practical way the nexus between extrasubjective movements and the acts (active feelings) with which it must produce them, and over which it has acquired a habit.

[158] Cf. *La lettera del sonnambolismo artificiale* in the last volume of my works [*Apologetica*, Milan, 1840, p. 454].

CHAPTER 11

Propagation of the movement stimulated by the rational
principle and beginning in the body; the parts to which
it spreads

Article 1
Summary — Voluntary and involuntary nerves and muscles

365. From what has been said, we note:

1. The *rational principle* acts on the *sensitive-corporeal principle*.

2. It exercises this action in two ways: through the understanding or *intellective* sense and through the *will*.

3. Because the understanding is a passive and necessary power, and the will an active power, the intellective soul influences corporeal life in two ways, one *necessary* and one *willed*.

366. 4. It is no surprise therefore that physiologists distinguish two orders of nerves and muscles, voluntary and involuntary, and that the nerves are sometimes moved in two ways, voluntarily and involuntarily. In fact, I think it probable that all the nerves are subject to the power of the will,[159] although its control varies in proportion to our need to subject them to our will, and to their distance from the place (the brain) where our will directly operates by means of images, as we shall explain.[160]

---

[159] For example, Willis' accessory nerve produces instinctive movements, but when used to produce the movements necessary for the voice is clearly subject to the power of the will.

[160] In my opinion, simple psychological observation supplies us with arguments suitable for indicating the internal construction of our body. For example I can apply psychological observation to the question of voluntary and involuntary nerves by noting carefully what happens during convulsions. Convulsive movements certainly suppose a stimulus acting on the nerves, but the person subject to the convulsive movements does not feel the stimulus in any way. The movements arise in him suddenly, without his will and without his feeling their primal origin. We must say therefore: 1. certain nerves can be moved involuntarily; and 2. they give no sensation of the foreign cause or stimulus that moves them. This fact alone demonstrates that there are nerves which are either involuntary or can be moved by a cause

Article 2
Parts of the body where movements stimulated by the rational principle begin

367. We need to see where rational activity produces bodily movements directly. Is it in the nervous system alone or elsewhere as well, and does the nervous system itself communicate to other parts the movement it has received?

368. In the second case, the other parts of the body would not be connected to the soul but would simply be under its influence by means of genuinely animated nerves, which are the true seat of the soul. At the very least, the instinctive, sensitive principle would not be in those parts or connected to the rational soul.

369. To answer this question we must first distinguish between the soul's action on the body and the manifestation of this action through movements which can fall under our external senses and thus clearly reveal the action.

I have not always held the same opinion on the matter. My present opinion is that the rational soul probably acts in varying degree on all parts of the living body; the *fundamental feeling of continuity*, together with its *sentient principle*, is present in all parts. But either because a suitable organism is lacking or because of opposing forces, the feeling is not suited to direct *stimulation* by the soul in every part of the body. Consequently the *feeling of stimulation* is either totally absent or extremely weak and limited.

370. By *feeling of stimulation* I mean the organic movement suitable for producing a sense-experience.

371. This kind of feeling must be granted to the *fundamental feeling* itself, because in a living animal there is continuous movement (of physical continuity), which ceaselessly stimulates the feeling[161].

372. We can say therefore that where the *fundamental feeling*

foreign to the will. This second alternative seems to be nearer the truth because convulsive movements, when considered individually, can nearly always be carried out by an act of will. Voluntary movements are precisely those where the nerves do not feel a stimulus, as I discussed in paragraphs 346–348.

of stimulation is missing, that is, where parts are not susceptible to stimulation by internal, direct movements which produce feeling-experiences, sensitivity is apparently lacking. This seems to me to be the concept we must form of the parts of the human body which we called *insensible*.

373. According to our supposition, nerves are parts organated in such a way that they can admit the extension, frequency, rapidity and measure of the instinctive movements which generate sense-experience. Hence, although the fundamental feeling of continuity exists throughout the whole fabric of the human body, excitable sensitivity is absent in some parts. These are moved principally by the nerves on which the soul acts most effectively, that is, in pronounced muscular movements, rather than by the soul itself directly. This difference, I repeat, must evidently be attributed to the compact organisation of the body. When the intellective soul exercises its motor action equally on two parts of the body, one part moves incredibly quickly through internal movements, and produces stimulation of feeling or sense-experience; the other part is not susceptible to these wave motions, oscillations, etc. The first part consists of a fibre organated with its fluids to produce such mobility; the second part, which is not so suitably organated, either resists the impulse and causes it to terminate uselessly, or is moved while keeping the same texture in its smallest parts.

374. Granted this, we must say that the movements initiated by the intellectual principle and suitable for being known by us begin in the nerves and, following special laws, spread to the other parts of the human body.

375. But further investigation is still required to find the parts of the nervous system where movements produced by the intellectual principle begin.

The general answer is that they are determined by the nature of the special movements produced by the rational principle. But their general classification can be of two kinds, as follows.

[161] *AMS*, 318–322.

Article 3
Continuation — Location of movements stimulated by the rational instinct and by the will — The double nervous system

376. We have seen that the rational principle acts in two ways, as *instinct* and *will*. Two nervous systems, the *ganglionic* and the *cerebro-spinal*, correspond to these two ways in the human body. When the rational principle produces movements *by means of the instinct*, the ganglionic nervous system is directly affected, but when it produces movements *by means of the will*, its action is in the cerebro-spinal system. This needs to be explained.

377. The cerebro-spinal nervous system is the instrument of the feelings we have called *shaped* or *surface*, that is, *external sensations* and *images*. These feelings supply the *matter* for our knowledge of extrasubjective bodies and their accidents, but they are certainly not knowledge. Although, strictly speaking, they are simply *signs* of the presence of a body, they are not arbitrary because they contain the action of the body itself.

Feeling is ours, not the agent's, although the agent through its action exists in our feeling, that is, exists in the very same surface space where we feel. This identity of space between the active agent and our passive selves makes us attribute the modification of our feeling to the body as proximate and quasi-formal cause of the modification. In this way the agent, different from us, appears coloured, odorous, etc. The extreme precision of the edges presented by shaped feelings and the amazing differences of the edges provide us with an extraordinary impulse to accept them as qualities of bodies. They thus become *matter* for our knowledge of corporeal entia.

378. *Knowledge* always precedes the *action of the rational principle* because the latter acts only through knowledge. But the knowledge present when the rational principle acts as instinct is not the same as that present when it acts as will. Let us suppose that someone has had some unexpected bad news, the sudden death of a dear relative, for example. He certainly uses his cerebro-spinal nervous system in receiving the sensible signs of the news. Whether he received the information by word of mouth or by letter, the sensations of hearing or of sight would

have revealed the sad event to his mind. We can also suppose that the dear departed came to his mind through image-packed memories, although these are not necessary for causing the sudden sorrow. The purely intellectual thought itself, which at that moment hardly had time or will to recall images, is sufficient; it causes the immediate withdrawal of blood to the heart, shown by pallor, reduced pulse, trembling, spasms and even syncope and apoplexy. These effects were not commanded by the will; they did not come from images resident in the cerebro-spinal system; the sole task of the images was to inform the understanding of the event. They came from the information itself given to the understanding. This information did not need to affect the brain beforehand, but immediately communicated its action to the trisplanchnic nervous system which controls the circulation, secretions, passions, that is, unshaped feelings.[162]

379. But this is not the case when we consider movements produced by the intellective principle as will, not as instinct. Whether this principle's act of will is spontaneous or deliberate, 1. it decides to will a particular movement, 2. it decrees this movement and 3. produces it.

380. The intellective principle cannot form the volition or decree pertaining to a particular movement unless it *conceives* the movement. The conceived movement towards which the will's decree is borne as its object is virtually nothing more than an extrasubjective movement. Only this kind of movement is perceived with distinct, shaped feelings suitable for attracting attention and fixing intellectual perception. On the other hand, it is very difficult to say that the intellect perceives the movement by means of a *subjective, prior feeling*, because a prior feeling, which is the product of the soul's very own energy, is hardly distinct from the greater feeling pertaining to the total energy of the soul. Only when the total energy passes into act and produces the movement does it distinguish itself by acting and become special energy. If the will therefore produces movements without knowing them, it must produce them, it seems,

---

[162] The great sympathetic system is certainly not the organ of shaped feelings which pertain to the brain and the spinal chord. It is however the organ and seat of unshaped, diffused feelings.

with the kind of volitions I have called 'purely affective'.[163] But even here the will's participation would be united with the instinct only after the latter had begun the movement and thus rendered distinct the energy of the soul which produces the movement. This energy would be drawn out of the total energy in which it was immersed. Only on this condition can the intellect perceive the separate, limited energy suitable as an object of the will.

381. Leaving aside this extremely obscure mode of the will's action, I shall speak only about volitions whose object are extrasubjective movements which the understanding can distinctly know and perceive. Relative to these volitions, I said that the object of the will, that is, the movement which it decrees, is presented to the intellect by means of images evoked only in the brain, the organ of the imagination. The will desires and decrees to execute this simple or complex movement which it preconceives with the help of the imagination. We need not discuss here the way in which animal forces are usually involved in the determination and execution of this act.

382. The imagination, which pertains to the cerebral system, presents to the understanding the simple or complex movement on which the will deliberates. The will executes its choice with a decree which pertains not to the phantasy but to the intellective, spiritual order. The decree is a practical judgment by which the will agrees that the movement is good and to be carried out. This practical judgment is the start of the act which carries out the movement.

383. How is it carried out? The movements which the rational principle produces as a result of a decree of the will must be distinguished into two classes.

Some movements, but not others, are accompanied either by a sensible, animal pleasure or by the satisfaction of a need. They are desired for the pleasure attached to them or for the need they satisfy. The other class of movements, which lack that pleasure or satisfaction, are not desired in themselves but employed as a means to obtain some good which is properly speaking the object of the volition. For example, human beings have a speech-instinct; the child instinctively repeats the sounds

[163] *AMS*, 612–635.

it hears; similarly birds reproduce the song of their species, etc. The movements of the vocal chords satisfy the animal's need and instinct; it seeks pleasure, and escapes the discomfort it would suffer if the instinct were suppressed. On the other hand, when a human being buys a book, the movements performed to obtain it are not the pleasant object in which his will terminates; his aim is possession of the book and the knowledge he hopes to gain from it.

384. The rational principle however proceeds differently when it carries out movements of the first and second class. In the first class, pleasant sense-experience and movement are so united that the former is the proximate energy initiating and producing the movement. The intellective energy need only stimulate and aid the pleasant feeling produced instinctively by the movement.

On the other hand, movements unaccompanied by a pleasant sense-experience must be produced directly by intellective energy not only without the aid of sense-experience but in opposition to it. I can for example move an arm or leg by strength of free will, even though the movement may be accompanied by pain.

All this is confirmed by consciousness.

385. No wise, intelligent person will say that it is unreasonable for us to attempt to deduce some conclusions about animal organism from knowledge of such subjective facts. These conclusions, which cannot be confirmed as demonstrated truths except by the surgeon's knife and physiological thought, concern the famous question mentioned above, the distinction between motor and sensitive nerves. Movements accompanied by sensation and initiated by sensation itself begin, it seems, at the root of the sensitive nerves, which consequently would have the double property of feeling and motion.

On the other hand, the class of movements produced directly by the will's command and without any sense-experience (which is the proximate cause stimulating and producing them), are apparently activated by the motor nerves. These nerves have only the property of movement, not of special feeling. If they do have the property of feeling, it is manifested only on a condition different from the property of the first class. In this case, the rational principle which moves the nerves does not stimulate them to feeling, and the movement given them is not a sensiferous movement.

386. This last hypothesis seems to me most probable and totally in harmony with the special sensibility proper to the cerebro-spinal system. In fact the sensibility of this system in a normal state is revealed only at the two extremities, that is, the external extremities by means of sensations, and the internal extremities by means of images. Hence, no special, distinct feeling is revealed throughout the total length of the nervous filaments. If we suppose that the commanded movement devoid of sense-experience begins precisely where images reside which re-present the movement itself to the intelligence, we immediately see why the movement is communicated from the nerves to the muscles without any sense-experience whatsoever, that is, without a sense-experience which of itself seems to stimulate and produce the movement.

387. Here the difficulty will be raised as to how brute animals, which are totally lacking a rational principle, can produce movements of the second class.

I reply: by means of the *unitive force*. Animals associate in their imagination movements of the first class with those of the second class. The sensitive principle, stimulated instinctively to produce movements of the first class, also produces those of the second whenever these are necessary for the first, that is, whenever the animal must produce the second in order to procure the sensitive satisfaction it looks for in the first.

388. We can show by another excellent demonstration of the simplicity of the sensitive soul that the second class of movements depends on the cerebro-spinal system or some part of it, and that the first class begins either in the ganglionic system or other parts of the cerebro-spinal system itself. The sensitive soul, seeking to procure the pleasure and avoid the pain connected with the movements of certain nerves, imparts movement to other nerves whose roots differ from those of the first class. But to do this its activity must be contemporaneously present and active in different parts and places. This presupposes that the sensitive soul is immune from the laws of space.

389. I conclude. The rational principle, acting as instinct, exercises a direct action on the ganglionic nervous system; as will, it exercises a direct action on the cerebro-spinal nervous

system. Both systems intercommunicate, as anatomists well know: the lateral ganglia of the great sympathetic system have multiple communications with the cerebral and rachidic nerves; the cerebral ganglia communicate with the pneumo-gastric system.

390. Accurate observation of the accidental differences between these nerve unions found in different individuals could greatly clarify the levels of the will's action, in different people, on the passions and on the movements of so-called organic life.

CHAPTER 12

Causes of the errors of the animistic school

391. In all the foregoing discussions we have always supposed that in the fundamental feeling there is only a totally simple, active principle which we have called 'sentient principle' or 'sensitive principle'. Hence, the sole cause of all animal phenomena must be seen in this principle. In the same way, the *rational principle* can act on the body only through the same principle of feeling.

In the *Anthropology* I demonstrated the existence of the sensitive principle, its simplicity and its immense activity over the body. I distinguished this activity into two branches, *life* and *sensuous instinct*.

Nevertheless deep-seated prejudices oppose this teaching, and in order to dispel some of these, I think I must pause here to discuss the *animistic school*. Although this school was closer to the truth than the others, its excess was disturbing, and made the world tend to the other extreme.

392. We have therefore two schools: the *materialistic school*, which claims that all phenomena apparent in the animal body are explained by the laws of matter, and the *animistic school*, which attributes all these phenomena to the rational principle. Both schools are erroneous because of the extremes to which they go.

The *materialistic school* is so crude and base that it cannot really do harm to our teaching, especially as we have already refuted it in many places. We need only submit the *animistic school* to a just critique and show how the truth lies midway between the extremes of the two schools.

393. All the errors of the animistic school can be reduced to one: its failure to see clearly that the cause of all animal phenomena is the *sentient principle*.

394. The principal causes of its inability to see this precise activity of the soul, to which the facts of animality should have been referred, were its failure to:

1. distinguish between subjective and extrasubjective phenomena;

2. see the specific difference between feeling and understanding.

3. distinguish the fundamental feeling from sense-experiences.

4. reflect that only the *term* of the sensitive soul is extended, and that the unextended principle (the soul) can *multiply*, but not *divide*, without harming its simplicity.

Let us look at each of these four causes.

Article 1
First cause

395. Kurt Sprengel says: 'The universality of organic effects, even in the vegetable kingdom, seems to be the strongest objection to the psychological system. Indeed, no supporter of the psychological system has been able to sufficiently refute this objection'.[164]

396. He is correct, but the objection loses its force in the face of what I have said, namely:

1. We simply need an hypothesis devoid of absurdity but capable of explaining this universality to show that universality cannot lead to any conclusion opposed to the psychological explanation of animal phenomena. There is nothing contradictory in admitting that *feeling* is individually united to the primal elements of matter. In the hypothesis, these elements would simply be the extrasubjective term of feeling.

[164] *Storia della medicina*, sect., 15, 1, 56.

397. 2. Even if we omit this hypothesis (which is not hot air, as it may seem at first sight), the objection can be demolished by the clear distinction between *subjective* and *extrasubjective* phenomena. This irrefutable distinction shows the total falsehood of the so-called universality of phenomena.

All thinkers who do not attribute feeling to vegetables, or to their parts or elements, must acknowledge that vegetables, although they certainly manifest extrasubjective phenomena consisting in movements similar to those seen in animals, do not manifest any subjective phenomena whatsoever of feeling. Because we perceive material forces as causes of movements, we have in the case of vegetables analogous causes and effects. It is difficult therefore, if not impossible, to demonstrate that the gentle, organic interaction of material causes cannot explain the movements of vegetables. On the contrary, the class of subjective or sensed phenomena which cannot in any way be explained by extrasubjective motive forces is found only in animals, and proper in them.

The real cause preventing an answer to this question until now is the very important line, which had not yet been drawn, between the two classes of above-mentioned phenomena. This cause however needs further investigation and we will return to it later.

Article 2
Second cause

398. The second cause preventing natural scientists from acknowledging the soul as the principle of animal phenomena was that the psychologists who first saw the need for recourse to a soul did not stop at the *sensitive principle*; ignoring the correct term, they introduced the *rational principle* into the discussion. Their excess was due to the fact that they never properly understood the essential difference between feeling and knowing, between sense and idea. Sensism was at the root of all their reflections, and even remains in those philosophies which today are vaunted as spiritual and rational. It is not easy to understand that the difference between *feeling* and *idea* is far greater than

one of degree or of accidental qualities. Feeling with its acts cannot be changed into idea. Acts and idea are two different and opposite entities; feeling is subjective, idea essentially objective. All modern philosophers, including Cousin and his disciples, find it impossible to conceive a feeling totally devoid of consciousness. They confuse the sensible element with the intelligible element, that is, they unconsciously and arbitrarily endow feeling with an intellective element. Because of this first error, they have at their disposition a feeling not present in nature, but formed by their own imagination. Starting from here they obviously have no difficulty in deducing all the functions of reason. All they have to do is develop the intellective germ they have planted in feeling of which, they say, it is a part.

399. At the time of Giovann'Alfonso Borelli,[165] Jan Swammerdam,[166] Claude Pérault,[167]and George Ernst Stahl,[168] the world was just emerging from Aristotelianism. It is not surprising to find that sensation and idea were not carefully distinguished. Aristotle's system took various forms with the

---

[165] †1679.

[166] †1680.

[167] †1688.

[168] †1734. It will be useful to indicate here the real error of Stahl's system. He deserves all respect, and his works are worthy of study. His error did not lie in upholding the identity of the sensitive and intellective soul in human beings, which is true; no one can reproach him for having written: 'We assert and profess that the very same soul, which performs rational acts or reasons, also exercises and administers feeling and movement as well as life' (*De febris rationali ratione etc.*). But he begins to err in failing to distinguish accurately between the intellectual and the sensuous orders. He claims that in sensuous actions every soul, even that of brutes, acts according to reason, and therefore by force of will, 'and indeed explicitly ACCORDING TO THE UNDERSTANDING it has of the thing present to it, and also ACCORDING TO THE WILL, which it generally has, of preserving and keeping its body or tentlike dwelling from corruption and annihilation' (*ibid.*). Consequently, the great man endowed feeling with intelligence, confusing the former with the latter. This sensistic rationalism of his would inevitably collapse with the development of the deadly germ within it. Anyone who grants intelligence to feeling does not elevate feeling but degrades reason, which he seems to elevate. Peace in the realm of philosophy is maintained only by observing very carefully the great borderline between feeling and intelligence, and preserving it unchanged. Wars always arise in philosophy when borders are crossed.

[399]

result that sensism, as well as the materialism of Pomponazzi and others, was drawn from it. The animists made the understanding part of their explanation of animal phenomena. They were incapable of conceiving pure feeling, that is, feeling without any knowledge joined to it.

400. Let us consider Borelli's confusion between the principle of feeling and the rational soul. As a former prince of 'iatromathematicians', he must be rightly placed at the head of modern animists. He recognised, before others, that animal phenomena must be explained by a principle of subjective activity.

401. In part of his very famous work *De motu animalium* he tries to show that it is possible for the movement of the heart to be produced *a facultate animali* COGNOSCITIVA [by the COGNITIVE animal faculty].[169] His argument however simply demonstrates that this movement results from the activity of the *sensitive principle*.

He notes that, when the principle of feeling (*animae sensitivae facultas*) is greatly affected by joy, the circulation speeds up, and when greatly affected by sadness, slows down. This fact undoubtedly demonstrates the *activity of the feeling* on the circulation, but Borelli, instead of being satisfied with this wholly true conclusion, confuses sensible activity with intellective activity and argues that the cognitive soul is the principle of the heart's movements. He considers feeling itself as an action of the cognitive soul; he says, *utraque enim pulsationis variatio fit ab apprehensione et persuasione quae sunt* ANIMAE COGNOSCENTIS *facultates* [both changes in the pulse are caused by intellectual apprehension and conviction which are faculties of the COGNITIVE SOUL]. He then adds, again confusing sensibility with the soul: *Ergo talis motus cordis fit a facultate sentiente et appetente, non vero ab* IGNOTA *necessitate* [This movement of the heart therefore springs from the sentient, desiring faculty, not from UNKNOWN necessity].[170]

402. We can see here the origin of modern sensism. The world had received an ancient inheritance (of which scholasticism was the last witness), namely, the prejudice that *feeling* was a kind of

---

[169] P. 2, prop. 80.
[170] *Ibid.*

knowing. In vain had St. Thomas said in certain places, almost in passing, that feeling was not in fact knowing; according to him, the expression was used only in a metaphorical way. His wise, but very brief comment was not enough to correct the wide-spread, mistaken way of speaking nor the erroneous opinion it brought with it.

Nevertheless, although his reasoning mistakenly confused feeling with knowing, Borelli grasped an important truth which had been accepted by the animist school but later rejected by scientists in general for the very same reason which provoked the acceptance of the error.

403. In fact, whenever an error is presented to the world accompanied by some truth, it is accepted because people pay attention only to the accompanying truth. Later, after the error has been accepted, the connection between error and truth is rejected because the truth, now seen as incoherent with the error that has prevailed, is not wanted. Lastly, a third, totally new stage comes: the whole is dismantled, the truth separated out from the error and retained, the error rejected. This is the kind of chemistry of opinions which I have tried, as far as I can, to apply to the most controversial philosophical questions.

404. But what contributed greatly to the deception of Borelli's fine mind was the fact that he considered the effect of passions in human beings and animals in a general way. When we receive unexpected, happy news that fills us with joy, our heart certainly beats hard; on the other hand, very sad news stuns us, and the heart sinks. But here we are dealing with information, which puts us into the intellective order. Information in the understanding has indeed the power to stimulate affections of joy and sadness, but it does not prove that we have the power to move or to directly slow down our heartbeat. If information influences circulation, it does so by means of the affections it first arouses in the human subject. These affections pertain to the order of feelings and are aroused even in brute animals not through the *information* animals may have but by virtue of blind instinct and the *unitive force* (I dealt with this at greater length in the *Anthropology*).

405. The intellective soul communicates with the *sensitive principle*, setting its activity in motion. All this happens within the subject. But the effects that modify matter and body as term

of the principle must be attributed to the activity of the sensitive principle.

406. Our next question, separate from the previous one but highly important, is: 'How does the intellective principle exercise an action on the sensitive principle?' Both questions, which are very different, must be dealt with by psychology. I began by differentiating them and indicating why they have so far been confused by the most serious scholars. This, I think, is the first step to reflection.

407. We need to continue our explanation of the causes prompting philosophers to accept intelligence (which they confused with feeling) as the sole means of explaining animal phenomena. As we shall see, they were led into error by the vestiges of supreme wisdom that are visible in the actions of animal instinct.

Galen's amazement at these philosophers and his repudiation of the Epicureans who rejected providence were justified.[171] He also made a very acute observation when he criticised those who gave the name 'nature' to the cause of generation and of other animal phenomena. Inventing a word, he maintained, does not explain facts.[172] However, he erred in attempting to explain how the substance which comprises first the embryo and then the foetus, and acts with such regular and complicated movements, was something non-rational.[173] He did not understand how we must be certain about the presence of an intelligent cause without confusing it with animal substance. In short, he neither distinguished the ultimate, creating cause (God) from the proximate cause (nature), nor conceived the proximate cause as feeling — feeling, although blind, is a most fitting servant of the divine intelligence that created it.

408. The great Stahl made the same mistake as a result of another truth which he had seen but applied badly. He saw that

[171] Stahl, admiring the very ingenious formation of the foetus and seeking its cause, says: 'This is why we do not believe Epicurus and others who think all things are done by chance' (*De formatione foetuum*).

[172] He speaks, in the work quoted above, about those who imagine 'they have said a great deal when they assert that the foetus is formed by nature. In fact they have merely repeated a word used by everybody.'

[173] Cf. *De foetuum formatione*. [*App.*, no. 4].

the understanding does many acts of which the human being has no consciousness. This was indeed a valuable truth but we cannot arbitrarily conclude from it, as he did, that animal actions are in fact the work of such non-conscious intellective acts.[174]

409. Stahl made two mistakes: 1. he wrongly distinguished non-conscious intellective actions from those which accompany consciousness, and 2. classified acts of animal feeling as acts of the non-conscious intellective soul. He very correctly distinguished reason (λόγος) from reasoning (λογισμός) but was totally wrong in attributing non-conscious acts to reason, and acts accompanied by consciousness to reasoning. The most attentive observation of our internal acts shows inductively 1. that we reason without any consciousness, and 2. generally speaking reveals the wonderful law that 'every act whatsoever of our spirit is unknown to itself and needs another act (reflection) for it to be revealed'.

410. Internal observation also exposes the second error, which classifies acts of feeling with acts of non-conscious reason. First of all, it is not true that everything occurring in our feeling is devoid of consciousness. On the contrary, 'we CAN be conscious of any feeling whatsoever'. If not, the feeling would not be OUR OWN because 'our own feeling' means precisely feeling of which we can become conscious. However, although we can become conscious of all our feelings, we do not in reality do so.

411. Feeling certainly does not include consciousness, which we have to form for ourselves through internal observation of feeling within us. Furthermore, we must distinguish our own feelings from those which can be in our body, but are not ours. Our own feelings consist of:

1. Those of which we can be conscious but are not, because we do not think about them.

2. Those of which we are actually conscious.

---

[174] Stahl claims that the reason which acts unconsciously is the same as Hippocrates' *nature*, which acts wisely but without reflection (ὀυκ ἐκ διανοίης); it is the φύσις ἀπαίδευτος, which Hippocrates describes as Ἀπαίδευτος ἡ φύσις ἐοῦσα καί οὐ μαθοῦσα τά δεόντα ποίει (ἐπίδημ., bk. 6, sect. 5). Cf. *Propedeuticon inaugurale, περί φύσεως ἀπαίδευτος.*

412. We also have feelings in our body which are not ours because we cannot in any way be conscious of them; entozoa are an example. We may conjecture that every corporeal element has such feelings which however lie outside our individuality. Only the first two classes, which do indeed pertain to us as individuals, are our own.

413. Turning our thoughts to the second class of feelings, of which we have actual knowledge, we can easily discern whether they are of a rational or non-rational nature precisely because we know them and are conscious of them. Consciousness in fact tells us that these feelings lack the characteristics of knowledge because they have no *object*, but only an exclusively subjective character. They are simple modifications of the subject; the knowledge and consciousness which accompany them does not pertain to them. This difference is what essentially separates knowledge from other entities: every cognition is an *act* that terminates in an *object* without being confused with it. Nothing like this is found in animal feeling, which is a purely subjective act and does not go out of itself to terminate in some distinct object, that is, one which it distinguishes from self. It is therefore an error to confuse feelings with rational acts of the soul, as the animist school has done.

Article 3
Third cause

414. The third cause for not recognising the true principle of animal phenomena was ignorance of the nature of the fundamental feeling, and belief that all feeling lay only in particular sensations aroused by extrasubjective stimuli.

415. The result was extraordinary. Galen, and many others after him, saw that human beings and animals move their muscles and nerves for the sake of their needs without knowing the nature or organisation of nerves and muscles. These philosophers and natural scientists thought it impossible for the human will to use wisely parts of which it was ignorant. Only the learned who studied anatomy would know this.

416. Those who reasoned in this way did not see first that anatomical knowledge is neither the only knowledge we can have of the human body, nor the most faithful, that is, it is not knowledge which truly lets us know the nature of the body. They did not see that external experience, which guides anatomists in their dissection and examination of bodies, is subjectively conditioned by the action of the external senses, the eyes, the touch, etc. The external senses do not present the nature of things but simply the phenomena resulting from two simultaneous causes: 1. the nature of the organs that have feeling and are the instruments of this kind of observation, and 2. the varying nature of the stimuli applied to the organs. Consequently, only phenomena are observed which contain much that is subjective and truly foreign to the proper, intimate nature of the observed body. These natural scientists, having failed to recognise the importance of this kind of observation, trusted blindly to extrasubjective observation as the sole, safe means to know animal-bodies.

On the contrary, the truth is that the body is known through two experiences, extrasubjective and subjective, of which only the latter indicates its real nature.

Subjective experience presupposes the fundamental feeling by which the sensitive principle feels all the parts of the body where the feeling is diffused. Although the external limits of these parts, shapes, etc, which are phenomena of extrasubjective experience, certainly do not fall within this feeling, the extension of the body is felt not only by the external sensations but equally by the fundamental feeling, although in a totally different way.

417. It is also true that this fundamental feeling is not knowledge but purely possible matter of knowledge. However, wherever it is, it presupposes the activity of the sensitive soul. We must no longer be surprised therefore that the soul uses the parts which it feels and invades according to the laws of its individual feeling and in favour of that feeling. A supreme intelligence has constituted this feeling in such way that it can, by its own action, attain wise ends. They are ends, however, only for the Creator; for the feeling, they are terms, conditions, attitudes, pleasant states to which it is continuously directed by its own natural energy, through which it exists.

Article 4
Fourth cause

418. Finally, the fourth cause of the error made by animists was their failure to distinguish the principle from the term of feeling, and their incapacity for forming a correct concept of a sensitive soul, whose essence lies precisely in being the principle, not the term, of feeling.

The failure to make such an important distinction resulted in enormities that contributed greatly to the discredit of their system.

Stahl, under pressure from Leibniz's objections, was forced to confess the necessity of such a conclusion.[175] But if this were true, either human beings would have two souls or the identical soul would share in materiality, extension and mortality! In reply Stahl, who was a religious man, does not hesitate to say that he awaits the immortality of the human soul not from its nature but from grace![176]

419. Furthermore, if the principle of feeling, which is unextended, is not distinguished from its term, which is extended, we have no means of knowing the teaching about the individuation of sensitive souls, nor about their faculty to multiply without dividing. Granted that this doctrine had not been discovered and that all animal phenomena were to be explained through recourse to the soul, what must we say about certain phenomena which all the disputing parties accept as animal, but occur in the body for some time after the death of the animal, for example, irritability or counter-distension of the muscles? Robert Whytt, who restored the animistic system in Scotland, was quick to affirm that the soul's activity is maintained in these muscles and increases under stimuli![177]

---

[175] Leibniz, *Opera*, t. 1, p. 156.

[176] *Negotium otiosum*, pp. 102–103.

[177] *Opuscoli teoretici*, Berlin 1790, p. 252.

CHAPTER 13

The soul's activity on the extrasubjective body

420. Summarising what has been said, we have seen that:

1. The rational soul is united to the animal fundamental feeling through a natural, immanent perception.

2. Because the fundamental feeling consists of two elements, that is, the sentient and the felt, the rational soul is united to both.

3. The rational soul's union with the *felt* element is the same as its union with its own subjective body; through this union the soul becomes passive because the body is passive.

4. Through its union with the *sentient* element, the soul is active, and can act on this principle which governs the felt or body. Thus it can act on the body.

5. The sentient principle in animals is that which constitutes the sensitive soul.

6. The sentient principle's indivisible union with the felt element is the union we have explained at length in *Anthropology*.

421. While demonstrating these things I only touched upon the extrasubjective body. But an explanation of the nexus between soul and subjective body is also an explanation of the relationship of the soul with the extrasubjective body. The extrasubjective body is substantially the subjective body, although possessed of other appearances because of the different mode and potencies through which we perceive it.

However, I do want to add something here. Philosophers have never really known what the subjective body is. They have always conceived corporeal substance wrapped in the phenomena given by external, extrasubjective experience. When they asked the question, 'How does the soul act in the body and viceversa?', they always understood by body the extrasubjective body. Hence their predicament.

To avoid this difficulty we must demonstrate the relationship between the two bodies which we perceive. When we know this relationship, we can easily understand how the soul's action on the extrasubjective body is exercised as a result of its action on the subjective body.

This gives us confidence that we can lift a part of the heavy veil covering the mystery of sensation. We will gain much light by explaining the nexus between extrasubjective and subjective phenomena, a nexus we have already found in the identity of the space where these two kinds of phenomena converge.

422. Let us grant therefore that a fundamental feeling exists, diffused through all the sensitive parts of the human body in such a way that it occupies the identical space as the body where the extrasubjective phenomena are manifested. For example, the nerve which I see with my eyes and touch with my hands (extrasubjective phenomena) is where subjective feeling adheres. This feeling is such that it makes its possessor feel the nerve naturally but in a different way, a direct way. Granted this, all movements produced in the nerve will show themselves to external observation as extrasubjective phenomena and also effectively modify the subjective feeling inherent in the nerve.

Note, however, that although we say a subjective feeling is diffused naturally in all the space occupied by the nerve, we do not mean that this space is outlined and shaped in the natural, fundamental subjective feeling. On the contrary, space is shaped and limited only through external sensation, which is extra-subjective phenomena. One of these phenomena is that of *surface sensations* which I discussed in *Anthropology* but, as far as I know, has never been considered by philosophers.

Surface sensations, properly speaking, are those which surround bodies and give rise to the forms, determined sizes and proportions of bodies; in a word, surface sensations furnish us with all the knowledge supplied by these elements. It is precisely in this way that the external world is, as it were, manufactured by our external sensitivity. On the other hand, no such perceptions are offered by the internal world locked within subjective feeling. The space occupied by the fundamental feeling, because unlimited and unrelated to other spaces, remains obscure and simple in appearance; it is unsuitable for stimulating attention. This space, I repeat, is that same space which the external sensations later define, shape and in a certain way illumine and distinguish from the totality of space. In it the corporeal organ to which feeling adheres receives movement.

[422]

423. Let us suppose that this body or corporeal organ changes place without any relative movement of the molecules or particles that compose it. Certainly, nothing would happen in the internal feeling inherent in the body that would indicate the place-change to an observer. The change of place is sensible only through the relative position of the external bodies which is presented to us not by the subjective fundamental feeling but by the accidental sensations and extrasubjective phenomena.[178] If, however, internal movements arise in the living body to which feeling adheres, if for example a nerve retracts or extends because it has a certain animal elasticity or contractility, the feeling inherent in the nerve will be restricted to a smaller space or diffused into a greater space. Note carefully, I do not mean that feeling in the nerve presents movement to our consciousness; movement, I repeat, is known only in virtue of extrasubjective phenomena. In other words, the rapid shortening and lengthening of the felt nerve must necessarily produce a modification in the fundamental feeling; the nerve's activity must be stimulated because the stimulus forces it to change its disposition. When feeling is stimulated in this way by foreign energy, and its activity shaken up, stimulated and intensified, it must produce a felt modification, because every activity of feeling is felt.

424. But what manner does this modification take? What phenomena are presented by this sensitive activity aroused from its quiet state? It is impossible to say *a priori*; only experience can inform us. Thus, we know from experience that such phenomena are transient sensations, colours, sounds, odours, tastes, sensations of touch, etc; they are therefore *stimulations of feeling*, of the fundamental feeling.[179] Although it was difficult to explain

[178] Cf. *NE*, [vol. 2, 806 ss.].

[179] Black is said to be the absence of colour. This is definitely true because colour means various sensations in the eye when struck by rays of light, or the aptitude of bodies to absorb some luminous rays and reflect others, or even the light rays themselves. In none of the three of these meanings can we say that black is colour. But is black simply the absence of light rays in such a way that the word is a pure negation? I do not think so. I hold that black is a feeling, and properly speaking is the *fundamental feeling of the retina* which, when stimulated by appropriate movements, displays its activity in colours. If the reader were to close his eyes lightly in a dark place so that no light penetrated and then concentrated his attention on observing whether he was

how movement of a body could produce these stimulations in a feeling that is not body, the difficulty seems to disappear once we have found a fundamental feeling which, adhering essentially to the body, diffuses itself in the space of the body. However, we must note that to draw certain special feelings from the fundamental feeling, it has to be acted upon and aroused by particular stimuli in accordance with particular laws and movements, and in particular organs to which it unceasingly adheres.

425. I say 'particular laws' because not all movements of the organs stimulate the fundamental feeling in such a way that sensations are aroused. For this, certain conditions are necessary, for example, a nerve apparatus, one kind of stimulation rather than another, a given rate of vibrations. All this is still mostly unknown.

426. Let me add an observation about the undeniable fact that several organs must concur in the production of one sensation. For example, to produce sight, the concurrent action of the optic nerves, the lobes of the cerebrum and the cerebellum, the optic thalami, etc. are required. This necessity of such a complex apparatus of organs to produce one, simple sensation will cause no surprise if we meditate carefully on the following truths already discussed:

1. The sentient principle is one and simple.

2. Sensation requires an aroused activity of the sensitive principle, the real cause of sensation.

3. The whole of the fundamental felt element in all its extension is in the unextended sensitive principle, not as one extended thing in another extended thing, but as the felt in the sentient. We have called this a 'relationship of sensility'.

conscious of any difference between the state of his eye devoid of all stimulation and that of one of his fingers, for example, relative to the feeling he experiences, he would notice, I think, a different feeling in both parts and will assign the feeling of black to the eye but never to the finger. It will be objected that this happens because he remembers the sensation of colours experienced by the eye and not by the finger. But I do not think this is the case. The difference between the feeling in the eye and in the finger would be imaginary. On the contrary, it seems to me there is a real difference of feeling which precludes completely any comparison with the previous state. Furthermore there is no reason why the pure absence of colour must give the feeling of black, rather than no feeling at all.

4. The sensitive principle is stimulated, aroused, actuated by internal movements produced in the organs, which are parts of the felt.

5. These movements, although varied and pertaining to different organs, all tend to a single effect, the stimulation of the sensitive principle by the contraction, intensification and successive dilation of the felt element, its term.

6. Although every intensification and dilation is followed by some modification of the feeling and of the activity of the sensitive principle, it causes no surprise that movements of a certain multiplicity, variety, frequency, etc. are required to explain particular sensations in the sensitive principle.

427. All these facts seem to shed great light on the origin of sensation, which was inexplicable before the discovery of the distinction between subjective and extrasubjective phenomena. To explain sensation is to solve the great question of the interaction between soul and body. Human thought, limited to the sphere of extrasubjective experience, strove vainly to invent hypotheses, without ever finding a real communication between spirit and body.

Consequently, philosophers divided into two classes. Some counterfeited the concept of the spirit and made it extrasubjective; they imagined it as a very subtle body which escaped the senses, and thus made possible reciprocal action between the spirit and cruder bodies. Others were well aware that this explanation destroyed the spiritual ens; it was the kind of materialism which could explain a mechanical relationship, but never a feeling-based relationship. Thus, they denied any physical influence between body and soul, and in its place either dreamt up various hypotheses[180] or more wisely called the

---

[180] Descartes stripped the soul of any power to act on the body: his disciple, Malebranche, invented the system of occasional causes; Leibniz, the system of pre-established harmony. In doing this, the three great men had glimpsed a beautiful truth which they were unable to describe and formulate. They had glimpsed that *subjective* and *extrasubjective* phenomena differed specifically. Desperate to find a nexus between the phenomena, they had recourse not only to gratuitous hypotheses but hypotheses that basically included several absurdities. The cause of their errors lay in their insufficient observation of nature. When internal observation or consciousness of what happens in us is scrupulously noted, it indicates the existence of a simple

problem a 'mystery' and, with this fine, decent word, put a stop to further discussion amongst themselves and amongst all popularisers who wanted to pursue the matter further.

Readers will find it interesting, I think, if I comment on the strange thinking which the first kind of thinkers had to pursue in order to imagine how the spirit, like some kind of extremely fine air, entered our dense, bulky body through a succession of other intermediate, more subtle bodies. I will use Jean Fernel's exposition of these systems; for him they seemed undoubtedly certain.[181]

428. He says:

> The Academicians were the first to recognise as impossible that two very disparate natures could associate without the interposition of some suitable means. They thought that our spirit, formed by the supreme Artificer of things, clothed itself prior to its emanation and immigration into this dense, concrete body, with a simple garment, that is, with a kind of noble, pure, ethereal body similar to the stars. This body, which had an immortal, eternal nature, could never be detached and divided from the spirit, and without it the spirit could not dwell in this world. Then they surrounded the spirit with another body, still a tenuous, simple body but this time more impure, less noble and splendid than the previous one. It was not procreated by the supreme Artificer but con-created by the intermingling of elements, particularly the most tenuous, hence the name 'aerial' and 'ethereal'. The spirit, enclosed in these two bodies and banished like an exile into the third, mortal, decadent body — or rather into a dark, gloomy prison — became a guest on earth. Finally, after breaking from its prison and returning to the air and freedom of its homeland, it became a townsman and citizen of the gods [*App.*, no. 5].

These errors of the imagination necessarily resulted from the principle and an extended term in animal feeling. Once this FACTUAL truth has been discovered, all reasoning must cease and be satisfied with what it has found, if we wish to be disciples of nature. Now, this *fact* tells us that the simple principle and the extended terms form one single feeling in which the communication of the soul (principle) with the (extended) body is the most intimate and, I would say, the most *physical* imaginable.

[181] *De naturali parte medicinae*, bk. 4, c. 1 & 2.

failure to explain the communication of the soul with the body and from ignorance of the subjective nature of the body. The soul was therefore accorded an extrasubjective nature, but one so tenuous that it escaped the senses. As we see, the whole of ancient philosophy followed the same road. Let us continue with our overview of the history of opinions, still following Fernel, who now describes the opinion of Alexander of Aphrodisias:[182]

> Alexander of Aphrodisias confirms this communication of body and soul. He says that the spirit we have mentioned interposes itself as a very apt bond between the two, and through this interposition reconciles and contains the two opposite natures. Because the spirit is acceptable and suitable to both extremes, and not entirely devoid of body, it can on the one hand insert itself in the crude body and on the other, being tenuous and splendid, connect the body with the soul. Thus, sharing in some way in both soul and body, it intermingles the nature devoid of body with corporeal nature, the immortal with the mortal, the pure with the impure, and the divine with the earthly. All this, although it demonstrates that the communion between mind and body is accomplished only through the nexus of the spirit which interposes itself, helps to extend the communion to the other base parts of the soul. That part of the soul which is generated in mortal condition, although impure and not as open as the mind, is on such a higher level than the state of the earthly, concrete body that it cannot adhere to it without a bond.

Fernel, when describing Aristotle's opinion,[183] seeks to reconcile it with the previous opinions. He continues:

> This explains why Aristotle correctly taught that the *spirit* is contained in the foam-like, seminal body, and that *nature*, which corresponds proportionately to the element composing the stars, is contained in the spirit. He clearly indicates that the spirit interposes itself between the body and the divine nature as a kind of common bond. He also gives each base part of the soul as well as the mind a spirit of its own, asserting that every faculty of the soul shares in

---

[182] *In Problematib.*

[183] *De animal. generat.*, bk. 2, c. 3.

another body. This other body is more divine than the bodies called elements; its nature differs in nobility and darkness just as souls do.

Fernel, bearing in mind the previous opinions, concludes very solemnly:

If we wish to weigh and judge the arguments of Aristotle and the others, it becomes clear that every part of the soul has a certain spirit as its foundation, and that through this spirit the soul resides in the body where it carries out every function of its office.

By 'spirit' Fernel understands an extremely subtle body as a vehicle for innate heat, because *innate heat*[184] cannot exist without a containing fluid to which it can adhere.[185]

These philosophers were unable to conceive the subjective nature whose phenomena they saw. They strove vainly to attribute this phenomena to extrasubjective nature which they made so subtle that it escaped the external senses and provided no extrasubjective experience. But at least they clearly understood that the phenomena of soul must be explained by something alien to extrasubjective experience, although they were unaware of what lay beyond this experience. Nor did they understand that the laws of the extrasubjective body, even the most subtle and totally evasive of the senses, are essentially the same, and that the body does not change nature with its size, because size, whether great or small, is purely and simply an accident.

---

[184] He then applies himself to showing that this innate heat is not elementary heat, but something with its own proper nature.

[185] This is his proof of the thesis: 'Simple heat, as a quality, cannot permeate a body or be diffused in it without some seat and means of motion, as indeed we perceive it to be given to the individual parts from the heart through the arteries. Consequently it was necessary, I think, for it to be carried by some spreading fluid. But there was no humour suitable and able to pervade the whole body with such speed. Consequently heat needed some very subtle, substantially free-flowing and consistently swift matter which by its warmth would be friendly and familiar to heat. Now, because air, or if you prefer ether, is like this, it would most fittingly serve as a support for heat. Air always burns like ether, and heat is perpetually present in it so that one cannot be divided from the other.' He also notes how Plato sometimes calls spirit *materia calorifera* [calorific matter]. *De naturali parte medicinae*, bk. 4, c. 2.

Book 4

The simplicity of the human soul and
the questions to which it gives rise

[INTRODUCTION]

429. If human souls were bereft of bodies, no one would doubt their spirituality. Their union with the body is the cause of doubts about their simplicity and spirituality in minds that have not succeeded in coming to solid knowledge about the nature of this union. This is why I have used the previous book to explore it.

This important truth, the subject of so many disputes, was disentangled from the dross which impelled truly learned but somewhat impatient men to conclude without more ado that this union was an impenetrable mystery. As a result, the apparent difficulties of materialists have been overcome, and I have been able to support spirituality without plunging into errors of a very different kind that caused the fall of upholders of the spirit in their attempt to explain their truly noble and consoling dogma. Pre-established harmony, occasional causes, Berkeley's idealism, the Aristotelian act of the body, subtle bodies bordering on supposed tenuousness of spirit are the principal systems undertaking to explain the animal phenomena which appear in matter. All are errors giving rise to very dangerous consequences. The next step therefore is to harvest the fruit of the teachings developed in the preceding book and consider explicitly this essential characteristic of the soul called simplicity or spirituality. This is linked with extremely important questions such as the origin or generation or multiplication of the soul (the problem goes under various names) whose difficulty lies solely in conceiving how the soul, which is essentially spiritual and simple, acts in the body and receives action from the body, and is subject to experiences apparently similar to those undergone by matter, although there is only analogy or proportion between them. I shall begin by explaining at greater length than previously the direct proofs of the simplicity of the human soul.

[429]

CHAPTER 1
The meaning of simplicity

430. First, we must note that the word *simplicity* has been taken in various ways. It was first used to exclude *multiplicity*. In this sense it is equivalent to *unicity*.

Secondly, it was used to exclude *extension*, and in this sense came to stand for *inextension*.

Thirdly, it was used to exclude *materiality* (sensiferous force), and comes to mean *corporeity* or *spirituality*.

All these are ways which require the soul to be simple.

CHAPTER 2
Classification of the proofs of the simplicity of the soul

431. The proofs with which the simplicity of the soul can be demonstrated are usefully reduced to three great classes. They are derived:

1. from consciousness;
2. from the special properties of the soul springing from consciousness;
3. from the soul's activities, that is, from the need to presuppose the simplicity of the soul in order to provide a sufficient reason, or necessary explanation, of these activities.

CHAPTER 3
The simplicity of the soul shown from the properties with which the soul is furnished

432. I have already set out the direct proof drawn from intimate consciousness. The following demonstration of the soul's simplicity can be drawn from its properties.

We begin from the definition of the soul: 'The soul is the principle of feeling and understanding.' This definition shows immediately that the soul is simple. In other words, it shows that *multiplicity, continuous extension* and *materiality* have no place in the concept of soul.

But every ens has its own properties, through which it is determined and distinct from every other. The properties which specify an ens cannot be communicated to any other not pertaining to that species. If it were possible, the species of things would be confused. In fact, they are inconfusable because their distinction is founded in the intrinsic order of ens, which is eternal and immutable.[186] It is sufficient to prove, therefore, that the concept of soul and that of multiplicity, extension and materiality are specifically different to show that they are mutually exclusive, and that the soul is neither multiple nor extended nor material.

433. *Multiplicity*, I maintain is opposed to every real substance because no real substance is possible unless it is one. *Continuous extension*, as we have seen, is found only in what is felt and in what is sensiferous. But the soul is the sentient principle, and 'sentient' is specifically different from the concept of what is felt and what is sensiferous. The soul, therefore, has no extension.

In the same way, we can prove that the soul has no *materiality* because the materiality of the body consists in a force which violently changes what is felt. This change alone is known to us. But the force which changes and violently alters what is felt has an entirely different concept from what is felt, and one even more different from that which feels; it is brute force opposed to feeling. The soul, therefore, which is the sentient principle has nothing whatsoever to do with materiality; it is immaterial.

434. The same conclusion is reached it we take other properties such as *principle*. The nature of principle excludes multiplicity, extension and extended matter. The same result is obtained

---

[186] Christian Wolff defends the thesis: 'The attributes of one ens cannot be communicated to any other.' He proves it by having recourse to the *principle of sufficient reason* as follows. 'Imagine that an attribute, which ens A does not possess, is communicated to it. This attribute has no sufficient reason in the essential constitutives of the ens. Consequently, something is admitted without a sufficient reason. But this is repugnant. The attributes of one ens cannot, therefore, be attributed to another' (*Physiologia rationalis*, §45). The demonstration is irrefutable.

if we begin from the *identity* of the soul (cf. 140–180). There are, in fact, as many proofs of the simplicity of the soul as there are properties.

CHAPTER 4

The proofs of the simplicity of the soul from its operations in general

435. Finally, we can prove the simplicity of the soul because this simplicity is the single, sufficient reason for explaining its different operations. This can be done in three ways. We can demonstrate that the efficient principle of such operations must be simple from 1. their *nature*, through the manifest opposition between what is extended and the principle which has the extended as its term; 2. their *mode*, through the opposition between the extrasubjective phenomena included in the concept of matter and the subjective phenomena which pertain solely to the sentient subject; 3. their *term*, through the opposition between the multiplicity of subjective phenomena and the unicity of their principle.

There are indeed many proofs of the simplicity of the soul.

Each operation of the soul, when carefully examined, provides three proofs because we can show that the soul is simple by considering the *nature*, *mode* and *term* of these operations.

436. Indeed, once it has been demonstrated that a given operation cannot be produced except by a simple principle, this principle can no longer contain in itself anything opposed to simplicity. If it could, it would no longer be the principle of that operation, as we suppose it to be. It cannot be simple and not simple at the same time. Let us grant that the principle contains in itself something not simple. This non-simple element is no longer the principle of that operation, but something else. It is not, therefore, the soul. A single operation necessarily requiring a simple principle is sufficient, therefore, to show that the soul is altogether simple.

437. Proof of the simplicity of the soul drawn from intellective operations is much easier for the unbiased mind to understand because those operations reveal themselves as

obviously immune and pure from all material accretions. Even the ancient physicists, who clothed the soul with different bodily layers, as it were, of extremely fine atmospheric ether, were unanimous in recognising the mind as altogether incorporeal. For this precise reason, we begin from what is easiest, and first explain the proofs of the simplicity of the soul drawn from sensitive operations.[187] These proofs are of themselves quite sufficient to prove the simplicity of the human soul.

438. If it is shown that sensitive operations cannot be explained in any way without supposing them as effects of a simple cause, it is shown that the entire soul to which those operations pertain is simple. If the first sensitive principle, which is substantially identical in man with the first intellective principle, is simple, the human soul also must be simple because it is at one and the same time the first principle of feeling and knowing.

439. Lucretius himself felt the efficacy of this way of arguing, and tried to use it in favour of the mortality of the intellective soul which he deduces from the mortality of the sensitive soul:

> When, for the sake of a name, I go on to call it 'soul',
> and teach that it is mortal,
> you should believe the same of what you call 'spirit'.
> Together they are one.

To this I would reply that the sensitive soul does not die, but multiplies itself, as we shall see. In this case, neither does the intellective soul die. But our argument will be considerably strengthened if we put it like this. The sensitive soul is simple; therefore, the intellective soul also is simple. In other words, if the sensitive soul were extended and corporeal, it could be thought that perhaps the intellective soul might receive some extension and corporeity from it. But because the sensitive soul is unextended and incorporeal, it can be united to the intellective as simple to simple, without anything extended or corporeal arising from their union and identification.

---

[187] Italian philosophers such as Riccati and Garducci, have already used this fount to provide various proofs of the simplicity of the soul. Garducci shows, in the last of his *Lettere ad un filosofo italiano*, that bodily renewal is proof of the spirituality of the soul.

CHAPTER 5

Proofs drawn from the passive and active operations
of the soul

440. I have shown elsewhere that sensitive operations require a simple principle. A multiple or extended principle could not produce them without contradiction.[188] Sensitive operations, however, are of two kinds, *passive* and *active*, and I restricted myself to demonstrating the simplicity of the sensitive soul from the passive operations of feeling. Similar proofs can, however, be drawn from the active operations of instinct.

441. Proofs of the simplicity of the soul deduced from both passive and active animal operations are divided into three classes. Each of the following considerations shows equally that the sentient principle is simple.

1. The sensation of the extended-continuum cannot take place in any way without the presence of a simple principle capable of feeling in itself, and all at once, total continual extension.

2. Extrasubjective phenomena of the body manifested contemporaneously with sensation are different from and opposed to it. These phenomena are multiple; the contemporaneous sensation is single. The actions of the extrasubjective body, such as the movements of the nerves, etc., cannot therefore be the immediate cause of sensations, as we have seen. They can only be phenomena in parallel with them, or their indirect cause.

3. The same principle of feeling experiences several sensations. This sensation of what is multiple cannot be explained unless we admit a simple principle capable of embracing in itself, and all at once, all those various modifications.

442. The first of these three classes of proofs distinguishes and totally separates the soul from the subjective body and from what is *extended*; the second excludes from the soul all *materiality* proper to the extrasubjective body; the third excludes from the soul all *multiplicity*. All three considerations are susceptible

---

[188] *AMS*, 92–134.

of further development. I shall indicate only the development possible to the first two.

CHAPTER 6

Development of the proof of the simplicity of the soul from the nature of the continuum

443. I have already used the first proof, drawn from the nature of the continuum, in *Anthropology*. It could, however, be illustrated more fully with the authority and speculations of the ancients on the need for a simple principle to contain the body, which otherwise would dissipate into nothing.

It is a property of the extended body that every assignable part in it is outside and independent of every other, just as it is impossible to assign a part of the body within which more and more parts cannot be assigned. Such a substance, however, is absurd if the parts are not united and contained by a simple principle. 'That which cannot be thought' is absurd. But the first parts of the body are not found existing in themselves; in every assignable part, a smaller part is outside all the others in such a way that there is no extended part which is everything in itself. Only simple points are *in se* but, as unextended, they are neither body nor parts of an extended body. Consequently they cannot form anything extended whatever their multiplicity. We have to conclude that either what is extended does not exist or, if it exists, does so only in a simple principle which brings it together.

444. This formed the ineluctable argument of the Alexandrian Platonists. Nemesius offers it in the following form:

> The arguments used by Ammonius, master of Plotinus the Pythagorean, are sufficient to refute all those who affirm that the soul is body. He said: 'Bodies change of their nature. Indeed, they disintegrate and divide infinitely. But if nothing immutable remains in them, they need something to contain and connect them, to bind them together, as it were, and hold them in. This is what we call *soul*. If the soul is indeed a body of any sort, even the most subtle of

bodies, what will its container be? We have shown that all bodies need something to contain them, and so on *ad infinitum* until we arrive at something which is altogether devoid of body'.[189]

Those who can follow this argument will profit by the study of philosophy. Anyone who absolutely cannot follow it should abandon the subject.

445. We should not believe, however, that this way of arguing is peculiar to the school of Alexandria. It is part of the inheritance received by this school from the first Italic philosophers.

Xenophanes, in beginning to speak about *unity* as a necessary element in the explanation of the nature of all things, cannot be credited with distinct ideas. Aristotle testifies that he did not explain whether he was talking about unity of matter or unity of concept.[190] But to have noticed even in general and indistinctly the need to have recourse to some *unity* to give consistency to nature was at least to have glimpsed that there could be no body without something simple to contain it.

446. Xenophanes was succeeded by Parmenides and Melissus in Italy. These both upheld the principle of unity, but the former, according to Aristotle's conjecture, maintained that it proceeded from reason; the second wanted to find it in matter itself.[191] It seems that both forgot *sense*, Parmenides by falling back on intelligence, Melissus by halting at *matter*. Sense and intelligence were still not accurately distinguished from one another. Parmenides confused sense with reason; Melissus, sense with matter. Nevertheless, both saw that something *simple* was needed to explain nature.

We see from Aristotle's later remarks in the same place that Parmenides included sense under reason. According to Aristotle, Parmenides affirms that ens is one, and that non-ens is nothing.

> But he was constrained to pursue things which appear, and thought that the *one* depended on reason and the *many* on sense. As a result, he posited two causes and two principles,

[189] *De natura hominis*, c. 49.
[190] *Metaph.*, 1, c. 4.
[191] *Ibid.*

hot and *cold*, as it were, *fire* and *earth*. The one, that is, what is hot, he posited with ens, the other with non-ens.

How could Parmenides declare that fire was a condition or property of ens, which is one through reason, unless he considered fire or heat as the principle of life produced in great part by breathing air, which is then broken down through contact with the blood by means of an operation similar to combustion? Here it is obvious that animal life, or the sensitive principle, intervened in the ens and in the *one* which, according to Parmenides, is dependent upon reason. But this sensitive principle is precisely that which, through its simplicity and unity, enables bodies to be one, that is, enables them as such to be something, to be that which they are, extended bodies.

447. Zeno of Elea, another light of the ancient school of Italy, succeeded Parmenides and Melissus. Careful consideration shows that his arguments against the existence of movement are all reduced to the principle: 'That which is extended has no unity in itself.' If, therefore, we prescind from some simple principle containing the body and making it one, no bodily phenomena can be explained. In this case, the body is a complex of contradictions and absurdities.[192]

448. This argument, drawn from the nature of the continuum, is similar to that developed by St. Augustine,[193] St. Thomas[194] and many others, and drawn from the existence of the entirety of the soul in all parts of the body. Modern authors have denied this truth only because, having abandoned internal observation and the witness of consciousness (the only authoritative witnesses in reasoning about the soul), they preferred to work through abstract reasoning. They *imagined* the soul as a kind of tiny, tenuous body residing in a determined part of the body. This is, of course, very far from the truth. The soul, the sentient principle, clearly does not reside in some determined point of the body, but is present wherever it feels. Its nature is entirely

---

[192] Cf. C. H. Lohse, *Dissertatio de argumentis, quibus Zeno Eleates nullum esse motum demonstravit, et de unica horum refutandorum ratione*, Halle, 1794.

[193] *De Trinit.*, 6 [8].

[194] *S.T.*, I, q. 76, art. 8.

reduced to the immanent act of feeling to which no element, alien to that act, can be added. That the whole soul is in every part of the body where it feels simply means that it receives and possesses in itself that which is felt. This argument about the simplicity of the sentient principle is reduced, therefore, to the first argument about the unity of the continuum. In fact, the continuum is only such because it resides in what is simple. This was St. Thomas' way of conceiving it. He affirmed constantly: 'It is the soul that CONTAINS THE BODY AND MAKES IT ONE rather than the opposite.'[195]

449. Paulinus of Aquilea, a notable 8th century Italian Father of the Church, wrote in a similar vein when he maintained that the soul

> wonderfully rules the whole continuous, separable, divisible mass of the body. Diffused throughout the whole body, the soul vivifies and animates it and, like a point at the centre, preserves its own individual dignity without breaking up into the qualities of something else. Although incorporeal, the soul through the body disposes all things corporeally while the substance of the body, although corporeal by means of an incorporeal creature, that is, the soul, fulfils the bodily actions.[196]

[195] *S.T.*, I, q. 76, art. 3.

[196] *Adversus Felicem Urgelitanum*. — St. Gregory Thaumaturgus, in his still extant *Disputazione dell'anima*, posits the principle that, 'the soul is known directly through its own actions (*eam ex propriis actionibus cognitam habemus*).' The proper action of the soul is to give life to the body. St. Gregory, therefore, asks how the soul gives life to the body. He shows that if it were joined to the body as one solid adheres to another, it would not animate the whole, but only those points which it could touch; if it were mixed with the body as one fluid is mixed with another, it would be divided in parts and would no longer exist as the one, same soul which simultaneously enlivens all the parts of the body of an animal. We have to say therefore that it is whole and entire in all parts of the body and, while remaining one, enlivens them all. — But body joined to body increases in mass; the soul existing in the body does not swell it, but vivifies it. The soul is not the body, therefore, but devoid of body'.

Development of the proof drawn from the opposition existing between extrasubjective phenomena accompanying sensation, and sensation itself

450. We come now to the second of the proofs I have indicated. It could receive great support from the work of students of anatomy and physiology if we were prepared to compare in an orderly fashion the extrasubjective phenomena (of matter) with the corresponding phenomena of feeling, and note their contrasts. Let me give a little example of such comparison.

1. The nerves, to whose movements the sensation responds, are composed of very fine filaments, called nerve-fibres, which now and again communicate with one another in the form of a plexus. It is also asserted that every nerve-fibre has a delicate, transparent covering called a neurolemma. The extrasubjective phenomenon which immediately precedes or accompanies a sensation is not, therefore, the movement of a single fibre, but of a bundle of innumerable fibres. If the sensation were a mechanical or material effect of movement, it would either be or represent a multitude of different movements. But this is not the case; the sensation is single, and a simple principle is needed in which and in virtue of which the sensation originates. It cannot arise in multiple little fibres disturbed contemporaneously by many distinct movements. Consequently, the statement, 'The impressions of external things received at the nerve-extremities are carried to the brain' is altogether inexact, although repeated endlessly by many authors. What are these impressions? The idols of Epicurus? No one would dream of such a thing today. They can only be movements which are not carried to the brain, but communicate with it. In other words, they extend along the nerve-fibre as far as the brain. Once and for all, therefore, we have to substitute the quoted statement by another: 'The whole nerve-fibre, or nerve-substance of the fibre, moves but unless the motion continues to the brain there is no sensation.' There is no doubt that the impression itself cannot be carried to the

brain because it is not something capable of being carried. It remains where it began, in the extremities; it is only the beginning, the impetus of motion that has been received. Granted this, there is nothing in the extrasubjective phenomena parallel to the sensation except longitudinal motion (whether this comes about mechanically or dynamically through solid filaments or through liquids is not important here) to the brain. But the sensation, that is, the corresponding subjective phenomenon, has no length, nor is it felt in the brain. It is felt in the extremity to which external force was applied. The extrasubjective phenomenon, therefore, provides extension, the subjective none. The former requires different movements in different parts where no subjective phenomenon is manifested. This subjective phenomenon, therefore, is not the extrasubjective phenomenon nor a merely material or an immediate effect of what is extrasubjective. If it were, it would have to manifest the image and nature of the extrasubjective. But motion, without the presence of a principle of a totally different nature, cannot produce anything except motion, nor can extension offer anything except extension.

451. According to physiologists, extrasubjective phenomena are even more complicated. The sensible nerves are bound together and in certain ways depend upon one another. If these mutual dependencies are removed, the phenomenon of sensation is no longer manifest. Magendie discovered through repeated experiments that the sensitivity of the head, and particularly of the face and its cavities, depends on the fifth pair of nerves. If this nerve is cut before it leaves the cranium, the face feels nothing.[197] Moreover, he also believed he had demonstrated that the principal seat of the sensorium and of the special sensories is not properly speaking in the brain or the cerebellum. He offers the following experiment.

> Remove the lobes of the brain and of the cerebellum of a mammal, then see if it feels. You will easily note that it is still sensitive to strong smells, to tastes, to sounds and to taste impressions.

He concludes:

[197] *Précis Elémentaire de Physiologie, De la sensibilité.*

It is obvious, therefore, that the seat of these sensations is not in the lobes of either the brain or the cerebellum.

An even more extended and complicated mechanism is shown in the extrasubjective phenomena that precede or accompany the subjective phenomenon of sight. Magendie reports:

> The experiments carried out by Rolando and Flourens show that sight is terminated if the cerebral lobes are removed. If the right lobe is removed, the left eye no longer sees, and vice-versa [*App.*, no. 6]. — Damage to the optic thalamus of mammals is also followed by loss of sight in the opposite eye. Although I have never seen damage of the anterior optic or quadrigeminal tubercle alter the sight of mammals, this effect is very clear in birds. — Thus, the parts of the nervous system necessary for the exercise of sight are manifold. Exercise of this sense requires integrity of the hemispheres, of the optic thalami, perhaps of the anterior, quadrigeminal tubercles and finally of the fifth pair. Note that the influence of the hemispheres and of the optic thalami cross over, while that of the fifth pair is direct.[198]

It is clear that, if various organs concur simultaneously to bring about a single sensation, such as sight, these organs must have a single, simple principle in which the sensation has its existence. It is also clear that this simple principle cannot be any single organ because a single organ does not produce the sensation. Nor can it be all the organs together because the sensation is single, not multiple. A single, subjective phenomenon corresponds to many extrasubjective phenomena which inhere as modifications to different organs. The subjective phenomenon must, therefore, have a single, simple principle which receives a single, simple modification parallel to the multiple, distinct and extended movements.

452. Finally, there are many sensitive organs to which special classes of sensations correspond. If one or other of these organs is destroyed, one or other class of sensations is also destroyed, but not all; the organs serving to arouse sensation show a certain mutual independence. But the principle which feels is always

---

[198] *Ibid.*

[452]

the same; all sensations of different classes arise equally in it. Consequently, it cannot be a special organ, nor a modification of an organ. It must be such that it responds equally to all the organs. This is the subjective principle, to which unicity and simplicity pertain. As such, it is essentially different from the extrasubjective principle, to which the contrary properties of multiplicity and extension pertain.

CHAPTER 8

Some proofs, given by the ancients, for the simplicity of the soul coincide with our own

453. Let us compare these proofs of the simplicity of the sensitive soul with those given by the ancients. The older proofs will perhaps be clearer if expressed in our terminology. Certainly, I make no claim to originality in what I have said. I have only said it anew to render it more easily understandable to contemporaries.

I. One proof of the simplicity of the soul was deduced by the ancients from the soul's presence, whole and entire, in every part of the body, as we have seen. A 6th century author writes:

> Do you admit that the entire soul is diffused through all the individual members, or that a greater part of it is present in a larger member and a lesser part in a smaller member? — I think rather that it is entire in each member of the body. Although it is circumscribed in some way, I do not believe that it is in any way composed of parts because it remains whole despite any truncation of the bodily members.[199]

This proof is extremely convincing, granted proof of the soul's true presence in every part of the body per *contactum virtutis*. Doubts were raised on this point, however, which diminished persuasion of the proof, although a careful examination of the way in which the soul feels restores the balance and redoubles the force of the proof. Examination shows that

---

[199] John Maxentius, *Dial. 2, Contr. Nest.* (AD 505).

continuous extension can exist only in a non-extended ens. It certainly follows from this that the soul is in every part of its body. Indeed, its whole sensible body, as felt, is in the soul as in a simple principle through the relationship we called *sensility*.[200] We ought also to note that all the extrasubjective phenomena of life are manifested, as I said, in a body felt subjectively.

It is clear, therefore, that the soul gives the living body its wonderful unity:

> Wonder at our Maker, and at the way in which he united the effective force of your soul to the body. The soul moves into the body, as it were, and invades even its external particles. Infusing its power there, it draws the most distant members together in a single, harmonious, social concord.[201]

454. II. Aristotle argues for the simplicity of the soul from the fact that it knows all bodies indifferently.[202] He says that the soul, if it were some determined body, would not know other bodies. St. Thomas develops the argument in this way:

> Anything capable of knowing several things cannot have anything of them in its own nature. If it did, this would prevent it from knowing other things. So, for example, the tongue of a person suffering from some bitter, choleric disturbance cannot perceive anything sweet. Everything seems bitter to him. Similarly, if the intellectual principle had in itself the nature of a body, it would be incapable of knowing all bodies which, as we must see, all have a determined nature. It is impossible, therefore, for the intellectual principle to be a body. Likewise, it is also impossible for it to understand by means of a bodily organ. If this were the case, the determined nature of that bodily organ would prevent the knowledge of all bodies.[203]

The Scholastics had a great deal to say about this argument, although others have often found it inefficacious. My own opinion is that it is highly effective provided the foundation is

---

[200] *AMS*, 230–234.

[201] St. Basil, *Homil. in illud 'Attende tibi'*.

[202] *De Anima*, bk. 3, c. 5.

[203] *S.T.*, I, q. 75, art. 2.

clearly explained. The argument should first be directed to proving the simplicity of the sensitive principle, not the intellective which comes later as a consequence. The sentient principle is first to perceive real bodies; the intellective principle only apprehends and affirms them as felt. If the sensible perception of bodies could be explained by supposing the sentient, perceiving principle to be corporeal, the later intellective operation would cause no trouble; it would receive matter just as it was given to it. But proof that the sentient principle cannot be corporeal lies in this argument: if it were a determined body, it would never feel its own or other bodies' extension because it would not be entirely the same in every part, and consequently would not be any of the phenomena manifested in extension. In other words, it would not be able to feel at all. This is in fact the first proof that I gave of the simplicity of the sentient principle.[204] It is irrepugnable.

CHAPTER 9

How the sensitive soul can multiply but not divide

455. From knowledge of the simplicity of the sensitive soul we move to its indivisibility. Some Scholastics maintained that brute souls were extended and divisible in general.[205] Others distinguished between perfect and imperfect animals. The souls of the latter were extended and divisible; those of the former, indivisible. Suarez himself speaks in several places of divisible souls:

I have no doubt that they are present in many living things,

---

[204] *AMS*, 94–103.

[205] Scotus, *In IV*, dist. 44, q. 1, art. 1; Durando, *In I*, dist. 8, 2nd p. dist., q. 3, n. 10; Capreolo, *In II*, dist. 15, q. 1 *et ultimum contra ultimam concl.*; Marsilius [of Ingen], *In II*, q. 11, a. 1; and *De gener.*, q. 11 and 12; Egidius, *In I*, dist. 8, 2nd p., q. 5; Pomponazzi, bk. 1, *De nutriente et nutrito*, c. 4; Peter of Mantua, *De primo et ult. instanti;* John of Janduno, *De Anima*, II, q. 6; Apollinare, *De Anima*, q. 6, and John of Saxony, *De generat.*, I, q. 10 and 11.

and I think it extremely probable that they are present in all except man.[206]

456. It seems clear to me that these authors arrived at their opinion solely because they did not consider that the soul is only the principle of feeling (the sentient principle), and that such a principle has to be essentially simple. If not, it would not be a principle. Their mistake was not due to lack of ability, which was highly developed in some of them, but because the *method* of investigation was still not perfected when they flourished. Instead of examining the soul directly through internal observation, they reasoned about it without prior observation, applying the general principles of ontology, form, matter and so on. These principles cannot be applied to an ens still little known through observation. These writers foundered on the same rock which accounts even today for our metaphysical authors who, however, are far less excusable. They undertook to resolve the question: 'What *must* the soul be in order to satisfy our ontological principles' (that is, their prejudices), rather than the other question, the only one that the philosopher should propose: 'What is the soul?' Only from knowledge of what the soul is can the philosopher arrive at the true, ontological principles which express the order of being in general.

457. Observations had already been made in antiquity on the conservation of life in bodies that had been severed or divided into parts. Aristotle, a great observer, distinguished between perfect and imperfect animals. He very wisely said that the former were 'like many animals joined together'.[207] He also noted that tortoises whose hearts had been removed lived a long time.[208] Averroes reports that he had seen a ram going headless

---

[206] *De Anima*, bk. 1, c. 2, n. 19. Cf. also *Disput. Metaph.* d. 15, sect. 10, n. 32. — In chapter 13 of the first book of the *Trattato dell'anima*, he undertakes to show that the indivisibility of the souls of perfect animals can be maintained together with the divisibility of imperfect animals. Baldassar Alvarez adds a note, however, stating that Suarez did this solely because of St. Thomas, who holds this opinion about perfect animals.

[207] *De iuventute et senect.*, c. 50.

[208] *De Anima*, 1, text. 67, 93; *De brevitate vitae*, c. 3, and *De iuventute et senect*, c. 1.

and, according to Avicenna, had seen a headless bull take two steps.[209] Similar facts are reported by Tertullian,[210] St. Augustine[211] and others.

In place of the direct observation of the soul given by consciousness, we could apply an ontological argument to these external, extrasubjective facts, but this would inevitably produce errors about extension and the divisibility of sensitive souls. We would reason as follows: if a polyps, when divided into parts, becomes many living animals, the first soul has either divided or perished; in its place two other souls have been infused. Do these souls come from corruption of the first soul, or from matter, or were they created by God? There would be innumerable difficulties, and to solve them, we would be irresistibly tempted to say what seems easiest, that is, that the first soul has divided neatly into two halves.

458. On the other hand, if observation and right reasoning tell us that the soul's substance lies in the principle of feeling, must we not say that the sentient element is necessarily one and simple in every animal, and that there are as many sentient principles as animals? Surely, we will understand at once that the extended is simply the felt, and that only what is extended can be conceived as susceptible of division? Is it not clear that if division can take place solely in what is extended, the soul as sentient cannot be conceived as divisible but is in fact the very opposite of what is felt?

I know that some people will be surprised at this. An imperfect ontology invades minds; we all create our own ontology from the nature of bodies, as if these were the only *entia* from which to draw the nature and intrinsic order of every *ens*. Consequently, there are many objections, and they all begin with the phrase, 'How is it possible...?' But ignorance of how a thing can be does not make it impossible when it is a fact of experience. My reply is St. Augustine's straightforward logical reply to precisely the same argument. Evodius had countered St. Augustine's defence of the soul's simplicity with the fact that

---

[209] *Physicor.*, 7, text. 4.

[210] *De Anima.*

[211] *De quantit. Animae.*

when a polyps is cut in pieces, all the pieces remain alive:

> I first say that we may indeed be fully ignorant of how this
> happens when bodies (of animals) are cut up. But it should
> not disturb us so much that we reject many arguments
> which previously seemed clearer than the sun. We do not
> have to forsake all that we have solidly learned to the
> contrary and admitted as very true.[212]

In fact, possible objections against a truth, even if apparently
insoluble, can never destroy, with good logic, what is directly
and solidly demonstrated. On the other hand, every excellent
doctrine causes the greatest difficulties to the masses because of
its profundity and abstruseness. The wise either solve the difficulties or, if not, maintain the most firm conviction of the truth
they had previously known.

459. However, we will not find the matter as difficult to
understand as it first appears if we obtain our notion of the soul
and its activities solely from consciousness and internal observation. The results will then silence the presumptuous prejudices ceaselessly murmuring in our spirit because we will have
found what I have pointed out, namely:

1. That which is extended and felt can exist only in that
which is unextended, simple and sentient.

2. The sentient element and the felt element, having no
third thing between them, form one single, simple feeling which
has two poles, as it were, of which the unextended pole is the
principle, and the extended pole, the term.

3. The unextended sentient element is thus totally present
in every part of the extended felt, precisely because no part
could be felt if there were no sentient element, which together
with the felt element forms one, single feeling.[213]

4. The sentient is limited by the felt, which is the term of its

---

[212] *De quantitate Animae*, c. 31.

[213] St. Thomas shows that the soul is present throughout the whole body.
Otherwise the 'whole (that is, the composed entity) would not naturally be a
single thing but merely a composition of parts'. He also shows that the soul is
totally in every part of the body. Because of its simplicity, it must possess the
full perfection of its species wherever it is: 'Simple forms and substances
possess a perfect species *per se*' (not through 'the conjunction of essential
principles' which is how composed entities have it). *Q. de Anima*, art. 10.

act. Thus, the sentient must always be where the felt is. Contrariwise, where there is no felt, there is no sentient, because the latter feels only through the felt, just as the felt is felt only through the sentient, as I have explained above.

5. An extended, corporeal matter underlies or adheres to the felt, which is bound to and dependent on this matter.[214] If the matter is withdrawn or changes in extension, the felt also ceases or changes its extension.

6. An extended, continuous felt can therefore divide into many parts when its matter divides, and form two or more felt elements without any communication between them.

7. There is no *a priori* reason why the two or more parts into which the felt element of a particular extension divides should cease to be felt; feeling as such has no dependence at all on the quality or shape of the extension. Before a felt continuum divides into two, feeling (and therefore the whole sentient element) is present in every point of the extension. In the same way, it is natural that a feeling and the sentient principle remain in all the points of the divided, discontinuous parts.

8. The sentient principle, although existing totally in every part of every felt continuum, is one because the continuum is one and without parts. For the same reason, when the felt divides into many continua, sensitive activity multiplies, because it now resides not in a single continuum but in many, separate continua.

460. This multiplication of the sensitive principle is difficult to understand, because our phantasy easily imagines the principle as some kind of complete, subsistent being without a felt element, a kind of very tiny body. But this is not the case; we must rid ourselves of such an imaginary being and concentrate

---

[214] Suarez, although erroneously admitting some divisible souls, confesses that the dependence of some souls on matter does not necessarily mean they are divisible: 'There is no necessary connection,' he says, 'between the two properties of *divisibility* and *dependence on matter*. The fact that indivisibility is a consequence of immateriality does not prove that the former cannot be found without the latter. There is no repugnance between indivisibility and dependence on matter. In fact, greater perfection is required to make a form independent than to make it indivisible, as we have seen in the case of a spiritual accident, which is indivisible yet dependent. Indivisibility can therefore stand with dependence' (*De Anima*, bk.1, c.13: 9).

our attention on the nature of the thing, namely, that 1. in nature there is only the felt, 2. the sentient is essentially united to the felt as felt, and 3. the sentient feels the continuous felt without feeling itself, because an animal felt cannot reflect upon itself in any way; indeed the word 'self' is not applicable to it. If then the principle feels only the felt and is sentient only in so far as it feels, it is clear that when the felt divides into two continua, the sentient will feel them both; on the one hand it does not feel itself, and on the other, it cannot maintain its identity in both felt elements because they are divided. This is precisely multiplication.

461. We must therefore conclude that although every sensitive soul is simple and *indivisible*, it is also *multipliable*.[215]

CHAPTER 10

Continuation — Multiplication of polyps

462. When Trembley, in the last century (1740), and other natural scientists began to observe what the ancients had already noted, namely, that hydra and other polyps multiply by the spontaneous formation of buds and by natural and man-made parts, they were beside themselves in wonder, granted the imperfect concept of the positive nature of the soul until that time.

463. In *Anthropology*[216] I noted that the manner of propagation of polyps does not differ in any way from the common law of generation, a law which is equally wonderful in all animals, whether viviparous, oviparous, gemmiparous, fissiparous or

---

[215] St. Jerome agrees that the souls of beasts propagate *ex traduce* [by transference], that is, 'by transference of flesh', but denies this to the human soul: 'Do humans,' he asks, 'like animals, propagate by transference?' (*Ep.* 61, *ad. errores Io. Hieros.*). The expression 'by transference' however does not properly express the origin of sensitive souls. These multiply solely by *division of the felt* without needing anything else, although the division takes place in many ways according to certain conditions.

[216] 323–349.

otherwise multipliable. In fact, every act of generation takes place without exception 'through the detachment from the animal of some living part which retains life and becomes a new individual of the same species.'

The differences between the various ways of generation are simply the 'different ways that the part destined to be a separate living being and become a perfect individual of the species detaches itself from the animal,' and also the various conditions necessary for each detached part. These differences however are purely accidental; the same law always remains true, namely, that generation is simply 'the detachment from the animal of a living part which preserves life and is individuated.'

464. The whole question therefore is reduced to knowing 'what *conditions* are necessary so that a part which detaches itself from the animal, subsequently retains life and individualises'. In my opinion these conditions vary in different animals only relative to accessories and accidents, and can always be reduced to a single condition, to one specifically identical law, which I have explained elsewhere,[217] namely: 'Life is preserved in the living, detached part of an animal in all cases where some kind of composition of all mechanical, physical, chemical, organic and vital forces is verified in the part. These forces continuously preserve the matter of feeling in a state suitable for acting as the term of the *specific feeling* which constitutes the species of the animal.'

The variable term in this formula is 'the specific feeling which constitutes the species of the animal.' It must be the source of the varieties of animals and hence of the variations we see in the ways of propagation.

465. The essence of what is animal resides in feeling. Consequently the specific and truly philosophical classification of animals must be recognised in the variety of their fundamental feeling.[218]

---

[217] *AMS*, 326–331.

[218] St. Augustine also begins from feeling. He argues that the soul is totally in every part of the sensible body because the *sentient principle*, which is the whole soul, is present wherever the soul feels. He says of the soul: 'It is not diffused as a mass through local space, but is present in every single body, totally in the whole body, and totally in every part of the body. There is SOMETHING FELT BY THE SOUL IN EVERY TINY PARTICLE OF THE BODY, and

466. The variety of this feeling is deduced from the extrasubjective phenomena accompanying it. Although these are not its *direct effects*, they are phenomena collateral to those of feeling and thus *signs* indicating feeling. *Extension* however remains identical for both the extrasubjective, material phenomena and the subjective, feeling-based phenomena, as I have said. The feeling is diffused in the space where the corresponding extrasubjective phenomena appear (although the extension is felt in a different way). From this I concluded that the same single force produces feeling by acting in the soul and, by acting on itself (that is, on the matter of feeling), produces extrasubjective phenomena.

467. The fact is that certain living parts, when they detach themselves from animals, sometimes become living animals and sometimes perish. The cause of this difference is, as I have said, the following: in the first instance, the matter of feeling is maintained in its necessary, normal state so that it can be term of that particular animal feeling; in the second instance, the matter loses its normal state. The normal state consists in a suitable organisation, that is, an organisation able to preserve the unity of the feeling.

CHAPTER 11

Causes of death and of generation

468. At this point we encounter many important and subtle questions: FIRST QUESTION: How does living matter, detached from the animal, lose the normal state of organisation which makes it suitable for being the term of a single feeling? Before detaching itself, it certainly possessed the necessary organisation because it was felt, and the whole of the sentient principle, which is present where it feels, was in it. How can this state be preserved by a part that is detached?

It cannot be denied that a felt part, divided from an animal's body, has, considered in itself, a state of organisation suitable

although this may not be the case in the body as a whole, the soul FEELS AS A WHOLE because it does not withhold its totality' (*De Trinit.*, 6, 45 [8]).

for being felt; there is nothing to show that it loses this state simply because it is cut off from the rest of the body. But the sensitive principle, we must note, not only feels but is continuously active, producing continuous movements in the living body it feels. Consequently, this term of its feeling has a continuous, intestine movement which, as I said, puts the sentient principle under continuous stimulation.[219] These movements cause unceasing change in the most intimate organisation of the matter, causing it to pass incessantly from one state to another. If normal organisation is to be maintained, these new states must always remain normal states. In other words, the movement must keep returning on itself, renewing and even improving the organisation by changing but not destroying it. These movements produced by the soul are of two kinds, one of which springs from what I have called the *life instinct*, the other from what I have called the *sensuous instinct*.[220] In certain cases however movements of the *sensuous instinct* thwart those of the *life instinct*; they disturb and disorganise the body, which the life instinct strives to organise better. In this way the sensuous instinct becomes the *first cause of death*.[221]

469. Moreover, the life instinct, that is, the *organising* principle, must continually struggle with brute force.[222] The mechanical, physical, chemical and other processes of this force act ceaselessly beside and independently of the life instinct. Consequently, they sometimes work in a direction contrary to the organisation which the instinct strives to maintain. If, in opposing the organisation to which the life instinct tends, they

---

[219] This question is discussed in *AMS*, 318–322.

[220] *AMS*, 380–388.

[221] We can be convinced that the *sensuous instinct* sometimes causes death if we consider those cases where it produces death very quickly, particularly in animals (in human beings it is stimulated and peculiarly changed by the abuse of intelligence). Many insects, for example, die in the act of giving life to other individuals. The cause must be the sensuous instinct. Naturalists note that the fly, *tipula*, sometimes falls dead solely on approaching the female. Virey says: 'We must believe that to generate is to deprive oneself of life and shorten one's days; it is like making a will or demonstrating one's mortality, because life is communicated only at the cost of one's own life.'

[222] Elsewhere we shall see what I mean by brute force; here, it is sufficient to accept the common notion.

act with greater speed and vehemence than the instinct's organising process, matter obviously loses the organisation necessary for animal life. This is the *second cause of death*.

Death must always be attributed to one or other of these causes.

470. If we apply these theories to the phenomenon of death in general, we see why some living parts detached from the living body die shortly afterwards, while others continue to exhibit the phenomena of life for a varying length of time, but finally die. For example, some parts, still attached to the whole living body, die slowly; they undergo the processes of profound changes that brings them to death. This is the case with gangrene and paralysis. Some diseases (every disease is simply a series of the processes we are discussing) cause the whole body to die; others make it healthy. Finally, some parts detached from the animal remain constantly alive and build up the part that was removed from their organisation; or, if they have the complete part, develop and perfect it. This last case is called 'generation'.

The theories also help to see why some parts, detached from the body, continue to live while the body from which they detached themselves dies. For example, the male bee leaves its generative organs impaled in the female it has just fertilised, and dies; a great number of insects like the cockroach, ephemera, cochineal, etc., die after fertilisation. Here, new processes suitable for conserving life take place in the detached parts which make up a new individual. For the same reasons, processes follow with varying speed in the generating animal and cause its death.

CHAPTER 12

Causes of different organisation in animals

471. *SECOND QUESTION*: Why is the life instinct not satisfied with any kind of matter, and why, in order to activate the animal feeling, does it require matter to be organated in a given way? In other words, why must the term of the feeling be this particular

aggregation of matter, this particular choice or form and not another?

If it is true that 1. in the animal the soul is the only substantial form of the body, 2. the felt exists by virtue of the sentient, and 3. feeling constitutes the animal in being, it must also be true that the *specific* fundamental feeling, not matter, is the cause of a specific organism in the animal; matter itself is cause of the various kinds of feeling. If the aggregation of matter determined the complex feeling, every little bit of matter would have a corresponding complex-animal feeling. But if feeling determined each little part and aggregation of its matter, these parts or aggregations would correspond exactly in number to the fundamental feelings in question.

472. If the fundamental feelings constituting a corresponding number of animals are definite and determined, why are not all conceivable fundamental feelings definite and determined?

The answer is found in data supplied by internal observation and experience. One particular datum tells us that the state of the body varyingly influences the contented state of the animal's feeling, that is, the animal experiences pleasure or pain according to the condition, changes and movements of its body.

Every fundamental feeling is therefore bound by certain laws which, modifying the feeling, endow it sometimes with a mode of perfection, sometimes with a mode of deterioration. When a fundamental feeling is susceptible of a mode of perfection, its action will strive to acquire this mode, and distance itself from the opposite extreme. This perfect mode or state is certainly in the feeling, not outside it. Consequently, what is felt will be ceaselessly moved and modified by the vital principle and the feeling itself, provided that this is active and has a continuous tendency to adapt to and settle in its more perfect, natural and contented mode of being. But whenever the felt is moved and modified, the body, together with the matter underlying the body is moved and modified. Thus, the vital or sentient principle, by adapting, settling and arranging itself, can place itself in its most natural state and most pleasant mode of being. Its operation either organises the matter in which it is acting or to which it can extend its action through contiguity, or at least seeks to control and organise the matter as it pleases. Hence, the stamp of the species, the moulding energy and the reason why every animal reproduces another animal like itself must be sought in the fundamental feeling, the seat of animal activity.

473. This enables us to understand and explain the *vis essentialis* of G. F. Wolff,[223] the epigenesis of Aristotle, Galen, Descartes, Harvey, J. Turberville Needham and Müller, the *nisus formativus* of Blumenbach, Barthez and others, the *plastic forms* of Cudworth, the attraction of parts and the superstructure of the organs of Maupertuis, the power to create and organise the foetus which Stahl attributes to the soul, the *archeus* and the formative spirit of Van Helmont. Although these authors certainly do not agree fully, and often say what is manifestly false by expressing their thought in totally incorrect ways (for example Van Helmont's *seminal soul* located in the matrix), they do agree in one, undeniable truth: an organising principle exists in nature. I believe that this principle is the vital principle and the sensuous instinct acting in unison with it [*App.*, no. 7].

CHAPTER 13

The law according to which the sentient principle carries out the organising function

474. THIRD QUESTION: The following facts cannot be denied:

1. The feeling of the animal has different pleasant and painful states, varying in degree and kind.

2. The body, which is term of the animal-feeling, has, as experience tells us, a state corresponding to every state of the feeling. Indeed, the state of the animal-feeling is always determined by what it feels, and it feels only and always in the corporeal, extended element. Consequently the good or painful state of the sentient principle must obviously depend on the state of the corporeal extended unit, that is, of the felt.

3. Finally, the feeling is active, and this activity is directed to procuring the most pleasant and consequently (for the feeling) most natural state. The activity therefore must act in the body,

---

[223] *Dissertatio sistens theoriam generationis*, Halle, 1774.

term of the feeling, and produce all the animal's movements; for example, it explains why an insect placed on its back tries its hardest to upright itself into its natural position.

These three facts cannot be denied. Hence, our investigation must determine first the cause of an animal-feeling's contented state and then the cause of the other less pleasant states and states of increasing unpleasantness, and finally why the animal-feeling ceases to exist.

475. If we consider the fundamental, substantial feeling as a specifically determined ens, our investigation can have only one possible result: the reason for the feeling's different pleasant and unpleasant states lies in the feeling itself, that is, in the law of its nature, and proceeds directly from the intrinsic order of its constitution. Every ens has an interior order whose ultimate cause is the intrinsic order of essential being. Essential being and its order is the first fact containing the ontological, sufficient and ultimate reason for all other facts.

476. However, animal-feeling, although one and simple in its principle, presents to observation and analysis its own multiplicity and composition as a result of certain intimate actions and passive experiences. This gives us some indication that the reason for its accidents and vicissitudes is to be sought in its internal constitution. Let us try to glance, as it were, through the cracks and catch a glimpse of this nature.

477. I take for granted the following principles:

1. Animal-feeling is essentially pleasant; it is enjoyable activity. Consequently its entity diminishes as enjoyable activity diminishes (enjoyable activity is fundamental enjoyment).

478. 2. Feeling, that is, enjoyable activity or fundamental enjoyment, can be diffused more or less equally in a continuum while being centralised to some degree in a physical point or many points of the continuum, which would be centres of enjoyment and activity caused by incessant stimulation or other means. Centralisation and condensation of fundamental enjoyment means that it is more intense and vivid in one place than in another.

479. 3. The instinctive activity of continuous fundamental enjoyment is proportionate to the intensity of the enjoyment.

4. In more perfect animals, fundamental enjoyment is more centralised and intense, and functions of life more numerous. In

imperfect animals fundamental primitive enjoyment is less centralised and more uniformly diffused. Because many centres replace a single centre, the activity, functions and indications of life are sparser and less observable. In my opinion, this varying centralisation and intensity of fundamental primitive enjoyment gives rise to the *specific difference* of the fundamental feeling which constitutes the animal, and therefore to the basis for a philosophical distinction of the various classes or species of animals.

480. 5. A different choice of matter, its varying elaboration and primitive organisation corresponds in the extrasubjective world to different fundamental feelings. If suitable matter is removed or not correctly worked, or no fitting organisation is chosen, the fundamental feeling suffers to varying degrees and even ceases, that is, it breaks down into many feelings, having lost the unity of its term.

481. Granted all this, I am of the opinion that the specific agglomeration of the feeling posited by nature at the first moment of an animal's existence (or at least of the feeling considered according to its type) can never be increased by the animal's own activity. This activity is totally directed to preserving the agglomeration and so opposes destructive forces. It also tries to obtain pleasant, transient sensations (sensuous instinct) which, however, do not make the fundamental feeling more concentrated in some point; they are simply transient, second acts of the feeling itself.

482. It is of course true that animals develop, but I consider this development an effect of the activity by which the animal seeks to preserve itself (life instinct), that is, to preserve the *type of its fundamental feeling*. This activity is associated with that by which the animal seeks transient sensations (sensuous instinct) without any direct end regarding development and growth, to which they both tend. Although the fundamental feeling wishes to preserve itself in keeping with its type and to carry out its acts, that is, transient sensations, it can do so only by means of the vital movements which develop and perfect it for a short time. Once this period of perfection is past, however, the sensations cause it to deteriorate and age. Hence, development and deterioration, although natural consequences of the use of the vital and sensuous activity, are not the proximate end to which these two branches of animal activity tend.

[480–482]

483. We could also conceive the full development of the animal as a state of maximum perfection, and suppose that only in this state has the fundamental feeling attained its maximum intensity in keeping with its natural basic form. In this case we would have to assume that the constant type or specific stamp of the animal is *the proportional division of the feeling among the different points of its term*. In other words, it is the nature and characteristic of the harmonious action proper to the animal. Where there is a single sentient principle, there is a single, fully harmonious action originating in the feeling. But because the activity of the animal is greater where the feeling is greater, this action will have only one centre, if the feeling has only one centre. If on the other hand the feeling has many centres, the animal activity will also have many centres. Thus, varying degrees of activity in the different points of the felt will depend on varying degrees of feeling — we are of course speaking about the feeling of stimulation, which presupposes the feeling of continuity. Granted that this proportionate distribution of feeling remains equal, the characteristic of the harmony of animal activity will also remain equal in every state that the animal subsequently passes through in its development. This constant characteristic of harmonious activity can constitute the species of the animal.

484. If therefore we accept the proportionate distribution of feeling and activity as the distinguishing characteristic of species, we must acknowledge as a constant law that animal activity, at least if not thwarted by foreign forces and accidents, works neither to change nor improve this characteristic, primitive distribution of feelings and activity. Indeed, it tends to preserve and use it by deriving pleasant sensations from it. Later however the change takes place *praeter intentionem*, so to speak.

485. Granted this law, the following corollaries result:

I. Whenever the active sentient principle works to preserve the type of the fundamental feeling and to enjoy particular sensations, it acts in matter. Matter either resists and tries to withdraw by using its mechanical, physical, chemical and other forces, or obeys and co-operates in some way with the principle. In the first case, the phenomenon of pain begins, that is, the sentient principle battles with its matter and with matter's incipient domination, but is frustrated in its effort. The feeling, now placed in a condition contrary to its nature (which is essentially one of enjoyment), is truncated, reduced or exhausted by its ceaseless effort to attain the unattainable; it becomes downcast and suffers. In the second case however, contrary effects occur because matter obeys and brute forces co-operate with the aim of the feeling.

486. II. The fundamental feeling may lose out in the struggle. If so, the form of its species deteriorates. If further specific reduction of the feeling and its consequent harmonious activity are rendered impossible, the specific feeling also becomes impossible and the animal dies.

487. III. Granted however an animal whose specific characteristic is the equal diffusion of its feeling to the whole felt element without any reduction, such an animal ought to multiply into as many animals as the pieces that came from it, because the feeling which constitutes the species of the animal would be equally distributed in each. This would also help us to understand how the vital principle could easily repair wounds, if we granted the presence in every case of at least the external conditions necessary for nourishing the principle.

488. IV. In addition, animals in which feeling is concentrated in many centres with equal intensity, must, when dissected, easily multiply or reproduce like buds, because centres would remain in various quantities in each piece. Hence the law of their harmonious action and the proportion in which the feeling is divided remains the same. This explains the multiplication of infusoria, and removes any surprise at the strange way the tricod, or charon as Müller calls it, multiplies: its stomach, first transparent and then opaque, swells like a bubble and finally bursts with such force that the little animal explodes into more than a hundred pieces, each of which becomes a perfect tricode.[224] My theory is not unlike St. Thomas' explanation of the multiplication by severance of linked animals:

> Linked animals, when cut into pieces, live not only because the soul is in every part of the body but because their soul, being imperfect and capable of very few actions,

----

[224] *Histoire des verm.* etc., p. 83, n. 2511.

requires little diversity of parts, which is the case for each of the living pieces. Hence, the soul remains in the cut pieces, because the disposition which allows the soul the possibility of perfecting the body, is preserved in the pieces.[225]

489. V. Finally, if the vital, sensuous movements produced by the animal caused the feeling to change its centre or intension or type, a total change in the organisation would result, and, without dying, one animal would change into another. This is precisely the case of certain living species, for example, caterpillars that pass through a state of chrysalis to butterfly.

The VI. and most important corollary of the theory, however, is the possibility of spontaneous generation, which I will now discuss.

CHAPTER 14

Spontaneous generation

Article 1
Various opinions about the truth of spontaneous generation

490. 'Spontaneous generation', as we call it, is denied today; 'putrefaction', as the ancients called it, was greatly supported by them. But if spontaneous generation were a fact, it would be, according to our theory, part of the universal law governing the multiplication of animals.

If the organisation of something felt and, consequently, the matter of an animal body, were to break up, so that neither the unity of feeling nor the specific characteristic of the harmony of its actions could be preserved, the conflict between these actions would be such that instead of co-operating in preserving

---

[225] *De Anima*, art. 10, ad 15. Aristotle had said that these animals had only one soul in act and many in potency (*De Anima*, bk. 2, text. 20). This however does not explain the multiplication of souls by severance; it simply states the fact in Scholastic terms.

the unity of the felt, they would all go their own way, and each centre would strive to achieve independence.

This inner struggle between the various activities of the feeling would arise in virtually all the points of what is felt as extended. The resulting disunion and dissolution, which would explain the phenomenon of putrefaction, would also explain the formation of very tiny animals. The difference between this kind of multiplication and the other three or four would simply be this: while the other kinds propagate an animal of the same species or transform it, this breaks up the animal to compose, from its bits and fragments, other animals of a different species, a real *generatio aequivoca*.

491. In the middle of the last century, a Catholic priest in England revived the opinion of spontaneous generation, and attempted to prove it with microscopic experiments.[226] Since that time many natural scientists have maintained it, including Vrisberg, Otto Friedrich Müller, Ingenhousz, Bloch, Lamarck, Treviranus, F. Meckel, Rudolphi,[227] Bremser, De Blainville,[228] Fray,[229] Carl Friedrich Burdach, Della Chiaie,[230] etc.; it has now become, we can say, almost a common opinion among natural scientists.[231]

A footnote in Richerand's *Nuovi Elementi di Fisiologia* speaks about infusoria as follows:

[226] J. Turberville Needham, *Microscopical Discoveries*, London, 1745 — in French, Paris, 1750.

[227] *Entozoorum sive Vermium intestinalium Historia Naturalis*, Berlin, 1819.

[228] Appendix to Bremser's *Traité des Vers intestins*, p. 563.

[229] *Essai sur l'origine des êtres organisés*.

[230] *Compendio di elmintologia umana*.

[231] A recent opponent of spontaneous generation is D.C.C. Ehrenberg, whose work was translated into French by Manol under the title, *Traité pratique du microscope, suivi de Recherches sur l'organisation des animaux infusoires* (Paris, 1839). Prof. Medici accepts spontaneous generation of animals below insects but not of insects. In a learned letter written to Prof. Secondo Berruti, Medici maintains the spontaneous generation of insects (*Giornale delle Scienze Mediche*, Turin, vol. 6). The letter, which provoked an erudite discussion among many professors, is reported in *Rendiconto dei lavori della Società Medico-Chirurgico di Torino*, edited by Dr. Secondo Polto, n. 28, and also in vol. 1 of the *Atti* of the Society.

[491]

These living beings, invisible without a microscope, seem to be produced by direct or spontaneous generation. Nature gives them birth by heat and humidity. We do not know how she uses certain mysterious fluids, like the principle of electricity, but such causes can very probably convert a small gelatinous mass into an organised, living cellular network. Monads are certainly formed in this way, as are a great number of tiny, microscopic animals that teem and dart about in stagnant water. It seems that the heat of summer is indispensable to their production because they are not seen in cold weather; stormy weather also favours their multiplication. As Professor Lamarck has very carefully observed (*Filosofia Zoologica*, vol. 2), modern thinkers seem to have rejected all too absolutely the opinions of the ancients relative to spontaneous generations. Certainly, complex animals like the bee cannot emerge from a putrefied bull, but the same cannot be said about beings with a primitive design of organisation. Monads, among infusoria, and the byssus, among the first families of algae, seem to be the direct production of humid heat, helped by the influence of electricity.[232]

Article 2
Does the opinion of spontaneous generation favour the materialists' system?

492. Materialists saw spontaneous generation as a proof of their system. Motivated by this second end, they tenaciously upheld it and proclaimed victory.[233] For the same reason, thinkers who admitted the spirituality of the soul attacked the opinion.

493. Both sides are mistaken. If the fact of spontaneous generation is really present in nature, we do not have to say, as Cabanis does, that pure matter itself acquires life by its own

[232] *Nuovi Elementi del Richerand migliorati da Bernard Seniore, tradotti dal D. Paolo Dall' Aqua*, pref. §5.

[233] *Système de la Nature*, vol. 1, c. 2. Diderot, *Pensées sur l'interpretation de la Nature*, §12, 58: 2. Robinot, *Vue philosophique de la graduation naturelle des formes de l'être*, Amsterdam, 1768. De la Mettrie, *Abrégé des systèmes — L'homme plante*, and other authors of this persuasion.

effort.[234] Rather, we must say that it was already alive, and that the principle of life which was in it acted in its matter to produce the organism. This important fact would itself be very clear proof of an immaterial principle.

494. A doctor of the Broussais school, in reply to Becquerel's question, 'How does inorganic nature become organic nature?'[235] says: 'Spontaneous generations could be of great help in answering the question. If it were true that *dead* matter could take on organisation through its own forces, the question would be mostly answered.'[236] But spontaneous generations would never demonstrate that matter was dead; on the contrary they would show clearly that it was alive.[237]

495. All that is needed is a clear understanding of the concept of body or matter; both are the term of feeling. This is the only idea we have of them without the intervention of the imagination. The term of feeling requires a feeling principle, and this principle must be totally simple; if it were extended, it would be term. The problem therefore is reduced to our acceptance of the idea of body and matter at the very moment we acquire it, before we change it with our imagination. The question, presented clearly in this form, is answered at once because we see that wherever there is feeling, there is an essentially simple soul.

---

[234] *Rapports du physique et du moral de l'homme*, Dixième Mémoire, première sect., §2.

[235] Becquerel, *Traité de l'électricité et du magnétisme*, vol. 1, p. 430.

[236] He immediately added: 'The spiritualists have understood this very well. Consequently, they do their utmost to make the contrary opinion prevail.' M-S. Houdart, *Études historiques et critiques sur la vie et la doctrine d'Hyppocrate* etc., Paris, 1836.

[237] F. Berard added some wise footnotes to the *Lettera postuma di Cabanis sulle Cause prime* (Paris, 1824). In a footnote on p. 60, he says, 'In the production of living beings there is a real vicious circle from which no escape is possible. One living being, or part of a living being, is necessary for producing another. The production of life always presupposes life. To make living organs, living matter is necessary, and to make living matter, living organs are necessary. A living being can be made only once, and all of a piece; if it is not perfect in itself, it cannot exist.'

Article 3
Animals considered by antiquity as emerging from apparently brute matter

496. In the book which contains the most ancient origins of the things of this world, God commands the earth to bring forth vegetables even before the sun and moon shine. After these two lights have been placed in the heavens, God commands liquid substance to produce reptiles, fish and birds; thus the waters and the air were populated. He next commands the earth to produce beasts of burden, snakes and animals according to their kind, and the earth obeys.[238]

It would be the greatest absurdity and totally gratuitous to conclude from this that material substances which produce animals at God's word were entirely devoid of life. Moses himself says that the spirit of God fertilised the waters from the very creation of matter.[239] Some of the older Fathers understood 'spirit of God' as the spirit of life, animator of things.

497. We can see the reason for the phrase, 'fertilise the waters', that is, liquid rather than solid matter, if we note that only subtle matter is suitable for the spontaneous generation of animals. I will give an explanation for this later.

498. St. Theophilus, who became bishop of Antioch in 168 AD, declares that Moses

> understands the spirit passing over the waters as the spirit which God gave creatures for generating living things, like the soul given to a human being. God united a tenuous thing with a tenuous thing (both spirit and water are tenuous) so that the spirit could fertilise the water, and then the water with the spirit could pervade everything and fertilise the creature.[240]

An authority as ancient as this is solemn authority.

---

[238] Gen 1.

[239] 'And the spirit of God moved over the waters' (Gen 1: 2 [Douai]). The Hebrew word translated as 'moved' properly speaking means 'incubated'.

[240] The Latin translation, which is all I have before me, says: '*Spiritum autem qui ferebatur super aquas, eum intelligit quem dedit Deus creaturae ad viventium generationem, velut animam homini, tenue cum tenui conjungens (nam spiritus tenuis et aqua tenuis) ut spiritus aquam,* AQUA AUTEM CUM SPIRITU (not water alone, as the materialists imagine) *omnia pervadens creaturam foveret*' (*Ad Autolyc.*, 2, 13).

499. The fact that material substance, fertilised in this way, can be organised by the living principle into various forms according to circumstances, is not materialism.

When Cuvier studied fossil bones, he found many kinds of animals that had completely disappeared (the palaeotherium, anoplotherium, anthracotherium, plesiosaurus, megalosaurus, pterodactyl, ichthyosaurus, etc.). Evidently, the temperature of the globe, the fecundity of the earth and circumstances influencing organisation must have differed from those of today. These vanished species, so different from what we have now, were considered as the product of the earth invested with a different power, in different atmospheric circumstances, etc. Whatever opinion we follow in these things and no matter how erroneous it may be, it will never favour materialism. Even if a mastodon or a rhinoceros, formed all at once, emerged out of the soil, the only thing we could reasonably induce was that a vital principle was in the soil as the hidden organiser of those great bodies.

CHAPTER 15

The hypothesis that all particles of matter are animated

500. What has been said implies that life or the sensitive soul can be united to matter even in the absence of external, extrasubjective phenomena of life. In this chapter I will first propose the hypothesis that feeling is united to all the elementary particles of matter, and then determine whether this entails fatal consequences.

501. The hypothesis could certainly be false, and cannot be admitted until verified by the most accurate experiments of fact. On the other hand, I can find no argument which demonstrates its absurdity. Some claim that it can be used to support *materialism* and *pantheism*, but in my opinion they are wrong because they make arbitrary additions to the hypothesis which denature it.

Article 1
The hypothesis that all particles of matter are animated does not favour materialism

502. First of all, it is clear that materialism cannot in any way be legitimately deduced from the hypothesis. We need only consider that if every particle of matter has some feeling conjoined with it, the extended particle is simply the term of this feeling. On the other hand, feeling requires a simple principle as its essential constitutive.

Article 2
The hypothesis does not favour pantheism

503. In the case of pantheism, the presence in the universe of a greater or smaller number of animated substances is completely indifferent. Provided these substances are created, and totally distinct from the Creator, pantheism is excluded.

504. In the second place, an hypothesis which grants feeling to the first elements of matter must not be confused with the hypothesis of the world soul conceived by the ancients. Even this hypothesis, although erroneous, does not necessarily imply pantheism, provided the world soul is created. But the hypothesis about an animator of the first particles implies more, namely, that there are as many souls as individual particles or groups of particles. These souls are either individually distinct or at least apt for being distinct and multiplied by means of separation. Consequently they could never be confused with the divine substance, which is most simple and in no way multipliable.

505. In the third place, corporeal feeling is truly distinct from intelligence, and blind. God however is essentially intelligible and intelligent. He cannot therefore in any way be confused with a sensitive soul.

506. In the fourth place, the sensitive soul is simply the sensitive principle, with matter as its term and in natural opposition to the principle. These two things (principle and matter) have different natures. It is therefore impossible to reduce all things to a single nature or substance, as the pantheists do.

[502–506]

507. These facts clearly indicate that if anyone wished to deduce pantheism from animation of the particles of matter, he would have to confuse 1. what is contingent with what is necessary; 2. what is multipliable with what is unmultipliable; 3. feeling with intelligence (he would have to be a sensist),[241] and 4. the sensitive principle with its felt term. Pantheism in fact is nothing more than absolute confusion, honoured with the title of 'system'.

508. Synthesis in the human mind precedes distinction of concepts, just as chaos in creation precedes the distinction of parts in the universe. It comes as no surprise therefore if pantheism appears at the beginning of all philosophies. Not that confusion is necessarily natural to the human mind. What is natural is that the mind begins to think in great generalities and perceives real things as a single, varied thing, so to speak. But in composing a philosophical system out of these first, poor materials, human beings grow proud and, confident of what they can do, rush headlong into error and invent pantheism. Nevertheless, because every error has its origin in some truth, it will be helpful to consider the deviations of the human spirit in order to discover evident consensus or some general inclination of the whole human race. This may serve as an indication and characteristic of truth. In fact, it cannot be denied that there was always and everywhere a very great inclination in the human mind to suppose that matter was animated, although the concept has been overlaid with errors.

---

[241] Virey rejected spontaneous generation because he was afraid of falling into pantheism. It is an important observation that sensists are much closer to pantheism than others, precisely because pantheism abolishes all differences, and sensism abolishes the difference separating feeling from intelligence.

Article 3
Opinions about the animation of the particles of matter

§1. *Indian philosophers*

509. India, where life in all areas of nature seems so fertile, indefatigable and luxuriant, was inevitably the country in which universal animation would be imagined more easily.

510. Moreover, the cause of animation was attributed to a universal spirit. There is a sense in which this unity of life would not be foreign to the truth; it is the way the East thinks. The Scriptures themselves speak of 'a spirit of life', which animates every living thing.[242]

In fact, granted that sensitive life multiplies with the division of living continua, all living matter must surely be conceived as united and organated, and consequently animated, as it were, by a single soul.

But once we lose sight of the multiplication of this soul through the division of its term, and claim that the soul preserves its unity even when the continua are divided and no longer have contact with each other, we fall into error; we have failed to acknowledge the multipliability of the soul and the plurality of souls.

511. Indian philosophers however added a much more serious error to this: they stopped at the world soul, accepting it as God, creator of all things. From that moment nothing could prevent them from descending into pantheism.

512. It is not difficult to acknowledge that matter exists solely in relationship to feeling. In feeling, the soul (the sentient element) is the active principle in which and by which the extended exists as felt. This very easily paved the way for *emanationism*.

If we accept the hypothesis of emanationism, all beings would have to share in the living substance of the first being from whom they are supposed to be derived.

513. The *Code of the Laws of Manu*, describing the origin of the world, says:

---

[242] [Douai] Gen 1: 2; 6: 3, 17; Job 12: 10; Ps 103: 29; Eccles 3: 21; Ezech 1: 20, 21; 10: 17; 37.

He who can be conceived only by the spirit, and eludes the organs of the senses, is eternal, without visible parts. He is THE SOUL OF ALL BEINGS, the incomprehensible one, who unfurls his own splendour. He resolved in his mind to make different creatures EMANATE FROM HIS SUBSTANCE.[243] He therefore produced water in which he placed an active seed.[244]

From this seed posited in the water, he himself emerged under visible form or like a supreme Soul (*param-atma*). From this supreme soul emerged 1. intelligence; 2. consciousness or 'myself', and 3. feeling diffused in the sensitive, active organs, and also a common, inferior sense. This explains the origin of all beings.

From the supreme soul, he (Brahma, the creating energy) drew the internal sense (*manas*)[245] which exists and does not exist for itself; from this intelligence, he drew consciousness (or that which produces 'myself') which admonishes and governs interiorly. From the supreme soul he also drew the great intellectual principle and the five organs of sense for perceiving external objects.
When he (Brahma) had used the emanations of the supreme spirit to suffuse the smallest particles of the six, extremely active principles,[246] he formed all beings.[247]

All beings therefore, like feeling, intelligence, consciousness

[243] Avya Kritarupat, which they translate as 'from his form not yet revealed and manifested'. This could mean from 'prime matter' or from the 'eternal possibility existing in the word'.

[244] Bk. 1, 7–8. Nevertheless, the Code of Manu distinguishes between animate and inanimate beings.

[245] I interpret the word *manas* as internal sense or feeling, basing myself on the poem of Ishvarakrishna, which is the compendium of Sankhya philosophy and mentions *Manas* in the 17th. distich: '*Manas* or interior sense shares substantially in the double nature of these two series of feelings' (that is, of the five organs of perception and the five organs of action). 'It judges, compares and is called 'sense' because of its affinity with the other senses.'

[246] These six principle are the five senses formed from the five subtle particles or elements. The sixth is the triad resulting from internal sense, intelligence and consciousness. Cf. the poem of Ishvarakrishna quoted above, distich 29.

[247] *Manava-Dharmasastra*, c. 1: 14–16.

and the five subtle particles or elements which compose the five senses, came from spiritual principles, and must all be accompanied by life and feeling.[248]

Hence it is no surprise that eventually feeling is attributed to plants:

> All these plants multiply from a seed or a cutting. They are enclosed in the obscure quality[249] and revealed in a multiplicity of forms or causes of their previous actions. Having an interior feeling, they are subject to pleasure and pain.[250]

In a word, the whole universe is, in this system, the Creator himself under a particular form.

> Because the six imperceptible molecules contain the six successive emanations of the supreme being,[251] the wise men called his visible form *s'ariram* (receiving the six). The elements, with their active faculties, penetrated this visible form, as did the triad (*manas*),[252] the inexhaustible spring

---

[248] Material elements cannot subsist on their own. Ishvarakrishna says, 'Like an unsupported picture or a shadow without solid body, subtle being or body lacking support cannot subsist without the different element' (distich 41). Later he says: 'Body cannot subsist without conditions or modes of being. The development of conditions and modes of being, like manifestation, can never subsist without body. A double creation (intellectual and elementary) is therefore said to proceed from body and conditions.'

[249] The *obscure quality* is explained in Bk. 12: 26, 29 where it says that its distinctive sign is *ignorance*. It is defined as 'a disposition lacking the distinction of good and evil, incapable of discerning objects, inconceivable and unappreciable by consciousness and the external senses.' Hence in this philosophy, the distinction between *brute* and *animated beings* is reduced to this; in brutes the faculty of knowledge is present but hidden. Ishvarakrishna says, 'This body, formed for use of the soul, behaves like an actor: according to inclination, it clothes itself sometimes in the original conditions of intelligent principles, sometimes in the derived conditions or non-intelligent principles. It all depends on the union between the procreating nature and its essential virtue' (distich 42).

[250] *Manava-Dharmasastra*, c. 1: 49.

[251] The six successive emanations are the triad (internal sense, intelligence, consciousness) and the five elements from which the five sense-organs are made.

[252] The triad, too, is included in '*manas*' which sometimes means the internal sense alone, principle of the triad, because the internal sense is understood to contain consciousness and intelligence which emanate from it.

of beings that have corporeal organs. This universe was formed from the most subtle parts of these seven principles,[253] that is, from parts manifested under a visible form and endowed with a great creating energy. The universe is change of what is unchangeable.

514. The life of all beings and of all the molecules composing the universe is mentioned, among other places, in the *Isha-Upanishad* of the Yajur-Veda, where we read in the translation of J. Pauthier:

> This universe and all that moves in it[254] is full of the energy of the Being that gives order. Surely, no one who acknowledges that all beings are in the universal Soul can see anything foolish in this? Let my breath of life be absorbed in the universal and MOLECULAR SOUL of space.[255]

According to this system death is simply the dissolution of the external form; feeling never perishes. Individual souls pass

---

Cf. the *Uttara Mimamsa*, bk. 2, c. 4.

[253] Here, seven principles are mentioned in place of the previous six. The six, having emanated, corresponded to the six emanations; the seventh is the emanator. Ishvarakrishna's poem says, 'The procreative root is uncreated. The great one or intelligence and the other procreative and procreated principles are seven' (distich 3). The first procreator is thus included in these principles. He is precisely the one manifested in the universe in his visible form, and consequently is the first, fundamental principle of the world. The six emanations are mentioned in the *Code of Manu*, bk. 1, 74–78: 'At the breath of this night, Buahora, who had fallen asleep, was woken, and upon waking, made the spirit (*manas*, the triad) emanate which essentially exists, and does not exist through external senses (first emanation). The *spirit* (the triad), moved by the desire to create, effects creation and gives birth to air, which the wise men consider endowed with the quality of sound (second emanation). The air undergoes a change and becomes the vehicle of all odours, pure and very strong, whose known characteristic is tangibility (third emanation). Next, a metamorphosis of air produces fire, which gives light, dispels darkness, shines and is said to have the property of visibility (fourth emanation). Then fire undergoes a change to become water, whose quality is taste (fifth emanation). Finally, from water comes earth, whose quality is odour (sixth emanation). This is how creation is effected at the beginning.'

[254] Note carefully that Indian philosophy explains *motion* by appealing to the first spiritual being, and gives the universe a soul.

[255] 1: 7, 17.

[514]

into the universal soul when the aggregation of their matter is broken up. There is nothing but change in the universe. This explains the distinction between the corruptible *universe*, subject to destruction, and the incorruptible principle and the imperishable elements[256] which properly speaking constitute its intimate substance.

515. This very ancient way of explaining the phenomena of the world demonstrates how antiquity was convinced that phenomena cannot be reasonably explained by recourse to brute causes as our modern materialists maintain.

The explanation also shows the foundering rocks of pantheism, emanationism and the transmigration of souls. These errors can so easily be espoused if such a delicate question is not approached with the greatest perspicacity and caution. It is clear however that they are not the necessary consequence of the hypothesis that corporeal elements are indivisibly united with a feeling whose term they constitute. This feeling would not always be one, and would not emanate from God as if it had something of his own substance. Created from nothing, the feeling could not be confused with matter nor with the intellective principle which in human beings is superior to matter.

§2. Greek and Italian philosophers, and those of other nations

516. From the East, we turn to Greece. Here, nearly all philosophical schools admitted the opinion of a world soul. Plato, Heraclitus and other schools each conceived it in their own way, but all agreed that the world was animated.

517. Many attributed life in the strict sense to the elements; among them, Empedocles. Sturz writes, 'Empedocles considered every element a spirit or soul.'[257] But Empedocles took the

---

[256] 'Subtle beings (the elements) are durable, but those born from father and mother (organisms) are perishable and return to nothing' (Ishvarakrishna, distich 39).

[257] Empedocles, §9, 15. Aristotle, *De Anima*, 1, 1: 2.

matter to extremes and deified the elements. Plato also predicated sense of the elements.[258]

According to Plutarch, Democritus 'believed that all things, even dead bodies, share in a soul. Clearly therefore they always have a share of heat and feeling, most of which however has evaporated.'[259]

518. This opinion of the animation of the world was received by the Italians. Virgil presented it in magnificent verse, Cicero in most elegant prose.

519. I said that one of the errors which did harm to the opinion of a world soul was its constantly maintained unity. Another was the inability to draw a line between sense and intellect. This meant that a universal soul was posited which was both sensitive and intelligent. When errors of this kind penetrated the Church they became heresies.[260]

But spontaneous generation was not opposed by the Fathers of the Church. They sometimes explained it by having recourse to a primal animation of certain corporeal molecules.[261]

520. The Italian philosophers of the 17th century re-asserted the hypothesis of universal animation but, failing to distinguish between the sensitive and intellective soul, fell into the error of a single world soul. Telesio wrote a small work entitled *Quod animal universum ab unica animae substantia gubernetur* [Animality is governed by a single soul-substance].

521. Francis Xavier Feller wrote:

> Anyone who happily mingles systematic ideas with truths

---

[258] Πρῶτον μὲν οὖν ὑπά ρχειν αἴσθησιν δεῖ τοις λεγομένοις ἀ εί (Plato, *Timaeus*).

[259] *De Placit. Phil.*, bk. 4.

[260] According to St. Jerome it is heretical to admit a rational soul joined to all things. Commenting on the words of St. Matthew, 'He rose and commanded the winds and sea', he writes: 'In this passage, we understand that all creatures sense their Creator. The things rebuked and commanded sense the one who commands, not in the erroneous way imagined by the heretics who consider all things animated, but because of the majesty of the Creator who makes things that cannot sense us sense him' (*In Matth.*, c. 8, 5).

[261] St. Augustine held the same opinion: 'Certain hidden seeds of everything that visibly and bodily comes into being are concealed in the corporeal elements of this world' (*De Trinit.*, 3, 8. Cf. St. Thomas, *S.T.*, I, q. 115, art. 2).

God poured out universal, seminal matter on the earth for the preservation and reproduction of species, and simultaneously attached to it this neutral substance whose nature we do not know and of whose existence we have only some idea. This substance would be suitable for animating organic bodies and would exercise its activity as soon as it was present in a being composed of organs where it could use its forces. But outside this being, it would remain inactive and in a kind of inertia. This idea, which makes the state of nature extremely simple and allows the most general, all-embracing explanations, agrees almost completely with what Cardinal Tolomei, Fr. Kumeth, Himheim, M^r Le Cat, etc. have written about the argument. Bossuet[262] and Fr. Kirker follow the same opinion in their writings.[263]

However, this addition of a neutral substance of the kind suggested above, as a sort of minister of animation, is merely the addition of one entirely gratuitous hypothesis to another. All we need suppose is that feeling is attached to the elements, and at once we have a satisfactory explanation of the facts of spontaneous generation and of the various manifestations of life, movement and organising process throughout the world.

522. After Van Helmont proposed his *archeus*, the philop}hers and doctors who called themselves 'Neo-Pythagoreans' arrived on the scene. They spoke about a *common soul*, which they distinguished from the intellective soul. One of their principal errors was the *transmigration* of this soul. We must note however that the transmigration of a purely sensitive soul is not only erroneous but absurd, because such a soul cannot transmigrate from one body to another without detaching itself from the first, and it cannot do this without perishing or losing its identity.[264]

523. We can say therefore that the hypothesis of the animation

---

262 *Discorso sulla storia universale*, 2 part., n. 1.

263 Kirker, *Mund. subt.*, 2 part., p. 337: 'This hypothesis, strangely distorted by Carra in his *Nuovi Principî di Fisica*, concerns the origin and nature of the human soul.' Cf. also Sennert, *Medicina practica*, bk. 6.

264 Cf. M. A. Sinapius, *Theoremata et quaestiones etc.*, c. 5, which speaks about 'the outpouring of spirits and the transmigration of the common soul according to the modern Pythagoreans'.

of matter was never clearly presented free from errors and arbitrary additions. If we brought together all who have posited it in so many different ways, without counting the errors added to it, we would find it common to all the principal schools of philosophy in all ages, as follows:

1. Materialists agree with it. For them, the cause of life and feeling is a force attributed to matter. Their only error is their inability to distinguish between this force and matter itself.[265]

2. All those who admitted or admit a world soul agree with it. Their only error is to make this soul intelligent and independent; they also exclude plurality of individuals.

3. *Pantheists* and *emanationists* agree with it. They err solely by making souls parts of the divine substance, or even the divine substance itself arranged in various ways.

4. Naturalists agree. They suppose a neutral substance, a biotic fluid, a weightless *quid* invading and suffusing everything, animator of everything. They err simply by admitting an extra substance in nature, of which neither the existence nor the power is proved.

5. Pythagoreans throughout the ages, or rather all the most ancient schools, agree. They admitted a common soul which individuates or transmigrates, but erred by adding transmigration to the above-mentioned errors.

6. All the various kinds of *idealists* agree. For them, matter is a modification of spirit. Their only mistake is to confuse term (matter) with spirit (principle), what is sensible with what is intelligible.

If all these systems are stripped of their errors, we find a fundamental opinion common to all, namely, the need to suppose animated matter.

§3. *German and English philosophers*

524. The hypothesis that life is joined to the elements of

[265] Geo. Freitag, professor at Groningen, undertook to demonstrate against Sennert the activity of the elements and the origin of form and of the brute soul of matter. Cf. his *Novae sectae Sennerto-Paracelsicae detectio et solida refutatio* (Amsterdam, 1637).

matter was fostered and at the same time corrupted more than ever in Germany, the homeland of transcendental idealism.

The impetus given to German philosophy by Schelling's *Ideen zu einer Philosophie der Natur* is well known. Kant, who took a great deal from Leibniz's system of monads, also made a contribution. Leibniz himself had to some extent been preceded by the Englishman, Glisson (d. 1776), who in turn had been preceded by our Italians, Telesio, Bruno, Campanella, Cardano (d. 1576) and others. I will discuss Francis Glisson's presentation of the theory.

525. He begins by stating that the concept of substance can be applied only to that which has three faculties, *perceptive*, *appetitive* and *motive*.[266] Then, taking for granted that bodies are substances, he tries to demonstrate that material substance itself has these faculties.

In Chapter 15, he had already dealt with the distinction between *natural perception*, which he attributes to material substances, and *sensation*. It is here that he reveals his total lack of understanding of the nature of *sensation* and how it differs from *intellection*, with which he confuses it. At the same time he at least glimpses something of the truth, if not the truth itself. For example, in comparing his *natural perception* with *intellectual perception*, he indicates the following difference:

> The former (natural perception) is a necessary, simple faculty tending directly to action; the latter (intellectual perception) is, as it were, doubled or judged, and terminates in action by means of free will. In my opinion, intellectual perception presupposes natural perception which it contemplates inflexibly as it were, and therefore perceives the perception of it (He should have said 'perceives that perception').

---

[266] 'I say therefore that all substances, properly so called, that is, subsisting in themselves or by their own effort, have A KIND OF VITAL NATURE; they are endowed with three basic faculties, perceptive, appetitive and motive' (*De natura substantiae energetica, seu de vita naturae eiusque tribus primis facultatibus perceptiva, appetitiva, et motiva naturalibus, etc.*, London, 1672, c. 16). Glisson saw that a body without life could not be conceived, but he made no distinction between life and body. He did not see that body is simply the term of a sentient principle, a real term endowed with its own activity in opposition to the vital activity united to it.

I myself have indicated this important difference between *sensitive* and *intellectual perception*. The former is simple and involves no judgment; the latter is double and accompanied by a judgment. Although the Englishman's authority confirms my teaching, he did not see that *intuition* is prior to *intellectual perception*. Intuition, which involves no judgment, is *objective*; *sensation* and *sensitive perception* are subjective and extrasubjective.

526. Moreover, Glisson glimpsed the *objectivity* of intellectual perception when he saw that its *objectivity* was a necessary condition for the existence of will and of freedom. He said:

> The second difference (between, for example, intellective perception in an angel and natural perception) is this: an angel's intellect can represent the object to its will 'with a kind of objective indifference', so that its will exercises its free choice over the object by choosing or not choosing it. If the eligible object is not presented to the will with some kind of indifference, freedom cannot be exercised relative to it; the choice remains predetermined and necessitated by the unbending dictate of the intellect.

Here, I agree with Glisson. He attributes to the object of the intellect, as such, an indifference that can be removed by the will, which thus renders the object good or bad for itself. I have called this function *practical reason*; it freely causes one object rather than another to be better for us and to prevail.

527. But when Glisson tries to distinguish between *natural perception* (which corresponds to what I have called *fundamental feeling*) and *sense* (which corresponds to my *sensation*), he shows his lack of clear and distinct ideas, because he knows neither the distinction between extrasubjective phenomena and subjective facts, nor the other distinctions mentioned above.

Glisson therefore assigns the following differences to his *natural*, or as he calls it, *animal perception*:

1. It is homogeneous and inorganic, whereas sensitive perception is organic. — This difference, however, is purely extrasubjective and does not imply an internal difference between the two perceptions.

2. It is simple, whereas sensitive perception is composed

and, as it were, doubled because it is a perception of a perception. — Here he failed to observe that sense does not turn back upon itself. It is always most simple, although *perception*, in so far as distinct from *sensation*, contains an extrasubjective element. In this sense it can be said to be composed of two elements, but never of a perception which has another perception as its object. Perception, in which there is only a term but never an object, is always single. Consequently, because Glisson did not recognise the essential simplicity of sensation, he later had to endow his natural perception with a kind of duplicity which led him into intricate, subtle and totally useless arguments.

3. Hence he even endows sense with judgment: 'Sense includes a certain kind of implicit judgment about the thing perceived.' Again, he confuses sense with *intellective perception*, although in sense the thing perceived is not even an object (a judgment can be made only about an object) but an element which, relative to the sentient principle, has the concept of matter or of term. The activity of the sentient principle exists only with its term and, because it is individual, cannot multiply itself nor judge the element that it needs in order to exist.

4. Glisson, still on the same mistaken path, grants to sense the possibility of erring, even though error pertains only to judgment, that is, to a function of reason.

5. He believes that sense can contemplate an object: 'The perceived object is contemplated as something outside oneself.' And he is so far from conceiving sensation and sensitive perception in their purity and simplicity that he invariably and arbitrarily adds some intellectual element. Consequently, in speaking about his *natural perception*, he invariably uses expressions which are applicable solely to *intellective perception*; he furnishes his natural perception with a SELF, and the faculty to represent itself, its causes, its effects, etc.[267]

528. But this is no surprise — I say quite openly and honestly that I have never found a philosopher able to form the concept

---

[267] 'The OBJECT (of natural perception) is its own entity which REPRESENTS ITSELF AND ITS CAUSES AND EFFECTS together with all the INFLUENCES brought to bear by other things, such as association, co-operation, consent, dissent, etc.' (*op. cit.*, c. 15).

of *simple sensation* without adding to it something intellective or material.[268]

Article 4
Does the hypothesis of animation contradict common sense?

529. There are certain questions about which common sense says nothing, because they do not present themselves to the minds of the majority of people. One example is the question of the animation of the first elements, which is discussed only in philosophical circles.

530. Indeed, although common sense divides bodies into animate and inanimate, it says nothing about the problem under discussion. It is speaking only about life as seen by our exterior senses, without any intention of discussing the other question: 'Can a latent life, some kind of sensitive principle, be united to certain bodies that lack animal organisation?'

531. In any case, the common distinction between animate and inanimate bodies remains solid. We must not change the common use of these words, except to give them a wider, truer meaning within the sphere of philosophy. An inanimate body can be defined as 'that which gives no signs of life due to lack of suitable organisation', or 'a body without organisation which, as such, is inanimate'. An animate body can be defined as 'that which gives signs of life', or 'a body with organisation which, as such, is animate'.[269] In this way, philosophical opinion is fully reconciled with common sense.

---

[268] Among modern Italians who have attributed properties of life to the elements or to the molecules of bodies, we find, in addition to Forni, Anton Giuseppe Pari, *Ricerche analitico-razionali sopra la fisica, l'analisi, e la vita della molecola chimica di prim'ordine ecc.*, Milan, 1834.

[269] In my hypothesis, the life of the organism would be a life of stimulation; the life of a simple element would be simply a life of continuity. Common sense has never examined, nor does it know, whether a life of continuity exists. I will throw greater light on this later.

Article 5
Does the hypothesis of the animation of the elements harmonise with the progress of the natural sciences?

532. But what do observers of nature have to say? The history of natural sciences certainly shows that the more we observe and experience, the further the realm of life extends. The sensitivity granted by Haller to certain parts of the body was extended by physiologists to other parts indefinitely. The discovery of polyps, infusoria, the spontaneous movements evidently manifested by globules of blood, etc., and innumerable other discoveries confirm the presence of life in a limitless number of bodies which seem and are at first considered totally inanimate. Ehrenberg thought he recognised that different rocks, particularly the rotten-stone, were made out of animal shells. Mault believed he had discovered that dental tartar was virtually a composite of little animals.

Payen and Mirbel claim that plants are a mass of numerous, microscopic creatures. When presenting a volume on plant physiology to the Academy of Sciences at Paris in February 1844, Payen said:

> Among the many facts I have observed, there seems to be a universal law which has led me to view plant life in a new light. If I am not mistaken, everything that we can see directly or magnified in plant tissue in the form of cells or vessels is simply protective casings, containers and channels in which animate bodies, that produce these things by secretion, reside, maintain and transport their food, as well as deposit and leave secretions.

Article 6
Apparent life and latent life

533. The hypothesis of the animation of the first elements of bodies thus coincides with the hypothesis, admitted universally today by physiologists, that there is latent life which produces no stimulated, external phenomena if the conditions necessary for their production are lacking.

[532–533]

But why are some phenomena considered to manifest life, and others not?

The only answer is our own experience, the sole criterion for distinguishing the phenomena; the only rule we follow is what we observe in ourselves, and then use to judge other natural beings. For example, we note the sounds we make when we feel acute pain, and experience great pleasure. The quality of the sounds, or of others analogous to them, are a sign which makes us conclude that beings who in similar circumstances make similar noises, experience pain or pleasure. We look at our own organisation and note how our bodies are structured, how our sensitivity is joined to nervous filaments, how different parts of our bodies contract on occasion of feelings; we see the kind of phenomena that accompany feeling or its cessation in our bodies. We then infer that a similar feeling must be present in beings where the same or similar things occur. But this is always a relative yardstick. It is not certain proof that life cannot exist under other forms, life which, although certainly different from our own, is nevertheless life and feeling.

Article 7
Three forms or levels of sensitive life: life of continuity, of stimulation and of self-renewing stimulation

534. The hypothesis, when considered in all aspects, indicates three kinds of feeling:

1. A feeling whose sole term is extension. This would be attributed simply to the individual elements of bodies.

2. A stimulated feeling whose term is extension but combined with intestine movements. It is not immobile extension, like the elementary term. This kind of feeling requires multiple, contiguous elements and movement. It requires therefore some kind of composite, dependent at least upon aggregation, if not organisation.

3. A stimulated feeling in which the stimulation is maintained by reproducing itself with some variation on the same theme. This requires a true organism in which intestine movements can be perpetuated.

[534]

The three kinds of life therefore that we must carefully distinguish are:

1. The life of separate, individual, mutually independent elements.

2. The life of united elements, that is, aggregated but not organated.

3. Finally, life which manifests external phenomena of its own and requires full organisation.

Let us consider each separately.

§1. *The first kind of life (non-apparent): a feeling of continuity*

535. If we imagined a single element of matter, extended and perfectly solid, as I think the first elements are, it would give no sign of life. Even if it could act on our senses, which is impossible owing to its smallness, it would not give us any sign of life nor provide itself with any movement nor receive any movement in itself. At the same time, however, its sentient principle would be simple, and the term of this principle would be the tiny space determined by the element. If we suppose the matter of the element to be uniformly dense throughout, the felt term would be homogeneous and uniform. On the other hand, if the density varied in the element's different strata or points, there would be difference of intensity [*App.*, no. 8]. In this minute life the characteristic of *continuity* would be fully present.[270]

---

[270] Glisson, in his work *De vita naturae* quoted above, acknowledges that the cohesion of his sentient or (as he calls them) percipient elements results from their continuity: 'The elements, which perceive the utility they enjoy from their mutual union, love or desire their union. Consequently they strive to preserve the union by adhering together. This internal cohesion is simply movement, or movement which results from continuity, and is used by nature to preserve continuity. By the natural means of perception and desire, therefore, cohesion is first grounded IN CONTINUITY' (c. 34, n. 22). However, we must note that according to us it is sufficient for the elements to be continuous at some point of contact, which excludes the question of void and filled space.

§2. *The second kind of (non-apparent) life: a feeling of simple stimulation*

536. If to one animate element we add other animate elements, we can readily conceive new phenomena. Let us suppose that the elements are differently shaped. Held together by their own attraction or retention, the polyhedra they form will vary according to the shape of the elements. If we suppose that their shapes are regular, the polyhedra will be regular.

These regular polyhedra however will differ from each other not only in shape but also in density and consequently in specific weight. This will be clear if we bear in mind that the following two accidents depend on the different forms assumed by the first elements that unite:

1. The points of contact will vary in quantity, with the result that the closest union will be among elements that have larger surfaces touching.

2. The intervals inside the crystals will vary in size, so that the greater the empty space enclosed by the surfaces of each elementary crystal, the smaller the specific weight or attraction of each crystal.

537. If at first only two elements unite, their bination must result in molecules whose properties differ from the first elements. This difference will increase markedly with ternation, quaternation, etc, of the first elements.

538. If we suppose that the first elements, even when in contact, unite with a force less than the force which makes the matter of each element perfectly solid, we would immediately have new vital accidents. In these molecules the continuous felt element, to which corresponds a single sentient principle, is more extensive than in the first elements. If these molecules resulted from only two or three elements, perpetual, internal movement[271] could certainly never begin; there would be no

---

[271] I say 'perpetual' because two or three elements placed in contact would draw as close together as possible through mutual attraction, even though their centres of gravity were not in maximum proximity. But their movement would cease as soon as they had found the position required by their mutual gravitation. I assume that the cause of the attraction or gravitation is, as I will explain later, the activity of the sentient principle.

vital movements. But if the two or three elements were moved by an external impetus without dividing, the adjacent surfaces would rub against each other, and in this case the uniform feeling diffused throughout the elements would necessarily receive stimulation. It would not be absurd therefore for a sensation to arise in the feeling, in the absence of all extrasubjective phenomena.

Moreover, granted that the two elements no longer had their centres of gravity in the closest possible proximity, due to violence from outside, it would not be absurd to imagine that they were impelled to re-establish the previous equilibrium of forces by the activity of the feeling which invests them.

539. The feeling diffused in the two elements is single, due to their continuity and, while repugnant to separation from them, tends to unite itself to them, keeping them united and in immediate contact at the greatest number of points possible. It does this through the activity of that organising function I call 'retention', which I will discuss later.

540. Here we would have the characteristic of *stimulation*, in addition to that of *continuity*. But the stimulation would only be momentary and accidental because it would lack a system of successive stimuli to keep the elements of the little group in continuous, regular and harmonious movement.

§3. *The third kind of (apparent) life: a feeling of perpetual stimulation*

541. In the life of two or three, or certainly of a few elements united in a single molecule, we have 1. continuity, and 2. the possibility of stimulation, that is, two characteristics of life. But in this case, the stimulation, dependent on the external force which makes the elements slide and rub against each other without separating, would be momentary. It would arouse only a transient sensation, which could not be sustained by the spontaneous activity of the sensitive principle.

Hence the external phenomena of animal life are possible only on condition that living elements join together in a sufficient number. These elements would compose a machine of varying complexity and of such ingenuity that stimuli could be reproduced by the mutual action of the organs. In their turn the stimuli, perpetuating the movement, would arouse feeling. Feeling, once harmoniously stimulated, could maintain both the continuity of the parts and the unity of the organism; it would spontaneously assist the harmonious movement which would stimulate and maintain feeling in its very stimulation.

Article 8
Different organisation is the cause of the varieties of life

542. From these observations we conclude that *organisation* (which is itself a production and development of feeling) causes the varieties of natural beings and the different kinds of phenomena presented to our observation. Hence:

1. Composites of just a few elements can manifest only mechanical, physical and chemical forces. Their true cause is very probably the feeling inherent in the first elements which, through lack of suitable organisation, is unable to manifest itself in another way.

2. In composites of several elements, a certain regularity of organisation must begin to emerge. This is seen in minerals, and in similar aggregations visible principally in metals.

3. A more complex composite must result in plant organisation which of course lacks all organs similar to those with which human beings express pleasure, pain, instincts, etc. But their organisation contains a system of self-reproducing stimuli. All that is lacking are the external signs of feeling which human beings experience and express. If there were feeling in plants, we would be incapable of knowing its degree of unity, centralisation and stimulation.

4. With a more fitting organisation, the phenomenon of *irritability* or *contradistention* is *manifested*. This phenomenon, although incapable of revealing to us with certainty the existence of feeling, comes close to doing so both because of the similarity manifested by the movements of irritable, contradistensive bodies with spontaneous movements (which arise from feeling), and because the composition of these bodies resembles that of felt organs.

[542]

5. Finally, an even more complex and perfect organisation manifests extrasubjective phenomena, commonly called animal phenomena. Properly speaking, these phenomena confirm for us the presence of feeling, of the continuity of the term of feeling and of the unity of action of the feeling itself. Such unity is capable of dominating all movements, which derive from it their continuity and direction but not their principle. These movements reproduce the stimuli which re-arouse the feeling when it loses its state of excitation, and return it to its previous state.[272]

Article 9
Sensitive and insensitive parts of the animal

543. Moreover, the system under discussion indicates that not all the parts of an animal body are necessarily felt by the same individual, that is, form parts of the fundamental feeling itself. Some of these parts could have a feeling of their own which would, nevertheless, be necessary for constituting the extrasubjective machine where the arousal of the feeling must be reproduced or continually re-activated by stimuli which need not be term to the fundamental feeling of the animal.

544. The system also shows how some insensible parts of a body can become sensible, or viceversa, provided the feeling proper to them is communicated to and in continuity with the total feeling or, if separate from the whole feeling, at least co-operates with the organic unity.

545. Finally, the system shows why certain organs or parts of the human body seem to enjoy a life of their own, and are subject to death before others.[273]

[272] Chemistry, which has still much to do, supplies us with valuable facts in confirmation of these ideas. Minerals often result from only two kinds of elements; plants from at least three, but the animal body requires at least four kinds of chemical elements: oxygen, hydrogen, carbon and nitrogen. The last element is not necessary for plants. It is certain therefore that the phenomena of feeling are never presented to our external observation without a complex, multiple organisation.

[273] The ancients were aware of this partial life proper to some parts of the

Article 10
Important questions still to be solved

546. Difficult questions now arise, full of those enigmas which accompany all natural investigations. Nature itself is an enigma, resulting from numerous enigmas.

How does the feeling proper to an element, a molecule, a rudiment, an organ have continuity and union with the fundamental feeling of other elements, molecules, rudiments, organs? Is the continuity of parts sufficient, as we have supposed? Is this continuity sufficient to make the lesser feeling lose its individuality? Does it perhaps individualise itself through the maximum stimulation effected at a point of the continuum where, consequently, the vital activity accumulates, that is, the *intensity* of the feeling which is the centre of all the harmonious movements? If there are various centres, are there many sentient individuals in the same continuum? And can each of the different movements which continue from these centres independently of each other be so harmonised that they do not break the continuum into many continua? Is this not the case with polyps, gemmiparous, fissiparous animals and entozoa? If so, does each of the sentient principles have the whole continuum for its felt element?

Article 11
Direct proofs of the life of the first elements; these proofs make the hypothesis practically certain

547. Granted spontaneous generation, we must admit that the

human body. Aretaeus describes the matrix as follows: 'It would perhaps not be incorrect to view the uterus, the female organ, which is situated in the middle of the female ilium, as an animal. It moves backwards and forwards in the direction of the ilea and resembles the xiphoid cartilage in its movements sideways, left and right, sometimes to the liver, sometimes to the intestines. We could say that the uterus, in the human being, is like one living animal inside another' (*Delle cause e dei segni de'mali acuti*, bk. 2, c. 11, translated by Francesco Puccinotti). Galen speaks about the opinion of some doctors who considered every muscle as an animal in its own right: 'Indeed one of them said that our will perceives every muscle as a kind of animal, and that it draws and twists the tongue to the shape suitable for a sound or apt word.'

[546–547]

elements, or certainly the molecules of which the new tiny animals are composed, are already animate. Otherwise, materialism is inevitable, for we would have to say that life and feeling are produced from brute matter, which is absurd. The term of feeling is in fact the opposite of its principle. If the extended term produced the principle, which is essentially simple, the effect would be unlike and contrary to the cause, a violation of the ontological principle 'that every cause must produce an effect similar to itself'.

548. In the second place, if the elements lacked feeling, they would have no existence of their own, but only extrasubjective existence, relative to another subject. They would thus be impossible, absurd beings, pure illusions. It is certainly true that 'possibility is indeed thinkability; what cannot be conceived cannot be' (*in the principle of cognition*).[274] But a being that is a mere relationship with another cannot be conceived; when a being has a relationship, there must be some thing in it which constitutes the term *a quo* of the relationship. But if the element did not feel, it would be nothing in itself and could not be the subject or the term *a quo* of the relationship. It could not be thought, and being unthinkable, would not be. It would simply be a false appearance.

549. Observation provides two facts: 1. generation happens much more easily in the microscopic world than in the world of large bodies, and 2. spontaneous generation takes place only in the tiniest animals. These facts are highly probable proof that life is joined to the first elements. If so, the two facts are immediately explained. If life is joined to the first elements, it is self-evident that, while they remain unorganised, they are free to combine in the way more suitable to their life instinct (I will discuss this law of formation in the second part), forming without any difficulty organated individual animals. On the other hand, bodies which are already composites cannot organate themselves into animal form because the organising elements cannot move freely within them.

550. Now, all generation, even that of larger animals, always takes place by means of *humidity* and *heat*. Fluids are therefore the first living things and organisers, precisely because their

[274] *NE*, vol. 2, 559–566.

elements and molecules are mobile and, by organating themselves in different ways according to circumstances, bring animate composites into being.

551. A fifth proof of the animation of the elements is supplied by internal observation, which tells us that sensation extends in a continuum.[275] This fact is also proved by reasoning. If it were not true, we could not have any idea of the continuum.[276] But we do have the idea of the continuum. Therefore the extended felt must be continuous. Now, where something is felt, there is feeling; feeling and felt are two indivisible things.[277] That which is sentient is thus in all the assignable points of a felt body, and must consequently adhere to the first elements, that is, to the smallest continua of matter.

552. Whenever the argument permits, I shall give other proofs as confirmation of the life of the elements. Anyone who understands them thoroughly will see that the hypothesis ceases to be a hypothesis and becomes, it seems to me, another demonstrated truth.

553. It is not my intention however to solve these most intriguing questions. I think a philosopher has done enough by determining which hypotheses concerning these mysterious questions do not involve logical contradiction or contradict other metaphysical truths or the experimental data daily furnished more abundantly by the physical sciences.

CHAPTER 16

Unlimited space as the term of sensitive souls

554. In *Anthropology* I showed that a limited portion of space cannot be conceived unless we also suppose that solid, unlimited space is felt. I think I have demonstrated with this and various other arguments that all the phenomena manifested by corporeal feeling suppose every sensitive soul to have solid,

[275] *NE*, vol. 2, 846–870.
[276] *AMS*, 94–103.
[277] *AMS*, 258–261.

unlimited space, or if we prefer, *unmeasured* space as its nature-given term. Corporeal, felt terms originate in this unlimited space and extend into a limited space contained within determined borders.

555. If we add to this doctrine the teaching about the animation of the elements, then the corporeal elements I have described approximate in some way to Leibniz's monads, which represent the universe. My elements, or rather my sentient principles, would certainly not represent the universe in the way Leibniz attributes to his monads. This great man claims that they represent the universe with all that it contains of both corporeal and spiritual beings; my sensitive principles encompass only solid, unlimited, unmeasured space in which corporeal beings subsist.

556. After reaching the opinion which I have just explained (it was not achieved lightly but only after long reflection and by logical necessity), I must ask myself whether a sentient principle could exist which felt only solid, unlimited space, and if so be an individual. Although obviously a question of pure possibility, it is not without its usefulness. Time is not wasted when we clarify concepts connected with those immediately required by philosophy. I maintain that the concept of such a sentient principle does not in itself involve absurdity. And if there were such a principle, it would certainly be an individual, in view of the simplicity and reality pertaining to the nature of a principle, particularly this principle.

557. There is however a rather important consequence: could there be only one of these individuals? If there were two principles with an identical term, such as unlimited space, they could not in any way have some distinct reality, because reality is the principle of individuation.[278] Therefore they could only be one, not two principles. The fact that they could not have a different reality is proved as follows. Their only activity or reality is that which they receive from their terms. If with our imagination we added some other reality, they would no longer be pure principles as our hypothesis supposes. If therefore the term is one and identical, the reality and activity of the principle co-relative to it must also be one and identical. But solid,

[278] *AMS*, 782–788.

unlimited space is one and identical. Therefore the principle which is referred to such a term must also be one and identical. This ineluctable argument is rather difficult to accept because the human mind so easily inclines to consider the principle as having some other appendage; the mind cannot see how a pure principle can be an ens, a substance, unless something else is attributed to it in addition to the sentient, perceiving act. The appendage would then be the difference used for distinguishing the imagined principles. But if the thinker strives to remove every arbitrary addition from the concept of principle, he will at once see the efficacy of my reasoning.[279]

558. Granted this, what relationship would exist between the single principle and the sensitive souls of bodies? These would arise and individuate deep within the principle by means of new terms, that is, corporeal terms. The initial principle could, in a certain but improper sense, be called the 'common soul', or better, the 'common principle of sensitive souls' (of corporeal feeling).

559. The individuality of these souls would remain intact, but they would have a proper act and an act common to them all. The former would constitute their own reality and substance, and hence their substantial difference. The reality proper to each would thus be the principle of their individuation. This agrees with St. Thomas' teaching, which is valid for merely sensitive souls, that matter is the principle of individuation of souls. There is nothing contradictory here. But we must discuss more extensively the individuality which constitutes them.

---

[279] This teaching is coherent with the other that a continuum, whether large or small (prescinding from stimulation) can have only a single sentient principle. From this fact I deduced the multiplication and concentration of sensitive souls. The teachings support each other because they have the same proofs.

CHAPTER 17
Individuality

Article 1
The concept and nature of individuality

560. Etymologically, 'individual' means 'indivisible'. According to this meaning, every essence, species and genus can be called individual, because they are supremely indivisible.[280] But the word 'individual' is more commonly used to mean the *indivisibility* of real entia, many of which frequently correspond to a single essence or a single species. This is the meaning I will use in this discussion.

561. A *real ens* is indivisible to the extent that it is one. But there are as many kinds of unity as there are different kinds of individuality and therefore individuals. Even an aggregation of several entia, when conceived mentally as a single, complex ens, can be called individual. This is however only a *mental individuality*, the individuality of a concept applied to reality. I am not speaking about this mental, artificial individuality, whose foundation is the unity of a concept; with the concept we think multiplicity *per modum unius* [as if it were one], as the Scholastics say. I am speaking about *real unity*, whose foundation is reality itself.

562. Real entia can be many, but each must be one. Indeed, if we suppose that a real ens is several entia, we contradict ourselves; if they are several, they are not one. A real ens must be one because the two parts of the division are identical. If the ens that was one, becomes two, there is no longer one ens, but two, each of which is one. Hence, every real ens, as ens, is one, and as one, is indivisible.

563. If real ens is indivisible, what is the origin of the concept

---

[280] St. Thomas distinguishes four kinds of individuals: 1. single, 2. most particular species, 3. most general genus, and 4. immediate proposition (*In 2, Met.*, Lect. 4).

of divisibility? The word 'divisibility' can be taken in a proper sense, or in an incorrect sense where it means *multiplicity*. In its proper sense, divisibility has its source in the mind or, more generally, in *perception*. For example, space is one and indivisible. But the human mind can think a limited space, and in doing so seems to divide space, because it restricts its consideration to that portion of space and divides it from the rest of space. But this action has in no way truly divided space; in itself space is totally indivisible. In fact, even when I draw in space an imaginary sphere, a metre in diameter, I do not stop space extending outside the sphere, as it did before I imagined my spherical space; nor do I prevent the space outside the sphere from continuing uninterruptedly from the space occupied by the sphere. The same can be said if a sphere limiting space is a real, corporeal sphere. Divisibility therefore in its proper sense is not real, but relative only to the actions of the perceiver.

564. Take a piece of continuous matter and divide it into two parts. Is this a true division? Strictly speaking, it is simply a *multiplication* which gives two individuals instead of one. To be a true division, I would have to have a divided individual. But I do not have a divided individual; I have two individuals. These two individuals that I have produced are certainly not parts of the same individual, because the two portions of continuous matter, being divided, form two wholes, not a single whole. They are not parts therefore, because the whole of which they may be parts does not exist. Can they be considered as parts of the whole that existed before the *division*? They certainly can — but only *by the mind*. Only consideration by the mind makes them parts of the whole; they are not parts when already divided, nor are they parts when united, forming one single continuum. Divisibility of matter therefore is again a way of thinking proper to the human mind and relative to its actions.

565. But could any matter be considered as an individual before the division? Is continuity sufficient to give unity to the being called matter? This question will be considered more deeply when I speak about matter. For the moment, it is sufficient to note that the individuality of matter is at most very imperfect; matter, as such, has no unifying principle. The individuality, the unity, of a real ens is found, properly speaking,

only in an ens which has the nature of *active principle*. The word 'principle' contains in its very concept unity and indivisibility. But the only *entia-principles* are sensitive entia and intellective entia. I must therefore speak about their individuality.

566. Sensitive principles and intellective principles are real individuals. They are first acts and, in the order of their own feeling, independent. However, although second acts are dominated by first acts and receive their unity and individuation from them, it is not absurd to conceive that a second act could arise deep within a first sensitive act. This would be an immanent act, and dominate the very act from which it arose. In this case, having become independent, it would constitute another individual. I say that the independence must be in the order of feeling, which means that the individuating feeling must not have another greater feeling dominating it with its activity. Let us apply these principles about the nature of individuality to the present discussion.

Article 2
Individuality of the human being in so far as it is rooted in intuition

567. We will begin with the individuality of human beings. It is not difficult for us to understand that no animal can have the particular *individuality* proper to a human being, who is a rational-animal subject.

568. Human beings receive their individuality from the intuition of being in general which constitutes them intelligent.[281]

---

[281] I have shown in *Anthropology*, 782–788, that reality is the principle of individuation. Human beings are *realities*. To know what individuates us, we must look for what constitutes us as real beings. In any case, relative to indeterminate ideal being, I have to say what I said about space: although we can conceive as possible an ens whose sole act by nature is the intuition of indeterminate ideal being, there could be only one ens of this sort. Our mind, if it forces itself to conceive two entia (which it thinks it can), is deceived. It would either think the same identical ens, or would add some other differentiating act to it, which is contrary to the hypothesis. Cf. *Teodicea*, 617–634, for the law of *excluded equality*.

This intuition is a most simple act and, by nature, alien to space, just as being, which is *per se* object, is most simple and unextended. Now the principle intuiting being is, in us, identical with the sentient principle. For this reason I called this single root of the two principles 'rational principle'. The sentient principle of human beings, potentially identified with the intelligent principle, is perfectly one, simple and alien to space, which pertains to the term of its act (to the felt). The singleness and simplicity of the immanent, intellective first act, therefore, constitutes human individuality.

569. A very important characteristic which distinguishes human individuality from the individuality of animals is rooted in the nature of ideal being, which informs all human beings. Ideal being is inexhaustible; even more, it is immutable and unmodifiable. Hence, it informs us without undergoing any change or restriction in itself. Strictly speaking, it is we who are brought into union with it, not it with us. It is in itself, and has no union with other things, although they may be in union with it; this union is relative to them, not to it. They feel improved by the union, and this feeling, which forms the union, is located not in ideal being but in the intuiting being.

570. Only when we understand all this, and cease to apply to ideal being the concept of union drawn from the reciprocal union of finite things, will we understand how reflection is possible. As intellective beings, we are informed by ideal being and exist through it. Nevertheless we, who exist through ideal being, rediscover ideal being, and in it contemplate ourselves informed by ideal being. This is precisely reflection.

Reflection presupposes 1. an intelligent principle whose form is ideal being and 2. ideal being in which we see ourselves informed by ideal being.

Ideal being has two tasks in reflection: it is the *form* of the intelligent principle which it constitutes; it is the *means* by which the intelligent, subsistent principle is known. As I said, ideal being is applied to itself by means of its inexhaustible or immutable nature.

571. Reflection is the origin of our consciousness or knowledge of self. *Myself* is posited by means of the different actions I have already indicated. Thus human individuality is perfected by self-consciousness. We feel and know ourselves; we know

and tell ourselves that we are a single principle (consciousness of individuality). This individuality is not in animals; it can be known only by human beings.

Article 3
Individuality in animals

572. The individuality pertaining to animals must be found in feeling, in the unicity of the sentient principle. I have distinguished a non-stimulated, uniform feeling[282] and a stimulated feeling. We have therefore two principles of individuation.

573. If a non-stimulated fundamental feeling were evenly diffused in a given continuum, the individuality would clearly consist in the single sentient principle in which the whole continuum exists. As we said, the continuum would not be continuous and one, unless it existed in what is simple.

574. But if some movements took place in the continuous aggregate of several elements, the stimulated feeling would increase in intensity in some points of the aggregate. Now, because the sentient principle is most active where it is most intense, it is most present where it is most active. In our case, the sentient principle is single, and, in so far as it extends to the whole continuum, individuated. But it has two acts: one with which it pervades the whole of the felt continuum, the other with which it concentrates in a particular part or different parts of it. The sentient principle is therefore individuated, and becomes dominant and independent, in proportion to the intensity with which it is posited in act.

---

[282] Glisson and others hold that there are degrees of absolute density in matter independent of the degree of porosity. I can only consider this opinion as a mere possibility. In fact, the porosity or intervals between the elements seems to me to explain sufficiently all the density we can observe. But granted the graduated density of matter in the smallest elements, we must suppose that their fundamental feeling also increases by degrees. In this case, the centre of the atom would be the seat of the greatest degree of uniform feeling, and this would be a third basis for animal individuality, a third principle of individuation.

[572–574]

575. We must now distinguish different cases. First, let us suppose that a greater intensity of feeling, stimulated by movement and limited to a tiny space, arises in a uniformly felt continuum. Individuality will be present because the feeling acquires the individuality of stimulation, and the individuality prevails through its intensity. It is founded on the act with which the principle feels more intensely and works more actively in this tiny space than elsewhere — a principle that feels more can also feel less, but not vice versa.

576. Now let us suppose two tiny spaces in the same continuum, in each of which the intensity of feeling has reached the same level. The individuality of feeling will not be lost; instead there will be two individuals in place of one. The act of greater intensity adhering to one tiny space cannot be the act of greater intensity adhering to the other because the intensities are equal. Nevertheless, in keeping with the principle that whatever feels more extension can feel less, the sentient principle that feels in one of the tiny spaces will assume the continuum into all its feeling, while sentient principle adhering to the other tiny space will do the same. This is a case of one and the same body animated by two souls united with each other, two individuals substantially joined together, as for example in cases of bicephalous offspring, annulates, polyps, gemmiparous and fissiparous animals, etc.

577. A third case can be supposed. Feeling, in a given continuum, could be concentrated and stimulated in different tiny spaces and to different degrees. If one of these stimulated, concentrated feelings were stronger than the other, it could be the centre of an instinctive activity so great that, suitably organised, it could dominate the activity of all the other feelings. Controlling and regulating its activity for its own good, it would bring about harmonious movements, capable of holding everything in unity. In this case, there would be a single animal of varying perfection even though there were several individual feelings, existing in the same body, which could not manifest their individuality externally because they would be subject to the other feeling. This is probably the case with all those beings we call animals, particularly the more perfect. Although separate feelings, and instincts relative to these feelings, exist in animals, only one feeling prevails and dominates. In a healthy

state, this feeling keeps in harmonious co-operation all the movements of the various organs that compose the body.

Article 4
Human individuality in so far as it is founded
in the perception of an individuated animal feeling

578. We must now consider the individuality of the animal joined to and fused into human individuality. Animal feeling is joined to intelligence through the *fundamental perception* that I have described. Consequently, its individuality is fused into human individuality.

579. We see again that only human beings can be conscious of their animal individuality. Hence, if in the same body there were lesser feelings which could be individuated, we could only be conscious of the all-pervading feeling we naturally and habitually perceive.

580. Parts whose movement did not modify the fundamental feeling which we habitually perceive and of which we can be conscious, would not be felt by us.

581. Here we see once more the reason why not every movement produces a sensation.

582. This will be better understood if we consider the following. First of all, it is a law of the fundamental feeling that although it extends to certain parts, it cannot reveal to us the locality of those parts;[283] the word 'locality' simply means a relationship between parts determined by surface sensations. Experience itself shows that not every movement in parts felt by us produces sensation. The retina, which is very sensitive to light, can be lacerated without our observing any sensation. Again, although the laws of *sensiferous movement* are little known, we could conjecture as follows. Every part of the human body is formed of molecules of varying composition. First, there are the elements; these form molecules of the first level, which form second-level molecules; these in turn form third-level molecules, and so on. According to the hypothesis

---

[283] *AMS*, 154–180.

we have suggested and are discussing, feeling always adheres to the elements. But does it adhere to first-order molecules and of all the succeeding orders? In other words, is the feeling of every molecule of any order in continuity with the feeling of another molecule, or is it continued by the elements alone and by certain determined molecules which cannot change their relative position unless the elements composing them change their relative position? I think it very probable that molecules are simply an organisation suitable in some way for the intestine movement of the elements.[284] I have laid down, as a condition for stimulation, that the elements to which feeling adheres and which are in contact with one another, must rub against each other and thus frequently change the extended continuous term of feeling. Hence, I do not stimulate any sensation if I stimulate a membrane composed of fiftieth-order molecules in such a way that the molecules, but not the elements, move and rub against each other, and if this elementary movement is not propagated to the centre, which is the term of the dominant feeling constituting the human being. But whenever I am able to arouse an internal movement in the elements so that the movement is propagated and in continuity with the central, intestine movement, I determine the sensation proper to a human being and capable of entering human consciousness. In fact, sensation is not caused by the absolute movement of the body and organs,[285] but by the relative movement among the felt elements, a movement which must be in continuity with that of the centre. If the intestine movements of the elements were limited to a part of the body without extending to the centre, a stimulated feeling would arise different from the all-pervading feeling because the movement would lack continuity, just as the feeling of continuity multiplies when the continuum divides and becomes discontinuous.

583. Only on these conditions does aroused sensation refer to the individual feeling of the human being, the all-pervading, fundamental feeling amongst all the feelings aroused in the

---

[284] If, when a molecule moves, no movement arises in its internal parts, and if feeling adheres to these parts, stimulation of the molecule's external parts cannot continue.

[285] *NE*, vol. 2, 804–809.

human body. Here we have, I think, the probable reason why the stimulation of the nerves must be propagated to the brain, granted that WE, who are the rational principle of the all-pervading feeling, are to sense it. This means that if such a sensation is felt where the stimulus is applied, that part also is included in the felt term of the all-pervading feeling. But to be included, the part must communicate with the centre, because the human fundamental feeling receives animal individuality from the centre, that is, from the unity and continuity of the term of the all-pervading feeling. If the part is divided from the centre, it pertains to another feeling.

584. For stimulation therefore to produce an individual sensation, the following is necessary: a movement must take place

1. in a felt continuum;
2. in the elements to which feeling adheres; and
3. the movement must be propagated to the seat of the individuality of feeling, that is, to the location of what is felt. This felt element corresponds to the greatest fundamental feeling and is individuated by virtue of its density, in such a way that the sentient principle feels an uninterrupted, continuous motion (that is, in the continuum).

CHAPTER 18
Living fluids

585. Today there is much discussion about the life of the fluids which circulate in animal bodies and account for eleven-twelfths of the weight of human bodies. What we have said may offer a solution to the question.

The following is clear:

1. These fluids can live with a feeling different from ours, of which we cannot be conscious.

2. It is not absurd to think that they, or a part of them, are terms of our own fundamental feeling of continuation. But granted that the sensitivity pertaining to our individuality is joined to their elements, not to their molecules, no stimulated feeling would arise from them. Because the fluids are pliable and

there are no stimuli, the elements composing their molecules are not displaced. This explains the apparent absence of feeling in the fluids: their molecules themselves may rub against each other, but this does not imply similar friction between the elements which continues as far as the centre of human feeling.

586. I will use another author's words to present the reasoning that leads many learned people to acknowledge vital properties in these fluids. The fact, if verified, will confirm the theory that explains the fact. Adelon says:

> Initially, vitality of the fluids was universally accepted. The reason was the rapidity with which the fluids corrupted when separated from the living body. — The theory also took for granted that every fluid was in continual intestine movement by which it maintained and renewed itself. For example, in haematosis, the blood acted analogously to a solid procuring its own nourishment.
>
> Later, the Montpellier physiologists went further, and unhesitatingly placed vitality of the fluids in the sensibility by which all the solids of a body are said, by abstraction, to be animated. They based their theory on the following considerations:
>
> 1. A general instinct affirms that there is life in the blood: the principal actions of animal economy tend to the formation and renewal of this fluid. It is the substance which repairs the organs, and the continual stimulus necessary for their activity. With its loss, life ceases.
>
> 2. Certain substances introduced into the blood, even in small quantities, modify it with a rapidity too great to be attributed to chemical action, fermentation, putrefaction or the action of solids modified by these substances. We must admit therefore that these substances act directly on the vitality of the blood. Boerhaave and Van Swieten, for example, report that a little scammony immediately caused coagulation of the blood; Felice Fontana injected the vessels of a living animal with the venom of a viper and witnessed the animal's immediate death and coagulation of the blood, an effect not found in a dead animal. Similarly, in medical practice, we see that astringent, weakening and antiphlogistic drugs, even in small dozes, produce such immediate effects disproportionate to the dose that the only attribution possible for the effects

is a direct action exercised on the vitality of the fluids. For example, a grain of nitro in a drink is very refreshing, yet the dose is so small that the effect cannot be physically explained. In the opinion of those who positively support this system, the vitality of the fluid has evidently been modified, and the part receiving the action has then defused the impression to the whole of the fluid. As proofs of this assertion, they note that Schulz and Benefeld stopped haemorrhages in other parts of the body by stiptic injections in the mouth, and that Fracassati injected a stiptic liquid into a dog's crural or jugular vein and saw all the blood coagulate immediately. They also base themselves on the authority of Treind, who attributes the power of resolvents to a direct action on the vitality of the fluids, and on the authority of Pringle who used this to explain the action of antiseptics which, he thought, forestalled the putrefaction of the blood by strengthening its vitality. According to Barthez, whose words we are quoting, all these facts seem to prove that there is consensus between the various parts of the fluids, which are therefore impregnated with life.

3. Affections of the soul modify the condition of the fluids; this fact cannot be contradicted. Boerhaave and Mathes observed that a nurse's milk was so altered by anger that the children she was nursing became epileptic. Anger often imparts to an animal's saliva the quality of transmitting rabies and of increasing the harmful strength of poison in venomous animals. Clearly, in all these cases, the fluids are affected so suddenly that the affection cannot be explained by the intervention of solids.

4. Observations seem to have demonstrated in the fluids conditions of temperature different from those in the rest of the body, and hence stemming from the vitality of the fluids. Hunter says he found that the blood's temperature differed from the body's; Borelli and Morgagni say that by blood-letting they have extracted totally cold but uncoagulated blood. Hewson and Dehaïn say that they have found blood to differ in colour, heat and density in different parts of the body

Finally, supporters of the vitality and sensibility of the fluids boost their system by saying they have sometimes seen, in health and in illness, the fluids share in the state of the solids. Thus, they note with Spiegel that in weak constitutions blood does not coagulate so easily, and mention that Stahl and Cullen claim to have seen blood become inflamed due to a general spasm, and that some epileptics have given a very liquid blood before, and a very dense blood during an attack.[286]

587. I am far from agreeing that there are corporeal substances separate from our body which, when applied to the body, immediately act on its vitality. In my opinion, body can act only on body; and a foreign body, as body, can act only on one's own body.

When our body, which is the term of feeling, is modified in this way, the feeling also must obviously be modified, increased, stimulated and even multiplied.[287] I have already suggested that the activity of the feeling whose term is the body could act directly on the feeling of the passive body.[288] The more I have observed the phenomena of animal nature, the more probable it seems to me that a living body has a double action on another living body, an action of matter and of feeling.

588. Indeed, according to the hypothesis, it is the feelings that unite and form a continuity when living molecules come into contact; it is the feelings that concentrate and individualise, and with their individuation make other feelings dependent on them, and govern the intestine movements of the continuum they pervade. Between these feelings there is sometimes harmonious, sometimes hostile interaction and communication.

589. Consequently, although the fluids of the animal body are insensible to the animal itself, they can be alive and invested with feeling as terms of the feeling of continuity, although their movements cannot stimulate feeling or produce sensation. Either their friction is not that of living elements, or the stimulation does not reach the centre where the seat of the all-pervading feeling is located. Alternatively, they can be terms of another feeling different from that of the animal to which they are thought to pertain.

The microscopic observations of blood globules by modern scientists seem to confirm that the fluids of the human body, or

---

[286] *Dictionnaire des Sciences médicales*, Art. *Humeurs* [Paris, 1818].

[287] *AMS*, 247–257.

[288] *Ibid.*

some of them, can be terms of another feeling. I quote a well known Italian doctor:

> Gruithuisen found that blood globules of animals whose heart has been removed are the seat of a particular movement called 'oscillatory'; the movement really looks like an oscillation, as if all the blood were finding its balance. Haller observed something similar in dying animals when the impelling force of the heart diminishes or ceases. Döllinger saw the same in young animals when their substance was converted into blood. Moreover, Heidemann noticed a slow *contraction* in blood globules that makes them turn in on themselves. This happens when they come to rest. These movements cannot originate from the heart or the vessels; they are proper to blood itself, where they foreshadow the first manifestations of vital movement. They are the steps taken by nature to raise matter gradually to a more elaborate, organised composition and to greater vital properties.[289]

590. It is indeed strange to hear some who deny the life to the fluids and speak only of solidism in medicine. If they bore in mind that liquids existed before solids, they would not make this mistake. Liquids precede solids in the formation of nature and in the generation of animals. This fact further illustrates the very ancient principle, which characterised the Ionic school: 'Liquid is the principle of all things'. Moreover, we must not forget the numerous observations made about the successive formation of the animal:

> The vescica proligera of the ovum contains a globular humour which on its own is incapable of the regular changes necessary for the formation of the foetus. But if a globule of the prolific male fluid is united to it, various reactions are immediately stimulated among all the globules and elements of the liquid containing them. At once the first rudiment of a seed is formed, to which other globules of the vescica proligera and of the vitelline fluid unite. These globules, which continue the same series of reciprocal reactions, decomposition and composition,

[289] Bufalini, *Fondamenti di Patologia analitica*, Milan, 1833, p. 268.

begin to form a granulated, gelatinous substance. Continuation of the same process changes this substance into cellular tissue. Next, the vessels, whose purpose is to distribute the nutritional humour, begin to appear. After this, all the other tissues are constituted, and the different organs and viscera formed, as described by Wolff and our own Roland.[290]

591. The life of the liquids will also explain assimilation by nutrition and the reproduction of some parts of the body:

This is the only way that the reproduction of parts amputated or destroyed by illness takes place in higher animals and in human beings. The reproduction always begins with the exhalation of a watery liquid rich in globules hardly perceptible with the most powerful microscope. The liquid becomes gradually denser and changes into a granulated substance as a result of the metamorphosis undergone by both the organised globules and the liquid containing them. New globular liquid continues to exhale and spreads among the grains, where it undergoes new metamorphoses. A cellular tissue is now produced, and the fluid deposited between its cells begins to flow with some regularity. The process that gave rise to the primitive tissue continues, and reciprocal actions multiply in proportion to the emergence of more complex tissues. Finally, new vessels, muscular fibres, nerves, etc., are formed.[291]

592. In the four kinds of known generation (viviparous, oviparous, gemmiparous and fissiparous), the particles of liquid giving life to a new individual detach themselves from the body. But because this very significant fact is so normal, we do not sufficiently reflect on it, although it alone, in my opinion, seems to prove that life is joined to the fluids. Our attention is stimulated more by another fact, namely, that vestiges of life are observable in particles which separate from bodies by accident rather than in accordance with the laws of generation as we know it.

---

[290] *Sulla generazione spontanea e sulla natura dei Zoospermi. Lettera del Prof. Secondo Berruti al Prof. Medici* [1st Dec. 1842].

[291] *Ibid.*

After Buffon,[292] who supposed the existence of organised molecules, many others tried to solve this problem.

In Italy, Professor Botto made special observations of the movements of animal and vegetable globules suspended in various liquids.[293] These movements could not, it seems, be explained solely by mechanical, physical, chemical and other laws:

> Organised globules move extremely rapidly, sometimes seeming to search for each other, sometimes to avoid each other. Occasionally, two globules that have established mutual contact suddenly separate. At other times two joined globules never separate, but undergo a metamorphosis by which they constitute a single body, a single substance that has clearly less mobility than the globules that compose it. This substance now becomes a centre to which various other globules move and, on arrival, almost immediately disappear. The metamorphoses they undergo not only increase the volume of the substance but change its shape and nature.[294]

593. We must not conclude from these observations that some action between the globules takes place at a distance. As I have said, I find no proof making me admit attraction between distant bodies; in fact, the contradiction I find in the concept induces me to deny it. The globules in question could have an intestine movement moving them from one place to another. Swimming in a fluid whose particles, it seems to me, are in contact with each other and endowed with feeling, they could quite easily extend their action to other globules swimming in the same fluid. This would be possible through the action of the feeling, which in the fluid itself would be continuous, although it could increase to such an extent in individual globules that they would become centres of greater action.

[292] Cocchi had already observed globules of blood and called them 'very lively, swimming' globules, after Malpighi had discovered them.

[293] *Observations microscopiques sur les mouvements des globules végétaux suspendus dans un menstrue*, J. D. Botto, professor of physics, Royal University of Turin, *Memorie della R. Accademia delle Scienze di Torino*, Serie 2, t. 2, p. 437.

[294] Berruti, *Lettera* quoted above.

594. In any case, we must reflect that different relationships are possible between the all-pervading feeling and other partial feelings. These relationships cease only when the continuity of the sensitive molecules ceases. Whenever these sensitive molecules, either in groups adhering to a centre of feeling or individually, separate from the animal body, they constitute other separate, individual feelings. But before they divide totally, their feeling can be united in varying proximity to the all-pervading feeling and governed by it, or at least influenced and maintained in a certain activity by it.

595. An animal's all-pervading feeling can contribute in many ways to the preservation of other individual feelings. All these ways can be reduced to two: a subjective way, which directly stimulates and activates the feelings until they acquire the intensity necessary for being individuated, and an extrasubjective way, which supplies the centres with food or applies extrasubjective stimuli suitable for maintaining stimulation.

596. In the first, subjective way, an animal's all-pervading feeling directly stimulates feeling in one of its parts with such force as to individualise it. This is what happens in the generative act, at least of the most perfect animals endowed with sex. In my opinion, the feeling present in the particles, which become a new individual, receives from the generative act that precise degree of enrichment necessary for their individuation. The individuation is of course aided by the separation of the seminal substance from the individuals to which it pertained, although it does not entirely detach itself from the female individual, to whom it adheres less than before.

597. The second, extrasubjective way offers many examples, above all in the foetus, which receives not only food but red blood from the mother. I do not know whether the mother extends her own fundamental feeling to that of the foetus or stimulates it directly, but if she did, it would help to explain maternal love. In any case, the foetus is supplied with red blood, impelled forward by the maternal feeling through the umbilical vein. This feeling maintains the interuterine life of the foetus by supplying the incessant, principal stimulus that produces the life of the foetus.

598. Many animals in fact live in other animals. Their life is so bound to the animal containing them that they die with it. They

are never found in corpses and die when taken from the body in which they live, although they contract for a time in warm water. We do not yet have sufficient data to determine how their life depends on the life of the larger animal, but the all-pervading feeling could directly communicate its own stimulation by extending its continuum into them. If this is not the case, the all-pervading feeling must, by means of its activity and the actions it produces in the whole body, at least supply these tiny living things with food and, very probably, with the extrasubjective stimuli which keep their feeling restricted to the level of intension necessary for it to be constituted an individual.[295]

599. Indeed, observation reveals that although some of these animals live only in healthy animals, and others are found only in diseased animals, the law governing their production and conservation is the same. The all-pervading feeling, when healthy, is active and produces movements in bodies different from those produced when it is ill. Hence, it must aid the development of different centres and produce different organisations within the sphere of the total organisation.

600. Among animals inhabiting healthy living bodies, sperm hold first place:

> When semen begins to corrupt, infusoria (which differ greatly from sperm) often develop, as in other fluids. Again, healthy semen gives rise to more numerous and mobile sperm, and to greater physiological activity of the organs that secrete the semen (these conditions are the opposite of those required for the spontaneous development of entozoic infusoria). As soon as the semen shows signs of putrefaction, the sperm disappear and immediately infusoria begin to appear. Animal parasites develop in young individuals that are weak, malnourished, of poor constitution, exposed to the inclemency of the seasons, etc., but sperm appear only when the body is almost fully

[295] If an all-pervading feeling exists whose term is a given stimulated continuum, and if in this continuum another tiny composed entity exists with organs whose internal movements are suitable for ceaselessly stimulating feeling but not for propagating the stimulation to the seat of the all-pervading feeling, then this fact alone makes the little entity a tiny individuated animal, as I have said.

developed; their ease of reproduction increases in proportion to the robustness and nutrition of the individual in which they are seen. They diminish in quantity, however, and even cease to exist, through the action of causes which weaken health and thus favour the development of parasites.[296]

Sperm are not only proper to the healthy body, they also seem necessary to it, because they seem necessary for generation. Berruti continues:

Can we justifiably consider the presence of sperm in semen as an accidental phenomenon, when we see that they never exist in the semen of infertile animals, and that their presence in it is a sure criterion of its capability to fertilise? The experiments of Prévost, Dumas and Lallemand[297] clearly prove that when the semen is filtered from its sperm, it becomes totally incapable of fertilising. On the other hand, the smallest portion of the substance remaining on the filter, principally made up of sperm, is sufficient to fertilise many eggs.[298]

[296] Prof. Berruti, who describes the matter better than I could, denies that sperm are animals; he attributes to them only the quality of *organic molecules*. But I think this is simply a question of words. There is spontaneous movement in sperm, which presupposes feeling, an individual feeling, and therefore an organisation. These, I think, are characteristics of the animal properly speaking, and must be distinguished from divided, animate, but not yet organated elements.

[297] Lallemand's important articles on sperm can be read in the *Annales des Sciences naturelles*, t. 15, pp. 30, 257, 262.

[298] I think Roland's opinion most probable. He says that the nervous system is given by the father, the cellulo-vascular system by the mother. This opinion is very close to that of Galen, who holds that the male semen turns into brain whose formation, he supposed, preceded that of the heart. Prévost and Dumas proposed the further hypothesis that only the sperm are used in fertilisation and converted into the nervous system. They note that the linear form of sperm has a bulbous extremity which would become the brain, and a tail which would change into the spinal cord. This hypothesis is opposed by the objection that while a system divided from others cannot remain alive, sperm continue to live. The objection however, does not seem to carry much weight. The essence of the animal is perhaps totally in the nervous system, while other parts are extrasubjective supports and stimuli, or at least parts where only the feeling of continuity is diffused, not the feeling of stimulation (at least in its normal state), which is the characteristic of the animal. The

It seems therefore that these tiny animals are as essential to the larger animal that harbours them as the generative faculty is.

601. Animals that seem to develop in bodies because of ill health, or that seem to produce ill health, are of many kinds: entozoa, mange-worms, lice, etc.:

> Every animal species has its particular entozoa which cannot live in a different species. They perish as soon as they leave the body where they originated. — Every internal organ of a body can breed only a particular kind of entozoa. Among these are hydatids or vesicular worms which have been divided into five major classes, each of which has been further subdivided. They all preserve their life through the influence of the life of the larger animal in which they live. Their division and separation takes place by means of the parenchyma of the organ in which they develop and by means of the membranes and vesicles which contain them. The vesicles' walls seem to have so great an influence in limiting the internal stimulation proper to these tiny animals that the stimulation cannot be extended or communicated to the larger animal which harbours, feeds and stimulates them,[299] and perhaps applies some of its own stimulation. This limitation must contribute to the individuation of these tiny fundamental feelings. The vesicle itself that forms each hydatid must contribute to the limitation. Furthermore, a more or less consistent, insensitive tegument which encloses all

nervous system cannot live by itself because it needs nutrition and stimuli. Sperm, however, receive stimuli and nutrition from the animal in which they live or into which they pass during fertilisation. Even if they show themselves to be alive when taken out of their natural habitat, it is only for a short time, and probably because they receive some nutrition or stimulus from the fluid into which they are put for observation. If, as Lallemand believes, sperm are originally all globular in form and later acquire a tail, this simply demonstrates that they also have a certain growth. We must note that, according to Czermak, there are as many species of sperm as of animals endowed with the prolific fluid.

[299] When the species of hydatids called egg acephalocysts, bud and grain acephalocysts, form in a part of the body abundantly supplied with a network of cells, they are seen to be surrounded by a more or less thick layer of cells from which they receive many blood vessels. This layer must supply nutrition, stimulation and perhaps participation in the stimulation enjoyed by the fundamental feeling of the host animal.

entozoa certainly seems to limit their organisation and their fundamental feeling to quite a small space, for which the walls of the tegument form a kind of dividing line.

In the case of the mange-worm,

the researches of Cassel, Raspail and Ranucci seem to prove that the worm almost constantly accompanies mange and in most cases is found not in the mange pustule itself but at some distance from it. It quickly moves away, forging a passage under the epidermis, to nest at some distance from the pustule. — Another species of this worm was discovered by Roland, Martinet and Murny in certain tumours on lepers. Dr. Simon of Berlin also recently discovered and described a third species of worm lodged in human hair follicles.[300]

Arguments to prove the spontaneous generation of lice in healthy children and in those suffering from phthiriasis were put forward by Fournier,[301] Sichel,[302] Burdach[303] and others:

Every animal species is subject to a particular variety of lice. Often, an individual of a determined species of living animal, quite separate from all the other individuals of its species, is seen to be pestered by lice proper to its species. Thus, after Patrin had hatched partridge's eggs under a hen, the lice on the partridges were those proper to partridges, without a single louse proper to hens.

602. All these living creatures seem to be generated from the larger host animal in both healthy and diseased states. Spontaneous generation is clearly much more evident at the break-up of the organisation of dead animals and of plants. When such substances are infused into a liquid, very many forms of spontaneous generation can be observed:

Infusoria of various species are obtained, depending on the variety of the infused substances and the different

---

[300] *Gazzette des Hôpit.*, 29th Nov. 1842. *Observations sur les acares vivants dans les follicules pilleux de l'homme*, Dr. Gustave Simon (of Berlin).

[301] *Dictionnaire des sc. med.*, art. *Casrares*.

[302] *Historiae phtirialis verae fragmentum.*

[303] *Traité de physiologie*, t. 1, p. 39.

conditions of the water and air, which play a part in the effect of the infusion. Thus, the infusion of a vegetal or animal substance lacking nitrogen will produce plant infusoria rather than animals. On the other hand, the infusion of an animal or vegetal substance rich in nitrogen but with little carbon will produce animal rather than plant infusoria. The infusion of different animal substances produce different infusoria, as Gruithuisen demonstrated. He observed that infusoria produced by musk differ from those produced by pus.[304] The change in state of an organic substance is sufficient to produce infusoria of a different species. Thus Spallanzani saw that the infusoria produced by boiled clover seed differed from those obtained from unboiled seed.

To explain all these facts we must suppose, it seems, that feeling is present in every element of matter, and that the composition of these little feelings together with the harmonious unity of their stimulation and accumulation — a composition and unity produced by the activity of feeling itself and by the laws governing composition and unity — produce these kinds of vital organisms and animals.

CHAPTER 19

Animal death

603. The foregoing supposition means that death for the larger, observable animals would simply be the dissolution of their fundamental feeling. Their individual existence would perish because of the loss of the organic composition suitable for the stimulated feeling which individuates the fundamental feeling.

604. Nevertheless in this event the primal, elementary feeling

[304] 'Gruithuisen (*Organozoonomie*, Munich, 1811, p. 164) says that he obtained a corresponding variety of infusoria by changing his experiments in a great number of ways.'

would not cease to exist. It would simply be composed differently, accumulated and stimulated, or, after dividing down to the elementary state, would receive other individuations, and thus cause the existence of other animals and living elements. This would explain spontaneous generation; indeed all generation would be reduced to a single law.

605. Metaphysicians, I am sure, would consider this not only as very possible and without harmful consequences, but as probable, if 1. they began their reasoning from internal observation of the consciousness of their own feeling; 2. they realised that without this observation, which makes them conscious of their feeling, the sensitive soul could not be known; 3. they accepted that the soul is found only in feeling and is defined as a feeling principle; 4. they acknowledged in this feeling principle an extended, variable, divisible and multipliable term; and 5. they noted that the principle exists only by adhering to its term, and multiplies when the term multiplies.

606. Note, however, that the intelligent soul is a higher principle. Intelligent being therefore cannot lose its identity and individuality through the loss of corporeal feeling, as I will explain later at greater length.

607. It may perhaps be objected against the universal law which I have discussed that no animal has yet been obtained by uniting purely inorganic substances. I know that some chemists claim to have obtained a rudimentary organisation by making purely inorganic substances interact but, leaving this aside, I maintain that the objection does not necessarily destroy the universality of the law I have proposed. It has already been demonstrated that certain, extremely simple aggregations of elements cannot give observable signs of life, even if they had it.

Whether elements joined in such a way as to acquire the wonderful organisation without which life cannot be seen or manifested externally by continuous, extrasubjective movements, need a pre-existent organisation as a kind of suitable machine in which the second composition can be elaborated and ordered, is a separate question.

608. Finally, it may be objected that according to this theory animal death would only take place as a result of disorganisation. Nevertheless, in certain corpses there is no sign of disorganisation. I reply:

[605–608]

1. Disorganisation can evade observation, as in fact often happens[305].

2. If life adheres to elements so minute that they escape human observation, the break-up of organisation may indeed be unobservable.

3. Finally, all observations carried out so far to discover which disorders in organisation cause death were made on human corpses. In human beings however there is a principle superior to the body. We cannot demonstrate as impossible that this principle has the power to divide spontaneously from the body without any preceding organic decomposition, although in this case, I think, a momentary alienation rather than a true separation must take place.

609. I must add here that the hypothesis of life in the first elements would reconcile two apparently contradictory opinions expressed by the best authors who, we must believe, had no real intention of contradicting each other so grossly.

The most brilliant minds thought that the immortality of the human soul could be proved from its being the life of the body. They argued that 'because the body receives the life of the soul, it is by nature dead. But the soul, which gives life to the body, cannot cease to live because it itself is life.'[306] This way of

---

[305] Cf. Houdart, *Etudes historiques et critiques sur la vie et la doctrine d'Hippocrate etc.*, bk. 3, sect. 2, which reports some facts about corpses in which disorganisation was accidentally found only at a later stage.

[306] St. Augustine writes: 'There are those who have found that the substance (of the soul) is not a kind of corporeal life but a LIFE WHICH ANIMATES AND VIVIFIES THE WHOLE LIVING BODY. Consequently, they have tried as best they could to prove that the soul is immortal BECAUSE LIFE CANNOT LACK LIFE' (*De Trinit.*, 10, n. 9). By 'body', he always means, he says, that which is extended 'whose location in space is less than the whole of space'. He thus excludes the sensitive principle, the soul of animals, as a body. Prior to him, St. Ambrose had said: 'The soul which creates life does not receive death' (*De mortis bono*, c. 9). Later, Cassiodorus uses the same argument: 'Authors of secular works have proved in many ways that souls are immortal. According to them, everything that vivifies something else is itself alive. The soul is therefore immortal because it vivifies the body and is itself alive' (*De Anima*, c. 8). St. Bernard argues in the same way: 'The living soul is certainly life, but only and exclusively of itself. If we want to speak about it correctly, we should say that it is life rather than living. Consequently, the soul when infused into the body, vivifies it. Here the body is alive through the presence of life, but it is not itself life' (*Super Cant. Serm.* 81); he thus

arguing is very solid, and valid for both the human and the animal soul. It demonstrates that the principle which gives life to the body, whether joined with intelligence or not, cannot perish.

The same eminent authors, who argue in this way, teach that the souls of animals perish. How then can they be reconciled with themselves?

610. The answer is: by the theory of life of the primal elements of matter, a life distinct from the organic-stimulated life proper to animals. Primal, hidden, initial life, which never perishes, pertains to the elements, and the argument given above fits it most aptly. But the patent life of animals does not consist in the primal feeling alone; it requires in addition stimulation, which must be continuous and regular. In other words, it requires organisation which reproduces a harmonious stimulation in a perpetual cycle. Hence, when the organisation is destroyed, the animal perishes. But although its very own life perishes, life remains, that is, the principle of its life or the soul adhering to the primal elements into which the organism breaks up.

611. The other argument for the immortality of the soul, deduced from the spontaneity of movement[307] applies equally to the sensitive and the intellective principle. Under suitable conditions, both have an ability to move of themselves. This argument is certainly efficacious but for proving the immortality of the life of the primal elements not the immortality of the individual intellective soul.

612. It is no surprise therefore that many of the ancient philosophers, unable to distinguish between the *stimulated life* of animals and the *quiescent life* of the elements, had maintained the immortality of both human and animal souls. Among such philosophers were the Indian Buddha or Shakyamuni, who said that animal souls differed only relative to the subject in which

concludes to the immortality of the soul. This kind of reasoning was common to the Platonic philosophers; cf. Proclus, *Theol. Platon.*, bk. 3, c. 1 and 21; bk. 4, c. 184–189; Iamblichus, *De Myst. Aegypt.*, sect. 8; Macrobius, *In Somn. Scip.*, bk. 2, c. 13–17.

[307] St. Athanasius uses the argument in this way: 'If the soul moves the body but is not itself moved by something else, it must be moved by itself, and after the body has been placed in the ground, the soul continues to be moved by itself' (*Orat. contra idola*).

[610–612]

they were present. Hence, these philosophers again made the mistake of distinguishing the *subject* of the soul from the soul itself.[308]

There are other, equally impressive arguments favouring the opinion that atoms are animated, but I will deal with them as corollaries of truths yet to be explained (cf. 459–460).

CHAPTER 20
The source of animal life

613. We can now improve and perfect the definition of animal. I have defined animal as 'an *individual* creature, materially sensitive and instinctive'. However, 'individual' needs clarification. What has already been said shows that the individuality of the animal consists in an all-pervading feeling governing all the feelings defused in a given felt extension. This explains the difference between *living elements*[309] and *animals*.

614. The elements have feeling alone; the constitution of an animal requires four conditions: 1. continuous feeling, 2. stimulation, 3. organisation which perpetuates stimulation, and 4. unity between organisation and stimulation resulting in a superior, dominant feeling. This feeling, greater than all others in the same continuum, dominates all the sensitive activities and thus individualises the sentient ens.

615. The question can therefore arise: 'Is there something particular in nature which provides animal stimulation and acts

[308] Naigeon, *Philosophie ancienne et moderne*, vol. 1, p. 245. Many Platonic philosophers argued in the same way: the soul is the principle of movement; therefore the souls of animals, they concluded, must be immortal. Cf. Plutarch, *Adv. Colot.*, and *Romul.*; Apuleius, *De Deo Socrat.*; Maximus Tyrius, *Disp.* 27–28; Plotinus, *Aenn.* 4, bk. 7; Macrobius, *In Somn. Scrip.*, bk. 1, c. 17, and Huet, *Alnet. Quaestiones*, bk. 2, c. 8.

[309] Buffon's expression, 'organic molecules', is inappropriate. If the molecules are organic, that is, organated in such a way that stimulation is perpetuated (this is the only composition of molecules that merits the name 'animal organism'), they are tiny animals.

as principal agent in the formation, restoration and development of organisation?'

It really does seem that, for many animals (perhaps for all), something particular, oxygen, is present.

In fact, if any part of warm, red blooded animals lacks oxygen, it gives no signs of animal feeling. This shows that without this stimulator the greatest, individuating feeling no longer has sufficient activity to preserve or exercise its dominion in them.

616. It is a very ancient opinion that animal life has its seat in the blood. I understand this as meaning that oxygenated blood is the stimulant of the individuating feeling in human beings and in other organated animals that have a certain perfection.

One famous author misinterpreted Genesis when he rendered the phrase 'the blood of lives' (*sanguinem animarum vestrarum*)[310] as 'the blood is life'.[311] Similarly, in another place we read that the life of the flesh is in the blood (*anima carnis in sanguine est*),[312] but not that the blood itself is life.

617. The same opinion is claimed for Homer, from whom Empedocles and many others took it.[313] It was certainly introduced into the *myths*, where we read that souls of the dead could remember things of the present life only by absorbing the vapour of blood, or blood itself. This opinion must have been to some extent the origin of the victims offered to the dead. The

---

[310] Gen 9: 4 [5, Douai].

[311] De Maistre, *Eclaircissement sur les Sacrifices*, c. 1. He also says incorrectly: 'Blood was the principle of life, or RATHER blood was life.' On the contrary, blood is not life; life is united to blood. Again, he translates inaccurately Lev 17, 10 ss., where it says that life is in the blood, not that the blood is life.

[312] Deut 12: 23 says, 'For the blood is for the soul. And therefore thou must not eat the soul with the flesh' [Douai]. This, it seems, must be understood to mean that animals have *living blood* in place of the rational human soul because the stimulating virtue of animal life is united to the blood. The sentence that follows, about not eating the soul with the flesh, must evidently be understood as not eating the substance which contains the stimulant of animal life.

[313] Tertullian, *De Anima*, c. 5: 'Empedocles and Critias form the soul out of blood.' Cf. Sturz, §15 for other places in ancient authors who discuss Empedocles' opinion.

following passage, preserved for us by Stobaeus, is from Porphyry:

> Now, among those who beyond the river have been divested of the sense of human things, only Teiresias preserves it. But the others in the underworld know only with an infernal knowledge. They can speak about human things only by absorbing the vapour of blood, just as souls that have absorbed blood have knowledge of human things. Although Teiresias himself has the sense of human things, he converses with living beings only after absorbing blood (of sacrifices). Homer, and many others after him, thought that human prudence was in the blood. Many of the more recent authors confirm this, and teach that when the blood is inflamed by fever or bile, it produces imprudence and foolishness. Empedocles also considers the blood as the instrument of prudence:
> > In the flow of blood,
> > Prudence has her seat;
> > Prudence which for us is blood
> > Swelling the heart and despatched in streams.[314]

Nevertheless, we see in all this that the sensitive soul is continually confused with the intellective soul.

618. In Italy, Pliny repeated the opinion that the soul is in the blood.[315] It has recently been re-stated by Rosa,[316] and, in England, more recently by Hunter,[317] who laid down this very helpful proposition: 'Organisation has nothing in common with life.'

619. Unfortunately these famous observers of nature did not see the difference between continuously stimulated life, for which suitable organisation is indispensable, and simple,

---

[314] Stobaeus, *Eclog. Phys.*, bk. 1, c. 51. Authors who quote Empedocles sometimes say that according to him the blood is the soul, sometimes that the soul has its seat in the blood, sometimes that it originates from the blood, and sometimes that the blood is the instrument of the soul or the first living thing. The passages of ancient authors can be found in the collection carefully assembled by Sturz in his *Empedocles*, §14.

[315] *Hist. Nat.*, bk. 12 [11], cc. 60 and 70.

[316] Cf. Gian. Rinaldo Carli, *Opere*, vol. 9.

[317] John Hunter, *A Treatise on the Blood, Inflammation and Gunshot Wounds*, London, 1794.

quiescent life, which consisted solely in feeling. In any case, I think we can safely gather from their experiments that the stimulating principle of stimulated, animal life is in the blood.[318]

620. But this is not all. The experiments of Bichat proved that only red blood, not dark blood, has the power to stimulate human animal life. Now we know that blood becomes red through the oxygen breathed in by an animal from the atmosphere, but we still need to know whether, in the case of fish and other cold-blooded or white-blooded animals, the stimulation which posits their life in act comes from oxygen taken from water or from elsewhere.

621. The atmosphere then is, for many animals, a kind of reservoir and perennial fount of animal life. Empedocles seems to have seen this. According to Theodoret, Empedocles says 'The soul is a compound of ethereal and aerial substances', whose seat, according to Empedocles, is in the heart.[319] Why the heart? Because the blood, laden with oxygen, passes from the lungs to the heart. 'Empedocles,' Cicero writes, 'thinks that the soul is the BLOOD FLOWING INTO THE HEART.'[320] Here, oxygenated blood flowing to the heart is clearly distinguished from the blood which the heart pumps to the unoxygenated extremities. Moreover, because the decomposition of air in respiration is a kind of combustion and produces heat, Empedocles considered the soul to consist principally of fire, and maintained that minds were alert or sluggish in proportion to the heat of the blood.[321]

622. Even authors like Anaxagoras, Anaximenes, Archelaus and Diogenes of Apollonia,[322] who attributed to the soul the nature of air, seemed to have accepted or glimpsed the same thing, as did all those authors, like Parmenides, Leucippus, Democritus and Heraclitus of Ephesus, who attributed to it the nature of fire. For Heraclitus, fire contained the elementary

---

[318] Hunter, according to *Recherches Anseatiques* (vol. 6, p. 108), placed in the list of truths the opinion that blood is a living fluid.

[319] Theodoret, *Graecarum affectionum curatio*.

[320] *Tuscul.*, 1: 9.

[321] Cf. the places mentioned in Sturz's *Empedocles*, pp. 446–447.

[322] Stobaeus, *Eclogae Physic.*, bk. 1, c. 40.

principle, that is, the *substratum* of everything, the universal agent. He therefore granted that the elements were animated by this principle,[323] and it seems he identified, or united, light with fire.[324] Empedocles, I think, must have taken many of his opinions from this source, which demonstrates that philosophers who seem to hold contrary opinions can sometimes be reconciled, just as I have reconciled those who consider the soul aerial with those who consider it fire.

623. The very etymology of the words 'animal soul' [*anima*], 'intellective soul' [*animus*], 'spirit' [*spiritus*], etc. — they all mean aerial substance — seems to prove that those who first formulated them, formulators and common-sense itself, thought that the animal, in breathing, drew in its life-motor from the atmosphere.

624. Perhaps this opinion is among those which go back to the origin of the world. Scripture calls the soul 'breath'; the soul was infused by breath from the mouth of God.[325] Commenting on these passages, Tertullian says: 'The soul is substantially breath, but from its effect it is called spirit because it breathes.'[326] This led him to his error about the materiality of the soul, which St. Augustine later soundly refuted.[327]

625. If ancient scientists had been content to teach that the animal draws the principal stimulant of life from the atmosphere, they would not have been far from the truth. But having confused the intellective principle with animal life, they went astray at the first step.[328]

---

[323] Aristotle, *Metaph.*, bk. 1, c. 3, 7; *De Mundo*, c. 5; Simplicius, *In Phys. Arist.;* Clement of Alexandria, *Strom*, 5.

[324] 'Parmenides and Leucippus (speak) of fiery nature. Democritus referred to the fiery compound of things perceived by reason; they had a globular as well as a fiery form. According to Heraclitus, this became the body of the light of nature' (Stobaeus, *Eclog. Phys.*, bk. 1, c. 40).

[325] Gen 2: 7; Is. 42: 5; 47: 16.

[326] *De Anima*, cc. 7–8; *De Resurrect. Carnis*, c. 11.

[327] *Ep.* 190; *Liber de Haeres*, 86; *De Gen. ad litt.*, bk. 10, c. 24.

[328] St. Gregory Nazianzen refutes this error in a poem about the soul:
Another opinion indeed is known to us
Which, while I see the light of day, I would never admit.
There is no mind common to me,
Which is pursued by all,

CHAPTER 21

The simplicity of the human soul relative to the intellective principle

626. Here, we consider the human soul as intellective and as *simple*.

Simplicity is a negative property, because it excludes what is multiple, extended and material. Nevertheless, it can greatly help our knowledge of the nature of the soul, because we consider it not by itself and abstractly, but in the soul's acts and operations, which give us some positive cognition. Knowing the soul positively through feeling and consciousness, as I have said, we can obtain reflective, scientific cognition simply by seeing how the soul *differs* from other things, and principally from bodies. This cognition is also composed of differences, revealed in the soul's negative properties, which exclude from an ens all that it is not.

627. I maintain that none of the soul's intellective actions could be carried out except by a simple principle. Consequently, there are as many proofs of the soul's simplicity as there are intellective actions. Each proof, when carefully analysed and meditated on, is so totally convincing that our investigation would never end if we wished to identify each individually. So I will deal with the intellective soul as I dealt with the sensitive soul when I limited myself to only a few of the soul's actions, although its simplicity can be shown by an analysis of any animal action. In the present case, I will limit myself to considering the kind of simplicity of principle required to produce the first intellective actions.

628. I. The intellective soul is a subject that intuits being in general. Intuition is a simple action because its object is simple;

> And which wanders about in any regions,
> So that all mortals breathe it in and out.
> Nor is it present in those nourished by this air of life,
> Or felled by death. This is stupid talk
> For air is now infused in some, now in others, etc.
> *Carm. 7.*

in fact, *being in general* is outside space and time.[329] But a subject that intuits being in general receives its form from intuited being. Therefore the intelligent entity, whose activity totally terminates and resides in intuited being, is a principle outside space and time, totally simple and spiritual.[330] Hence, intuition clearly demonstrates the simplicity of the intuiting soul.[331]

This is the fundamental proof of the spirituality of the intellective soul. It is taken from the soul's first act, from its formal being, and includes all other proofs. Thus, if the other actions of the rational, intellective soul must be simple, the ultimate reason for their simplicity lies in the simplicity of the first act, from which second acts derive and develop.

629. II. The intuition of specific and generic essences proves the same truth. All these essences are simple, immune from space and time. Their sole difference from being in general are the few determinations with which they qualify being.

630. III. But what deserves our closest attention is the following. The simplicity of the intellective soul is confirmed even more strongly by the very thing which at first sight seems to prejudice its simplicity and indeed was used as the basis for some objections against it.

---

[329] *Rinnovamento*, bk. 3, cc. 43–45.

[330] This basically explains why 'understanding is an act which cannot be exercised through a bodily organ, in the way that vision is exercised', as St. Thomas says (*S.T.*, 1, q. 76, art. 1, ad 1).

[331] This excellent proof is not new. Francesco Suarez presents it clearly in these words: 'The sufficient object of the intellect IS ENS IN SO FAR AS ENS OR AS TRUE. This means that the intellect is a power of a higher order, beyond all feeling, a spiritual power, without any corporeal organ. WE KNOW FROM METAPHYSICS, and now from the argument given here, that the intellect attains all created, corporeal and spiritual entia, substance and accidents, even the uncreated God himself, and all other things which, if they are to come within the compass of a single power, must be accepted under some common concept. This concept can be only that of being, whether intelligible or real. It is therefore the concept of the sufficient object of the intellect. The first consequence is clearly seen and known in itself, namely, that the faculty embracing such a general object is outside feeling. — As I said, feeling or the cognoscitive faculty (Suarez names this incorrectly), which is organic and material (these are the same), is an extremely limited faculty because of matter' (*De anima*, bk. 1, c. 9, n. 3).

The simplicity of the sensitive principle was proved from the nature of the continuum which, I said, presupposes something simple in which the continuum exists. The sensitive principle unifies *extension* which is presented as something simple to the understanding. *Number*, however, receives its nature of number from the unity and simplicity of the intellective principle, which grasps many things simultaneously with an extremely simple act. Only a mind can unify many things into a single group, can number them and abstract from them the concepts and theory of numbers with a simple act which embraces the many in the one.

631. IV. The previous argument, which proves the simplicity of the soul from the fact that the soul can consider many things simultaneously, with the same act and in one idea, leads to another proof of the simplicity of the intelligent principle. This proof, which I have mentioned elsewhere,[332] is drawn from a syllogism and from all the acts of reasoning. Without a totally simple spirit, human beings could not make comparisons, find the differences between things, determine what is suitable and unsuitable, order means to an end, etc. All these actions presuppose a principle that embraces many things in the unity and simplicity of one and the same idea.

632. V. This leads to the argument drawn from human freedom. Human freedom requires a simple principle capable of choosing among many things. The argument, used by St. Thomas,[333] was put forward by Suarez in the following way:

> All material agents of which we have experience act by necessity of nature, and all animals by natural instinct. This is shown by the fact that all things of the same species have a determined action and a uniform mode of action. This kind of determination therefore results from materiality. Consequently, the rational soul's mode of action, which is totally different, comes from immateriality.[334]

633. VI. Aristotle and his followers, the Scholastics, observed most perceptively that the condition and power of a body is so

[332] *NE*, vol. 2, 670–671.
[333] *C. G.*, 2: 65.
[334] *De Anima*, bk. 1, c. 9, n. 35.

limited and particularised that it admits only certain modifications and experiences which mutually exclude each other — a red body cannot simultaneously be another colour. Hence, the acts of a body do not extend beyond the little power present in the first act of the body itself. But the case is totally opposite relative to the power of the intellective soul. The intellective soul can understand, compare, etc. everything, even what is most contradictory, when presented in the required way. It cannot therefore have a corporeal nature. This proof is substantially Aristotle's proof considered in its essentials and presented in a precise form.[335]

The reason why the cognitive nature of the soul can embrace everything is that its first act, which determines its power, is informed by ens in general. Ens in general embraces virtually all entities and thus has a primal power which extends to all entia. On the other hand, body has no object distinct from itself; it terminates totally in itself, in its particular nature. The sensitive principle also has corporeal extension as its term. Its power therefore is limited to the modifications of which the extended felt element is susceptible. But the extended felt element, that is, the body, is limited in the way I have said. Hence, the sensitive principle remains limited by the very limitation of the body which constitutes the term of its first act.

634. VII. Another, very evident proof, often used by the ancients,[336] can be reduced to the previous proof. The

---

[335] Aristotle's argument, although basically solid, was defective in the form in which he presented it. This perhaps explains why it has been abandoned in modern times. The principle taken by the Scholastics as the basis of the demonstration was: 'That which can know some things, must not contain any of them in its nature' (St. Thomas, *S. T.*, 1, q. 75, art. 2). But the principle is not valid because the soul also knows the soul, even though it has the nature of soul. Another principle must be substituted: 'The acts of an ens do not extend beyond its first act, which determines its power.' But the first act of a body extends solely to having certain modifications, and nothing more at a given time. Even if these modifications were cognitions, which they are not, they would be few and determined, in contrast to the action of the soul, which is capable of knowing any ens whatsoever and many entia at the same time.

[336] Cassiodorus says: 'Although burdened by bodily mass, the soul weighs opinions with keen curiosity, considers heavenly things in depth, delicately investigates natural things, and even desires to know the most difficult

intellective soul conceives spiritual *entia*, for example, itself, angels, God. It can love these and desire each as a good for itself.[337] But the extended body, as extended, cannot exercise its action outside extension or attain anything outside it. The intellective soul is therefore incorporeal.

635. VIII. Finally, the *action of reflection* which the soul exercises upon itself is a very clear proof of its simplicity and incorporeity, because the body performs no action upon itself.[338] Again, however, this proof is a consequence of the first. Indeed, the faculty by which thought reflects upon itself comes from the nature of *being in general*, object of the faculty's first act, which constitutes it as intelligent. This object is so universal that it embraces every entity, including the entity of the soul and of all its acts. In this object the soul can find itself, its acts and its objects. This is reflection. Furthermore, because being is the object of the soul's intuition and the means of reasoning, the soul can apply being as a means of reasoning to being as the object of intuition and thus reflect upon being itself. By means of being, it can reason about being.

CHAPTER 22
The simplicity and oneness of the rational soul

636. If the sensitive and intellective principles are simple, and identify in the rational soul, the rational soul is simple.

properties of the Creator himself. If the soul were corporeal, it could never look at or see spiritual things with its thoughts' (*De Anima*, c. 4).

[337] St. Gregory Nazianzen says: 'The soul differs greatly from the body. Just as the body is fed by what is corporeal, the soul is fed by what is incorporeal' (*Apologetica*). Suarez, after referring to St. Gregory, adds: 'Tertullian (*Liber de Anima*, c. 6) tells us that this was one of the strongest arguments of the philosophers, particularly the Platonists, for proving that the soul is incorporeal. "Some philosophers," he says, "judge all bodies by what is corporeal, but the incorporeal soul by what is incorporeal, that is, by the study of wisdom." Gregory Nazianzen uses the same argument, taking it from Ammonius. Marsilio. Ficino does the same (bk. 8, *De Th. Platon.*), "The soul is fed by incorporeal, eternal truth", and therefore is incorporeal' (*De Anima*, bk. 1, c. 9, n. 18).

[338] St. Thomas uses this proof, *C. G.*, bk. 2, c. 49.

In fact, as I said, *myself* who performs an act performs all acts. *Myself* who acts through the body in one space, acts in all the other spaces where it wants to act. *Myself* who acts at one time, acts at other times. *Myself* who suffers is *myself* who acts. *Myself* who feels is *myself* who understands; *myself* is always the same, one and most simple *myself*. Hence, *myself* the human rational soul, is shown to be simple and spiritual, by its perfectly constant entity amid varying accidents (cf. 140–180).

637. On the one hand, the simplicity of the soul, of every soul, is certain and manifest; on the other, the supposition that the soul is extended is seen as manifestly absurd. Nevertheless, despite the unassailable proofs that the human being is one, and can have only one soul, a kind of doubt returns to weaken our conviction about the truths we have found. The following considerations explain the origin of this doubt:

1. The proof of the unity of the human soul deduced from consciousness, that is, from the unity of *myself*, does not settle the doubt that outside *myself* but connected with it, there could be another sensitive soul.

2. Consciousness does not show that all the actions done in a human being are done by *myself*, and that *myself* is consequently the only operative principle in the human being. On the contrary, many things happen in human beings which *myself* cannot do, and others happen which *myself* directly opposes, such as the movements of our lower part pertaining to animality. Finally, certain vital actions, like the circulation of the blood, are almost entirely outside the free dominion of our rational part, and hence carried out by another principle.

3. Human beings, when acting intelligently, seem different beings when acting as animals. Sometimes, in their desire to lose themselves in sense pleasures, their intellectual functions are suspended. They could not desire this if they were merely rational souls.

4. The proof deduced from the oneness of the principle of intelligence and of sensation demonstrates only the existence of a single intellective principle, whose action is sometimes associated and identified with the animal principle (in any case, not every sensitive act must always be attributed to the principle of intellective acts). But this does not prove that the animal principle does not sometimes manifest and have its own activity. In

[637]

these cases, the animal principle differs from the principle of intelligence.

Influenced by these reasons, some weighty philosophers apparently attributed two souls, one intellective, the other sensitive, to the human being. Nearly all contemporary physiologists, guided by substantially the same or similar reasons, distinguish between the human soul and the principle of animal life.

638. These difficulties are not to be despised and have some foundation, but prove nothing against the thesis of the oneness of the human soul. The question, 'Is the human soul one and simple?' differs from 'Does the soul, although one and simple, have two different activities divisible from each other, but joined in such a way that during the state and act of union, the principle of one identifies with the principle of the other, that is, they have a single principle called "soul"?'

639. The proofs I have put forward show that both questions must be answered affirmatively:

1. The proof deduced from the unity of *myself* demonstrates that, if something happened in the human being which could not be attributed to the intellective principle, the activity would not be another human soul. It would be an activity not pertaining to the human soul.

640. 2. The proof drawn from the fact that sensitive acts can sometimes be reduced to the understanding principle shows that in this case the principle of the two kinds of acts, sensitive and intellective, is a single principle, and that this single principle is the single human soul. Everything that remains outside this single principle therefore does not constitute a human soul.

3. I have conceded that the sensitive principle, considered in itself, differs from the intellective principle. However, I said that these two principles are capable of uniting in a single principle, not perhaps in the way that two mathematical points, having come together and united, become a single point, but at least in the way that two straight lines joined end to end, have only a single, not a double starting point.

641. 4. I said that the foundation of the union of the intellective and sensitive principles is the *fundamental perception of the animal feeling*. This perception is an act of the intellective principle which now acquires the title 'rational'. Indeed, granted this perception, the intellective principle

becomes simultaneously sensitive, although it feels in another, higher way than the merely sensitive principle feels. The intellective principle perceives the substantial feeling (term and principle) under the nature of ens, that is, as a mode or act of ens (because the substantial feeling is itself a special actuality of being in general). Now, the intellective principle could not perceive the feeling as ens, unless it perceived it as feeling. Hence what it perceives is feeling-ens.

On the other hand, the sensitive principle has as term that which is felt as felt, and not as ens, nor as feeling (principle and term). The sensitive principle, which is identical with the intellective principle, is precisely the intellective principle itself which, perceiving the *ens-feeling*, feels its term (the felt element) with a feeling enclosed in the ens, its proper object. The sensitive principle, however, in so far as it simply adheres to the extended term and producing feeling — and consequently perceives neither the ens nor itself — does not identify with the human soul and is not the human soul. It is to this principle that those movements must be attributed which are carried out in the human being without the co-operation of the intellective principle, or contrary to its will.

642. 5. In this way, the purely sensitive principle does not lose its activity, because the union is effected by means of a permanent intellective perception which does not alter the nature of the thing perceived, although it can act on it and even dominate it. Thus, the felt element can be term simultaneously of the purely sensitive principle and of the intellective-sensitive or rational principle.

This explains how two powers, that of the purely sensitive principle, and of the perceptive or rational principle, can act on the identical *felt element* and even come into conflict.

This also explains how the *sensitive* and the *perceptive* (or rational) principles can influence each other. If the purely sensitive principle, through its own spontaneity (granted a suitable stimulus), changes its felt element, the term of perception is also changed. In this case, it is able *indirectly* to modify and move the act of the rational principle. On the other hand, if the rational principle wants to change the *felt element*, which together with the sentient principle it actually perceives, it does so by acting directly on the sentient principle. Although perception, when

[642]

actual, does not change the nature of what is perceived, the perceiving element has the force to act on it and change it. Thus, when I actually perceive an external body by touch, I can change the body because the actual perception joining it to me provides the occasion for doing so. This explains why human beings can change their own body, which they perceive directly as felt. We have therefore resolved the first, second and fourth objections.

643. 6. The third objection is concerned with people who abandon themselves willingly to sense-pleasure. We must not believe that in doing this they lose their immanent, fundamental perception (despite the suspension of their reflective acts). It is not true that sensation alone remains. Pure sensation, cut off from everything else, cannot be desired by human beings, by rational principles. In a case like this, human perception is reinforced, and the feeling comprised in the perception becomes the object of desire. It is not a question of desiring mere sensation. The first act desired among rational acts is that of intense perception, which is sought even to the point of sacrificing other reflective acts.

644. 7. Finally, it will be helpful to note that in perception the rational principle is not so much *active* as *receptive*, although it has and communicates the form, which makes it the informing cause.[339] If the fundamental perception alone is considered, it is difficult to see how the rational principle is also the principle modifying feeling. But if we go further and reflect that every actual perception endows the rational principle with an *active faculty* (corresponding to the receptive faculty of perception), through which it can be a cause of modification in what is perceived, we will see how the activity of the rational principle on the animal felt element is not as actual and permanent as the fundamental perception itself. The rational principle can in fact begin and end its act, and it is therefore a potency, not an act. As long as this activity of the rational principle remains in a state of potency, the sensitive principle can act independently of it and modify the animal feeling. These modifications are all received by the perceiving principle in its receptivity and informed by it, that is, they are reduced to a rational condition.

645. To these observations let me add another about Plato's

---

[339] *Informing cause* is not the same as *active cause*.

definition of human being as, 'An intelligence aided by organs'. It is defective, as I have shown,[340] but here I want to discuss what is true in it, the part that suggested it to Plato's mind — the errors of great men, as I like to repeat, are simply great or subtle truths, but disguised and imperfect. Aristotle, followed by the Scholastics, found Plato's definition defective because it apparently united intelligence to the body as *mover* and not as *form*.[341] But is it entirely wrong to consider intelligence rather as *mover* of the body than as *form*?

The answer certainly depends on how we define and determine the nature of intelligence and of organic body. The definition is defective precisely because the two terms are used without this determination.

But if we replace the generic term 'intelligence' with 'intelligence perceiving animality', and organic body or 'by organs' with 'animal', the definition would be corrected and become 'an intelligence which aided by animality itself, naturally perceives animality'. In this case the relationship between this kind of intelligence and animality could be that between mover and moved, because the rational form given to animality is already expressed by this determination of the intelligence. The fact that animality occurs twice in the definition would cause no difficulty; in reality, animality, that is, substantial animal feeling, has two modes of being in humans: it is present as perceived in the rational principle, and thus informed by this principle; and it is present in itself as mere feeling, and thus moved.

646. Human beings are thus composed of two parts, one their essence, the other their condition. These two parts would be the rational soul and living body, not *soul* and *body*. In Scripture *spirit* and *flesh* seem to correspond to these two parts, because the word 'flesh' means living flesh endowed with feeling, not dead flesh.

We must now discuss the origin of the intellective soul, a question much debated by ancient philosophers and by the Fathers of the Church, but later abandoned by modern thinkers, who were exhausted by such long investigations and disheartened about finding a solution.

---

[340] *AMS*, 24–26.

[341] Aristotle, *De Anima*.

CHAPTER 23

The origin of the intellective soul

> The divine he made with his own hands,
> but ordered his children
> to make what is mortal.
>
> Plato, *Timaeus*, 69

647. If we had to explain only the generation of a purely sensitive soul, as in animals, the difficulties of the problem would be far less. We have already seen that the soul is multipliable through the division of its felt term (cf. 455–499), and that this kind of multiplication does not in any way affect the soul's simplicity. But in the case of an intellective principle, the difficulty increases immensely.

648. Aristotle himself noticed this. In his work on the generation of animals, he first says that their souls do not come from outside and cannot exist without a body, because all their actions are done with the aid of a bodily organ. And then, speaking about intelligence, he adds, 'Only the mind is added from outside; it alone is divine, because bodily action has nothing in common with its action.'[342]

In fact, the most influential philosophers have all acknowledged that there is something divine in the human being, that is, something which only God himself can give directly. Elsewhere Aristotle says, 'Among animals, only the human being shares in divinity,'[343] and when speaking about the life of contemplation he does not hesitate to affirm that it 'exceeds human nature'.[344] Here he means that human beings can in their contemplation pass beyond the limits of their nature and attain divine things,

[342] *De Generat. Anim.*, bk. 2, c. 3.

[343] *De Anima.*, bk. 2, c. 10.

[344] *Ethicor.*, bk. 10, c. 8.

such as ideas. He adds that 'human beings do not live in this way because they are human, but because there is something divine in them';[345] also, 'This (intellective principle) differs from the composite human being as much as its action differs from the action of other kinds of power. But if the mind is a divine element relative to the human being, the life proceeding from this element is divine relative to human life.' Hence he teaches that 'we must not think too much about mortal things but, as much as possible, make ourselves immortal.'[346]

649. This is why I said that human generation cannot be explained in any way without recourse to God.[347]

But this divine element, seen and acknowledged by all the greatest thinkers on human nature, still required accurate determination if it was not to be confused with anything alien to it.

650. The ancients were in fact content to say that the human mind was divine, but as far as I know they went no further.[348] When I investigated the matter myself, I found that two things had to be distinguished in the human mind, subject and object, as I called them. I saw that *subject*, because limited and contingent, could not in any way be called divine; only *object* could be ranked among divine things as something truly unlimited, eternal, necessary and furnished with other totally divine qualities. This object, standing immovably before the human subject, is being itself, in its ideal mode.

651. All we can say about this communication which the object makes of itself to the human subject is what St. Augustine said about the nature of the intellective soul, that is, it is 'close to the substance of God'[349] but is not itself divine. Indeed,

---

[345] *Ibid.*

[346] *Ibid.*

[347] *AMS*, 812–831.

[348] Sometimes the Alexandrian philosophers seem to touch the truth. The Valentinian heretics said that the human being was generated by λόγος and ζωή. But λόγος retained its double meaning of subjective reason and of objective reason (idea). Consequently they neither thought nor expressed themselves clearly, in addition to the vague errors they later added to their teaching.

[349] *In Ps. 145.*

as Claudius Mamertus stated so well, it is like God in the way that WHAT IS INTELLECTUAL is like WHAT IS INTELLIGIBLE.[350]

652. The object, that is, the form of intelligence, cannot therefore be generated. God himself unveils it to the soul which is thus made intelligent. He did this for all human nature when he infused a soul into Adam in whom human nature was contained. After this, human nature had only to multiply into many individuals by means of generation.[351] Just as God, at the beginning, gave fixed laws to all created things, so he gave this fixed law that every time human beings multiplied individuals through generation, *being* was present to these new beings in such a way that it drew and bound to itself their intuiting gaze.

653. The new individual before whom being shines must be a living thing organated in the same way as its generator. This organisation is certainly the most perfect that animality can have. In it, stimulation is probably supreme, the harmony of supreme stimulation perfect, and the central power of feeling at its highest level. The animal subject, having reached its extreme perfection, had to pass beyond the confines of animality and attain eternal things, the idea.

654. Between the specific perfection of this animal organism and the vision of being, there is no time lapse. At the precise moment that the human animal is formed in nature, it is made intelligent because admitted to the vision of being through a law of nature established by the Creator at the beginning.

655. Nor can the organism proper to the already formed human being ever be found without the intellective principle. The intellective principle, once united to the body, gives it its final formation and modification which thus makes the body fully proper to the human being. The intellective principle continues to exercise the same activity, influence and dominion over the body which I described when I said that the rational soul by acting on the body, gives it a certain actuality previously

[350] 'It is like (God) in the way that INTELLECTUAL LIGHT is like INTELLIGIBLE LIGHT; unlike God in the way that the changeable creature is unlike the unchangeable Creator' (*De Statu Animae*, bk. 1, c. 4). He calls the soul intellectual light in so far as it is enlightened by what is intelligible.

[351] *AMS*, 812–831.

impossible for it. Consequently, there must be an organism totally proper to the formed human being who cannot be without the intellective soul because the intellective soul, by informing the human being, bestows on him the last act. Animality and its organism must therefore be first brought to their greatest perfection so that the intellective, rational soul may be added. But then the intellective soul, by its very addition, imparts to the organism the sort of completion, actuality, kind of movement, vitality and life that could not be present in any purely animal ens.

656. Granted this, there is nothing contradictory in the multiplication of the *subject* under discussion through generation. The subject as subject (prescinding from the object) is simply a living creature.

But, we may ask, where does the animal principle acquire the power to intuit *being*? This power is created by being itself, when it joins itself to the principle. Essentially intelligible, being cannot join itself to any subject without being understood; its being joined consists in it being understood. Being therefore has the power to create intelligences. As Aristotle would say, 'A sentient principle can, without contradiction, be intelligent in potency; it can, without contradiction be raised to a state of understanding.' A sentient principle is simple; it is not a body. On the contrary, body is its term. If another term is given to it, its activity is necessarily widened. It must therefore be conceived as a capacity to receive, like a remote potency drawn into a new act. At the beginning, it was given an extended term; now, it is also given an unextended and, by nature, superior term. But if this second term cannot be confused with the first, it cannot be modified by it. In short, the second term is an ESSENTIALLY knowable object, with the result that the sentient principle has in this way become intellective. Having been actuated in another principle, it has certainly lost its previous identity as principle. This transnaturation however, when correctly understood, contains nothing contradictory.

657. Just as St. Thomas said that the sensitive soul is an act of the body (this is true provided that by 'act' we understand 'principle' of the body which is respectively term), so we can say that intelligence is an act which originates from the sensitive soul. This is indeed true provided we add that this act

constitutes a subject, independent of the body and of the sensitive principle, and sustained now by a new, imperishable term.

658. This solves another difficulty which may be stated as follows. 'In the human being there is only a rational soul. But the human being is also an animal and as such has a sensitive principle. The nature of the animal and of the sensitive principle is to multiply through generation. This universal law of animal cannot be nullified by human beings, who also generate. If therefore the individual animal generates and multiplies in this way, the rational soul which is one and, in human beings, identical with the sensitive soul, must also multiply.' In reply, I say that this is in fact the case, as long as we presuppose the first law which decreed that universal being be united to all individuals of human nature, a law that was fixed by God when he breathed the breath of life into Adam.

659. In fact the Fathers constantly attribute the origin of human souls to that first act. 'Human beings,' says St. Athanasius speaking generally, 'received their soul from the divine in-breathing. Hence they know divine things, pursue and understand heavenly things, are rational and endowed with a mind.'[352]

This also confirms the opinion of Athanagoras that 'the soul, because it does not generate a soul, cannot claim the title of genitor; it is the human being who generates a human being'.[353]

[352] *In questionibus de Anima.*

[353] *De resurrectione mortuorum.* Prudentius expresses himself in an extraordinary way on the origin of the human soul:

> Souls do not bear souls,
> But by a HIDDEN LAW
> NATURE DIFFUSES its work
> So that small vessels breathe,
> And the vital SPARK IS PRESENT to those destined for it.
>
> *In Apotheosi contra Ebionit.*

[658–659]

Book 5

Immortality of the human soul

and

death of the human being

[INTRODUCTION]

660. The previous book entailed hard work. Its inevitably difficult questions about the simplicity of the soul, a truth which, as we saw, is easily confirmed by numerous direct, impugnable arguments, leave unsolved any number of obscure, mysterious investigations that remain in the mind like seeds. Already fertile, they are nevertheless enclosed as it were in extremely hard shells which remain unopened until warmed and incubated by the mind with persevering, generous love. Although at first suspicious, the mind comes to rejoice in them as it beholds its off-spring come forth alive; it recognises them clearly as the true issue of the beauty of truth.

The reader will have greater reason to take comfort from the work he has done, and from that which still remains, to the extent that his intellect is already well prepared and disposed to consider the immortality of the intellective soul, the noble truth and object of this latest book. Immortality is the condition on which human dignity depends, just as it is the condition of the happiness to which human beings continually aspire with irresistible, unconquerable longings.

We are indeed mortal of our own nature, but we desire immortality and avidly seek to be certain of it. Nothing disturbs us more than doubt or suspicion that immortality may not be our lot.

It is true that reason and experience show our body to be corruptible and destined to dissolution; God's revelation alone provides us with a secure promise that our body will one day be restored to us free from subjection to death. Nevertheless, the little that philosophy can tell us about this matter is a delightful and extremely precious truth. Philosophy can indeed show that our better part, the intellective soul, is of its own nature immortal and not subject to disintegration. This truth must be for us a joyful anticipation and herald of everything else we can expect from the magnificent generosity of our Creator. Let us start to consider this argument, therefore. It is the delicious fruit which we have cultivated and brought to maturity through our previous investigations.

CHAPTER 1
The concept of death, and the concept of annihilation

661. If we are to rise to a discussion about immortality, we first have to descend to the consideration of death which, bound up with the beginning of life, that is, with generation, was our subject towards the end of the preceding book. As we know, clarity of concepts is the foundation of all clear reasoning. We have to begin, therefore, by reminding ourselves of the concept already given of death (cf. 135) as the cessation of bodily animation. Granted this, death cannot be conceived in any way as something undergone by souls, but only by bodies. We have already proved that souls, whether sensitive or intellective as well, cannot cease to exist through death (cf. 134–139, 602–605).

662. We still have to ask if there is any other way in which souls can naturally cease to exist. Can they annihilate themselves or be annihilated by some change occurring in nature in virtue of the agents which constitute nature, or of a positive act on the part of the Creator? We shall first look at the question relative to sensitive souls, and then in relationship to intellective, rational souls.

CHAPTER 2
Can sensitive souls cease to exist?

Article 1
Sensitive souls cannot cease to exist through any action on the part of natural forces

663. What has been said before about the nature of sensitive souls leads us to distinguish them into what we call *elementary souls*, whose term is the elementary continuum, and *organic souls*, whose term is the organated continuum, agitated internally and stimulated by continual movements. The second kind

of souls springs forth in great number from the former of which they are actuations and individuations but from which they differ. The former, however, have everything needed to be called 'souls', that is, they have: 1. a sentient principle, which is the essence of the soul; and 2. an extended term, which is the essential condition for the soul itself.

The general question, 'Do souls annihilate themselves?', deals properly speaking with elementary souls. The fusion of organic souls into elementary souls through the dissolution of the organated body transforms souls, but does not deprive them of existence. This opinion is a middle way between that which requires the annihilation of the souls of beasts and that which declares them immortal.

664. I think that the impossibility of the annihilation of elementary souls through natural agents can be demonstrated by several arguments, two of which run as follows:

I. If sensitive souls, that is, sentient principles, could separate from the continuum, they would certainly annihilate themselves because their natural condition and essential relationship would be lacking. But what we have said about the nature of matter, whose existence cannot be conceived except as term of the sentient principle, shows that in such a case matter would be annihilated with them (*Anthrop.*). But it is admitted by all that matter, which can experience various changes, cannot be annihilated by causes acting in nature. The same must apply to sensitive principles, which are essentially relative to matter.

II. There is a direct conjunction between sensitive principle and its term, that is, with matter. No natural agent which acts as mediator in bringing about or assisting the conjunction forms part of the concept of this conjunction, which is brought about through the reciprocal actions and passions of the unextended, sentient principle and the extended, felt term. If, however, every other agent is extraneous to this conjunction, nothing can act on it, nothing can remove it. The dissolution of the bond can only come about either through the work of the sensitive principle itself or through that which can act upon it; or through the work of matter or that which can act upon it. But the sensitive principle and matter which are joined cannot spontaneously divide because no ens can annihilate itself. Their conjunction is natural to them, and their natural activity is directed to actuating and maintaining it. No other activity is present in them. If disunion is possible, it must arise therefore from some extraneous activity on the sensitive principle, or directly on matter. But these actions also are impossible.

It is impossible for a natural agent which operates on the sensitive principle to disunite them. Nothing acts on the sensitive principle except the intellective principle. But the intellective principle has no power over the sensitive principle except that of moving it to its operations (cf. 291–305). These operations do not, however, include that of self-destruction by disuniting itself from matter. Disjunction is not obtained in this way. Nor through the other because nothing acts on matter directly (with the exception of the sensitive principle) except matter itself. But material forces applied to matter have no other power than that of dividing it or uniting it in itself through motion. But dividing it or uniting its parts does not influence the conjunction that the sensitive principle has with matter. There is no agent in nature, therefore, which can make elementary souls cease to exist.

Will these souls be destroyed by direct action on the part of the Creator?

Article 2
Sensitive souls are not destroyed by the Creator

665. Natural theology offers us this proposition (confirmed by Revelation): 'Nothing created is annihilated by God.' Indeed, it is not fitting for the Creator to annihilate his own work which, precisely because it is his, is respected and loved because of the respect and love that he has for himself.

Sensitive souls, therefore, do not perish in any way.

Article 3
Confirmation of the existence of elementary life

666. At this point we can see that the hypothesis of feeling connected with the primal elements of bodies receives new support. If life were separable from bodies, it would perish.

This, however, would contradict the thesis that nothing is annihilated of all that has come into existence through the hand of the Creator.

On the contrary, if it is true that 1. every material element has a sentient principle essentially joined with it, and 2. several sentient principles identify as a single principle when a number of elements unite in virtue of the continuum and of other laws (some of which we have explained), it remains true that created feeling never perishes. All that occurs through the decomposition and recomposition of bodies is continual, varied modification expressed in countless different forms. These changes, foreseen and preordained by the sublime wisdom of Providence, have to be directed to bringing the spirit of life, which animates the world, to an ever better state and condition, to ceaseless perfection.

667. The thesis, 'nothing is annihilated' strengthens the hypothesis of the animation of the elements of matter. In the same way, the identical thesis receives new probability from the theory of animal generation. If it is true that animals *are multiplied* by division of the felt continuum according to certain laws, it is clear that the contrary must also be true; that is, life is *simplified* when appropriate union takes place between several felt continua. This is simply the inverse activity of generation. If one is admitted, the other cannot be excluded.

CHAPTER 3

Origin and confutation of metempsychosis

668. The death of the animal being, that is, of the animated organism, is not destruction, but modification of feeling. It is simply dissolution of the *individual* or of the *organic soul*, that is, of the harmonious feeling of stimulation, continually reproduced, possessing a centre of prevalent activity, whose organisation is an extrasubjective manifestation.

At this point, it will help if we consider the origin of *metempsychosis*. It would seem necessary to attribute such a system, for the most part at least, to inability on the part of the first philosophers to distinguish the intellective from the sensitive principle,[354] and to their way of looking upon the human being as a more perfect animal, nothing more. Because they believed in spontaneous generation and observed the frequent occurrence of similar facts in nature, they concluded that all corruption was generation and that the dissolution of one animal led to the formation of others from the previous animal's sections. This appeared to be transmigration of souls. Hermias, a 2nd-century Father of the Church, mocked the pagan philosophers in his attractive booklet for their uncertainties and contradictions. In doing so, he touches on their teaching about the vicissitudes of the human soul:

> At one moment, I am immortal and rejoice in my immortality; at another, I become mortal and feel sad. When I am mingled with determinate bodies, I change into water, air, fire; a little later, I am no longer air or fire, but beast or fish. When my turn comes, I have dolphins as brothers. But if I look at myself, I see my body and am terrified. I no longer know what to call myself. Am I man, wolf, bull, bird, serpent, dragon, or chimera? These students of wisdom have changed me into every kind of beast on earth, in the sea, in the air. I am polyform, wild, tame, dumb, noisy, brute and endowed with reason. I swim, fly, cleave the air, crawl on the ground, run and sit down. Here comes Empedocles, and he makes me a bush![355]

669. These philosophers made a twofold mistake.

1. They dealt with human beings as though they had only a sensitive soul, as mere animals;

2. Many of them did not realise that the individuality of feeling ceases with the death of the animal, and that what remains is the feeling possessed by the surviving continua.

---

[354] Aristotle noted this (*Physic*, bk. 4, text. 52, and 57). St. Thomas also: 'The ancients were ignorant of the power of understanding, and did not distinguish between sense and intellect. As a result, they thought that there was nothing in the world except that which could be apprehended by sense and imagination. And because only body falls within the imagination, they thought that nothing else existed except body, as the Philosopher says — This was the error of the Sadducees who maintained that spirit is non-existent' (*S. T.*, I, q. 50, art. 1).

[355] Hermias Philosophi, *Gentilium Philosophorum irrisio*, n. 2.

However, Heraclitus 'the *Obscure*' seems to have glimpsed this truth. He posited a common, universal soul with which particular souls were fused. The Stoics who followed him said the same[356] but made another mistake by insisting that this soul was one only; there were not as many souls as there were continua. From here, they passed to another error about the soul of the world; and to yet another, but much more serious error, when they affirmed this soul to be God himself.

CHAPTER 4
The concept of human death

Article 1
Death in human beings consists in the cessation of the primal perception of the fundamental feeling

670. We have excluded these errors as a result of understanding animal death. We can now investigate the nature of human death.

Common sense tells us that this consists in the separation of soul from body. This is indeed correct, but what is this separation?

After having seen where the union of the rational soul and the body lies, we can go on to understand their disunion. Once we know the bond that forms human life, we know what loosens that bond; we can explain its cessation.

The bond tying the intellective soul to the body consists, we said, in a natural, immanent, intellective perception of the fundamental feeling and, consequently, of the body. When this primal perception of the fundamental feeling ceases, the human soul is cut off from the body, the body is dead, the human being is dissolved.

---

[356] Aristotle, *De Anima*, 2.

Article 2
The conditions giving rise to the primal perception and consequently to human life

671. To further clarify this truth, let us sum up the fact comprising the composition of the human being, and its conditions.

1. A subject exists whose act is provided with two terms, one of which is felt and extended, and the other, intelligible being. This subject is called a) sensitive principle, or animal, in so far as its term is that which is felt and extended, and b) *intellective principle* in so far as its term is *intelligible being*.

2. The intellective principle has *being* as term. Its object, therefore, is every entity comprised in being in general. It even has feeling as object under the relationship of *entity*. The *intellective principle*, which to this extent, has feeling as entity for its object, is called principle or *rational soul*. Feeling, however, contains the sentient animal principle and what it feels, that is, the body, the felt. Thus, the first perception of the fundamental feeling includes the perception[357] of body, that is, the union of the intellective soul with the body and simultaneously with its proximate animating principle.

3. But what is the condition according to which the subject, besides being animal, becomes intelligent? The requirement, as we said, is the acquisition on the part of animal feeling of greater specific perfection, greater unity and harmony, through the most suitable organisation. Determining this unity and harmony is a profound investigation which I do not intend to undertake here. Moreover, I do not think I am capable of it.

---

[357] We have already noted that this first perception is first-level *perception*, that is, simple *apprehension* without any explicit, actual *affirmation* (cf. 268–271). Actual affirmation is an operation which follows much later when the rational soul becomes aware that the body is an ens *per se*, distinct from the sentient principle. At this point, affirmation does not add *cognition*; it confirms the previous apprehension. Moreover, this confirmation is not something added as objective, but a new disposition taken by the subject relative to what is known. Completing the perception by raising it to its final level simply requires activity on the part of the subject which produces in itself an actual state of *persuasion*.

CHAPTER 5

How human nature is constituted

672. Let us ask instead why the intuition of being is given only to a subject whose animality possesses such perfection of feeling and therefore of organisation.

If we were content to refer to the will of the Creator, we would be affirming something very true and just which, however, would not help in the solution of the question. Properly speaking, we should ask whether the Creator saw some reason of natural necessity or at least of fittingness for establishing things in this way.

673. It is obviously fitting that the dignity of ideal being should be manifested to a perfect, not an imperfect animal subject. We see that the whole of nature is governed by the following law: 'Imperfect things are brought to perfection through successive grades.'[358] Granted this, it was fitting that bodily feeling should be left to progress through the gradual scale of perfection proper to it. Only when it reached the final level as a result of optimum organisation, beyond which the perfection of the sentient principle may not go, should it attain a new perfection by going out of itself and reaching the object which lifts it to the condition of intelligent being.

674. It would be more difficult, however, to show that this was required by some necessity of nature. That is, if someone, having considered the nature of the sensitive principle and the idea, noticed that this principle could not intuit the idea without its first having acquired the best possible specific organisation; or again, in the case of such organisation, thought that the idea should be unveiled and manifested. Some probable conjectures can be made about both propositions, as follows.

It is possible to conjecture that an animal principle cannot intuit the idea before reaching the greatest power of animality by supposing that every power of a sensitive principle which

[358] I have spoken about the wisdom of this law in *Teodicea*, bk. 3, c. 20.

has not reached its greatest specific potency remains suspended and absorbed in its tendency to obtain the state of organic perfection it lacks. Consequently it is unable to ascend to the vision of ideal being, which is *per se* essentially intelligible and everywhere present (if being is not seen, the defect lies in the subject which is powerless to turn to it). In fact, if we suppose that the virtue of a sensitive principle is entirely absorbed in organising matter, nothing remains with which it can actuate itself towards ens. But after the specific perfection of the organism and feeling has been fully achieved, the principle no longer uses the power and force which it employed in the labour of *organisation*. At that point it encounters being, which is everywhere present, as I said, and renders itself intelligent by taking being as its term. I repeat, we have to consider that being is everywhere, and everywhere intelligible, because it cannot be otherwise; this is its proper essence. If, then, we posit the existence of some universally sensitive power (some subject) which is capable of seeing everything present to it, this power will feel being, which is never lacking, and simply by feeling being will be made intelligent. The only condition required is that the power is not occupied and totally taken up with something else. The nature of the sentient principle is determined by what is felt. The nature of being, however, is such that when felt it renders the sentient principle intelligent precisely because it is the intelligibility itself of being, and as such essentially objective and unable to mix with anything else. To understand this fact, it is sufficient to suppose that the power or sensitive principle, which I call subject, can terminate its act in everything present, but that its limited power sometimes draws the act to a close through exhaustion, and sometimes provides it with the vigour needed to feel intelligible being.

675. This thought will be still better grasped if we consider the nexus between *body* and *ens*, rather than the power of the sentient subject which tends to increase as much as possible and, having reached its highest grade, finds the force needed to push its act outside matter. *Body*, term of the act of the sentient principle, has different levels of being, and is apprehended successively by the sentient principle in these different levels.

At the first level, it is like some *extended-sensible thing*. As long as the sentient principle apprehends the body only in this way or, as we said, under the relationship of sensility, such apprehension renders the principle sentient, not intelligent.

At the second level, the extended-sensible called body is an *ens*. It is rendered intelligent and rational as soon as the sentient principle apprehends the body as ens. Indeed, to apprehend the body as *ens* means simply to apprehend it as a certain determined, limited realisation, that is, as a certain term of the act of being.[359] If, then, we suppose in the sensitive principle a first tendency to apprehend the body to the greatest degree possible, it will follow that after having apprehended the body, that is, the extended-felt, in its greatest perfection, the sensitive principle will tend to apprehend the felt still better in its entity, and in virtue of this instinct be led to apprehend it in ens in general, which is what *forms* the body-ens, an object whose principle is indeed ideal being (called initial being) and whose term is the extended-sensible. In a word, the tendency to apprehend the body will lead the sentient principle to apprehend it as ens, and thus be led from the extended-sensible to its essence which pertains to being in general, and consequently to see being itself in general. This is the way in which it seems possible to explain the passage made by the sentient principle from the order of mere sensitivity to the order of intelligence, that is, from a less to a more perfect state.[360]

It is the sentient principle's need to become rational which makes it intellective; it is its need to perfect itself relative to the apprehension of its proper term (the body) that urges the sentient principle to the ideal essence which is *per se* intimately united to every sensible reality and which through such union becomes ens, that is, object.

The sentient principle cannot therefore apprehend the body

[359] We say that what is *real* (as we think it) is the term of an act of *ideal essence*, according to the principle posited by St. Thomas: 'Every participated thing is related to what participates as its act' (*S.T.*, I, q. 75, art. 5, ad 4). *Subsistence* is a participation of *essence*, and is therefore called an act of essence. More correctly, however, it is a term of its act. *NE*, vol. 3, *app*. no. 6.

[360] Clement of Alexandria uses this principle to prove against the Platonists that the human soul is not sent from heaven. If this were the case, God would make it pass from a more to a less perfect state, which is not fitting. 'The soul is not sent from heaven to those things which are inferior. GOD MADE ALL THINGS ACCORDING TO WHAT IS BETTER' (*Strom.*, bk. 4).

at its highest level of being except by pushing its power beyond the body to a more ample term in which the body is contained and rendered intelligible. This term, in which the body is present with its essence, is being in general.

CHAPTER 6

The intellective soul never loses its individuality; it is immortal

676. Although *being in general* contains the essence of body, it is not true that body contains being in general. The greater contains the less, but not vice versa. The sentient principle, therefore, has acquired through this progress a new term of its activity, a term superior to and independent of body. This term is *per se*, is ideality itself.

677. But the term of the active principle is that which determines its nature. The sensitive principle, having acquired a new term, has changed nature. It has acquired an infinitely more noble nature; it has attained a perfect, divine form.

678. The following ontological law is worthy of consideration: 'Every ens tends to preserve and perfect itself through the very power by which it is. No ens, therefore, has any power directed to self-destruction.' This law is proved in ontology, which provides it for us here. If, therefore, no ens, no nature destroys itself, every destruction undergone by entia comes from outside, from extraneous activity.

Again, every complete ens is a simple principle and has a natural, immanent term. The principle is, if it is in touch with its term; but if its term is removed, the principle ceases. The natural, immanent term is the condition of the first act through which the principle is, according to the known law of synthesism. Stripped of all its terms the principle becomes a mere abstraction, a mere capacity, an ens similar to the *first matter* of the ancients, who supposed it to be devoid of all form. All that remains is the creative potency of God, which is not some determined external ens. The destruction of a contingent ens comes about only through the destruction of the term in which its first act ends.

679. What is the term of the ens which we know as 'man'? We have already seen that the terms are two: the body, and being in general. The only extraneous entia capable of destroying these terms are God Almighty and contingent things. As far as God is concerned, we have already presupposed that he does not annihilate anything that he has created. The destruction of human beings cannot, therefore, come from him. But can the activity of contingent things play any part in the destruction of human nature? Can they do anything to destroy the two terms of the first act through which the human being is? The body of the human being, one of the terms, is a complex of elements organated in the most perfect, specific manner, and thus individuated. It is true of course that the forces of nature can dissolve this organisation, and as a consequence destroy with it the animal feeling proper to the human being. But no force of nature can do anything relative to being in general, which is impassible, immutable, eternal and not subject to the activity of any ens. Hence, the power with which human beings intuit being in general cannot perish. This power, this first act, is the intellective soul which cannot therefore cease to exist in its own individuality; it possesses its own individuating reality,[361] a fact which we normally express by saying that it is immortal.

680. The human intellective soul arises originally, therefore, from the bosom of the sensitive soul of which it is a power. But this power has become its principal act and has acquired immortality as soon as it has attained being in general, which is totally imperishable, unchangeable and eternal.

CHAPTER 7

The first thing that human beings understand

681. We can draw the following corollary from the theory

[361] I have already shown that reality is the principle of individuation in *AMS*, 782–788.

expounded in the previous chapter. Indeed, the Scholastic opinion, expressed by St. Thomas, can be given an interpretation which renders it true. He says:

> The FIRST thing understood by us in our present state of life is the QUIDDITY OF SOME MATERIAL THING which is the object of our intellect.[362]

From what we have said, it is clear that the sensitive principle, when it has reached its perfection, tends to know the *nature* of the body (the QUIDDITY OF SOME MATERIAL THING). In other words, it tends to perceive the body *as an ens*. Consequently, the first *real object* of the intelligence is the body.

682. It may be objected that our fundamental perception does not, properly speaking, make the body the object, but the animal feeling. This is true. Nevertheless, if we consider that the sentient principle is indivisible from what is felt, and that as a result we perceive it in the felt and with the felt, it follows that the felt body, the live body, is truly the term of perception.

683. It will also be objected that St. Thomas is speaking about the extrasubjective body perceived with the five special sensories. But I do not claim that the opinion I have put forward is exactly the same as that of Aquinas; I simply say that the two opinions come close to one another. Note that my opinion offers the reason why intellectually we perceive an external body almost through instinct as soon as it acts on our sensory organs. This reason lies in the first, immanent perception. Because the rational principle perceives the fundamental animal feeling through nature, it must also perceive its modifications and the action of any foreign force upon it. This is why I said that the Scholastic proposition receives from the theory I have expounded an interpretation which renders it true.

684. There is a final objection: what is first understood by us is not the body, but being in general through which we understand the body. My answer is that at the deepest level this is the teaching of St. Thomas. I say that we perceive the body with THE IDEA OF BEING; St. Thomas, following St. Augustine, says that the human being perceives the body WITH THE LIGHT OF THE FIRST TRUTH. In fact, St. Thomas makes the same objection:

[362] *S. T.*, I, q. 88, art. 3; and q. 84, art. 7; and q. 85, art. 1; and q. 87, art. 2, ad 2.

That IN WHICH we know all other things, and through which we judge them, is known first, as THE LIGHT is known by the eye and the first principles by the intellect. But we know all things IN THE LIGHT OF THE FIRST TRUTH, and through it we judge all things, as St. Augustine says.[363]

St. Thomas does not deny that we know things in the light of truth. He affirms it unequivocally.

We understand and judge all things in the light of the first truth in so far as THE LIGHT ITSELF of our intellect is a certain impression of the first truth.[364] But the same light of our intellect is not related to our intellect as THAT WHICH IS UNDERSTOOD, but as THAT WITH WHICH WE UNDERSTAND.[365]

that is, the means of knowledge. What I have done is to show that this *universal means of knowledge* is *being in general*. This was my aim in *A New Essay concerning the Origin of Ideas* where I attempted to clarify what the ancients had said obscurely. Note that St. Thomas concedes that the impression of the light of eternal truth is the principle 'BY WHICH WE UNDERSTAND', and also concedes that 'that in which all things are known is what we KNOW FIRST'. When he says, therefore, the *quiddity of the body* is what is first understood, he is speaking about another way of knowing, different from the other according to which we first know the light of the intellect, of being. What I have done is to name appropriately these two ways of knowing by calling one *intuition*, the other *perception*. I also said that being in general is what we first know through intuition; the body is what we first know through perception. Thus, St. Thomas is reconciled with himself.

---

363 *De vera Relig.*, c. 3.
364 He had shown this in the *Summa* itself: I, q. 12, art. 2.
365 *S.T.*, I, q. 88, art. 3.

CHAPTER 8

Why the human soul no longer perceives the body when the organisation is dissolved

685. Let us sum up what has been said about the death of the human being.

1. The soul apprehends the body successively as sensible and as ens. In this apprehension of the body as ens, the soul intuits being and in it the felt-body. The power of the soul, in raising itself like this to its final degree of activity, does not lose the degrees it has already acquired. Consequently, while it perceives being in general, it continues to perceive the body as sensible and hence to perceive it in being as ens.

2. The most elevated act of the soul, that is, the intellect, continues to dominate all inferior acts, and thus becomes the substance of the soul. Substance is in fact the first act of an ens, to which all other acts are appended. It is the first act dominating all others, which exist through and in the first act (cf. 52).

3. It seems that at the beginning of human generation the act of the sentient principle does not possess its final act, that is, the act which brings it into being by rendering it intellective and rational. At least this was the opinion of the ancients, and of St. Thomas. In the order of generation, therefore, it seems that the sentient act is anterior in time to the intelligent act. When human beings are fully natured, however, the act which was last is the first of the human ens. It is the act which prevails in the ens, and that on which other acts depend. Thus it becomes substance.

4. In so far as it is sensitive, the soul feels the body; as intellective, however, it perceives the felt body. In this way, the union between the intellective soul and the felt body comes about through a natural, immanent perception.

5. At the death of the human being, the intellective soul ceases to perceive the felt body but does not cease to intuit being in general, which constitutes it as intellective. It remains, therefore, without a body. The separation of soul from body is called 'death' in the human being.

6. In other words, that which according to the order of generation was the first act of the soul, but has then become a subordinate act, ceases with the death of the human being. The act which according to the generative order was the last to be formed has become by nature the first, and has acquired the condition of substance, subject and person.

686. Human death does not, therefore, remove the identity of the principle which, by losing a term, undergoes change in its nature, that is, substantial but not personal change (cf. 190–195). The identity of such a principle consists in the conservation of the intellective substance, and hence of the same subject and same person.

687. But why, we may ask, does the human soul no longer perceive the body after the body's dissolution? From what has been said, we can come to some conclusions. We have considered the human soul united to the body in its three special acts: 1. in the act with which it feels the sensible body; 2. in the act with which it intuits ens in general; 3. in the act with which it sees the body in this ens in general, that is, with which it perceives the body as ens. The last two acts begin under certain conditions, and subsist under certain conditions.

The condition on which the soul passes from the act with which it feels the body as sensible to the act with which it feels the body as ens and thus first intuits ens, is this: bodily feeling has attained its specific perfection. But the breakup of the organisation leads to the breakup of the perfect, human feeling into several imperfect feelings, none of which is capable of possessing a principle suitable for intuiting ens. These new, sensitive principles, originating from the destruction of the human body, no longer have any aptitude for seeing ens. None of them, therefore, is the human soul; they have lost their identity with this soul. On the contrary, once the act which intuits ens has been posited, it no longer needs the animal feeling, from which it is altogether independent, for subsistence. This act is the human soul, which formerly was identical with the sensitive principle.

688. Just as different sensitive principles can be unified in a single principle, so a given sensitive principle can be unified and identified with the principle of the intellective act. But just as a sensitive principle can multiply, so it can be separated from the

intellective principle. In this case, it loses its identity; it is no longer a human principle, which remains the principle of the act intuiting being. Where there is an act, there is a principle; and where there is a principle, there is a subject, a substance. And such is the separated soul.

689. Care must be taken to understand correctly the way in which I speak of the identification of the sensitive principle with the intellective principle. I do not mean that the former is confused with the latter. What identifies it in some way is rational perception in which a single thing is made from what is perceived and the perceiver, without confusion between the two elements. Perception presupposes the prior existence of that which has to be perceived, which in our case is feeling; perception perceives *feeling* under the relationship of entity. It seems, therefore, that the rational principle feels, although it is not the proximate principle of feeling.

In a word, the essence of the human soul is to be intelligent and to perceive the body only when a sentient principle of body is identified with this essence and becomes one of its faculties. Simple feeling is not a human, but an animal act. The human being does not feel until he knows in some way that he feels; nor does he know he feels unless he apprehends the body as ens, that is, the essence of the body. Such apprehension is an act of the rational soul, which is his soul.[366]

---

[366] This explains St. Gregory of Nyssa's excellent distinction between the human soul and the principle of sensitive life. This principle is not the human soul except in so far as it is apprehended and perceived rationally by the human soul. 'That soul is perfect which is endowed with the power of INTELLIGENCE and REASON. Whatever is not of this nature can indeed share a common name with the soul, but in fact it is NOT THE SOUL. It is only A CERTAIN FACULTY OF LIFE which, by common consent, is given the name *soul*' (*De hominis opificio*, c. 15).

CHAPTER 9

Why the human soul is joined to only one body, and to this body rather than that

690. If we consider that the intellective principle is cut off from the law of space, there is no reason why it should be determined to join one body rather than another, or one body rather than many. But the sufficient reason determining the intellective principle to be joined to one rather than another body is found in the way in which I have explained the formation of the rational principle. As we saw, it was first a sensitive subject, an animal, which then continued to perfect itself until it attained being in general.

The animal subject, however, is determined by the continuum (that which is felt), and thus bound to space and to a determined space. In addition, it is a law of the animal subject that it cannot terminate in several divided continua. On the contrary, given several continua, the subject, or sensitive principle, multiplies. The intellective act, when it originates and gives existence to the intellective soul in the depths of the individuated corporeal feeling, remains bound in its formation by the same laws of the sensitive principle which lay at its root. It cannot, therefore, perceive, or inform, any other animal feeling or other body, except that of which, at the start, it was act and form.

CHAPTER 10

Can the intellective principle abandon the body spontaneously in the absence of disorganisation?

691. So far I have left suspended the question: 'Can human death occur without disorganisation in the body?' As part of our summing up, let us see whether we can draw some probable solution simply from the principles already posited. I said that the animal principle, if it has reached its greatest potency through the specific organisation of the felt (body), rises to the

perception of body as ens and consequently to intuit first ens in general (in logical, if not chronological order), granted the law laid down by God in the primal institution of human nature.

It follows from this that animal feeling, as long it retains its specific perfection, cannot on its own account separate itself from the intellective soul which has arisen in it. But if it retains such perfection while the organisation remains intact, it follows that human death cannot take place without some organic lesion. In this case, does the fundamental feeling always retain its perfection while the organisation remains intact?

There is no doubt that the unity and harmony of this feeling cannot be altered unless the organisation suffers some damage. This is the extrasubjective phenomenon which corresponds to the unity and harmony.

692. Possible doubts therefore can be reduced to the following:

1. Can the intellective principle alienate itself from bodily things to such an extent that it exhausts all its power in incorporeal things, either through contemplation or through love?

I reply that it cannot do this naturally[367] because the natural object is a purely ideal being not entirely satisfying to the spirit, which the idea draws totally to itself. Moreover, a nature whose act tends to perfection cannot destroy itself. Finally, if the soul could abandon the body spontaneously without disorganising it, the individual animal feeling remaining in the abandoned body would give rise once more to an intellective soul. But because there would be no interval in time or nature between the new activity and the old, the new would simply be the old activity increased in force. This occurs in all those persons who

---

[367] Supernaturally? The Scriptures say, in several places, that the vision of God, if given to a person in this life, would cause him to die. This is undoubtedly true, not because the vision of God would bring destruction to the person, but because it would be incompatible with the disordered body that results from original sin. As far I can see, therefore, the action exercised by the soul on the corruptible body would disorganise it if the soul, still dwelling in the body, were to behold the Almighty. The very act which aims at ordering and rectifying the body would disorganise it because the body in its present state is irreparable prior to its dissolution. The perfect body, however, would not be damaged but through the beatific vision attain supreme, transcendent perfection.

have been enhanced and developed through the loving contemplation of eternal truths. The intellective soul, therefore, cannot separate itself spontaneously from animality.[368]

693. 2. Does the intellective principle abandon the body through disgust at seeing itself united to a corrupt body? This cannot happen naturally for the same reasons.

694. 3. Can death take place through pure spasm, without organic-specific alteration? If this were the case, would not the life instinct cease to act and to animate the body?[369] As far as I can see, there is no doubt that extreme pain can be present without any alteration to the specific organisation, and solely as a result of nervous movements that do not specifically alter the organism. In fact, complete disorganisation brings about the cessation of pain.

I doubt whether this pain would be sufficient to hold back, as it were, the activity of the life instinct to such an extent that the spontaneous act with which it stimulates the organated body would cease. It seems to me that the feeling of the continuum could never cease in every case. But if it did, an immediate, profound disorganisation of the body would follow because the life instinct itself gives to organisation its final act. Hence, although there may not be obvious signs of disorganisation in corpses, their presence should be granted. Indeed, disorganisation would have to start in this way in the structure of the elements themselves, and thus be totally imperceptible at its very beginning.

Let us suppose that pain was so great that the life instinct ceased producing any feeling of stimulation, and that the organisation remained for some moments totally intact. In this case, it would seem that a momentary suspension of life would

---

[368] The appropriate development of the soul has been taught from the first masters onwards. St. Bernard says: 'The soul has to develop and expand if it is to be capable of God (*capax Dei*). — It develops, therefore, and expands, but in a spiritual way. It develops not in substance but in virtue' (*Super Cantic.*, Serm. 28). — John of Salisbury wrote about the development of the soul in a similar fashion: 'It develops, therefore, in reason and intellect alone, not by multiplication of parts or greater quantitative extension. It expands in its desire for good, and its distaste for evil, and remains simple in nature' (*Polycr*, bk. 3, c. 1).

[369] On the life instinct, *see AMS*, 371–384.

take place because the intellective soul no longer perceives the perfect, harmonious feeling. Life would return, however, when the pain ceased. Moreover, the intellective soul which would perceive the body anew would not be different from before. Because the intellective soul is immune from place, it would be neither nearer to nor more distant from the body. Indeed it (the intuitive act) would always have remained an act of the same sentient principle whose term is the continuum of the organated body. This sentient principle would have suspended its perception, but not its intuition, by withdrawing its stimulating activity. On renewing this activity, it would restore to the soul the corporeal object, that is, the body felt by the perception of its essence.

695. None of this prevents the rational soul, with its spiritual passions of sadness, joy, desire, and so on, from exerting great pressure on the organisation. This pressure may either destroy the organisation more or less quickly, or preserve it for varied lengths of time if, as a result of other causes, it tends to become disordered. In fact, experience shows that a painful or joyful surprise can cause disorganisation and give rise to apoplexy.

696. On the other hand, I have no doubt that life is sometimes prolonged solely by domination on the part of the power and force of the intellective principle over the sensitive principle. Without this dominion, the sensitive principle would perhaps withdraw itself from the action which individuates and stimulates it. My opinion is strengthened when I read the description of the death of Jacob given in the book of Genesis. The old man, feeling his forces ebb, calls his sons to his bed and, drawing on his fading energy, speaks to them forcefully and at length. The sacred writer brings the conversation to an end with the words: 'When Jacob finished charging his sons, he drew up his feet into the bed, and breathed his last.'[370] Why didn't death surprise him before the end of his long discourse? Why, when he had finished, was death so swift? Why did he 'draw up his feet' so tranquilly and die so spontaneously?

This lengthening of life through the power of the intellective soul has been observed by several doctors, one of whom writes that the soul 'on the brink of expiring sometimes waits to instruct an heir about various dispositions, or awaits an

[370] Gen 49: 32.

[695–696]

expected friend to say goodbye and to hand over safely to his relatives his good name.'[371]

Confirmation of this will be found in animals which never give signs of certain phenomena that in human beings provide prior warning of death. Only delirious humans say they want to change residence and go elsewhere, and try to do so by getting out of bed and fleeing. Feverish sailors often throw themselves into the sea as a result of this desire to go elsewhere. All this pertains to the intellective soul which, when feeling unwell, tries to change its condition through its own activity. This effort produces in human animality an attempt to go elsewhere.[372] The merely sensitive soul never tends to change its condition: it simply relaxes its individuating act a little more. The phenomenon of which we are speaking is never found in beasts.

697. This provides confirmation that the intellective soul has a feeling of its own immortality.[373] People suffering from tuberculosis, although at the final degree of marasmus, do not foresee their imminent dissolution. They seem to want to live for a long time, and have projects for the future. This must be attributed to the vivacity with which the organ of phantasy endures in them. It is not properly speaking a feeling that gives them this hope but thought, which is happy to hide behind images, without however allowing them to be genuinely persuaded of their recovery.

[371] At this point, Nicholls adds a note in which he refers to other authors who give examples of deferred death.

[372] As long as the intellective soul is united to the animal principle, its acts although merely intellective draw in their wake some modifications of animality and some corporeal movements. Such acts are, for example, those of delirious people who want to go elsewhere.

[373] This was rightly considered an argument for the immortality of the human soul. Francis Nicholls writes, in the *Praelectio* we have already cited: 'Provided all other things are taken into account, the most obvious argument for the immortality of the soul is found here: the soul seems to want to leave an uncomfortable for a more comfortable place on the basis of trivial reasons as though happier pastures existed where, like a fastidious guest, it would be more at home'. Various cases are told of death deferred through acts of will, amongst them that wonderful fact narrated by Nicholas Pechlin, p. 396. — There have been pious persons who did not die without receiving permission from their spiritual director. I could name one myself.

CHAPTER 11
Why human beings find death repugnant

698. This also explains the repugnance that we feel to death, that is, the repugnance the intellective soul experiences in feeling the loss of the animal feeling which it apprehends naturally.

Death in the animal takes place through the disorganisation of the body or through extreme pain. The act with which the soul vivifies the organic body is that through which the *life instinct* produces stimulation, organisation and the individual feeling; at the same time, this instinct has a natural tendency to posit itself in this fashion. Granted these things, animal repugnance to death must be proportioned to the force of the life instinct. Death, therefore, is the extreme evil for an animal, whose repugnance to it must be proportionate to the act by which the animal exists.

699. But the rational principle perceives feeling as the entity which it is. In other words, the rational principle is either content or suffering when it perceives feeling. Everything the animal suffers at death is therefore perceived by the rational principle, to which death must be as repugnant as it is to the animal principle. There is a difference, however. The rational principle, in addition to the activity by which it perceives the animal feeling, has another, more noble activity, which endures and with which it can console itself for what it loses. The rational principle suffers loss, but it does not perish; the animal loses everything and perishes.

700. Moreover, perception of the body is the first act of the rational principle, the first act of reason, the act in which the rational principle is given the *reality* it knows naturally. But the perfection of every being consists in its act: 'A thing is, in so far as it is in act.' But every ens has some force through which it is. This force, through which it is, is that which makes the cessation of being repugnant; it is an instinct for being, and therefore for self-preservation. The rational principle, if impeded from carrying out the first natural act which makes it what it is and contains virtually all other acts, must experience extreme

repugnance in seeing itself so impeded. This repugnance to seeing the body subtracted from the rational principle must be as strong in that principle as the force which naturally impels it to the act with which it perceives the animal feeling and posits itself as rational. The rational principle, therefore, must feel extreme repugnance at having to separate itself from animality, although this separation does not entirely remove its first act. There still remains the act with which it intuits being in general, the act through which it is intellectual and moreover apprehends pure space (cf. 554).

CHAPTER 12

Does the separated soul retain any inclination to unite itself with the body?

701. It is a theological opinion that the soul separated from the body preserves some tendency to reunite itself to the body.[374] Has philosophy anything to say about this? It would seem at first sight that such a question about the state of the separated soul lies outside the boundaries of philosophy. At a deeper level, however, we find that philosophy can say something about it, at least by way of not improbable conjecture.

702. It would seem that, if philosophical reflection enables us to know 1. the elements constituting the human soul, that is, the rational soul; and 2. the elements it loses at human death, we should also know what elements remain after the removal of those which death eliminates. Thinking about the question,

---

[374] Theologians are divided on the question, 'Does the separated body desire to unite itself to the body?' There are three principal opinions. Scotus denies this appetite. Suarez denies what he calls an elicited appetite: 'It is very probable that the separated soul led by the natural reason does not desire, with an elicited appetite, reunion with the body except through a certain strong longing, and under conditions which seem impossible, naturally speaking.' But he does admit a 'certain natural aptitude' which he improperly calls 'natural appetite' (*Tract. De Anima*, bk. 6, c. 10). St. Thomas, whom I follow, admits a true inclination, a true natural appetite, for which he gives proof in *S.T.*, I, q. 26, art. 1, ad 6; *De Spirit. creat.*, q. 4, art. 5; *De potentia*, art. 2, ad 5; and elsewhere.

however, we immediately finds ourselves following a path of reasoning that seems to lead our thought to a conclusion contrary to the theological opinion we have just mentioned.

The rational soul loses its bodily term through death. All that remains to it is the sole term of essential being. But every activity and reality of a principle is determined solely by its term. No activity can remain in the rational principle, therefore, except that through which it intuits being. Hence, if the bodily term is altogether removed from the rational principle, the sensitive principle itself no longer remains; the intellective principle rests in the idea; no activity remains which can possibly be a principle inclining it to take up the body once more. The very memory of the preceding body must be entirely abolished because the memory of bodies cannot be preserved without some vestigial phantasm of them. The phantasm itself ceases, however, when the brain, the appropriate organ of fantasy, is lost.[375] This seems to be how reasoning can proceed, but it is defective because it forgets an important fact about the human soul already indicated by us.

703. I have shown that every sensitive soul which has as its term a body occupying a limited portion of space must first have as its term (in logical order) pure, solid, unlimited space. This is necessary because an unlimited space is included in the concept of the limited corporeal space which is term to a feeling. Feeling cannot be thought without the concept of unlimited space (cf. 554–559). Consequently, the rational soul, which is sensitive and intellective, must have the same term of simple, unlimited space. What happens, then, at death? Simply the dissolution of the corporeal organism, and consequently the dissipation of the organic-corporeal feeling. All that perishes is the organism and its relative feeling, nothing more. The body, however, which limits space is essentially different from the space that is limited; this space is altogether independent of the body. Space, therefore, cannot be taken from the soul simply because the soul has lost its bodily term. The rational soul which has lost the body must, therefore, still retain two terms:

---

[375] I am speaking of the separated soul according to its nature, and prescinding from anything else it could obtain in the next life through divine disposition. Cf. the appendix to *Teodicea*, 48–49.

1. essential being which renders it intellective; 2. pure, unlimited space. It follows that with this second term it still maintains a certain relationship with the created universe whose extension it feels.[376] But we have seen that the principle which feels unlimited space is the root of the corporeal sensitive principle (cf. 558). It is as it were the principle of the sensitive principle, the remote principle of feeling. Here we have already arrived at a very satisfying conclusion: the human soul separated from the body still preserves its radical potency for feeling.

704. But this is not sufficient. We have to make use of the following ontological or cosmological theory: 'Principles have existence in accordance with their term; but once in existence they have their own activity relative to those same terms.' This theory is proved by intimate observation of any subject. Although a subject or principle cannot be conceived as existing without its term, it is certain from experience that, in existing, it can carry out different activities and exercise different functions relative to its term. We shall speak more at length about this important truth in the second part. But, granted this, there remains in the separated soul the identical subject which was present before the soul ceased to perceive the body. There is nothing repugnant, therefore, after the cessation of the actual perception of the body, if this identical subject, receptive to activity, retains its habitual dispositions and tendencies. Moreover, since bodily sensation is an act of a principle which has space as its term, there is nothing to prevent this same principle from preserving an inclination to the preceding act, that is, to its preceding perception. Its tendency in this case is rather like that of the eye which, having seen an object, can continue to look in the same direction and with the same intensity even when the object has been removed and the eye sees nothing more.

705. In my opinion, it is certain that something similar to what is said of the eye can be said of the intellective principle, which remains identical in the separated soul. This principle already had an inclination towards perception of the bodily

---

[376] The words used by St. Paul to describe death are highly appropriate: '*Praeterit enim* FIGURA *huius mundi*' (1 Cor 7: 31). The word *figura* indicates strictly speaking the limitation of the space making up the bodily substance, not space itself.

feeling, and the inclination must remain in it (as we said about the sensitive principle of space), although it no longer has any matter over which it exercises the inclination. In fact, the perception of the natural, corporeal feeling included: 1. the sensitive principle of space with its term, space; 2. the sensitive principle of body with its term, body (as we saw, this principle is an act individuating the prior principle); 3. the intuitive principle of being. Only the second of these three elements ceases with the separation of the body. The intellective perception of the feeling of space remains, that is, the intellective perception of the principle and term of this feeling. But the principle of this feeling preserves the actuality which puts it in relationship with the body. Consequently, the rational principle remains, and it remains with its inclinations because it perceives a sensitive principle inclined towards its bodily term.

706. This teaching also shows why the separated soul preserves its own individuality through nature. A principle which had pure space as term, and no other reality in itself, would have to be one, and thus without the individuation proper to a principle feeling the body (cf. 557). But, as soon as some activity tending to the body were added to the principle, the new activity or reality would individuate it. Matter, as I said (cf. 564), is divisible and consequently multipliable of its nature in such a way that one portion of matter is not another.

It is precisely from this relationship between the intellect and matter that St. Thomas proves the individuation of matter and consequently a plurality of intellects.[377] This truth led the Scholastics to assert that matter was, generally speaking, the principle of individuation. This proposition is far too general, as I mentioned elsewhere. In fact, every *reality*, whether material or spiritual, when it can be distinguished, is already *per se* a principle of individuation. St. Thomas realised this, and corrected the principle with various limitations. One of these affirms: 'Form is individuated through itself.'

The intellective soul separated from the body remains

---

[377] 'The intellective soul, just like an angel, has no matter from which it can arise. Nevertheless, unlike an angel, it is the form of some matter. So, according to the division of matter, there are many souls of a single species. But in no way can there be many angels of a single species' (*S. T.*, I, q. 76, art. 2, ad 1).

individuated, therefore, primarily because of the perception that it preserves of the feeling which reaches out to space. In turn this feeling is individuated as a result of the activity which it preserves towards the bodily feeling.

707. Here I must not overlook an extremely important observation: the individuation of the intellective soul, and that of the sensitive principle, are brought about under very different conditions. The sensitive principle is individuated directly through the separation of matter because it is connected through its own essence to the elements. Every elementary feeling is therefore a different individual when the elements are separate and discontinuous. If two groups of elements were to compose a completely equal organisation, there would be two, equal, organic feelings, but not a single identical feeling. Consequently, the intellective souls which perceived these organic feelings would be two, not one, and would remain two as separated souls. But if, on the contrary, the Almighty were to change the organism in the case of an intellective soul which perceives the organic feeling, and did so by substituting another, totally equal organism without any change in the perceived organic feeling, the intellective soul would be totally unaware of the change which has occurred solely in the matter, not in the feeling which is all that the soul directly perceives. The soul would not therefore lose its identity in any way through such change. Experience shows the same thing. The matter composing the body changes with age without detriment to the identity of the soul. Indeed, not only does the matter change, but even the organic feeling, although never specifically. The individuality of the intellective soul does not originate directly from the individuation of matter as such, but from the individuality of the feeling. Only when several feelings exist are there several intellective souls, which are referred to the feelings, because an intellective soul can perceive only one, not two or more organic feelings. The intellective soul, although already originated and constituted through itself, draws its origin from one organic feeling alone.

708. But after all this, the individuality of the already constituted intellective soul draws its individuation from another source. It carries out some rational acts with which it sends out new activity and thus differentiates and individuates itself by

acquiring the additional reality in which the activity consists. The terms of these acts may indeed cease for the separated soul once it has lost the organic feeling. However, the soul, by remaining identical, retains that activity through the principle we have indicated, namely, if a constituted principle exists, it has its own proper activity independent of its term (cf. 707). So, although all the cognitions received in the present life in dependence upon bodily organs may naturally perish relative to the soul, the acquired activity of the soul is retained. And this is sufficient to individuate it.[378]

709. Several objections can be made to this teaching, but they are not insoluble, as far as I can see. I shall mention only those which appear most relevant and, by clarifying them in my answers, fill out the teaching itself.

Objection 1. — You have said that the intellective soul retains perception of the feeling of space. In this case, do the elements of the body (which dissolves), elements which have their own bodily feelings, remain deprived of these feelings?

Reply. No. The feeling of space remains equally united with the intellective soul and with the surviving elements or organisms. Because this feeling is of its nature one, it can be multiplied, that is, remain united both to the subject, to the intellective soul, and to the sensitive, corporeal principles separated from the soul. It preserves its singularity and identity in itself, but can be joined to several subjects which individuate it. There is nothing contradictory in this, nor anything out of harmony with the nature of sensitive principles.

710. *Objection 2.* — You have said that when a term is identical, and when the principle referred to it has no other reality than that which comes to it from its being principle of that term,

---

[378] In the Platonic system, soul is simply something which moves body. Consequently, when separated, it does not retain any tendency towards body. On the contrary, Platonists consider body as a prison for soul. Although conscious of the disorder which is at present so noticeable in humanity, they failed to realise that this is not nature but the effect of original sin which has corrupted the whole man and changed him for the worse. They look upon the union of soul and body as an *imperfection*, a punishment. But this is absurd, and simply proves the erroneousness of this system.

then this principle itself must be one and identical. But intellective souls have identical being as their term. There can only be one of them, therefore, not several.

Reply. That is true, but once the principle has been put into being, it can have a reality and activity of its own different from that included in the naked concept of principle. As soon as this principle carries out some activity of its own, it immediately acquires individuation from this activity. There is a plurality of human souls both because they have as their terms distinct organic feelings, and because they have their own rational activity, which is carried out in the acts of reason they engage in from the very first moment of their existence. If, however, we supposed the existence of intelligences different from human intelligences, they would certainly lack a principle of individuation if they had only identical intelligible being as their term, and all intuited it at the same level, without any other activity or reality except that which sprang from this intuition. They would be one, because only a single reality of such a nature can be conceived. We can deduce from the objection, therefore, only that souls, besides having something in themselves which individuates and distinguishes them, all retain a common, mysterious bond, a subjective root, common both on the part of sense and of understanding. This root establishes the unity of the human species even in *reality*, and is in great part the reason for the empathy felt by individuals of the same species. And this explains why at certain moments, human beings appear to be a single human being.

711. *Objection 3.* — If separated souls retain an inclination to the fundamental, corporeal perception, this will prove an impediment to their happiness.

Reply. Revealed doctrine teaches that the souls of the just who receive their eternal reward find all things in God through Christ. If we consider the soul in itself, without the additions it receives from divine goodness or divine justice, we have to say that as separated from the body it remains imperfect precisely because it is deprived of its natural act. But we also have to add that it does not feel any pain because no habitual tendency is painful if it makes no effort to be satisfied. In our case, all such effort has been removed because of the removal of the corporeal term. No one can make himself act without the term of his

[711]

activity. The effort itself needs something for its own formation; it is never made relative to nothing.

CHAPTER 13

The preceding teaching about the union of soul and body avoids the opposite errors

712. Let us pause for a moment to consider how the teaching I have developed about the connection between the human soul and body corresponds to the facts and, at the same time, avoids the contrary dangers on which other systems have foundered with various degrees of damage. I shall not repeat what has been said or, if I do, I shall place it in a new light.

713. Systems about the union of the human soul with the body normally go to one of two extremes. Some were conscious only that the human soul is single and, in their endeavour to unify it, neglect one of the two active principles in human beings, that is, either the sensitive or the intellective principle. As a result, they did not grasp the knot of the union between these principles. Others, considering only the twofold aspect of these two principles of action, ended by separating them and thus positing several souls in the human being.

The first group can be divided into three systems, which are either erroneous or imperfect. Some could not explain the union of the rational principle and the body, and reduced everything to the sensitive soul. I totally exclude this sensistic system. I have shown at length the specific difference between the sensitive and intellective principles by examining their specifically different terms, that is, *being* in general, and that which is *felt*.

714. Others fixed their attention exclusively on the rational principle and saw clearly that this is what is proper to human beings. However, they were unable to reconcile the sensitive with the rational principle, and said that the sensitive soul reasoned by feeling. Feeling itself was knowledge, that is, people feel with their intellect. Plato sometimes seemed to have conceived things in this way. This *rational system* is defective in the same way as the *sensistic system*. It removes the specific distinction between the animal-sensitive principle and the rational principle.

715. Finally, there were others who although they realised that feeling is not understanding, and understanding not animal feeling, affirmed that they were two immediate activities of the same soul. They began from true principles, that is, from the principle that the intellective soul 'virtually contains inferior forms',[379] and from the other principle, 'of each thing there is one substantial being and one substantial form'.[380] They tried to avoid the error of two souls in the human being, of two or more substantial forms.

But a great difficulty follows if feeling and understanding are merely two activities of the intellective soul. Feeling is not understanding, sense is not intelligence. If these two things were to be in the soul as part of its essence, two forms would compose a single form, which is repugnant to the unity of form. On the other hand, feeling cannot exist without a subject if it is a simple faculty of the intelligence. In this case, beasts have to be made either intelligent or machines. It is, however, gratuitous to maintain that in beasts a subject is added to this faculty. Because feeling in man and feeling in beasts, considered as feeling, is of the same nature, the addition of a subject would mean adding something other than feeling to feeling in beasts, in which we see only feeling. On the other hand, the soul is intellective only in virtue of its acts of intelligence. If intelligence is of the essence of this soul, it cannot be the direct principle of feeling. A directly sentient being is not intelligent in so far as it is sentient; it is not the intellective soul. Moreover, intelligence cannot perceive feeling if feeling is not already formed. A principle is required which will form feeling (a principle which will feel) and thus furnish intelligence with matter of perception.

716. Again, if the intellective soul were the proximate, direct and single principle of feeling, it would follow that sensations and animal movements would always be acts of intelligence. This is the opposite of experience; in human beings, sense is at work without preceding intellective acts.[381] This shows that the principle moving them is not always the intellective soul. We have to

[379] *S.T.*, I, q. 76, art. 4.
[380] *Ibid.*
[381] Cf. *Conscience*, 89–93.

find, therefore, a system in which man is furnished with a single soul, a single substantial form, and in which there remain two active principles of feeling and understanding. These principles must not be connected in such a way as to constitute two souls, but at the same time must not be so separate that sense can move without the intervention of intellective activity.

717. Philosophers who wanted to maintain this second condition often fell into the opposite error present in the systems already mentioned. In other words, they wanted to posit several souls in the human being.[382]

I do not mean that when the whole of antiquity distinguished *soul* (*anima*) from *spirit* (*animus*), it intended to posit two souls in the human being. Common sense did not pass any opinion on the matter. It admitted the distinction which it found expressed in language itself, but it did not bother to decide the question. For myself, I consider the use of these two words or their equivalents as a witness from the human race in favour not of two souls, but rather of two active principles in the human being, each one of which has its own proper activity. One, however, receives the other in itself and dominates. Let me offer some authorities to clarify this distinction between the two active principles.

718. Scripture continually distinguishes *flesh* and *spirit* as adversaries. And it certainly speaks of the flesh not as dead but as alive.

St. Paul distinguishes the soul from the spirit when he speaks of the word of God as 'piercing to the division of SOUL and SPIRIT.'[383] And in a fragment of Plato's *Timaeus*, we read: 'He shut intelligence in the SPIRIT, and SOUL in the body.' Flavius Josephus says: 'He (God) sent into man SPIRIT and SOUL.[384] In

---

[382] Gennadius says that this error of two souls was common in Syria. 'We do not say that there are two souls, as James and other Syrians write. There is not an animal soul which animates the body and is MINGLED WITH THE BLOOD, and another spiritual soul which provides reason' (*De Ecclesiatic. Dogmatib.*, c. 14). Origen also, in his *De' Principi* (3: 4), seems to posit two souls, and says that when Scripture mentions *flesh*, it has to be understood as the *soul of the flesh*. It is certain that it has to be understood of the *sensitive principle*, but this is an activity, not a distinct soul in the human being.

[383] Heb 4: 12.

[384] *Antiq. jud.*, bk. 1, c. 1, ‡2.

Juvenal we find: 'At the beginning, the common maker furnished them with a SOUL only; to us he gave a SPIRIT also.'[385]

An illustrious Savoyard, who is perhaps too inclined to follow the two-soul system, brought forward the authorities I have just transcribed. In the following passage, he speaks both of the ancients and of certain physiological facts which show the existence of two activities in human beings, although they do not in any way demonstrate the existence of two souls.[386]

> In antiquity, it was thought that there could be no bond or contact between *spirit* and body. For the ancients, *soul* or sensitive principle was a kind of *proportional median*, or intermediate activity, where the spirit rested, as the soul rested in the body.[387]
>
> Lucretius uses an ingenious comparison when he compares the *soul* to the eye, and the *spirit* to the light of the eye.[388] Elsewhere, he calls it the *soul of souls*.[389] Plato, with Homer, calls it the *heart of the soul*,[390] an expression repeated by Philo.[391]

[385] *Sat.*, 15: 148–149.

[386] De Maistre, *Eclaircissement sur les Sacrifices*, c. 1.

[387] Malebranche, Leibniz and many other noble, modern intellects thought the same. They had not penetrated the nature of the subjective body, nor formed any idea of body except that given by extrasubjective experience which (properly speaking) makes us feel only a dead body, not the life of a body. On the other hand, there could be no proportional median between the extrasubjective body and the intelligent spirit. Moreover the sensitive soul, which adheres essentially to the body, does not exist divided from it because no principle can exist without a term. If these thinkers had arrived at the concept of a *substantial feeling* with a simple principle and an extended term, they would have seen that the intellective principle communicates directly not only with the principle (soul), but also with the term (body). It does not communicate, however, with the body separated from its immediate principle, but with the single feeling in which the sensitive principle and the body are inseparably united. Note again that the sensitive principle, called 'soul' by the ancients, is not properly speaking soul except when it is alone, as in beasts. It is not soul when united to the intellective principle as in human beings.

[388] Lucr. 3: 409 ss.

[389] *Ibid.*, 276.

[390] *Theaet.*

[391] *De Opif. mundi*, in Justus Lipsius, *Phys. Stoic.*, 3, diss. 16.

Jove, when he has decided in Homer to give victory to a hero, has weighed the decision in *his spirit*;[392] he is *one*; there can be no struggle in him.

When a person knows his duty and fulfils it without hesitation on some difficult occasion, he is like a god, beholding the occurrence in his *spirit*.[393]

But if he has agonised at length between his duty and his passion and is now about to commit some inexcusable violence, he has deliberated *in his soul and in his spirit*.[394]

Sometimes the *spirit* reproves the *soul*, making it blush on account of its weakness. — 'Come on, soul', it says, 'you have gone through worse than this.'[395]

Another poet offers a very pleasing dialogue about this kind of struggle. 'My soul', he says, 'I cannot grant you all you desire. Just realise that you are not the only one who wants what you love.'[396]

Plato asks: 'What does it mean when we say that a man has conquered himself, or that he has shown himself stronger than himself? At one and the same time, we are saying that he is stronger and weaker than himself. He is weaker, yet he was also stronger. Both are affirmed of the same subject. But the will, granted its *unity*, could no more be in contradiction with itself than a body could move simultaneously with two actual, contrary movements.[397] No

---

[392] *Iliad*, 2: 3.

[393] *Iliad*, 1: 333.

[394] *Ibid.*, 1: 193. — There is no doubt that it is always the rational principle which deliberates in favour both of duty and of passion. The rational principle, however, is oppressed and tempted by another, contrary activity which is mostly sensitive.

[395] *Odyss.*, 20: 18. 'Plato, in quoting this verse in *Phaedo*, sees it as one power speaking to another.' — However, it is the same intelligent spirit which reproves itself. In other words, it reproves its own intelligent will. The animal principle is incapable of reproof or encouragement. Nevertheless, the intelligent spirit could not complain and encourage itself unless it were passive in relationship to some foreign power which stimulated and tempted it.

[396] Theognis, *Inter vers. gnom.*, edit. Brunkii, v. 72–73. — Everyone of us knows the *Capricci del Bottaio*, which are dialogues between Justus and his soul.

[397] Plato, *De Rep.* — This proves only that the will can be moved by contrary motives placed before it by the intellect. The intellect, without ceasing to be one in itself, apprehends several contrary things because they

subject can unite itself to two simultaneous contraries.[398]
'If man were one in himself', as Hippocrates so admirably says, 'he would never be ill.' The reason is simple: he adds: 'because a cause of illness cannot be conceived in that which is one.'[399]

Cicero, in writing 'when we have to command ourselves, we mean that reason has to command passion', either understood passion as a *person* or did not understand himself.[400]

Pascal certainly had Plato's ideas in mind when he wrote: 'This duplication in human beings is so clear that some people thought we had two souls. A simple subject seemed to them incapable of such sudden changes.'[401]

None of these observations can demonstrate the duplication of the human soul, although they do indicate two active principles and, if you wish, two lives.[402] Lactantius' *'inextricable'* difficulty[403] consists in finding a system in which the two active

are all contained in being in general. Nevertheless, the argument shows that there is in human beings a *feeling* which is not the *rational soul*, but actually opposed to it.

[398] This principle of Aristotle (*Catheg. de quant.*) does not impede the possibility present in the intellect for perceiving opposite things, and the desire of the will for them. Even opposite things converge in being, in which the intellect perceives them and in which they are SINGLE THINGS.

[399] *De nature humana.* — Hippocrates' opinion has nothing to do with the two soul-theory because illness exists even in beasts. The duplication which produces illnesses in animals is that of soul and matter, of principle and of the term of feeling. The organic term can break up into different elements. The organic body, even granted that it is a continuum, virtually contains plurality.

[400] *Tuscul.*, 2: 21. — The famous author errs here. In using 'command' at this point, Cicero means 'to put in order'. If something is put in order, it does not have to be a person, although it is necessary that a person be the one who puts things in order.

[401] *Pensées*, 3: 13.

[402] Man's twofold life is admitted by ecclesiastical writers. Lactantius will serve as an example for them all: 'Because man is made up of two things, body and soul, one of which is earthly, the other heavenly, TWO LIVES are attributed to him, a temporal life assigned to the body, and an eternal life for the soul' (bk. 7, c. 5).

[403] 'There is another, INEXTRICABLE QUESTION. Are the SOUL and the SPIRIT the same, or is there something by which we live, and something else by which we feel and know?' (*De opif. Dei*, c. 18).

principles remain distinct in man, but nevertheless avoid the error of two souls. I think that the system I have proposed satisfies this condition.

719. In fact, I have said:

1. The union of soul and body comes about through a natural, immanent perception by which the rational principle perceives the *animal, fundamental feeling*. The physical nexus in the perception is such that *ex percipiente et percepto fit unum* [perceiver and perceived together give rise to a single thing]. Nevertheless, although the union between perceiver and perceived is physical and results in one, composite substance, its components retain a real distinction (but without separation). The perceived is not the perceiver, nor is the perceiver the perceived.

2. Rational perception is an act of the *rational principle* and consequently proper to human beings who, as we said, are defined as 'rational subjects'. Hence that which is united as form to the animal feeling is the rational soul, the only soul proper to human beings.

3. What is perceived is known; the rational soul, therefore, knows the animal feeling. To know it, the soul must share in it; otherwise, it would not perceive it. Consequently, feeling (but not mere, naked feeling) is present in the rational soul. What is present is feeling in its condition as *ens*. The rational principle, therefore, is also sensitive, but not in the way that the animal principle is. The latter is a direct principle of feeling; the former exists at a much higher level in so far as it perceives being at all its levels and therefore at the level of animal-feeling. This explains the truth of St. Thomas's affirmation: the rational soul 'CONTAINS VIRTUALLY the sensitive and nutritive soul.'[404]

4. At the same time, the purely sensitive principle, although perceived, preserves its difference from the rational, perceiving principle in so far as the former is the direct principle of animal feeling (what is perceived is not confused with what perceives). This becomes clear if we consider that animal feeling, if it did not exist, could not be perceived by the intellective principle. That which is perceived has to exist. Feeling is not made to exist by the rational principle but by the direct principle of feeling

---

[404] *S.T.*, I, q. 76, art 4.

itself (which makes feeling exist). This explains the dissolution of animal feeling without the intervention of the rational principle. Once the dissolution has taken place, animal feeling is no longer perceived and death of the human being intervenes. If animal feeling were produced directly by the rational principle, it would never cease. If a cause continues, the effect continues. Death in this case would be inexplicable.

5. This explains the struggle that occurs within man, and presupposes two activities. Activity remains in the perceiver and in the perceived, although both are joined substantially in the perception.

6. It also explains the dominion that the rational soul must have of its nature over animality. In the union between perceiver and perceived, the active part is played by the perceiver. This becomes even clearer if we consider that here we are dealing with *rational perception* in which what is *perceived* (the animal feeling) is apprehended under its condition of *ens*. This apprehension is more intimate and perfect than that with which the sensitive perceiver perceives matter, on which it depends in part as a third, foreign (extrasubjective) activity. The direct agent in what is felt, that is, in the body, is the sentient principle. Consequently, the rational principle dominates the body through the dominion it has over the sentient principle united to it through perception.

7. We notice at the same time that alterations and changes independent of the rational activity can arise in animal feeling as a result of the action proper to the sentient principle and of the action of (extrasubjective) matter. These passions are not attributed to man as to their cause because man is only the rational principle. The rest are conditions and appendages.[405]

8. The rational principle, therefore, is the sole, substantial form constituting the human being and containing in its power

---

[405] Notice here that physiologists view the vitality of the body as possessing a principle distinct from the rational soul. This is true in part, although they exaggerate this independence through their ignorance of psychology. Barthez is a good example. He says of the animal principle: 'It is absolutely independent of the thinking soul, and even of the body, in all probability' (*Nouveaux éléments de la science de l'homme*). Nevertheless, if Barthez means by this independence a real distinction only, his language, but not his thought, is inexact.

the other forms. The sensitive principle *as such* pertains to the *matter* of the human being, not to the *form*. As the form of man is the rational principle, so the matter which remains informed is not the dead body, but the live, animal body, that is, animal feeling, which is informed through perception and thus elevated to the condition of *ens*, object of the rational soul, and modified in various ways by the action of the soul.

9. Even more can be said. Animal feeling, whether perceived or not by the intellective soul, is identical. It does not duplicate itself by being perceived, but simply exists in two modes, that is, in itself and in the perceiver. But the perceiver if it does not alter the nature of animal feeling while it perceives, does not alter its principle and its term. The principle of animal feeling is, however, an extremely simple activity. By perceiving it, therefore, this principle perceives the activity in itself, as ens. The perceiver, simple as it is, receives in itself the perception of another activity, which itself is simple. The identification of the two principles, sensitive and intellective, lies here, and the principle arising from the two identified principles is the rational soul united to the body. As an ancient author said:

> One and the same spirit is called SPIRIT relative to itself, and SOUL relative to the body. — It is called soul in so far as it is the life of the body; spirit in so far as it is the life of the spiritual substance.[406]

10. Because the two activities are identified to the extent that one contributes to increasing the power of the other, the sensitive activity can cease without cessation of the rational activity. Scripture, in fact, teaches us to lose our *soul* in order to save our *spirit*. 'In this life', says our ancient author, 'the SOUL is lost to save the SPIRIT.'[407]

11. The distinction between the two activities is not destroyed as a result of what I have said, that is, that the first intellective act arises in the depth of animal activity and is as it were a new actuation of the same subject. On the contrary, although it proves that the principle of both activities is the

[406] *Tract. super Magnificat.* Amongst the works doubtfully attributed to St. Augustine.

[407] *Ibid.*

same as a result of their common origin, it does not prevent their being specifically and infinitely different. The nature of an activity is always formed by its term, not by its generative, imperfect beginning. Here, the term is as varied as the variation between the felt, extended element and being in general. Once intellectual and rational activity has originated, an entirely new nature, an imperishable substance, is present which is so different from sensitive nature that it would be altogether separate from it, were it not united through perception. It is perception which unites the two terms, that is, *animal feeling* and *intellective being*, and thus impedes separation between intellective and sensitive power.

I shall now add some further proofs which confirm the perpetual duration of the intellective soul.

CHAPTER 14

Further proofs of the immortality of the human soul

720. I have demonstrated the immortality of the human soul by starting from the principle: 'The nature of every subject is determined by its term' (cf. 676–680). The human soul, by having as its term being in general which of its nature is eternal and impassible, must itself be eternal. All previous proofs of the immortality of the soul are reduced to this. I shall add here, however, the principal proofs of which nothing has yet been said expressly.

721. I. The immortality of the soul was proved by its possession of a heavenly, divine element. The presence of this element in the intellective part of the soul was recognised, although what constitutes it as divine and heavenly was not clearly expressed. Lactantius, for instance, writes:

> Body and soul originate as united and associated. The body, formed of earthy consistency, seems almost the vessel of the soul, which takes its being from subtle, heavenly nature (*a caelesti subtilitate deductum*). Nevertheless, when some force separates them (the separation is called 'death'), each returns to its own condition: what was made

of earth becomes earth, and what sprang from heavenly in-breathing remains and flourishes always. The divine in-breathing is everlasting.[408]

Prudentius offers the same argument in verse:

The work of the mouth,
GOD'S BREATH, fiery vigour, dies not.[409]
The being he forms, flowing from the high throne of the Father-Creator,
HAS THE POWER OF FLUID REASON.[410]

722. II. The immortality of the human soul was proved in the second place by the soul's lack of contrary elements (destruction always arises by way of struggle between contraries). Now, every substantial subject has a principle and a term, which determines its nature. Contrary elements cannot be present in the subject's principle which can only be a simple activity. Struggle, therefore, can only be found in the term. This, indeed, is what occurs relative to animal life. The multiple, organic term, that which is extended, receives opposing agents which are able to tear it apart and destroy it. The intellective soul, on the other hand, having as its term *being* which embraces everything under the same relationship of entity, does not oppose elements because in it even contrary entities are unified and rendered equable. The argument that intelligence does not admit in itself any struggle between contraries and consequently is not subject to death is thus reduced, as always, to a discussion totally dependent on intuited *being*.

[408] Bk. 7, c. 12.

[409] The whole of sacred antiquity agrees in making the divine element present in the soul come from God's first in-breathing to Adam in whom all human nature was included. For me, this element, as we saw, is *being in general*.

[410] *Hymn.*, 3. — Henry Suso also proves the immortality of the soul from the divine element present in reason: 'The soul lasts eternally ON ACCOUNT OF ITS DIGNITY AS A RATIONAL BEING AND ITS DEIFORM POWERS because God, in whose image the soul is formed, is the superessential mind and intelligence' (*In Appendice quarundaum sublimium quaestionum*, c. 15). Aeneas of Gaza says that every rational act done by the soul is an argument of its immortality: 'All art, all knowledge, action too and contemplation, are able to show superabundantly that the human soul is immortal' (*In Theophr.*).

Vincent of Beauvais sets out the argument in the following way:

> Notice that the soul, considered *according to its origin*, that is, in so far as it has being, can be and is contingent and corruptible (contingent) of its nature in the sense that it can return to nothing if the will of the first ens does not prevent this. But considered according *to its essence or substance* it is incorruptible because it does not result from contrary elements, nor is there anything contrary to its nature which could corrupt it.[411]

723. III. The normal argument, which proves the immortality of the soul from its simplicity, is similar to the preceding. It is not sufficient to prove that the soul is simple in its principle; the soul of beasts is also simple in its principle. To validate the argument, we have to go further and prove the simplicity of the term on which its nature depends. We have to appeal to *being in general*, the most simple thing of all.

The argument from simplicity was developed by St. Irenaeus[412] and St. Gregory Thaumaturgus, and repeated by all their successors. This is what St. Gregory says:

> The soul, not having a body, is simple, that is, not composed nor possessed of many parts. But as far as I can see what is simple must be immortal. How shall I show this? Listen! Nothing corrupts itself; if it did, it would be unable to last right from the beginning. Things which become corrupt, are corrupted through contraries. Indeed, that which becomes corrupt, disintegrates; that which disintegrates, is composite; that which is composite has parts; that which has parts, has different parts; and that which is different is not the same. But the soul is simple and not composed of many parts precisely because it is neither composite nor destructible. It follows that it cannot be corrupted; it is immortal.[413]

He says several parts, if they exist, must be different because if they had no difference their multiplicity would be indiscernible,

---

[411] *Speculum historiale*, bk. 1, c. 34.

[412] Bk. 5, c. 7.

[413] *De Anima*.

and altogether non-existent. If, however, the parts are different, the ens composed of them would not be the same, nor entirely equal to itself. Granted differences, contraries must be admitted. But there is no difference in the object of the intellect which conceives everything in the unity of the same being. The holy bishop of Neo-Caesarea rises almost to the speculations of the School of Elea.

724. IV. A fourth, extremely powerful argument, drawn from the rights of justice, was used not only by Greek philosophers, but by ecclesiastical writers such as Origen,[414] Lactantius,[415] Leontius[416] and others. Seeing that rights were not always safeguarded in this life, they realised that another life must exist in which equality will be re-established between the overabundance enjoyed by the wicked here below, and the undue suffering of the good. But how are we to explain why justice must be triumphant? Because, I say, justice is of its nature immutable and eternal. But this eternity proper to justice is based solely on the eternity and immutability of being which shines in the human mind, as I showed in my moral works.

725. V. Socrates, in *Phaedo*, used the same kind of argument to prove the immortality of the soul. He reasoned that man, made for justice, which he could and should love, must be immortal because he was made and ordained for something immortal. He tries to show that the body is a kind of veil separating the understanding from the glorious vision of justice to which it is naturally united. This means feeling and confessing a holy God, the *unknown God* of the Athenians.[417]

[414] *Super Cantica.*

[415] Bk. 3, c. 19.

[416] *De Sectis*, Art. 2.

[417] The intimate sense of moral good as something eternal for which human beings are made has great influence on the spirit of upright men and women. Whether real or imaginary, the discourses of the dying Socrates inserted in *Phaedo* demonstrate this truth. If they are invented, Plato would never have expressed them so wonderfully unless he had believed them to be highly likely and totally in conformity with the noble character of a person whom he wished to show as a type of the just man. Suidas affirms that the philosopher Hermias felt the same way. 'He was alert and very sharp. So much so that he is said to have stated on oath to the dying Egyptian (brother Theodotes) that the soul is immortal and immune from annihilation. The

726. VI. The term of human understanding, as we said, is being, and thus immortal. This immortal essence, which informs understanding, provides it with its nature. It is not surprising, therefore, that understanding possesses the feeling of its own immortal nature. From this feeling we can draw a new proof of the truth of which we are speaking because the feeling, as the work of nature, does not err or deceive. Human beings ceaselessly manifest this feeling of their own immortality in actions and lasting undertakings which go beyond the present life, in their love of future glory, in their contempt for death and even in suicide, of which only humans, not animals, are capable. And, we may add, in the force of thought and spirit which is often characteristic of dying people. St. Athanasius says:

> The soul, when it has entered the body and been bound to it, neither contracts nor accommodates itself to the smallness of the body. Often, it remains alert with its own forces when the body lies in bed deprived of movement. It goes beyond the condition of the body, as though wandering away from the body, yet still within it, as it imagines and beholds superterrestial things. Often, it meets saints and angels outside earthly bodies and, sustained by its purity of mind, manages to reach out to them. Surely it will have an even clearer idea of immortality when the Almighty, who has joined it to the body, separates it from the body?[418]

727. VII. These totally natural feelings, if not suffocated and extinguished in vice, give rise to the universal agreement amongst all peoples about the immortality of the soul. And this is yet another effective, persuasive argument for this truth.

very integrity of life, which is contrary to bodily nature, gives the soul this confidence as it reflects on itself and notices, at one and the same time, the separation of body and soul, together with its manifest immortality' (under the entry *Hermias*). If this feeling of the immortality of the soul is so strong in upright, virtuous people, how does the notion of mortality originate? It springs from vice, from wickedness, which makes flesh the object of our thought. The light of decency, and consequently our feeling for what is immortal, is thus extinguished in thought.

[418] *Orat. contra idola.*

CHAPTER 15
Conclusion

728. So we have arrived at the end of the first part of *Psychology*. Despite the difficulty of our undertaking, we need have no regret, I am sure, about the effort necessary to attain self-knowledge in the light of our joyful, certain conclusion about the unending existence of our soul, our most noble part, through which we live and understand. This truth raises us above those enormous masses which, although they make up the universe, are destined to disintegrate. It shows that an immortal destiny awaits us as we survive the dissolution of matter. At this point, we can ask ourselves why our soul has been made, what is the end of its existence, what good is proportionate to its nature. We are now in a position to reply to these sublime, necessary questions (they are necessary because human beings are not satisfied to live in ignorance and uncertainty about them) as a result of our study of self which has brought us to indubitable certainty about the immortality of our own souls. It is indeed clear that only immortal, divine good is proportionate and fitting to an immortal being. Psychology has prepared and led us to the search for this good.

729. Some people, although they possess a great deal of self-opinionated knowledge, are enemies of wisdom, and hurl abuse at others who raise their minds above the senses to investigate more noble matters. Their restless, quite brilliant intellects are not content with complaining about the industry and diligence of high-minded people who, they think, are attempting the impossible and wasting their time in empty speculation. These intellectual back-biters imagine that considerations leading human beings to knowledge and possession of eternal things are all useless because they are not confined to increasing his temporal welfare. Their lassitude in shown in certain maxims and opinions which they enunciate as indubitable, and which all begin: 'It is impossible to know' and 'It is impossible to understand'. One very solemn maxim, repeated a thousand times, is this: 'The essence of things

cannot be known' and in particular: 'It is impossible to know the essence of the soul.' But when Zeno argued against the existence of movement, Diogenes moved — and proved him wrong.

For our part, we have dealt in these five books with the essence of the soul rather than argue about the knowability of its essence. Diogenes' argument was not truly effective because he contrasted a physical fact with metaphysical speculation, but his principle, 'That which is cannot be called impossible', was totally true. I think, therefore, that the first part of *Psychology*, in which I demonstrated the nature of the essence of the soul, has given us a great advantage. The only people who from now on will be able to say that the essence of the soul cannot be known in any way whatsoever are those who have first proved that this essence, which we have indicated by repeating the teaching handed down from generation to generation, is not in fact the essence of the soul. I trust that such people, jealous of the good possessed by the human race, will not be able to rob it of such a precious and extremely necessary truth on which rests the demonstrative certainty of our immortal life. Certainly, anyone who totally ignores the essence of the soul could never know through reason if the soul is immortal or mortal. The first part of *Psychology* has, therefore, provided us with a delightful and important harvest in which the essence and nature of the soul furnish indubitable proofs of its immortality, on which hangs our eternal destiny.

730. The destiny of the soul will in all cases be eternal, but it does not follow that it will be happy. Necessary justice, evident to all, promises eternal joy only to the virtuous soul, and a terrible threat to the vicious soul. Virtue, which perfects the soul, is the work of the soul itself; the same must be said of vice which corrupts and ruins the soul at its depths. It is obvious that the soul which has ruined and disordered itself cannot attain as happy a condition as the soul which has perfected, enlarged and ennobled itself as a result of its own noble, worthy activities. Ethics deals with these activities through reference to moral laws by distinguishing some acts as good and some as bad. But we have to consider them in themselves and in the activities resulting from them before we can look at them from the moral point of view. This is what I intend to do in the second part of

Psychology, which treats of the natural development of the human soul and shows how various, multiple activities originate from its essence. The second part of *Psychology*, which still remains to be tackled, will therefore provide as noble a service to man as the first. It will bring us to understand ourselves in those interior aptitudes and faculties whose appropriate use makes the possession of an immortal soul highly desirable and precious and which, by enriching us with virtue, assures for our souls a blessed, eternal destiny. Let us move on, therefore, swiftly and confidently to the new investigation we have proposed.

Appendix

1. (13).

The statement *'ideal being* is *essentially object'* excludes all philosophical errors about the starting point of philosophy. Amongst philosophers who hold these errors are:

1. *Materialists* (extra-subjectivists) who start from *matter* which they wrongly consider as thinking.

2. *Sensists* (sensual subjectivists) who start from *sensation* or from feeling, and suppose that to feel is to think.

3. *Subjectivists* (intellectual subjectivists) who start from *consciousness*, and wrongly suppose that known objects are modifications of the spirit and that the act of human knowledge, needing no intellective light to inform it, produces its own light.

4. *False objectivists* whose conclusion necessarily coincides with the first three errors. These objectivists fail to understand the nature of *object*, and imagine it as something *real*. It is not; an object can never be other than *ideal* because the mind is necessarily illuminated by an *idea*. What is *real*, on the other hand, is something thât needs illumination if it is to be known. What does 'being known' mean? It means 'being objectivised', being known in the *object*. All real things, therefore, are known through *ideas*, without which nothing is known. In other words, real things need two conditions if they are to be known positively: 1. they operate upon feeling and thus render themselves sensible; 2. after they are rendered sensible, the intelligent subject must apply the idea to this sensible thing and see it in the idea, or in ideal being. In other words, the subject sees the relationship of (formal) identity between the real, sensible thing and the ideal object. The real thing, therefore, remains unknown until it is *object*; the idea, however, never ceases to be the object of the mind, and would not even exist unless contemplated by some mind. It is, therefore, essentially object. But what is the real thing (that which is sensible) if it is not *per se* object, and comes to be known in the object (in the idea)? *Per se,*

it will be something subjective if it is real and sentient; it will be extrasubjective if it is real and sensed: such is matter. Hence, those claiming that the primal object of the mind is something real falsely apply the word, *object*, to *matter*, that is, *subject*. This class of philosophers should, therefore, be called *false objectivists*. Their mistake, as I said, coincides with the first three errors. It is one or other of them but disguised by the name *objectivism*. These philosophers misuse words and arbitrarily attribute what they call object to that which is *real* as though there were some kind of magic in their language enabling what is *real* to acquire the nature of object. What is real, however, remains exactly what it is: *matter* or *feeling* or *intellective act*. Matter is extrasubjective, as we said, while the other two elements are subjective. Philosophers of this kind propose a system called 'objectivism', a noble name, which contains in its depths either materialism, sensism or subjectivism, according to the way they intend to develop it.

But are we to say that we know Almighty God by way of ideas? Yes, in this life we know him through the way of ideas and affirmation as we know other real things. However, the cognition that we can have of God in this life (prescinding from the supernatural order) is negative, or ideal-negative, as I prefer to call it.

In the supernatural order, Almighty God is *perceived* supernaturally. This *perception* of God differs, however, from all other perceptions in the following way. In the perception of contingent things, *reality* is provided for man by a sense faculty different from the *intellect*; in the perception of God possessed by the blessed in heaven, the reality of God is perceived by means of *intellective feeling*. God's reality is in his very own ideality, something not difficult to understand if we keep in mind the principles according to which we see the essences of things in ideas. The essence of God, however, is necessary; it is also subsistent, never merely possible. The divine subsistence must, therefore, be perceived in the idea itself. But for this to take place, God must manifest his essence to the created intellect. Without this no created intellect can perceive Almighty God.

2. (77).

My lack of a reply to C. Mamiani's *Lettere* was taken by one person as contempt. But I do not despise anyone, still less such a learned fellow-citizen as Mamiani, whom I have often sincerely praised. I have to say, however, that many of those who honour me with their comments almost always express my feelings in words that do not truly express them. In this case, my reply would have to be a simple reminder of the expressions I used. If I did this for every individual, I would constantly be going over the same path. This substitution of expressions different from my own, and hence of different concepts, is found also in Mamiani's *Letters*, although he certainly is unaware of this. Let me give an example and, by breaking my intended silence, show my esteem for this exceptional Italian philosopher and man of letters. He finds intellective perception, as I describe it, impossible. He says: 'One of the terms must remain obscure and unknown by the very law of its nature. In fact, how will thought have information about the subsistent sensation, which is the real subject to which the predicate, the hypothetical ens, has to be joined?' (*Lett.* 4). But I have never used the expression '*hypothetical* ens.' I have mentioned 'possible ens', but not 'hypothetical ens', which is something totally different. Possible ens is eternal and necessary and the very opposite of hypothetical ens. It is also untrue that the predicate is, according to me, *possible ens*. The predicate is indeed ens, but ens in its common essence as ens. I have already said on several occasions that *possibility* is only a posterior relationship, added by mental reflection to innate ens (*NE*, vol. 2, 743–746). I said that it did not constitute the essence of ens. I also showed that the *essence* of ens is identical under the two forms of *ideality* and *reality*; the spirit finds it in both forms. It could not find it, however, in reality if it were not first given in ideality. Being is called 'ideal' only in so far as it is intelligible.

My reply to the other objection, 'One of the two terms remains unknown' in the primal judgment, is as follows. It is indeed unknown until this judgment has been made; but this judgment makes it known.

My reply to the other question, 'How will thought have

information about the subsistent sensation which is the real subject to which the predicate, ens, has to be joined?' is as follows. If thought had information about the subsistent sensation, the latter would already have been perceived, and there would be no need to add the predicate, which would have already been added. It is mistaken to suppose that knowledge of the subsistent sensation is needed to form the primal judgment. On the contrary, this altogether unknown sensation comes to be known and affirmed by means of the judgment, which of course has to be explained. But affirming the sensation means knowing it; nothing real is known unless it is affirmed.

— But are you not saying that between the subsistent sensation and the ens which is predicated of it there is a relationship of subject and predicate? Yes, I am, but this does not take place in any way prior to the judgment; if the judgment has not been concluded neither one nor the other is subject or predicate. These two words, subject and predicate, are an analysis of an already formed judgment; predicate and subject are never found outside a judgment. But when the judgment has been formed, not before, the subsistent sensation is certainly known. Then it is called 'subject' by the person who reflects on the formed judgment and with this act of reflection considers it as known, and notes that existence is predicated of it. The objection is apparently serious, but arises solely through incorrect understanding and incorrect expression of my theory of intellective perception.

The *synthetical judgment*, therefore, that is, the primal judgment, is not to be confused with the *analytical* judgment which comes about as a result of reflection upon the synthetical. Moreover, it is incorrect to make all judgments analytical, as Galluppi does when he speaks in general terms, affirming: 'Judgment is simply an analysis of a complex perception' (*Elementi di Psicologia*, c. 1, §8). — Cf. *Sistema filosofico*, 43–50.

3. (223).

My apparent departure here from the opinion of St. Thomas (who upholds the Aristotelian definition of the soul as an act of the body) should not cause surprise. In taking as our teachers all the holy doctors of the Church, it is I think a duty of lovers of truth to cling to the basic principles rather than the letter of their teaching. There are sometimes contradictions in the letter which are absent in the principles. In his time, St. Thomas was almost obliged to hold the teaching of Aristotle or correct it with caution. As far as I can see, Aristotle's definition of the soul cannot be upheld. Calling the soul *act of the body* appears to render it a production of the body; acts are produced by their subject. The image he uses of wax and a shape impressed on it (*De Anima*, bk. 2) shows that this criticism is correct. In fact, the wax in which the impression has been made is one substance, wax; the image is but an act, a simple modification of the wax. Thus, the soul would not be a substance, but a simple modification of the body.

St. Thomas was aware of this, and although he retained the Aristotelian definition, he was not prepared to accept its consequent error. In his own objection about the possibility of the intellect's being an act of the body, he replied that 'the human soul is an act of the organic body to the extent that the body provides an organ for it. Nevertheless, the body need not be the organ of the soul relative to every potency and power because the soul exceeds the proportion of the body' (*De An.*, bk. 2, ad 2). One part of the soul, the principal part, is not therefore an act of the body. Consequently, the Aristotelian definition does not express the essence of soul as a good definition should; if the essence were nothing more than an act of the body, the intellect would not be soul, nor pertain to the essence of soul because it makes no use of any bodily organ.

This is an invincible objection which certainly did not escape the insight of St. Thomas. He did not resolve the difficulty, but was content to safeguard the more important truth by replying simply: 'The possible intellect *is consequent* to the concept of soul in so far as the soul exceeds bodily matter. Hence although it is not the act of any organ, the intellect is not entirely outside the essence of the soul, but is that which is supreme in it' (*Q. De An.*, art. 2, ad 4). In abandoning Aristotle's definition, I think therefore that substantially I am upholding Aquinas' teaching. This is all the more necessary when we consider that intelligence is not a mere *potency* of the human soul, but a *part of its essence*, a substantial and specific part.

Galen complained that philosophers had not dealt with such an important question. He tells us that disciples succeeded their interminable masters without ever finding what they were looking for. But when he studied the question himself, the result was: 1. he could not explain the formation of the animal and the movements of the already formed animal without an intelligent formative principle; 2. but the baby moves without knowing of its own anatomy, that is, of the muscles it moves; as a result yet another intelligent principle is required, different from the former and able to control involuntary muscles; 3. one is forced to say therefore that either the intelligent principle which formed the animal remains in it even after the formation, or that every muscle is an animal in itself. He summarises himself in the following passage:

> This fact — that he had not found among the learned of his time anyone who could demonstrate for him the formative principle proper to the animal — saddened and forced me to look for some efficacious reason explaining the formation of animals and the complex work involved. But I have to declare here that I have not found any reason of this kind. I now exhort and beg practitioners of these noble sciences to investigate the subject and share freely with us whatever they wisely succeed in finding. We see children speaking and saying all the things we require them to say, for example, 'myrrh, knife and soap', without any knowledge of the muscles suitable for moving the tongue to pronounce such words, or (and this is more important) of the nerves of those muscles. I consider it highly credible and probable either that whatever forms the tongue remains in the formed parts, or that each part itself has been constructed and formed by yet another animal (another soul) who KNOWS the will proper to our soul's principal part. But when I see as a consequence that one soul must be brought to bear in the principal part of our reason and other souls in the individual parts, or that there is at most a common soul governing everything, I relapse into my primitive ignorance. Again, when I hear philosophers say that 'matter was animated from eternity, and renders itself beautiful by gazing on ideas', I reflect once more that there

must be a soul which formed us and now uses all our parts. But what militates greatly against this opinion is our ignorance of this soul that governs us and the parts which serve its desires and movements.

Later he says:

In the formation of the animal I see simultaneously a supreme wisdom and a supreme power. I do not accept therefore that the foetus can be formed by the soul inserted in the seed, that is, by the vegetative soul according to Aristotle, by the sensitive soul according to Plato, and by nature (not even the soul!) according to the Stoics.

Here and in other places of the famous doctor of Pergamum we note the following:

1. The best minds of antiquity saw the absurdity of animal phenomena being produced by a material, *brute cause*.

2. But because they did not know the nature of feeling, which they confused with intelligence, and wanted to avoid the absurdity of a *brute cause*, they went to the opposite extreme of supposing a *rational* cause.

3. They glimpsed that matter could be united to a feeling but not how it was united. Unable to conceive the concept of creation, they fell into the error of eternal matter.

4. They also glimpsed that feeling could be directed by nature to the intuition of ideas, but knew neither the unity of ideas nor the organisation, given by the Creator, which was necessary for the intuition to take place.

5. (428).

Indian philosophers tried to explain the interaction between soul and body in the same way. They enclosed the soul within a subtle form called *linga, linga-jarira*. Between this *subtle form* and the crude body, they imagined a connecting ring, a tenuous body, servant of the five organs. This was the teaching of the school of Kapila. Henry Colebrooke, in his *Saggio sulla Filosofia degl'Indú*, describes the teaching of the Vedanta school:

The soul is enclosed in a body as in a container, or rather in a series of containers. The first and innermost intellectual container (*vijnanamaya*), composed of the rudimentary part (*tanmatra*) or of simple uncombined elements, consists of the intellect (*buddhi*) united to the five senses.

The next container is the mental one (*manomaya*) where the interior sense (*manas*) is joined to the previous container. A third container, called the organic or vital container, consists of the organs of action and the vital faculties. These three containers or shells (*kosa*) constitute the subtle form (*sucma sarira* or *linga sarira*) which waits for the soul in its transmigrations. The internal basic element confined within the most intimate container is the causal form (*karana-sarira*).

The fatty body (*sthula-sarira*) which encloses the soul from birth to death in each stage of its transmigrations is composed of the densest elements formed by the combinations of simple elements in the proportion of four-eighths of the characteristic, dominant element and one-eighth of each of the other four. In other words, because the particles of many elements are divisible, they are in the first case divided in half; one of these halves is subdivided into quarters, the other is combined with a part (the quarter of a half) of each of the four others. It thus constitutes the dense, mixed elements. The exterior container, which is composed of elements combined in this way, is the alimentary container (*annamaya*), and as the seat of enjoyment is called the dense body.

The organic form assimilates the combined elements received through nutrition. It separates out the finest parts and rejects the bulkiest: earth becomes flesh, water blood, and inflammable substances (oil and fat) marrow. The fattiest particles of the first two are disposed of as excrement and urine; the particles of the third kind are laid down as bones. The finest or most delicate particles of the first part nourish internal sense; those of the second feed the respiration, and those of the third maintain speech.

This extraordinary coincidence with the Greek hypotheses shows either that philosophy must naturally arrive at such a hypothesis because it lacks the correct concept of subjective ens, or that Greek philosophy derives from Indian, perhaps through Pythagoras who, according to Laertius, Clement of Alexandria and Aelianus, travelled in India, or that Indian philosophy is more recent than is thought. Ward suspects that Indian writings are not older than 500 BC, and depend on the Greek. According to Ward, Gautama would be a contemporary of Pythagoras.

6. (451).

The second of the four demonstrations of the simplicity of the sentient principle given in *Anthropology* is based on the fact of the duplication of organs in certain sensories such as the eyes and ears, etc. and their corresponding simple sensations. The force of this proof, therefore, depends on showing that there are two sensory organs, and consequently two sensations received by the soul which then makes them one through its own simplicity. Roland's experiment shows that the optic nerves are not united in the brain, as some people suspected, but that there are two clearly distinct sight organs, not one. The proof becomes even more effective if we consider that the optic nerve of the right eye terminates in the left lobe and that of the left eye in the right lobe. Granted the twofold nature of these sensations, it is not surprising that Doctor Gall made every effort to prove that we always see with one eye alone. There is no doubt that the fact of our seeing simultaneously with both eyes must have been a severe embarrassment to a system as materialistic as his. Nevertheless, says Magendie,

> it has been shown, that the two eyes not only concur in vision, but that it is altogether necessary that both operate if certain acts, extremely important to sight, are to be carried out. — Let a ray of sun fall on a plate in a darkened room. Then take two pieces of very thick glass, each coloured with colours of the prism, and put them to the eyes. If your sight is good, and especially if the eyes are of equal strength, the image of the sun will appear whitish, whatever colour glass you use. But if one of your eyes is much stronger than the other, you will see the image of the sun coloured according to the colour of the glass you have put to the stronger eye. These results were verified in the presence of Mr. Tillaye junior in the physics laboratory of

the faculty of medicine. A single object, therefore, really produces two impressions. The brain nevertheless perceives only one of them (*Précis élémentaire de Physiologie, Action simultanée des deux yeux*).

The consequence Magendie draws from the fact he has noted is absurd. He concludes that the brain perceives only one of the two impressions. This is a clear proof of the incredible force possessed by educational prejudice in distracting the most perspicacious minds, despite every effort to avoid unproved assertions. The learned physiologist acknowledges that each eye receives not only a single, distinct impression, but an impression accompanied by sensation. He knows through his own anatomical experiments that each of the nerves terminates in a different lobe of the brain; nevertheless he asserts with the highest surety that the brain has only a single impression because of the presence of a single sensation! Anyone with a little common sense is capable of recognising here that the brain can neither simplify the two distinct impressions which it undoubtedly receives nor fuse the two sensations (which do not arise in the extrasubjective brain) into a single sensation; it can fuse them only in the subjective feeling, that is, in the soul. The simplicity of the soul is alone capable of explaining how two sensations, when having wholly equal positions in what is felt fundamentally, necessarily change into one because the space which divides them and makes them appear two is lacking. My own experiment, made without glasses, consists in fixing the eyes on a piece of paper painted with two columns of different colours. Cross the eyes so that one colour is superimposed on the other. The result is that one colour is changed by the other in the same way as different colours of transparent glass when imposed on one another. This is another proof of the simplicity of the soul (cf. *AMS*, 107).

Magendie himself has this to say about the twofold sensation given by the two ears:

> It has been said incorrectly that we use one ear at a time. When dealing with the direction of sound and deciding where it originates, we are obliged to employ both ears. Only by comparing the intensity of the two impressions can we recognise the source of the sound. If, for example, we completely block one ear when a slight sound is being

made some distance away in a dark place, it will be impossible to judge the direction of the sound which can, however, be recognised if we make use of both ears (*Précis élémentaire de Physiologie, Action simultanée des deux appareils de l'ouïe*).

How can he say, therefore, that the brain receives only one sensation?

7. (473).

The ancients, who attributed the generation of beings to *love*, acknowledged indirectly that the moulding force or the 'plastidinamia', as J. F. Lobstein called it (*De l'organisation de la matière dans l'espèce humaine*, in Millin's *Magasin encyclopédique*, 1804), must be found in *feeling* alone, because *love* is feeling. The Epicureans, who attributed this formative, organising virtue to matter without the intervention of the Creator, basically did no more than associate a feeling with matter. A clear demonstration of this is their claim that all worldly events are explained by the principle of love and by the sympathy and antipathy of things. Their imagination certainly confused the extrasubjective facts of attraction and repulsion with the real subjective cause (feeling), and interchanged these as they pleased. This prevented them from making a constant distinction between the concept of what is subjective and what is extrasubjective. But clearly, their use of the word 'love' is sufficient of itself to show that their thought started from the subjective principle. Indeed, some thinkers today have turned precisely to feeling and love to explain generation and, by extending their explanation to plants, have imitated the language of Epicureans. Virey, for example, has no hesitation in writing:

Animals and plants have life because they have received existence and organisation from the love of their parents. We all begin in the maternal womb; our life is simply an emanation of that of our parents, the fruit of their love; our existence has its source entirely in them, and the more ardent their love, the more energetic our life. Love is the force by which individuals produce descendants who are stronger and more active than those of very old or very young parents. As the sole source of life, love is the period of strength, energy, activity and reproduction. — In its widest sense, love is the principle of life of all organised bodies and alone presides over the generations. It is the generative Venus, celebrated in earlier time by philosophers and poets:

> Through you, every kind of living thing is conceived,
> And what has arisen has gazed on the light of the sun.
> Every kind of living things
> Follows you desirously in your alluring deeds
> Wherever you lead.
> You pierce their breasts with seductive love,
> Giving them the desire to propagate by nations down
> the centuries.
>   (Lucret., bk. 1)

Love therefore is the judge of the organic world. It orders the chaos of matter which it impregnates with life; it opens and closes at will the door of existence to all the beings it calls out of nothing and returns to nothing. Attraction in brute matter is a kind of love or friendship analogous to the love that reproduces organised being. The generative faculty is therefore a general phenomenon in the universe, manifested in brute substances by planetary and chemical attraction, and in organised bodies by love or life.

> Article *Générations* in *Nouveau Dictionnaire d'Histoire naturelle.*

8. (535).

A difference of density is difficult to conceive in a perfectly solid continuum. I prescind from it totally as something unproved and improbable, and simply note that, even granted a different density in the element, there would be no extra-subjective phenomenon of life unless there were some kind of attraction.

We could however advance another hypothesis, and suppose that in every first element there is a kind of centre corresponding to Boscovich's simple points. From this centre, there emanates *attraction* or *retention* which reveals its effect in a given proportion, for example, in inverse proportion to the square of the distances. It is true that in this case the element's density and solidity would increase in proportion to the proximity of its matter to the centre. But equally, if we supposed the elements to be of a fixed, extremely small size, they would be so dense and solid throughout that they could not be broken apart by any external force; they would be true atoms (physically indivisible). It is easy to understand the necessity of this effect when we consider that at the shortest distances attraction increases in an unimaginable progression. Against this progression, mechanical forces are practically infinitesimal, and can be applied only externally to an extremely minute part, because of the smallness and lightness of the atom itself. Similarly, physical and chemical forces are practically powerless, if we suppose that they all act (as I believe) according to the law which governs attraction in general, or present the outward appearance of acting in this way. In so far as these attracting forces have to be applied externally to the atom, the body which is applied to the atom is more distant from the centre of attraction than the matter of the atom is. The body therefore necessarily exercises less force on the matter than does the centre of the atom, which we suppose to be the centre of attraction. Furthermore, the attraction, if supposed from a distance (which is contrary to the way we perceive), can exercise on the atom only the minimum force sufficient for attracting the atom itself. Consequently, the whole atom, whose weight is as minute as its size, could be drawn but never smashed by these forces.

Nevertheless the *density* or supposed centre of attraction inside the atom seems suitable for explaining how atoms joined by contact, which I suppose possible, do not join in such a way that they become perfectly solid and inseparable.

Indeed, if the density of matter did not vary inside the atom, it would be difficult to explain how atoms, even when in contact, remain distinct and separable, without denying the contact (as some have done) and without having recourse to a repulsive force (which in my opinion must be derivative). But granted that the density increases in the atom in proportion to the proximity of the matter to the centre of attraction, we immediately understand how the internal matter cannot be further rarefied, precisely because, although still continuous and impenetrable, it is at its most rarefied near the surfaces in contact with the atoms. Hence, the matter cannot become denser because it is always held more strongly by the dense matter nearest the centre of the two atoms which are in contact.

We must leave the mathematicians to calculate the accuracy of these postulates and determine how small the primitive elements must be if they are to remain perfectly hard, that is, indivisible and clearly distinct from each other, even when in real contact.

Index of Biblical References

Numbers in roman indicate paragraphs or, where stated, the appendix (app.); numbers in italic indicate footnotes. Bible references are from RSV (Common Bible) unless marked †. In these cases, where the author's use of Scripture is dependent solely upon the Vulgate, the Douai version is used.

Genesis

1	*237*
1: 2 [Douai]	*238, 241*
2: 7	*324*
6: 3, 17	*241*
9: 4 [5, Douai]	*309*
49: 32	*696*

Leviticus

17: 10 ss.	*310*

Deuteronomy

12: 23	*311*

Job

12: 10	*241*

Psalms

103: 29	*241*

Ecclesiasticus

3: 21	*241*

Isaiah

42: 5	*324*
47: 6	*324*

Ezechiel

1: 20–21	*241*
10: 17	*241*
37	*241*

1 Corinthians

7: 31	*375*

Hebrews

4: 12	718

Index of Persons

*Numbers in roman indicate paragraphs or, where stated, the appendix (app.);
numbers in italic indicate footnotes. Bracketed numbers refer to the Preface*

Adelon, 586
Aelianus, *app.* no. 5
Aeneas of Gaza, *410*
Agrippa, *135*
Alexander of Aphrodisias, 428
Al-Gassali, 284
Alvarez, Baldassar, *206*
Ambrose (St.), *306*
Anaxagoras, 622
Anaximenes, 622
Andronicus of Rhodes, (3)
Apollinare, *205*
Apollonius of Tyana, 285; *98*
Apuleius, *308*
Archelaus, 622
Aretaeus, *272*
Aristotle, (3); 53–54, 114, 223–224, 399,
    428–429, 445–446, 454, 457, 473, 633,
    645, 648, 656; *37, 51, 102, 139, 225, 323,
    354, 355, 398*; *app.* no. 3
Athanagoras, 659
Athanasius (St.), 659, 726; *307*
Augustine (St.), 113–115, 117–120, 139,
    448, 457–458, 624, 651, 684; *144, 218,
    261, 306, 406*
Averroes, 274–283, 457
Avicembron, 284
Avicenna, 284, 457

Baldinotti, *(12)*
Barthez, 473; *405*
Basil (St.), *200*
Becquerel, 494
Berkeley, 429
Bernard (St.), *306, 368*
Berard, F., *237*
Berruti, S., 600; *231, 294, 296*
Bichat, 620
Bloch, 491
Blumenbach, 473
Boerhaave, A. K., *75*

Borelli, G-A, 399–404
Boscovich, *app.* no. 8
Botto, 592
Bremser, 491
Brougham (Lord), 32
Bruno, 524
Buddha, 612
Bufalini, *289*
Buffon, 592; *35, 309*
Burdach, C. F., 491

Cabanis, 493
Campanella, 524
Capreolo, *205*
Cardano, 524
Carli, G. R., *316*
Cassiodorus, *306, 336*
Cataneo da Imola, Andrea, *135*
Cheyne, G., *157*
Cicero, (2); 518, 621; *69, 400*
Claudius Mamertus, 651
Clement V (pope), *103*
Clement of Alexandria, *323, 360*; *app.* no. 5
Cocchi, 292
Coelius Rhodiginus [Ludovico Ricchieri
    of Rovigo], *135*
Cogevina, *135*
Colebrooke, H., *app.* no. 5
Condillac, 32, 93; *38*
Confucius, *86*
Cousin, 398
Cudworth, 473
Cuvier, 499
Czermak, *297*

De Blainville, 491
Dégerando, 94
Della Chiaie, 491
De la Mettrie, *233*
De Maistre, *386*
Democritus, 517, 622

Descartes, *(9)*; 286–287, 473; *75, 180*
Destutt-Tracy, *38*
Diderot, *233*
Diogenes of Apollonia, 622, 729
Dumas, *298*
Durando, *205*

Egidius, *205*
Ehrenberg, D. C. C., 532; *231*
Empedocles, 517, 617, 621–622
Epicurus, 450
Euclid, 33
Evodius, 458

Feller, F. X., 521; *35*
Fernel, J., 427–428
Fichte, 72–73, 80; *37, 129*
Ficino, Marsilio, *98, 135, 337*
Fontana, A., *(10)*
Fontana, F., *358*
Forni, *268*
Fray, 491
Freitag, G., *265*
Fyens, T., 302; *136*

Galen, 407, 417, 473; *273, 298*; *app.* no. 4
Gall, *app.* no. 6
Galluppi, *(15)*; 95; *app.* no. 2
Garducci, *187*
Gennadius, *98, 382*
Gerbert, 54
Giacomo di Forli, *135*
Glisson, F., 524–527; *270, 282*
Gregory of Nyssa (St.), *105, 366*
Gregory Nazianzen (St.), *328, 337*
Gregory Thaumaturgus (St.), 723; *83, 196*

Haller, 532
Harvey, 473
Heraclitus of Ephesus, 516, 622, 669
Hermias, 668
Hippocrates, 302; *174, 399*
Hobbes, *(14)*
Homer, 617
Houdart, M-S, *236, 305*
Huet, *308*
Hugh of St. Victor, *106*
Hunter, 618; *318*

Iamblichus, *109, 306*
Ingenhousz, 491
Irenaeus, 723

Jerome (St), *215, 260*
John Damascene (St.), *105*
John of Janduno, *205*

John of Salisbury, *368*
John of Saxony, *205*
Josephus, Flavius, 718
Juvenal, 718; *107*

Kant, 53, 524; *16*
Kirker, *263*

Lactantius, 718, 721, 724; *402*
Laertius, *app.* no. 5
Lallemand, *297*
Lamarck, 491
Leibniz, 280, 418, 524; *180, 387*
Leo X (pope), *103*
Leontius, (2); 724
Leucippus, 622
Lipsius, Justus, *396*
Lister, *156*
Lobstein, J. F., *app.* no. 7
Lohse, C. H., *192*
Lucretius, 439

Macrobius, *306, 308*
Magendie, 451; *app.* no. 6
Malebranche, 280; *180, 387*
Malpighi, *292*
Mamertus, C., 651
Mamiani, C., *app.* no. 2
Manol, *231*
Marsilius [of Ingen], *205*
Mault, 532
Maupertuis, 473
Maxentius, John, *199*
Maximus Tyrius, *308*
Meckel, F., 491
Medici (Professor), *231*
Melissus, 446–447
Millin, *app.* no. 7
Mirbel, 532
Müller, O. F., 473, 488, 491

Naigeon, *308*
Needham, J. T., 473, 491
Nemesius, 444; *98, 100*
Neo-Pythagoreans, 522
Nicholls, F., *371, 373*

Origen, 724; *382*
Orioli, F., *135*
Otto III, Emperor, 54

Paracelsus, *135*
Pari, A. G., *268*
Parmenides, 446; 622
Pascal, 718
Paulinus of Aquilea, 449

Pauthier, J., 514
Payen, 532
Pechlin, N., *373*
Pérault, C., 399
Peter of Mantua, *205*
Pez, *31*
Plato, (*9*); 516–517, 645, 647, 714, 718; *16, 185, 417*
Pliny, 618
Plotinus, *308*
Plutarch, 517; *308*
Polto, S. (Dr.), *231*
Pomponazzi, 399; *98, 135, 205*
Porphyry, 54, 617
Porterfield, W., 358; *156*
Prévost, *298*
Proclus, *306*
Prudentius, 721; *353*
Puccinotti, F., *273*
Pythagoras, (2); *app.* no. 5

Reinhold, 72
Ricamboni, 362
Riccati, *187*
Richarand, 491
Robinot, *233*
Roland, *298*; *app.* no. 6
Romagnosi, 287
Rosa, 618
Rudolphi, 491

Schelling, 524
Scholastics, 53–54
Scotus, *205, 374*
Seneca, *107*
Sennert, *263, 265*
Shakyamuni, 612
Simon, Gustave, *300*
Simplicius, *322*
Sinapius, A., *264*
Socrates, 725

Sprengel, K., 395
Stahl, G. E., 399, 408–409, 418, 473; *171*
Stobaeus, 617; *322, 324*
Stoics, 669
Sturz, 517; *313–314, 321*
Suarez, 455, 632; *100, 204, 214, 331, 337, 374*
Suidas, *417*
Suso, Henry, *410*
Swammerdam, J., 399

Telesio, 520, 524
Tertullian, 457, 624; *313, 337*
Theodoret, 621
Theophilus (St.), 498
Thomas Aquinas (St.), 113–114, 121, 207, 237, 255, 276, 282, 289, 293, 402, 448, 454, 488, 559, 632, 657, 681, 683–685, 706, 719; *6, 67, 83, 100, 104, 113, 206, 213, 261, 280, 330, 335, 338, 354, 359, 374; app.* no. 3
Tianese, The [Apollonius of Tyana], *98*
Townshend, 360
Trembley, 462
Treviranus, 491

Van Helmont, 473, 522
Vincent of Beauvais, 722
Virey, *221, 241; app.* no. 7
Virgil, 518
Vrisberg, 491

Ward, *app.* no. 5
Whytt, R., 419
Willis, *159*
Wolff, C., (16); 28–30; *186*
Wolff, G. F., 473

Xenophanes, 445–446

Zeno of Elea, 447, 729

General Index

*Numbers in roman indicate paragraphs or, where stated, the appendix (app.);
numbers in italic indicate footnotes. Bracketed numbers refer to the Preface*

Abstraction
being and, (25)
difficult task, (22)

Accident
defined, 52
nature and, 56
substance and, 98, 167; *84*

Act(s)
faculty and, 103
first
in general, 166, 170
of an ens, *335*
of body, *335*
of soul, 628
rational, 266, 275
second, 166, 170

Action(s)
entity and, 239
form and, 289
principle and second, 167–168,
175–176
see also **Operations**

Activity
entity and, 180
passivity and, 152
rational and sensitive, 255–263
sentient, 215

Affections
of rational principle, 310
spiritual, 339

Affirmation
apprehension and, 270
intellective operation, 143
perception and, 78, 268, 278

persuasion and, 269

Air
life from, 620–625

Analogy
foundation of, 21
God known by, 22

Analysis
abuse of, 3–4; *4*
knowledge and, 3

Anatomy
science of, 8

Angels
human soul and, 201–202
reasoning and, (28)

Animal
activity, 474–484
animals living in other animals,
598–602
constitution of, 614
defined, 613
feeling, 264–266, 270, 294, 329, 413,
715, 719; *180*
greatest feeling and other feelings of,
594–602
ideal being and, 673–674
illnesses in, *399*
individuality in, 572–577, 613
indivisible feeling, 254
movement in, 387–388, 716
passage of, to eternal things
(intelligence), 653–655, 671,
673–675; *app.* no. 4

phenomena of, wrongly explained, *app.* no. 4
principle of intelligence and animal principle, 637, 719
sensitive and insensitive parts of, 543–545
sentient principle and soul in, 420; *386*
source of life of, 613–625

Animality
in human beings, 645
intelligence and, 305
material school and, 392

Animation
signs of, 226
soul and, 223–226
see also **Universal Animation**

Animistic School
errors of, 391–419

Annihilation
death and, 661–662

Anthropology
psychology and, 10–11
see also **Supernatural Anthropology**

Apprehension
affirmation and, 269–270; *357*
perception and, 268; *357*
rational, 271

Archetype
defined, *24*

Art
internal act and, 357
practical cognition and, 356

Atom
attraction and density of, *app.* no. 8
feeling in, *282*
life and, 612

Attraction
between bodies, 593

Babies
ideas of bodies and, 324
movement by, 352

Bad, *see* **Evil**

Being
absolute, 231
cognition and, 41
consciousness and, 41–42
contingent, (16); *1*
essence of, *1*
eternity of justice and, 724
feeling and, 12–17, 41, 75
ideal, 54, 196; *2*; *app.* no. 2
intuited, 12–13, 172, 229, 233–247, 309, 628, 656, 672, 722; *21*
mental, *2*
object of human mind, 650–652
order of, 170, 176
reality of (defined), 54
relationship and, 548
sensibility of intuition of, 137–138
sentient principle and, 674–675
supreme, (29); *22*
three forms of, 22
ubiquity and intelligibility of, 674
see also **Being in general, Idea of Being**

Being in general
activity of any ens and, 679
body and, 675–676
divine element of soul, *409*
intellective soul and, 628, 633, 720
intuition and, 684
reflection and, 635
see also **Being, Idea of Being**

Black
fundamental feeling of the retina, *179*

Blood
life and, 616–621
will relative to circulation of, 360, 637

Body
action of, 587
alienated momentarily from principle, 608
anatomical, 221–222, 224, 267
animate and inanimate, 531
author's system about union of soul and, 719
being in general and, 675–676
concept of, 217, 495
defined, 51
ens and, 675

erroneous systems about union of soul and, 712–717
first thing understood, 681
insensible parts of, 372–373
intellect acting on, 306–310
intellective principle and, 308–309, 655
material, 220–221, 433
matter of, 218
matter of the soul, 219–225
perception and, 272–273, 671, 684, 700
plurality and organic, *399*
rational principle's action on, 307–310.
senses and existence of bodies, 82–91
sensible and insensible parts of, 543–545
sentient (sensitive) principle and, 630, 633; *266, 387*
separated soul and, 701–711
several individual feelings in same, 577
simplicity of sentient principle and, 454
soul and, 10, 24, 420–428, 448, 690
soul and dissolution of, 685–689
soul as form of, 226–230
space and, 703
subjective and extrasubjective, 272–273, 280, 299–300, 421–428, 453
two constitutive conditions of, 273
two souls in same, 576–577
union of rational soul with, 254, 420
union of sensitive soul with, 249–253
see also **Extrasubjective Bodies**

Brain
organ of corporeal imagination, 326, 381
pure idea and, 338
sensation and, 583–584

Caterpillar
change of state of, 489

Cause
creating and proximate, 407
effect and, 38
efficient and formal, 288
informing and active, *338*
occasional, 252, 280

Certainty
being and, 42
knowledge and, 39
persuasion of, 32

Chaos
parts in the universe and, 508

Codes of Law
Manu, 513

Cognition(s)
being and, 41
object and, 413
positive, 23, 325
practical, 355–356
principle of, 548
rational principle and, 310
rudiments of, 12, 15, 27
separated soul and, 708
truth of, *75*
see also **Knowledge**

Comparisons
spirit and, 631

Concepts
positive and negative, 197–198
relative, 38, 40
see also **Idea**

Consciousness
actions and, 408–409
being and, 41–42
feeling and, 410–413, 605
reason and, 409
reflection as origin of, 571
soul and, 45, 81, 459

Contemplation
intellective soul and, 692

Continuum
density of, *app.* no. 8
point and, 443
simplicity of the soul and, 443–449, 630

Convulsions
will and, *159*

Corporeal Principle
sensiferous force and, 86, 218

Correlative Teachings
certainty of, 38–40

Cosmology
absolute Being and, (29)
God and, (23)
psychology and, 24–26
science of perception, (21)
world and, (23)

Death
animal, 603–612, 668, 698–699
annihilation and, 661–662
causes of, 468–470, 719
concept of human, 670–671, 685
contempt of, 726
human repugnance to, 698–701
intellective soul not subject to,
676–680, 685–686
joy causing, 341
meaning of word, 135, 247
pain causing, 694
vision of God and, *367*
without disorganisation of the body,
691–697

Definition
essence and, 107

Demonstration
meaning of, 43

Deontology
ethics and, (19)
real ens and, (18)

Development
sufficient reason and, 163

Divisibility
meaning of, 563–564
of matter, 706

Duty
rational principle and, *394*

Element, *see* **Extrasubjective Element,
Felt Element, Primal Elements,
Multiplicity of Elements,
Understood Element**

Emanationism
first being and, 512

Empathy
within same species, 710

Energy
bodies as foreign, 273
see also **Force(s)**

Ens, Entia
acts of, *335*
body and, 675
complete, absolute, (13), (25)
essence of, *app.* no. 2
faculty of, 291
first act of, 685
good and, 330
idea of, (16)
love of, 334
mental, 1–2
ontology and, (25)
order of, 432
possible, *app.* no. 2
properties of, 432
real, (11), (19)
self-preservation of, 678
things as, 18
unity of, 1

Ens in general, *see* **Being in general**

Entity
joy and, 330
relationship of, 260, 264

Entozoa
greatest feeling and, 601

Error(s)
judgment and 528
of great men, 645
truth present in, 403; *22*

Essence
definition and, 107
positive, 108
specific and generic, 629
subsistence and, *359*
ultimate reason and, 46–47
what is real relative to ideal, *359*

Ethics
deontology and, (19)
soul and, 730; *16*

Evil
feelings and, 331, 335
sadness and, 329

Experience
  as sole criterion, 533

Extension
  body and, 225, 273
  continuous, 433
  extrasubjective, 225
  matter and, 220, 459
  sensation and, 441
  sensitive principle and, 630, 633

Extrasubjective
  bodies
    animation and, 224–226
    body and, 270, 300, 416; *387*
    matter of, 377
    movement and, 352–353
    perception of, 273
    soul and, 267
  element
    feeling and, 24–25
    first felt and, 210
  extension, 225
  force
    sensitive perception and, 53
  perception
    matter and, 217
  phenomena
    animation and, 226
    bodies and, 225
    differ, *180*
    feeling and, 466
    life and, 453
    sensations and, 441, 450–452
    subjective and, 397, 421–428
    vegetables and, 397
  term of intelligence, 209

Faculty
  act and, 103

Feeling(s)
  as ens, 291
  active feelings, 355
  activity and passivity in, 152–153, 215
  agent and our, 377
  agent and term in, 152–153, 171, 273
  animal, 329
  animal-fundamental, 266, 294
  atom and, *282*
  being and, 12–17, 41, 75
  centralisation of, 478–479
  consciousness and, 410–413
  corporeal, 325
  given by nature, 13

greatest, 594–602, 613–614
human being and, 136, 265, 689, 715
idea and, 278, 398
individualising of, 588
intellective operations and, 136–138
intellective perception and, 79
intellectual (intellective), 329, 361;
    app. no. 1
intelligence differs from, 715; *168*
intuited being and, 12–17
judgment and, 32
matter and form of, 215–216
myself as, 132
molecules and, 582, 594
movement and, 580–584
multiplication of, 709
observation and, 34
of continuity, *298*
of stimulation, 369–372, 483; *298*
oneness of, 147
our own feelings, 411–413
parts of body with or without,
    543–545
perception and, 90, 256, 278, 689
pleasant and unpleasant states of,
    474–475, 477–480
potency of, 215
primal elements and, 396
psychology and, 23
rational feelings, 329–342
reality and, (11); *108*
rudiment of cognition, 12
same body with several, 577, 579,
    594–597
separated soul and, 139
soul and, 79, 81, 247, 249–253,
    264–266, 707; *397*
sounds and, 78
spiritual and corporeal, 131
subjective, 13
subsistence of things and, 18–21
synthesism and, 34–35
things and, 256–259
thought and, *(8)*
truthfulness and, 18
two elements of, 146–149, 152, 251,
    253, 418–419, 459; *180*
universal, 346
willed and unwilled, 343, 347
  see also **Animal Feeling,**
          Fundamental Feeling

Felt Element
  feeling and, 146–149, 152–153
  feeling subject and, 161, 171

felt entity, 179
form of the sentient principle,
210–218
matter of feeling, 212
principle and, 152
removal of, 186, 190–191
sensitive nature and, 56
sentient activity and, 215–216
sentient element and, 184, 296, 459
soul and, 185, 297

Fluids
living, 585–602
see also **Liquids**

Foetus
life of, 597
maternal love and, 597

Force(s)
defined, 51
healing and disruptive, 303
human-synthetical, 328
life instinct and brute, 469
sensiferous, 85–86, 212, 217
subsistence and, 55
unitive, 387, 404
see also **Extrasubjective Force,
Energy**

Form
action and, 289
first active power, 206
substantial, 52
two kinds of, 238

Freedom
simple principle and, 632

Fundamental Feeling
alteration of unity and harmony of,
691
animal, 266, 294
animal phenomena and, 391, 414–417
everything virtually felt in, 172
locality and, 582
perception of, 266–267, 291–298, 670,
719
philosophers unaware of, 92–95
of continuity, 369
ordinary mode of feeling, 273
parts of body and, 543–546
perfect mode of, 472

proofs of, 96–103
rational principle and, 292, 683
soul and, 91, 267, 282, 420–425
space and, 422
species and, 465–466, 471–472,
479–489
stimulation and, 371–372

Generation
animal's greatest feeling and, 596
causes of, 468–470
human, 649, 652–655, 658–659
love and, *app.* no. 7
non-annihilation and, 667
sentient principle and human, 685
spontaneous, 489–499, 521, 547, 549,
601–602, 604
universal animation and, 549–550

God
analogical knowledge of, 22
communication of, 262
cosmology and, (23)
essence and subsistence of, 240, 242,
246
human generation and, 649, 654,
658–659
human knowledge of, 22, 240
ideas, and knowledge of, *app.* no. 1
object of human mind and, 650–652,
672
ontology and, (25)
philosophy and, (15)–(16)
soul as substance and, *83*
vision of, and death, *367*

Good
ens and, 330
human being and, 327, 329, 331–332,
335
immortality of soul and, 728
intimate sense of moral, *417*
universal feeling and, 346
see also **Moral Good**

Habit
internal act and, 357

Happiness
soul and, 730
see also **Joy**

Harmony
pre-established, 252, 280

History
science and, *1*

Human Being(s)
acting as animals, 637
animality and, 645
essential Being communicated to, 262
feeling and, 136, 265, 689, 715–716
first thing understood by, 681–684
harm to, 304–305
idea of being and, 569–570
individuality of, 567–571, 578–584
pure sensation and, 643
something divine in, 648
two parts of, 646
unity of, 264–265
unity of human species, 710

Human Nature
mode of constitution, 672–675
substance of the soul and, 204–230
see also **Man**

Idea(s)
abstract, 195
brain and pure, 338
feeling and, 278, 398
given by nature, 12
knowledge and, *app.* no. 1
negative, 246
objective, 13
pleasure and pure, 338
positive, 244
reality and, (11)
see also **Concepts, Idea of Being, Ideal, Ideality**

Idea of Being, Ideal Being
animal and, 673–674
final evidence of, 33
human being and, 569–570
myself and, 233
pure intellection, 336
soul and, 231–246
synthesism and, 34–35
see also **Being, Understood Element**

Ideal
defined, *24*
real and, 54
see also **Being**

Ideality (Intelligibility)
entity and, 180

Identity
change and, in a subject, 161–173
of sentient and intellective principle, 161–173

Ideology
being and, 23
logic and, (9); 23
psychology and, 12–23, 27, 37
science, *1*

Images
described, 320
idea and, 326
memory and, 327–328
movement and, 349
sense-experiences and, 321
thought associated with, 337
see also **Phantasms**

Imagination
existence of bodies and, 84
organ of, 381
perception and, 244

Immortality
happiness, human dignity and, 660
of the soul
agreement of all peoples, 727
contrary elements and, 722
divine element and, 721
dying people and, 726
essence and, 729
feeling of, 726
intellect and, 676–680, 697, 720
rights of justice and, 724–725
simplicity and, 723
term of understanding and, 726
see *also* **Separated Soul**

Individuality
concept and nature of individuality, 560–566
of animals, 572–577
of human being, 567–571, 676–680
of separated soul, 706–711

Instinct
activity of sentient principle, *147*
life, 358, 391, 468–469, 471, 482, 549, 694, 698
sensuous, 341, 391, 468, 473, 481–482
speech, 383
will and, 358

Intellect
being and, 199
body and, 306–310
darkness of, (2)
finite reality and, 308
infinite and, 237
opposites perceived by, *398*
possible, 277–278
pure, 306–310
truth and, 238
two actions of, 262
understanding and, 289
will moved by, *397*
  see also **Mind**

Intellection
corporeal images and, 336
elements of, 151
  see also **Intelligibility,
Understanding**

Intellective Operations
sensibility of, 136–137, 229

Intellective/Intellectual Perception
being and, 41
defended, 53; *app.* no. 2
feeling and, 32, 41, 79
individual and, 566
intuition and, 525
judgment and, 32, 41
objectivity of, 526
rational principle and, 568
real ens and, *19*
sensitive perception and, 525
theory of, 75

Intellective/Intelligent Principle
abandoning body spontaneously,
  692–694
animal movements and, 716
animal principle and, 637
being in general and, 628, 671, 720
body and, 308–309, 655
contrary elements in, 722
encouragement of itself, *394*
identity of sentient and, 161–173,
  228
immortality of, 439
individuation of, 708–711
momentary alienation from body,
  608
oneness of sentient and, 174–180
sensitive principle and, 364,
  438–439, 640–641, 664, 688–689

separated soul and, 705–706
simplicity of soul and, 626–635
sleep and, 362
soul and, 52; *386*
superiority of, 187–188, 247
  see also **Rational principle, Soul**

Intelligence
animality and, 305
feeling differs from, 715; *168*
form of, 208
increase of, 243
likenesses known by, 245–246
non-human, 710
object of, 209
  see also **Pure Intelligences**

Intelligibility
soul and, 240–247

Intuition,
being and, 234, 656, 684
defined, 53
feeling directed to, *app.* no. 4
individuality of human being and, 568
intellectual perception and, 525
nature of, 53, 232, 628
reasoning and, 241
subject and, 672
  see also **Being**

Joy
death caused by, 341
entity and, 330
feelings of, 329, 332, 335
pleasure in, 332
rational, 331
spiritual, 339
  see also **Happiness**

Judgment
analytical, *app.* no. 2
error and, 527
feeling and, 32
knowledge and, *app.* no. 2
perception as, 78
synthetical, *app.* no. 2

Justice
eternity of, 724

Knowable
two parts of, 14
  see also **Cognition**

Knowledge
absolute, 263; *125*
anatomical, 416
objectivity of, *app.* no. 1
rational principle and, 378
reality and, (11)
synthesisation of, 3
truth and, 39

Language
accuracy of, 80
mental activities and, 76

Life
apparent and latent, 533
body and, *265*
ever greater perfection of, 666
extrasubjective phenomena and, 453
intellective principle and
prolongation of, 696
of continuity, 534–535; *269*
of self renewing stimulation, 534, 541,
610
of stimulation, 534, 536–540; *269*
organisation and varieties of, 542
soul and organic, *105*
source of animal life, 613–625
suspension of, 694
three forms of sensitive, 534–541
see also **Feeling**

Likeness
knowledge through, 245–246

Liquids
precede solids, 590
see also **Fluids**

Locality
sensations and, 582

Love
generation and, *app.* no. 7
objective, 334

Man
history of, 9
meanings of, *87*
physiologists, psychologists and, 7
unity of, 6
see also **Human Nature**

Materialism
errors of, 392

Matter
annihilation of, 664
concept of, 495
defined, 214
divisibility of, 706
error of eternal, *app.* no. 4
feeling and, 467–468, 471, 480
felt element and, 459
first felt element as, 212–218
individuality of, 565
individuation of, 706
meaning of word, 213
organisation of, 467–469, 480, 486
sensitive principle and, 674
term of soul, (23); 664
see also **Body, Soul**

Memories
discussed, 325–328

Metaphysics
defined, (11)
meaning of, (1)–(30)
ontology and, (18)
physics and, (10)

Metempsychosis, *see* **Transmigration**

Mind
entity known by, 1
things known by, 57–60
truth and, 58
two things distinguished in, 650
see also **Intellect, Understanding**

Molecules
animation of, 519
as animals, *309*
feeling and, 519, 546–547 582, 588,
594
fluids and, 550, 585
human body and, 582
Indian philosophy and, 513–514
union of elements and, 537–541

Moral Good
intimate sense and influence of, *417*

Mortality
origin of notion of, *417*

Motion, *see* **Movement**

Movement
convulsive, *160*
feeling and, 580–584

instinctive, 358
propagation of, 365–390
rational principle producing, 336–341,
  351–390
sensiferous, 582
sensitive principle and, 359
spontaneity of, 315–319
subjective and extrasubjective, 350,
  352–353, 423; *155*
will and, 348–384

Multiplicity of Elements
oneness and, 150

Muscles
voluntary and involuntary, 365–366

Myself
as feeling, 132
concept of soul and, 61–81
defined, 55, 63
ideal being and, 233
simplicity of rational soul and,
  636–639

Natural Theology
absolute being and, (29)
being and, 22
infinite Spirit and, (26)
reasoning and, (21)

Nature
defined, 56
radical activity, 301
subject, substance and, 56
see also **Human Nature**

Nerve(s)
cerebro-spinal system of, 376–378,
  386, 388–389
ganglionic system of, 376, 388–389
instinct and, 376
motor and sensitive, 385
movement by, 373–374
seat of soul, 368
sensation and, 450–451
voluntary and involuntary, 365–366
will and, 376

Number
intellective principle and, 630

Object
eternal mind and essential, 211
knowledge and, *app.* no. 1

Objections
truth and, 458

Objectivisation
operation of, 114

Observation
error and, 244
feeling and, 34; *180*
perceptions and, 43
psychology and, 28
reasoning and, 30–31, 34

Ontology
ens and, (25)
God and, (25), (29)
metaphysics and, (18)
nature of bodies and, 458
strict sense of, (21)

Operations
intellective,
sensitive, 437–438, 440
see also **Actions**

Order
effected by person, *400*
see also **Supernatural Order**

Organisation
causes of different, 471–473
of matter, 467–469, 480
sentient principle and, 474–489
total change in, 489
varieties of life and, 542

Organs
simplicity of soul and double, *app.*
  no. 6
single sensation from several, 426,
  451–452

Pain
death caused by, 694
phenomenon of, 485

Pantheism
multiplication of sensitive soul and,
  503–508
sensism and, *241*

Passion
rational principle and, *394*

Pathology
physiology and, *5*

Perception
body and, 272–273, 671, 684
defined, 54
extrasubjective element and, 527
feeling and, 79, 90, 256, 278, 689
fundamental, 264–273, 294, 316, 328, 578, 641, 643, 670–671, 682–683, 719
in general, 268
intense, 643
of God, *app.* no. 1
of substantial feeling, 291
observation and, 43, 244
perceiver and, 292, 719
positive idea and, 244, 246
rational, 265–266, 291, 689, 719
rational principle and, 315–319, 644, 719
reality and, 68
same act as principle and term of, 79
theory of, 75–78
thing perceived not changed by, 642
understanding and absolute, 260–263
see also **Extrasubjective Perception, Intellective Perception, Sense-perception**

Perceptive Principle, *see* **Rational Principle**

Perfection
imperfect things brought to, 673
of every being, 700

Person
first principle, 199
order effected by, *400*

Persuasion
affirmation, apprehension and, 269; *357*
perception and, 268

Phantasms
corporeal feeling and, 325
fundamental feeling and, 279
sense-experiences and, 321–324
species and, 277–278
see also **Images**

Phenomena
subjective and extrasubjective, 397

Philosophers
errors of, 72

reasoning and, 30
sensism and, 31

Philosophy
definition, (7); 46
division of, (17), (20)
erroneous starting point of, *app.* no. 1
God and, (15)
Indian, *app.* no. 5
materialists and, (14)
meaning of, (1)–(30)
subjectivists and, (15)
universality and, (10)

Physics
metaphysics and, (10)

Physiology
pathology and, 5

Plants
animation of, *98*

Pleasure
pure idea causing, 339

Pneumatology
spirits and, (26)–(27)

Point
continuum and, 443

Polyps
propagation of, 463

Possibilities
reality and, 54
reasons of things and, (16)
relationship, *app.* no. 2

Postulates
two necessary, 13

Potency/Power
action and, 166, 170, 175
form and, 206
remote, 656

Prejudice
force of, *app.* no. 6

Primal Elements
nature of, 535
see also **Universal Animation**

Principle
  action and, 164–168
  activity of, 55, 702, 704
  feeling and, 575
  first, 199–200, 203, 229
  meaning of, *78*
  operation by simple, 435
  supreme, 205
  term and, 702, 704
  see also **Corporeal Principle,
    Intellective Principle, Rational
    Principle, Sensitive Principle**

Psychology
  anthropology and, 10–11
  cosmology and, 24–26
  defined, 50
  division of, 45–49
  empirical and rational, 29–33
  feeling and, 23
  ideology and 12–23, 27, 37
  matter and, (23)
  principle of, 107–124
  St. Augustine and the principle of,
    113, 115, 118–120
  St. Thomas and the principle of, 114,
    121
  science of perception, (21)

Pupil of Eye
  contraction of, 359

Pure Intelligences
  Chinese tradition and, *86*
  see also **Angels**

Putrefaction
  phenomenon of, 490

Rational Principle
  action on body, 307
  death and, 699–700, 702
  described, 307
  duty, passion and, *394*
  feeling and, 291, 689, 699, 719
  first principle, 228–229
  formation of, 690
  fundamental feeling and, 292, 683
  good and evil and, 331, 335
  intellect and, 307
  intellective principle and, 180, 189,
  knowledge and, 378
  matter and, 229
  movements produced by, 336–342,
    351–390

  perception and, 291–292, 315–319,
    700
  rational attention of, 319
  sentient principle and, 312, 568, 642
  things and, 264
  see also **Intellective Principle,
    Rational Soul**

Rational Soul
  animal feeling and, 316
  body and, 227, 292, 294–300, 369
  feeling and, 291, 719; *397*
  fundamental feeling and, 420
  harmful movements and, 301–305
  intellective principle and, 671
  intellective soul and, 228
  multiplication of, 658–659
  organisation of body influenced by,
    695
  positive cognitions and, 325
  simplicity and oneness of, 636–646
  see also **Rational Principle**

Reality
  defined, 54
  entity and, 180
  feeling and, (11); *108*
  idea and, (11); 54
  knowledge and, (11)
  perception and, 68
  theory and, *(6)*

Reason
  consciousness and, 409
  definition, 228
  ens and, 291
  error and, 527
  first principle and, 180
  practical, 526

Reasoning
  being and, 635
  feelings and, 35
  idea of being and, 34, 241
  observation and, 30, 34
  ourselves and, 15–16
  synthesism and, 34–36

Reflection
  acts known by, 409
  feelings and order of, 332
  idea of being and, 241, 570
  origin of consciousness, 571
  other faculties involved in, 338
  perceiving principle and, 265
  simplicity of soul and, 635

Relationship
  a being and, 548

Retention
  organising function, 539

Sadness
  feelings of, 329, 332, 335
  rational, 331

Science
  history and, *1*
  intuited being and, *21*
  object of, *1*
  principle of, 107–109

Sciences
  classification of, 1–5
  cognition and, 116
  complete and incomplete, 2-5
  deontological, (18)–(20)
  ideological, (20)
  ontological, (18)
  metaphysical, (20)–(21)
  philosophical, (17)

Scripture
  soul as breath in, 624
  'spirit' and 'flesh' in, 646
  'spirit of life' in, 510

Sensation(s)
  extended-continuum and, 441
  extrasubjective phenomena and, 441,
    450–452
  human beings and pure, 643
  intellective operation and, 229
  knowledge and, 32; *app.* no. 2
  locality and, 582
  movement and, 581–584
  several organs producing, 426
  surface, 422

Sense-experience(s)
  bodies and, 273, 321–322
  images, phantasms and, 320–324
  sentient principle and, 210
  shaped feelings and, 349

Sense-perception
  animals and, 317
  defined, 53
  intellectual perception and, 525, 527

Sense-pleasure
  fundamental perception not lost by,
    643

Senses
  existence of bodies and, 82–91

Sensility
  relationship of, 250, 258, 260, 264,
    426, 453, 675

Sensism
  erroneous system, 398, 713–714
  origin of modern, 402
  pantheism and, *241*

Sensitive Perception, *see*
  Sense-perception

Sensitive Principle, *see* **Sentient
  Principle**

Sentient Principle (Sentient Element)
  as individual, 566
  as potency, 656
  being and, 674–675
  body and, 675; *266, 387*
  continuously active, 468, 574
  continuum and, 574
  contraction of pupil and, 359
  elevated to order of intelligence,
    674–677, 691
  feeling and, 294, 459
  form of the, 210–218
  generation and, 685
  habit in, 317
  individuation of, 707
  instinct and, 391
  intellective principle and, 161–173,
    364, 438–439, 640–641, 664, 688–689
  limitation of act of, 674
  loss of identity, 656–657
  matter and, 674
  movement and, 359, 405
  multiplication of, 439
  organising function of, 474–489
  one principle out of several, 666–667
  oneness of intellective and, 174–180,
    228
  rational principle and, 312, 642, 719
  simplicity of, 630
  sleep and, 361
  soul and, 52, 420; *102, 387*

Separated Soul
  animal and,
  happiness of, 711
  intellective principle and,
  Platonists and, *378*
  rational principle and,
  sensitive principle and,
  space and, 703–706, 709
    see also **Immortality, Immortality
    of the Soul**

Sight
  simplicity of soul and, *app.* no. 6

Simplicity (of the Soul)
  ancients' proofs of, 453–454
  animal operations and, 441–442
  classification of proofs of, 431
  continuum and, 443–449, 573–574
  intellective principle and, 626–635
  meaning of, 430
  negative property, 626
  operations of soul and, 435–439
  properties of soul and, 432–434

Simplification
  of several sentient princples, 666–667

Sleep
  intellective principle and, 362
  intellectual feeling and, 361
  sensitive principle and, 361–362
  will and, 362
    see also **Somnambulism**

Somnambulism
  artificial, 362
  will and, 362

Soul
  activity and passivity of, 291–442
  addition or change to felt element of,
    192–195
  addition to understood element of,
    196–199
  angels and, 201–202
  animal souls and, 201, 203; *387*
  animation and, 223–224
  author's system about union of body
    and, 719
  body and, 10, 24, 249–254, 282, 309,
    448, 687
  body and separated, 701–711
  body as matter of, 219–225
  cessation of sensitive, 663–665

  consciousness of, 71–80, 605, 626
  constitution of, 200
  definition of human, 53
  definition of sensitive, 50, 432
  deprived of felt element, 190–191
  deprived of understood element,
    186–189
  development of, *368*
  dissolution of body relative to,
    685–689
  drawn to act, 191
  efficient cause of human being,
    288–290
  elementary, 663
  erroneous systems about union of
    body and, 712–717
  essence of, 104–106, 189, 200, 247; *40*
  essence of human, 689; *app.* no. 3
  ethics and, 730; *16*
  extension excluded from, 432–434
  extrasubjective body and, 420–428
  feeling and, 79, 90–91, 136–139, 247,
    264, 605, 707
  finiteness of, 234–238, 247
  first principle, 200
  form of human being, 204–207, 219,
    288
  form of the body, 226–230
  fundamental perception and, 267–271
  German philosophy and, 72
  happiness and, 730
  harmful movements and, 301–305
  human nature and substance, 204–230
  ideal being and, 231–234, 235,
    237–246
  identity of, 140–180, 247
  immortality of, 134–139, 609–612,
    660; *16*
  infinity of human, 235–238, 247
  intelligence and, *app.* no. 3
  intuition and, 233–234
  materiality excluded from, 432–434
  matter and, (23)
  mind and concept of, 61–68
  multiplication of sensitive, 455–467,
    488, 605, 663; *279*
  multiplicity excluded from, 432–434
  nerves as seat of, 368
  one body with two souls, 575–576
  one particular body relative to, 690
  operations and substance of, 127–130
  organic, 663
  organic life and, *105*
  origin of intellective, 647–659
  perfection and strength of, 340

positive cognition of, 626
pure intelligences and, 201
pure notion of, 69–81
rational principle and, 189, 291–292
reality of, 231–234, 247–248
sensitive, (23); 249–253, 294, 309, 420; *38, 387*
space as term of sensitive, 554–559
spirit differs from, 230, 717–718
spirituality of, 131–133
subject and substance, 181–183
substance of, 89–91
substantial essence of, 110
substantial feeling, 81
term of, (23); 247, 252, 605
thinking and, 286
transient acts and, 306
two activities of human soul, 638–644
unity of, 125–126, 264
vice and, 730
virtue and, 730
whole man and, 10
   see also **Immortality of the Soul, Rational Soul, Separated Soul, Simplicity (of the soul)**

Sounds
feeling and, 78

Space
body and, 703
external sensation and, 422
fundamental feeling and, 422, 709
sensitive souls and, 554–559, 703
sentient principle of, 556–559

Species
fundamental feeling and, 465–466, 471–472, 485
intelligible, 278, 282–283
phantasms and, 277
specific feeling and, 464–466, 471, 479–484, 486

Speech
instinct of, 383

Sperm
greatest feeling and, 599–600

Spirit(s)
encouragement of intelligent, *395*
psychology and, 26, 112
soul differs from, 230, 717–718

Spirituality, *see* **Simplicity (of the Soul)**

Spontaneity
law of, 317
perceptions and, 315–320

Stimulation
animal life and, 610, 614–615, 620
brain, nerves and, 583
life of, 534, 536–541
sensation and, 583–584
supreme, 653
vital activity and, 546

Subject
contrary elements and, 722
existence of, 671
intuition of being and, 233, 672–675
meaning of, *78*
oneness and simplicity of, 160
oneness of the sentient and the intelligent, 174–180
predicate and, *app.* no. 2
sameness of, 161–173
soul and, 182
substance, nature and, 56

Subsistence
contingent, 242
defined, 54
divine, 240, 242, 246; *app.* no. 1
essence and, *359*
force and, 56
things and knowledge of their, 18–21

Substance
accidents and, 68, 167; *84*
defined, 52, 168
false concepts of, 84, 87–88
first act, 52, 166, 169, 685
first, operative principle, 175
inanimate bodies as, 183
oneness of, 433
subject, nature and, 56
unchangeableness and permanence of, 169
without accident, 98

Suicide
humans, animals and, 726

Supernatural Anthropology
theodicy and, (30)

Supernatural Order
being and, 199
created being and, 240, 242
perception of God in, *app.* no. 1

Sympathy
individuals and, 710

Synthesis
abuse of, 3–4
concepts and, 508
principle of, 180

Synthesisation
knowledge and, 3

Synthesism
feeling and, 148–149
form and matter and, 41
principle and action, 165
reasoning and, 34–36

Theodicy
role of, (30)

Theology
object of, *1*
see also **Natural Theology**

Theory
reality and, *(6)*

Theosophy
science of, (22), (29)

Things
essence and reality of, 18–19
knowledge of subsistence of, 18–21
mind and knowledge of, 57–60
rational principle and felt, 264
reality and ideality of, 231; *app.* no. 1
senses and, 256–259

Thought
composition of, 328
feeling and, *(8)*
images associated with, 337
no organ of, 326

Transmigration
of soul, 515, 522–523, 668–669

Truth
being and, 42
error present in, 403; *22*

knowledge and, 38
mind and, 58
objections against, 458
understanding and, 260

Truthfulness
feeling and, 18

Understanding
absolute perception and, 260–263
agent and term in, 155–159, 171
external bodies and, *129*
immortality of the soul and, 726
see also **Intellection, Mind**

Understood Element
agent and, 155, 158
form of the intelligent principle,
208–209
intelligent subject and, 161
removal of, 186–189
understanding and, 158, 160, 171, 211
see also **Idea of Being**

Unity
entia and, 1
multiplicity and, 150
of sentient and intelligent principle,
174–180

Universal Animation
common sense and, 529–531
emanationists and, 523
German and English philosophers
and, 524–528
Greek philosophers and, 516–517
idealists and, 523
Indian philosophers and, 509–515
Italian philosophers and, 518–522
materialism and, 501–502, 523
naturalists and, 523, 532
of particles of matter, 500–553, 602,
604, 607, 609–613, 666–667; *97*
pantheism, 501, 503–508, 523
three forms of life of, 534–543

Universalisation
operation of, 114

Universality
philosophy and, (10)

Vice
soul and, 730

Virtuality
first principle and, 166

Virtue
soul and, 730

Volitions
purely affective, 380

Will
circulation of blood and, 360
contraction of pupil and, 359
convulsive movements and, *159*

first principle and, 180
instinct independent of, 358
intellect moved by, *397*
movements and, 351–364, 379–384
organs of secretion and, 363
rational feelings and, 343–350
sleep and, 361–362
weeping and, 363

Wisdom
unity of, (7)

Wounds
vital principle healing, 487